China under
Jurchen Rule

SUNY Series in Chinese Philosophy and Culture
David L. Hall and Roger T. Ames,
Editors

China under Jurchen Rule
Essays on Chin Intellectual and Cultural History

Hoyt Cleveland Tillman
and
Stephen H. West,
Editors

Foreword by Herbert Franke

State University of New York Press

Published by
State University of New York Press, Albany

© 1995 State University of New York

All rights reserved

Printed in the United States of America

No part of this book may be used or reproduced
in any manner whatsoever without written permission
except in the case of brief quotations embodied in
critical articles and reviews.

For information, address State University of New York Press,
State University Plaza, Albany, N. Y., 12246

Production by Marilyn P. Semerad
Marketing by Bernadette LaManna

Library of Congress Cataloging-in-Publication Data

China under Jurchen rule: essays on Chin intellectual and cultural history /
    Hoyt Cleveland Tillman and Stephen H. West, editors.
      p. cm. — (SUNY series in Chinese philosophy and culture)
    Includes bibliographical references and index.
    ISBN 0-7914-2273-9 (acid-free paper). — ISBN 0-7914-2274-7 (paper
    : acid-free paper)
    1. China—History—Chin dynasty, 1115–1234 2. China—Intellectual life—
960–1644. 3. Chinese literature—Sung dynasty, 960–1279—History and
criticism. I. Tillman, Hoyt Cleveland. II. West, Stephen H. III. Series.
DS751.92.S36 1994
951'.024—dc20   94-4812
                                                                                         CIP

10 9 8 7 6 5 4 3 2 1

To the memory of

William Hung
James T. C. Liu
Lien-sheng Yang

*and others who left their native land to share with us
the history and culture of China*

Contents

Illustrations	ix
Table of Dynasties	xi
Acknowledgments	xiii
Contributors	xv
Note on Romanization	xvii
Foreword	xix
Herbert Franke	
Introduction	1
Hoyt Cleveland Tillman and Stephen H. West	

I. Politics and Institutions

1. An Overview of Chin History and Institutions	23
Hoyt Cleveland Tillman	
2. The Jurchen-Sung Confrontation: Some Overlooked Points	39
James T. C. Liu	
3. Public Schools in the Chin Dynasty	50
Tao Jing-shen	

II. Religion and Thought

4. Confucianism under the Chin and the Impact of Sung Confucian Tao-hsüeh	71
Hoyt Cleveland Tillman	
5. Chao Ping-wen (1159–1232): Foundations for Literati Learning	115
Peter K. Bol	
6. Buddhism and Taoism under the Chin	145
Yao Tao-chung	

III. Literature and Art

7. Five Paintings of Animal Subjects or Narrative Themes and Their Relevance to Chin Culture ... 183
   Susan Bush

8. Jurchen Literature under the Chin ... 216
   Jin Qicong

9. Satire and Allegory in All Keys and Modes ... 238
   Wilt Idema

10. Chilly Seas and East-Flowing Rivers: Yüan Hao-wen's Poems of Death and Disorder, 1233–35 ... 281
    Stephen H. West

Glossary ... 305

Bibliography ... 333

Index ... 377

Illustrations

Figures

1. Chang Kuei (fl. mid-12th cent.), *Sacred Tortoise*. Handscroll, ink and colors on silk, 30 × 57.2 cm. Courtesy of the Palace Museum, Peking/p.186.

2. Chao Lin (fl. mid-12th cent.), *Six Horses*, detail. Handscroll, ink and colors on silk, 30.9 × 205 cm. Courtesy of the Palace Museum, Peking/p. 187.

3. *Ch'iu Hsing-kung and Whirlwind Victory*. Stone relief from T'ang T'ai-tsung's Chao-ling (ca. 636). Courtesy of University Museum, Philadelphia/p. 190.

4. Chang Yü (?) (late 12th–early 13th cent.), *Wen-chi's Return to China*. Handscroll, ink and colors on silk, 29 × 127 cm. Courtesy of the Jilin Museum, Ch'ang-ch'un/p. 191.

5. Chang Yü, *Wen-chi's Return to China*, detail/p. 192.

6. Liu Yüan (fl. early 13th cent.), *Dream of Ssu-ma Yu*. Handscroll, ink and colors on silk, 29.2 × 73.2 cm. Courtesy of the Cincinnati Art Museum/p. 193.

7. Liu Yüan, *Dream of Ssu-ma Yu*, detail, p. 200.

8. Attributed to Li Kung-lin (1049–ca. 1105), reattributed to Ma Yün-ch'ing (fl. 1229), *Vimalakîrti Expounds Buddhist Sutras*, detail. Handscroll, ink on paper, 34.6 × 207.5 cm. Courtesy of the Palace Museum, Peking/p.201.

9. Ma Yün-ch'ing, *Vimalakîrti Expounds Buddhist Sutras*, detail/p. 204.

10. Ma Yün-ch'ing, *Vimalakîrti Expounds Buddhist Sutras*, detail/p. 205.

Tables

1. Geographical Locations of and Textual Sources for Fifty-eight Chin Schools/pp. 54–55.

2. Enrollments of Chin Schools/p. 56.

3. Schools in North China during the Chin/p. 58.

Table of Dynasties

Shang ca. 1460–1045 B.C.
Chou 1045–256 B.C.

Western Chou 1111–771 B.C.   Eastern Chou 770–256 B.C.
Spring and Autumn 722–481 B.C.   Warring States 480–221 B.C.

Ch'in 221–207 B.C.
Han 202 B.C.–A.D. 220

Eastern Han 202 B.C.–A.D. 9   Western Han 25–220

Three Kingdoms 220–80

Wei 220–65   Wu 222–80
Shu-Han 221–63

Western Chin 266–316
Eastern Chin 317–420
Northern and Southern Dynasties 386–589

Southern 420–589

Sung 420–79   Ch'i 479–502
Liang 502–57   Ch'en 557–89

Northern 386–581

Northern Wei 386–534   Eastern Wei 534–50
Northern Ch'i 550–77   Western Wei 535–57
Northern Chou 557–81

Sui 581–618
T'ang 618–907
Five Dynasties 907–60

Later Liang 907–23   Later T'ang 923–36
Later Chin 936–47   Later Han 947–50
Later Chou 951–60

Sung 960–1279

Northern Sung 960–1127   Southern Sung 1127–1279

Liao 916–1125

Chin 1115–1234

Yüan 1260–1368

Ming 1368–1644

Ch'ing 1644–1911

Chin Emperors and Reign Periods

Emperor T'ai-tsu 1115–23
Shou-kuo 1115–17   T'ien-fu 1117–23

Emperor T'ai-tsung 1123–35
T'ien-hui 1123–35

Emperor Hsi-tsung 1135–50
T'ien-hui 1135–38   T'ien-chüan 1138–41
Huang-t'ung 1141–50

Prince of Hai-ling 1150–61
T'ien-te 1150–53   Chen-yüan 1153–56
Cheng-lung 1156–61

Emperor Shih-tsung 1161–89
Ta-ting 1161–89

Emperor Chang-tsung 1190–1208
Ming-ch'ang 1190–96   Ch'eng-an 1196–1201
T'ai-ho 1201–8

Prince of Wei-shao 1209–13
Ta-an 1209–12   Ch'ung-ch'ing 1212
Chih-ning 1213

Emperor Hsüan-tsung 1213–24
Chen-yu 1213–17   Hsing-ting 1217–22
Yüan-kuang 1222–24

Emperor Ai-tsung 1224–34
Cheng-ta 1224–32   K'ai-hsing 1232
T'ien-hsing 1232–34

Emperor Mo-ti
Sheng-ch'ang 1234   T'ien-hsing 1234

Acknowledgments

Many individuals and institutions have had a hand in the long prepartum history of this book. The initial conference on Culture under the Chin was held at the University of Arizona Conference Center in Oracle, Arizona, in December 1983. That conference was sponsored by the American Council of Learned Societies; we would like to acknowledge their early financial and moral support, especially as offered by Dr. Jason Parker. We have both received encouragement over the years from professors James T. C. Liu and Yü Ying-shih of Princeton University, Herbert Franke, president of the Bavarian Academy of Sciences, Tao Jing-shen of the University of Arizona, and Chan Hok-lam of the University of Washington.

Hoyt C. Tillman conducted his initial research on Chin cultural history under the auspices of the Academy of Sciences' Committee on Scholarly Communication with the People's Republic of China and the Department of Education's Fulbright-Hays Program, which allowed him to spend time in China, where professors Deng Guangming and Yan Buke of Peking University and Qiu Hansheng and Song Dejin of the Chinese Academy of Social Sciences provided helpful insights into the period. Portions of the manuscript were prepared under a grant by the Graduate College of Arizona State University, which awarded Tillman a Humanities Research Award. Thanks are due Bettie Ann Doebler and O. M. Brack of the Interdisciplinary Program in the Humanities and to Brian Foster of the Graduate College for their support.

Over the years, librarians at Peking University, Beijing Library, the Harvard-Yenching Library, Princeton, Columbia, Leiden, Berkeley, Oxford, Cambridge, Munich, and the University of Arizona have been gracious in providing access to their collections. We would like to single out Mrs. Ai-Hwa Wu at the Arizona State University Library and Mr. P. Y. Chang of the East Asian Library at Berkeley for their cheerful assistance through the years the project has been under way.

The manuscript has undergone many revisions. Earlier drafts were read by Conrad Schirokauer of City College of New York and others. We have benefited from their critical and constructive readings and suggestions. Alejandro Echevarria, Arizona State University, and Richard Everett also proofread early copies of the papers. Professor Peter Bol and Anthony Deblasi spent long hours compiling a draft Bibliography and setting it in English and Chinese. Rodney Ito and Langston Tillman helped solve problems of computer compatibility and worked their wizardry with balky machines and recalcitrant users.

The final copyediting was done by Deborah Rudolph, University of California, Berkeley. Her pencil and her mind, both sharp as needles, brought grammatical and citational consistency and clarity to the texts. Verena Tent-Braucher input the edited copy for typesetting. The final book was designed and set by Stephen H. West. Marilyn Semerad of SUNY Press provided helpful guidance during the final phase of manuscript preparation. Roger Ames and David Hall, editors of the series in which this volume appears, are due our gratitude for their belief in the value of the book, as is William Eastman, Director of SUNY Press.

A final note of thanks to our families and spouses for their constant support that allowed us, finally, to see this project through to the end. Perseverance has prevailed by virtue of the help and support of all of these people. And we have discovered a mutual friendship that has grown significantly deeper in respect, despite the impediment of a fetal lump of manuscripts that we have carried over a long period of gestation and now, at last, deliver.

Contributors

Peter K. Bol is Professor of History, Harvard University. He is author of *"This Culture of Ours": Intellectual Transition in T'ang and Sung China*, coauthor of *Sung Dynasty Uses of the I Ching*, and compiler of *Research Tools for the Study of Sung History*.

Susan Bush is Resident Associate in Research at the John King Fairbank Center for East Asian Research, Harvard University. She has written, among other works, *Chinese Literati on Painting: Su Shih (1037–1101) to Tung Ch'i-ch'ang* and has coedited *Early Chinese Texts on Painting* and *Theories of the Arts in China*.

Wilt Idema, Professor of Chinese Literature at the Institute of Sinology, Leiden University, The Netherlands, is the author of many works on fiction and drama, including *Chinese Vernacular Fiction: The Formative Period* and *The Dramatic Oeuvre of Chu Yu-tun (1379–1430)*. He has coauthored, with Stephen West, *Chinese Theater 1100–1450: A Source Book* and *The Moon and the Zither: The Story of the Western Wing*.

Jin Qicong, former head of the Shenyang Center for Research on Jurchen and Manchu Languages and Cultures, lives in retirement in Peking. He is the author of the standard Jurchen dictionary, *Nü-chen-wen tz'u-tien*, and, with his daughter, Jin Guangping, of a study of the Jurchen language and script, *Nü-chen yü-yen wen-tzu yen-chiu*.

James T. C. Liu (1919–93), late Professor of East Asian Studies, Princeton University, wrote many works on Sung history and culture, including *China Turning Inward: Intellectual-Political Changes in the Early Twelfth Century* and *Ou-yang Hsiu: An Eleventh-Century Neo-Confucianist*.

Tao Jing-shen is Professor of East Asian Studies, University of Arizona, and fellow of the Institute of History and Philology, Academia Sinica. In addition to his many works in Chinese, he has published *The Jurchen in Twelfth-Century China: A Study of Sinicization* and *Two Sons of Heaven: Studies in Sung-Liao Relations*.

Hoyt Cleveland Tillman is Professor of History, Arizona State University. His studies on Chinese intellectual history include *Utilitarian Confucianism: Ch'en Liang's Challenge to Chu Hsi* and *Confucian Discourse and Chu Hsi's Ascendancy*.

STEPHEN H. WEST, Professor of East Asian Languages, University of California, Berkeley, has authored several works on early drama and on Yüan Hao-wen. His works include *Vaudeville and Narrative: Aspects of Chin (1125–1234) Theater* and, with Wilt Idema, *Chinese Theater 1100–1450: A Source Book* and *The Moon and the Zither: The Story of the Western Wing*.

YAO TAO-CHUNG, Associate Professor in Asian Studies, Mount Holyoke College, has written extensively on Ch'üan-chen Taoism, including several articles on the history of the sect, its literature, and its relations with the Yüan court.

A Note on Romanization

Wade-Giles romanization is used for Chinese names and terms, the modified Hepburn system for Japanese. Circumflexes are used for macrons in romanized Japanese and Sanskrit.

Foreword

When the editors of this volume suggested that I contribute a few prefatory remarks, I accepted their flattering invitation gratefully because I realized that their book marks a new level in our comprehension of North China's cultural history under Jurchen rule. Previous Western studies on the Chin have largely concentrated on political and social aspects of the Chin state—no mean achievement considering the complex interaction of tribal traditions and Chinese patterns of governance. But even this basic elucidation of structural elements serving as a background for intellectual and cultural developments took a long time to emerge, in the West as well as in China. Under the Yüan and Ming, scholars tended to adopt a condescending attitude toward Chin literature and history. It was only in the seventeenth century that some attention began to be paid to the Chin as a distinct entity, for the simple reason that the Manchus, as linguistic and cultural descendants of the Jurchen, looked back with understandable pride at the exploits of their progenitors. In 1646, only two years after the foundation of the Ch'ing dynasty, an adaptation of the basic annals of the *Chin shih* was compiled and translated into Manchu under the title of *Aisin gurun-i suduri bithe* (Annals of the "Gold" state). In the good old days of nineteenth-century European sinology when knowledge of Manchu was still regarded as standard, this book was translated into French by Charles Joseph de Harlez as *Histoire de l'empire Kin ou Empire d'or* (Louvain, 1887). His translation remained for many years the only Western book devoted to the history of the Chin.

Chinese textual and commentarial scholarship, to which modern scholars are indebted for a galaxy of works that have led to a better understanding of Chinese dynastic histories, has for a long time bypassed the *Chin shih*. As late as roughly 1800 the first book of emendations to the *Chin shih* was published in China, followed by a few anthologies of Chin dynasty writings. But these efforts remained isolated. Only after World War II did a growing number of Chinese scholars turn to the study of the Chin period in all its aspects, with, however, an awkward consequence: it is at present so hard to keep track of all current publications, an inordinate amount of time could be spent reading secondary literature instead of the original sources. In Japan serious scholarly interest in the Chin began much earlier than on the continent, prompted by Japan's political aspirations in the Manchurian homelands of the Jurchen. Already prior to World War I, substantial books and articles, chiefly on historical geography, were published by Japanese scholars, some of them sponsored by the South Manchuria Railway Company, then an unofficial but most powerful agency in Manchuria. During the following decades Japan continued to show a lively interest in the Chin, resulting in many standard works, including several indispensable indexes. But in Western Europe the Chin remained a virtual *terra incognita* until about thirty years ago. The chapters on Chin in Otto Franke's *Geschichte des chinesischen Reiches*, vol. 4 (Berlin, 1948), have been for many years the most detailed survey of Chin political history since de Harlez in 1887.

It is unnecessary to point out the drastic change that has occurred since about 1960. A glance at the Bibliography in the present volume and, of course, at the articles themselves will suffice to illustrate the undeniable progress of Chin studies in many countries. Attention should also be drawn to the sometimes overlooked contributions of Russian scholars. They have done important spadework in the strictest sense of the word by excavating ancient Jurchen sites in the maritime provinces of the Russian Far East and thus supplemented the work of Chinese archaeologists on the other side of the border. Two comprehensive volumes on the Chin are due to M. V. Vorob'ev, *Chzhurchzheni i gosudarstvo Tszin'* (The Jurchen and the state of Chin) (Moscow, 1975), and *Kul'tura Chzhurchzheni i gosudarstvo Tszin'* (The culture of the Jurchen and of the Chin state) (Moscow, 1983). The latter presents a detailed conspectus of material culture, educational institutions, artistic and intellectual trends. The author's analysis underlines the nativist tendencies in Jurchen culture under the Chin and tries to show that in the twelfth and thirteenth centuries for the first time in history a Tungus people established consciously bilateral contacts with other cultural areas in the Far East. Indeed, even the early Jurchen can hardly be regarded as entirely barbarous; nor can the intellectual and artistic relations between Sung and Chin be viewed as if a cultural void had had to be filled by importing or adopting Sung elements.

It is not the least merit of this new volume that the cultural identity of North China is seen as a constitutive factor, an identity that drew much of its strength from the heritage of T'ang and Northern Sung. This has been largely overlooked in previous studies, but also in the image projected by traditional Chinese scholars, who, it seems, were prone to being overawed by the towering figure of Chu Hsi in the South. North China was in reality by no means and in no respect a cultural backwater, but rather "another China," certainly to a higher degree than the Liao and Hsi-hsia states ever were. No "iron curtain" separated Chin and Sung, only an insufficiently guarded border permeable by economic and intellectual contraband. Interaction and osmosis therefore helped to shape cultural life in the North. Repeatedly the individual authors of this volume have complained about the scarcity of sources on certain topics. It is indeed a fact that a great number of Chin writings have been lost, known only by their titles today. We can only speculate what the reasons for these losses are. It is not impossible that orthodox literati in later centuries did not think it worthwhile to preserve in reprintings or manuscript copies the productions of Chin writers (tradition always implies selection). A more realistic interpretation would be to ascribe this partial non-preservation to the physical destruction that afflicted the Chin state after the fall of Peking in a singularly chaotic and war-torn period of Chinese history. We must therefore be grateful for the impressive corpus of Chin Taoist literature that has survived in the *Tao-tsang*, documenting the new trends in Taoism that emerged in the twelfth century and enriched religious life in China for a long time afterwards, as Ch'en Yüan's seminal study of 1941 has shown. The contributions on religion in the new volume must also be welcomed, because popular religions like Taoism and Buddhism have perhaps, seen from a quantitative perspective, influenced the minds of more people than the philosophical ideas of the Chin intellectual elite trying to follow the Great Tradition in Chinese thought. The popular element in Chin culture is equally well represented in this volume's contributions on literature.

In concluding, I wish to congratulate the editors and contributors for their outstanding achievement. This collection of essays is evidence that the high degree of sophistication and expertise which we are accustomed to expect from Sung specialists has now been extended into a previously less developed field of study. It is now possible to perceive more clearly the contours of a distinctly northern cultural identity in the twelfth and thirteenth centuries, a period that can henceforth no longer be regarded merely as an unproductive transitional phase between the Sung and the Yüan.

Munich
August 17, 1992

HERBERT FRANKE

INTRODUCTION

Hoyt Cleveland Tillman and Stephen H. West

Although never well integrated into the cultural history of China, the Chin (Golden) dynasty needs to be appreciated as part of an enduring process of interaction between the northern and southern cultures of that land. These two cultures have traditionally been thought of as quite distinct: northern culture is conventionally held to be more rational, martial, and political, southern culture more romantic, peace-loving, and philosophical.[1] From the Southern Sung era onward, there has been a tendency among scholars of China to focus on the formation of cultural orthodoxy, identified with Tao-hsüeh, that developed during and after the Southern Sung. Attention has been concentrated on that evolution to the neglect of cultural developments in the North during the Chin, which has more or less been seen as the twilight preceding the dark night ushered in by the Mongol conquest. This neglect has been strengthened by the ascension of Yangtze valley culture in the early Ming and the general shift away from the predominantly northern cultural values of T'ang and Northern Sung toward the literary and artistic aesthetic of the South and the southern philosophical traditions exemplified by Chu Hsi. Conventional wisdom explains the shift as the triumph of orthodox southern culture; we propose that the paradigm of interaction and fusion common to other eras of cultural history applies to the Chin as well. Chin culture, we suggest, contributed significantly to the cultural unification of China under the three dynasties, Yüan, Ming, and Ch'ing, that spanned the last seven centuries of the Chinese empire.

Chin was a polyethnic state that ruled more of China and became more sinicized than any earlier dynasty founded by a foreign conqueror. The

Jurchen rulers wedded native customs and practices that had evolved among Tungusic tribal units deep in the forests of Manchuria to the institutional features of the Chinese bureaucracy and imperial system. The resulting offspring greatly influenced later Chinese political culture. The Jurchen, for example, were the first rulers to inflict corporal punishment on high officials at the imperial court. They also simplified the upper levels of government, creating the tripartite system of bureaucracy, Censorate, and army. Inherited and refined by later dynasties, this structure is still operative in Peking, where the Party now functions in a fashion analogous to the Censorate. It was the Chin that first established Yenching (modern Peking) as a principal dynastic capital. Although the Jurchen retreated back into Manchuria when they were vanquished by the Mongols in 1234, their descendants, the Manchus, benefited from Jurchen experiences and institutions when they founded the Ch'ing to rule over the whole of China. New religious trends and movements that developed during the Chin, such as Ch'üan-chen Taoism, also dominated the later centuries of imperial China. New forms of oral and dramatic performance—the farce play (*yüan-pen*) and the ballad form known as "all-keys-and-modes" (*chu-kung-tiao*), both discussed in Professor Wilt Idema's article—flourished in the major Chin cities. Clearly, the Chin dynasty represents a significant, if neglected, stage in the development of Chinese political, intellectual, and cultural history, and the scholarly community must now consider it as such.

The fact that the Chin state was established by foreign conquest has been the major factor in its neglect. The trauma of barbarian invasions and conquests that culminated in An Lu-shan's (d. 757) rebellion in the mid-eighth century has given the Chinese (i.e., ethnic Han Chinese) an understandable bias against the cultures that developed under conquest dynasties—especially in the case of the Chin, which coexisted with a native Chinese dynasty, the Southern Sung. In the eyes of traditional historians, no dynasty established by a people ethnically distinct from the Chinese could claim cultural legitimacy unless it was sole master of all under Heaven—and unless it eventually became sinicized enough to take on the mantle of Chinese civilization.

Among the many problems inherent in bringing the contributions of Chin intellectual and cultural history into focus, the issue of sources stands at the fore. Primary source materials are scarce compared to those available for other, roughly contemporaneous dynasties, particularly the Sung and even the Yüan. Limits appear in two fundamental ways. First, only a fraction of the 1,351 works of drama, poetry and prose, history and philosophy mentioned in extant Chin works still exists. Second, the literary corpus that has survived derives principally from only three localities other than the capital at Yenching: the south-central part of Shansi, Chen-ting (modern Ting-hsien near Shih-chia-chuang) in Hopei province, and Tung-p'ing in the western part of Shantung province. Such traditional cultural centers as Ch'ang-an (Sian), Loyang, or Kaifeng are hardly represented. This fact was not lost on Chin intellectuals. Liu Ch'i (1203–50), the chief chronicler of the period, for instance, joked with his friends, "Most eminent literati of the Chin came from the north.... When I was in southern precincts, I was talking once with some colleagues and I jested, 'From antiquity the renowned have come from the east, the west, and the south; but nowadays we should head for the north!'" (KCC 10.112). He might have been referring to Chen-ting, home to such scholars as Ts'ai Kuei (d. 1174), Chou Ang (d. 1211), and Wang Jo-hsü (1174–1243). Although Kaifeng became an important cultural center after the relocation of the capital there in 1214, Chen-ting and Tung-p'ing remained, along with Peking, the principal literary centers even until the early Yüan. Scholars from these areas were also treated as significant figures not only by the major literary critics of the period to survive the Chin—Yüan Hao-wen (1190–1257) and Liu Ch'i—but also by the compilers of standard histories during the Yüan, who drew on their writings for source material. Our confidence on this score should be somewhat tempered by the knowledge that they, like other critics and historians, often propagated their own schools of thought or lineages of affiliation to the exclusion of others. The tendency in traditional writing to give prominence to one tradition while ignoring or misrepresenting others should caution us not to construe the whole of Chin cultural development from such a limited number of sources, themselves bound by both geographical distribution and the predilections of collectors, editors, and publishers. Yet even though few in number and exclusive in nature, these works do not exist in a vacuum; relations in thought or style or theme are there to discover, if not as a whole picture, then as related fragments that have points of intersection and tangency.

The scarcity of source materials in part reflects what was surely a real cultural decline in the wake of both the Jurchen and Mongol conquests. Although the Jurchen captured the Sung capital at Kaifeng in 1127 and imprisoned the last two Northern Sung emperors, warfare between Jurchen forces and Sung loyalists did not cease until a peace was concluded in 1142. The remnant Sung court had set up a temporary capital at Hangchow (renamed Lin-an, "Temporary Resting Place") in the southeast. Cultural losses during this extended period of warfare were compounded by the exodus of most leading literati families to the South. While the Southern Sung court attempted to prevent printed texts from being exported to the Chin, the amount, number, and quality of Southern Sung texts actually to reach the Chin remains a matter of uncertainty. Chao I (1727–1814), the great Ch'ing historian and critic, suggests that few, if any, Southern Sung texts made their way north (*OPSH* 12.12). Refuting this argument, the modern polymath Ch'ien Chung-shu (1984, 158) offers evidence of citations of near-contemporary Southern Sung poets in the work of Yüan Hao-wen. Although our own investigations on this point are only tentative, they suggest a limited circulation of important texts. But caution is again the key word. The wide range of material cited in Wang Jo-hsü's forty-three-chapter critique of the literary and historical tradition, for instance, seems at first blush to suggest access to an enormous collection of primary sources in the classics, histories, and belles lettres. Many entries in the work, however, may be read as responses or counterarguments to essays that can be traced to one of two major Southern Sung compendia: Hung Mai's (1123–1202) *Jung-chai sui-pi* and Hu Tzu's (1082–1143) *T'iao-hsi yü-yin ts'ung-hua*. Hung Mai's work originally appeared serially: the first portion was edited for presentation to the emperor between 1174 and 1189, and the final editing of the entire work took place between 1208 and 1224. Hu Tzu's work was originally published in two separate volumes, the first in 1148, and the second in 1169. So while Wang Jo-hsü, who cites most widely from other texts, may not have possessed the works of each individual author he discussed, he at least had access to these two compendia within a few decades of their publication. Those Southern Sung works that are known to have been available in the North and that provided a (now) hidden stimulus for writers like Wang Jo-hsü are of particular importance in reconstructing the world of thought the Chin literati moved in; they demonstrate that the textual and intellectual interests of Chin scholars evolved along a path completely different from that of their contemporaries in the South.

Even though Chin was not extinguished by the Mongols until 1234, military disruption of civil culture had begun soon after the turn of the century with the menacing assaults of the Sung from the south and the Mongols from the north and west. By 1214 the Jurchen had had to abandon the principal capital at Peking to the Mongols and flee to Kaifeng just south of the Yellow River. The empire's longest continuous period of peace and normalcy thus lasted only about forty years, from 1165 to 1206, a period that might be called "High Chin," and civil culture thus had little time to flourish in the North under the Chin. The official *Chin History* centers its discussions of Chin culture around the reign of Chin Shih-tsung (r. 1161–89) and states that it was during the reigns of Shih-tsung and Chang-tsung (r. 1190–1208) that learning flourished (*CS* 125. 2713; Chu Chung-yü 1984). This era of relative peace was shattered by the Mongol conquest of North China, a protracted border war of some twenty years' duration (1213–34). The devastation wrought by the Mongols was so overwhelming, the crises of this era brought challenges that far exceeded any faced by the South during the twelfth and thirteenth centuries. Historically, a degree of turmoil and disorder has often provided a stimulus to cultural creativity, but rampant upheaval and violence can reach a point where mere survival leaves little energy for cultural pursuits. This period found its voice in Yüan Hao-wen, whose poems of death and disorder (*sang-luan shih*) are recognized as the greatest achievement of Chin poetry. Stephen West's article on Yüan's poems discusses the tragedy of the Mongol cataclasm and how it provoked these poems of lamentation even while it created in Yüan Hao-wen the resolve to chronicle the achievements of his fallen dynasty, a resolve that came to fruition in his *Collection of the Central Plain* (*Chung-chou chi*) and other works that provided much of the source material for the later *Chin History*.

The greatest literati of the Chin dynasty, those who were educated during High Chin, began to rise in prominence only in the 1190s and produced the body of their literary output during the crisis years of the early thirteenth century. This period of change from High Chin to Mongol conquest presents a curious mixture of political instability and bureaucratic reform. The focus of this reform was, as during the Northern Sung, the examination system. An enduring conflict noted in Liu Ch'i's writings is that between two classes of scholars, the literati (*wen-jen* or *shih*) and the examination candidates (*chü-tzu* or *chü-tzu pei*). He identifies the first class as comprising those who are broadly read in the classics, histories, and belles lettres, especially poetry, and the second as those who specialize only in the examination curriculum and the requirements of "regulated rhyme-prose" (*lü-fu*), an exercise in syntactic symmetry, tonal and metrical antithesis and parallelism, and the use of a highly refined diction. Between the decline of High Chin and the years before and after 1224, the examination system became particularly corrupt: the examiners effectively made regulated rhyme-prose the centerpiece of the exams, promoting or rejecting candidates on what was, in reality, only one of the several parts of the examinations. Liu Ch'i described the situation:

> The corruption of regulated rhyme-prose during the Chin is beyond description. The creations of writers of the Ta-ting reign period are full and substantial in both spirit and content; their scholarship is deep and broad and can still stand as a model. But after this period, Chang Hsing-chien [d. 1215] became chief examiner, and in grading [the examination candidates] he adhered strictly to the stipulated metrical and stylistic rules; he was tyrannical and assiduous in his fault-finding. Candidates who sat for the examinations during this period simply sketched out something that was loosely akin to the topic, vague, sometimes so much so that the language of the piece

was completely incomprehensible. Because of this, ... the air [i.e., the accustomed style and quality] of [compositions of] the literati gradually declined. In the grove of scholars it was said, "Whenever you begin a smaller piece of regulated rhyme-prose, you must say, 'The state—one desires to plan for its ordering; the emperor should understand [this with clarity], as if he had been burned by it.'"[2] When a transitional phrase was called for between passages, they invariably used the four-character phrase *k'o te erh chih* ["it can be assumed," "one simply knows"], so when real scholars see an examination candidate, they point him out and say, "Here's another 'one simply knows.'" (KCC 9.97)

Liu Ch'i's point here is not only that by its nature regulated rhyme-prose pushed the writer in the direction of hyperbole, florid language, and set, even stale, diction, but that the process of writing in this form robbed the young student of the ability to think properly. In mentioning their use of the phrase "one simply knows," he is pointing to the corruption of logic in text. This transitional phrase, unlike others that might normally include particles of summation or causation, describes the relationships between two sets of ideas as "self-evident." The writer is thus relieved of the responsibility of establishing authority for his views through either logical argumentation or reference to classical precedent.

It is important, of course, to realize that what Liu wrote about literature and the examination system is analogous to the moral and social order in general: literature and writing exemplify moral character and—by extension of the moral self into the public sphere—government, administration, and bureaucracy. The net result is that, in Liu Ch'i's mind, this decline of literature and personal morality exemplified the wholesale degeneration of the cultural Zeitgeist. Liu lays the blame for this at the feet of the Jurchen rulers, particularly Hsüan-tsung. He points out that after the southern crossing of 1214, Hsüan-tsung surrounded himself with sycophants and eunuchs who wielded great power, gradually divesting his prime ministers of all authority and efficacy (KCC 7.69–72). Moreover, under the influence of the powerful Shu-hu Kao-ch'i, the emperor began to promote clerks, whom he relied on to run the bureaucracy; and the literati, who as a class gained political power through the examination system, were thereby disenfranchised (KCC 7.72). Liu wrote of the effect of these policies:

The spirit of the literatus must be fostered in an unbroken fashion. For instance, in the Ming-ch'ang and T'ai-ho reign periods [1190–1208] culture [*wen*] was venerated and scholars were fostered. Consequently, literati of the age respected each other on the basis of boldness in speech and action. So when it came to the Ta-an reign period [1209–12], when northern troops penetrated our borders, many literati died in resistance, integrity intact. After the southern crossing, Emperor Hsüan-tsung used clerks [in the court bureaucracy] and suppressed the literati. Those bold in speech or action were expelled or punished. Those [who remained] in prominent positions were mostly weak-willed men who sought only either to avoid being charged with wrongdoing or to ingratiate themselves with others. During the T'ien-hsing [1232–34] usurpation [of Ts'ui Li], not one literatus died with integrity. But wasn't there something that had brought this about? (KCC 7.73)

In several places, Liu describes attempts at reform, primarily by Chao Ping-wen and Yang Yün-i, who supervised the examinations during the period after the southern crossing. These reforms did not, of course, go unchallenged:

Since the T'ai-ho and Ta-an reigns [1201–12], writings [produced] for the examinations had become corrupt. Now, those in charge of the examinations simply stuck to the rules of style and metrics, nurturing neither inner talent nor mind. Therefore, the texts that they selected were soft and weak, stale and rotten—[the candidates] simply did no more than what was necessary to pass. Those who possessed surpassing talent and expansive vigor or who delighted in what was new or extraordinary often met with expulsion or failure. So the air of culture declined more and more. When it came to Hsüan-tsung's southern crossing, at the beginning of Chen-yu [1213–17], a rescript was sent down abrogating the local first-level examination [*fu-shih*], and Chao "the Leisured" [i.e., Chao Ping-wen] became chief examiner for the Secretariat examinations [for the degree of *chin-shih*]. Those in charge received a piece of rhyme-prose from Li Ch'in-shu and were very fond of it. Now, although the style of his piece was a little loose in terms of metrical and grammatical rules, the rich vocabulary he employed was serious and solemn and lacked any touch of the vulgar or common. Consequently, he was chosen for the first position [in that category] and Ma Chih-chi was selected as top of the class in the category of discussion and policy. At this point the whole class of examination candidates began to raise a clamor. They [eventually] took their suit to the Censorate, submitting a complaint that the noble Chao had ruined the rules of writing; they also wrote poems satirizing him. Censor Hsü Tao-chen sent a memorial to the throne about it. The case was on the verge of undergoing a second investigation, but it died away after a long period of time.

At precisely this juncture, Ch'in-shu passed the palace examinations [*hung-tz'u k'o*] and was accepted into the Han-lin Academy. By that time, the multitude [of candidates] had been repressed, and they submitted.

During the Cheng-ta [1224–32] era, Ch'in-shu was again made chief examiner of the Secretariat examinations, and those in charge received the rhyme-prose of Shih Hsüeh-yu. They were greatly taken with it, and he was made top candidate. At this point the whole class of examination candidates again protested angrily. Now, Shih's rhyme-prose was even less bound by the rules than Li's, and it was solely on the basis of his learning and the force of his words that one could see that he was a great writer; moreover, the rhyme-prose used a number of animal names in parallel lines. The group of examination candidates said, "Do you know why the examiners took this rhyme-prose to be the best? Because it's so full of flavor!" They also said, "We should call Hsüeh-yu an animal trainer!" But Hsüeh-yu passed the palace examinations at precisely that time, and so the clamor died down.

Alas. The literati have so long been at peace in a position of baseness and so long accustomed to the vulgar that their fright and surprise at the sudden appearance of someone of extraordinary talent far surpassing their own is most understandable. The [purpose of the] examinations is primarily to select those in the world who possess heroic talent; metrical and stylistic rules are just a general guide. Some [examiners] will take this one and reject that one [following different criteria], so there is always a possibility someone will lament being left out. And Chao and Li did not simply go along with the predilections of the majority; they selected candidates on the basis of what they alone thought was right—so how can the clamorings of those who debate this point be worth comparing, one with another? (KCC 10.109)[3]

Not surprisingly, Chao Ping-wen's, Yang Yün-i's, and Li Ch'in-shu's efforts at institutional reform did not bear fruit. There was simply too little time. Try as they might, the reformers were unable to overcome what Liu Ch'i saw as a lack of strong leadership in late Chin intellectual life. Hsüan-tsung's policies were partially to blame, but the literati must share accountability.

Liu presents us with two important facts about the years between 1224 and 1234: the first is that the literati were then disenfranchised by those in power; the second is that there was a reform movement headed by men of moral worth that was just then beginning to gather steam. These two issues seem paradoxical until we look more closely at what Liu actually says. The reforms themselves are part of a basic instability at the nexus of late Chin culture. We find, for instance, that Liu mentions three major periods of reform within a space of ten years—this clearly indicates that for him there was no well-defined contemporary concept of the responsibilities and duties of the literati. We do not mean to imply here that Liu Ch'i argues for a rigid consensus; on the contrary, he seems to argue for a generally recognized field of values within which there is room for expression and implementation of literati ideals. For Liu Ch'i the constant change of examination curriculum, the bickering at court between scholars and students were symptomatic of a destabilization of the moral and cultural center of the state. His criticism of examination writing may be seen, we think, as indicative of his concern about the locus of responsibility for culture. In his essays it is clear that he sees that the disempowerment of the literati had debased their values. They were unable to muster authority, either by reasoning or by reference to classical sources, and thereby were unable to inspire their writing with any moral essence. The lack of allegiance to a central set of values also meant that the literati gravitated toward political power instead of moral authority, and, as Liu Ch'i points out, the consequent possession of power cut even deeper rifts between those in and those out of office:

> After the southern crossing, the air of the literati [shih-feng] became exceptionally insubstantial. Once they got on the registry of official service, they viewed the various students who had not passed the examinations as following a different road, and they might even go so far as to part suddenly from those who had once been close friends and associates. Sometimes, when those who were still civilians had affairs of importance, they would try several times to see those who were in positions [of authority]. But those in positions [of authority] would rarely answer their requests. Some even removed themselves to lofty mansions where their old friends could not get access to them. Li Ch'ang-yüan therefore became very upset about this and said, "Can they become the most arrogant of all literati in the world on the basis of one trifling pass in the examinations?" Many who had already passed the examinations were extremely angry when they heard this, and they managed to drive Li Ch'ang-yüan out of the Bureau of History and actually lodged a formal complaint against him. Can the air of the literati be like this? (KCC 7.76)

Instead of using their offical positions and moral authority to advance the cause of the *shih* as a class, these scholars accelerated the fragmentation of those who should have been united in their quest to reinstate and uphold the cultural order that was their heritage

The Chinese literati would probably have found themselves in a better environment for cultural creativity if they hadn't had to contend with problems introduced by the southern crossing. Still, it would be unfair to overlook areas of creativity that existed during High Chin and even during the declining years of the dynasty—creativity in the realms of religious thought, literature, and institutional restructuring. The level of scholarship in Chin China, more uneven in quality than that of either the Northern or Southern Sung renaissance, still had its high points, especially if we position thinkers like Wang Jo-hsü and Chao Ping-wen in a tradition of scholarship not particularly allied to Tao-hsüeh—one like Hung Mai's, which was heavily textual. We should not deny the positive contributions the literati made to civilizing alien rule in North China and continuing alternative forms of Confucian learning, ethics, and service.

In addition to the destruction and losses incurred during the conquests of North China, the attitudes of Ming and Ch'ing scholars and the regimes that ruled them have not favored the survival of Chin historical materials. Much was no doubt lost during the Ming simply because it was considered to be of inadequate significance to mainstream Confucian culture to be preserved or reprinted. Although the reigning Manchus of the Ch'ing dynasty were related to the Jurchen, after their conquest of China they did not call attention to their ancestry, cultural or otherwise. The Manchus wanted to present themselves to the Chinese as the custodians of Chinese culture, and little was to be gained from close identification with the Jurchen. Moreover, the Chin had been not only a short-lived dynasty, but one that was also geographically restricted to the northern part of China.

Modern scholarship has only recently begun to transcend traditional biases against the Jurchen and Chin history. In recent decades Chinese scholars have explored a wide spectrum of topics, which is evident even in a partial listing of the major publications in this field. Sun Chin-chi's (1987) book, for example, traces the history of the Jurchen beginning with the end of the Eastern Han and continuing through the Ming period. Sung Te-chin (1988) and Wang K'o-pin (1989) discuss various aspects of Jurchen society and daily life, including food, clothing, recreation, festivals, wedding ceremonies, and religious beliefs. Yü Yu-yen and others (1989) document surviving Jurchen folk tales. Jin Guangping and Jin Qicong's (1980) volume on the Jurchen language and Jin Qicong's (1984) Jurchen dictionary enhance our understanding of the language. Chang Po-ch'üan, whose (1981) book on economic development and (1984) historical survey are both well known, is currently writing a three-part work (1986–) on Chin history, an overview of historical sources, personages, social change, economy, government institutions, Jurchen military organization, wars with the Sung, and historical geography. Yü Chieh and Yü Kuang-tu (1989) explore the legacy of Peking as the Chin capital. Liu Su-yung (1987) provides a detailed biography of the dynasty's most outstanding emperor, Shih-tsung. Ts'ui Wen-yin gives us a modern edition of a major historical source for Chin history (*TCCC*). Li Shu-t'ien (1989) provides annotated transcriptions of Chin stele inscriptions. Chou Hui-ch'üan and Mi Chih-kuo (1986) have an annotated volume of literary selections from the Liao and Chin. Two important works on literature have recently appeared: the first, by Chao Chih-hui and others (1989), is a study of the literature of Manchu peoples and is devoted to Hsiao-shen, Po-hai, and Jurchen literature; the second, by Chan Hang-lun (1993), is a comprehensive history of Chin dynasty literature. Even though the late Ch'en Shu's major research centered on the Liao, he deserves special credit for developing Chin studies during his long tenure as president of the Chinese Association of Liao-Chin and Khitan-Jurchen History. Among other works, he edited five volumes of essays (1987–92) on Liao and Chin history. Although most research in the People's Republic of China has centered on ethnic culture, archaeology, socioeconomic history, and political institutions, more attention is currently being given to the subject of cultural development than in past decades. For example, at the 1991 Tatung conference convened by the Liao-Chin Association, there were even several papers on Confucianism.

Chin studies have also made progress outside the PRC. Besides several studies in Chinese by Tao Jing-shen (T'ao Chin-sheng) on Chin institutional, political, and military history, as well as a book by Yeh Ch'ien-chao (1972) on Chin legal history, other monographic studies include Yang Shu-fan's (1978) book on central government political systems. The volumes of essays compiled by Yao Ts'ung-wu (1971) and Wang Ming-sun (1981) are also noteworthy. Japanese scholars have made major contributions to the field, particularly to our understanding of the language, culture, and customs of the Jurchen people. Special notice should be taken of Toyama Gunji's (1975 and 1978) histories of the Chin, Mikami Tsugio's (1970, 1972, 1973, 1984) social and institutional studies of the Jurchen, Niida Noboru's (1944) work on Chin law, and Yoshikawa Kôjirô's (1974) pioneering work on Chin political culture. The history and teachings of Ch'an Buddhism are subjects of particular interest among Japanese academics because of the link between Ch'an and Zen. In the West, outstanding examples of scholarly contributions to the field of Chin studies would include Herbert Franke's social and political histories; Chan Hok-lam's studies of historiography; Morris Rossabi's (1982) monograph on the Jurchen during the Yüan and Ming; Gisaburo Kiyose's (1977) and Daniel Kane's (1989) studies of Jurchen language and script; J. T. Wixted's (1982) work on Yüan Hao-wen and Chin literary theory; and Tao Jing-shen's and Chan Hok-lam's works on political history and interstate relations. Special note should be made of the volume of translations on Chin society that Herbert Franke and Chan Hok-lam have been editing at the University of Washington. Even this partial listing of major works reminds us that the present volume is indebted to a growing scholarship on the Chin period. Still, compared to the state of secondary scholarship on the Sung or Yüan dynasties, Chin studies are markedly underdeveloped.

This underdevelopment is particularly pronounced in regards to cultural history. Although the limits of extant sources and the nascent state of the field restrict our progress, the present volume will take steps to relate aspects of institutional, intellectual, religious, literary, artistic, and social developments to the cultural matrix. Discussing these various areas of historical development should promote a greater interest in the culture of the era and help set the foundation for the eventual integration of the Chin into Chinese cultural history. In taking up this task, the authors of these essays have in a sense been influenced by one of the primary missions of the Chin intellectuals upon whom they have focused. For instance, Chao Ping-wen (1159–1232), in a memorial to Chin Chang-tsung, praised that emperor's efforts to "enhance the tradition of the Central Plain" (*FSWC* 10.9a). He was anxious, in other words, that the Chin strengthen its connection to the cultural tradition of North China. As Sung Te-chin (1990) documents, dynastic legitimacy was a major issue throughout the Chin, of both political and cultural import. The concern displayed in Chao Ping-wen's memorial reflects the seriousness with which Chinese scholars and regimes have historically viewed the question of legitimate dynastic succession. It was profoundly important that a dynasty be judged, by contemporary and future generations of historians and critics alike, to be or to have been in the mainstream of Chinese history. Being viewed as mainstream was crucial to a dynasty's legitimacy and also to the individual Confucian scholars who hoped their lives and literary works would be appreciated as contributions to the legacy of Chinese culture. Although we are not attempting to redress the placement of the Chin in the succession of dynasties, we generally do share the concern that Chao Ping-wen articulated, to consider the cultural developments that unfolded under the Chin as a part of the cultural history of China.

Although Yüan scholars edited the three histories of the Liao, Chin, and Sung nominally without settling the controversial problem of legitimate succession, their official *Chin History* in fact affirmed the Chin as the legitimate state. Specifically, legendary births are cited only for Jurchen ancestors and not for successors of the Sung or Liao royal houses; emphasis is repeatedly placed upon the arrival of envoys from the Sung, Korea, and the Hsi-Hsia (990–1227), a state founded by Tanguts in northwestern China; and references to the fall of the Southern Sung consistently employ terms of unification and pacification that imply that the Mongol Yüan had already gained legitimacy from their conquest of the Chin (Chu Chung-yü 1984). Thus, the Mongol editors broke with the tradition of according legitimacy only to Han Chinese regimes; moreover, they presented a positive image of a polyethnic state that regarded all its people ultimately as one family (Chang Po-ch'üan 1984, 11–13). Besides noting that the official history retrospectively accorded political legitimacy to the Chin, James Liu (1977) also observes that the Chinese contributors to the dynastic histories project sponsored by the Yüan court countered by establishing collective biographies of Tao-hsüeh Confucians in the official *Sung History* only and thereby set their claim to ideological orthodoxy. Historiographically, there was a clever compromise between the Mongol preference for the Chin and the Chinese affinity for the Sung.

In essence, we might say that this compromise by Yüan scholars left the status of Chin's legitimacy split by affording it a greater degree of political legitimacy but denying it cultural legitimacy. Especially given the fact that the political legitimacy accorded the Chin was not very explicit and could easily be viewed differently by Chinese historians and scholars, this recognition of the Sung as the inheritors of cultural orthodoxy relegated the Chin—and all cultural developments occurring within the boundaries of their empire and during their regime—to the fringes of Chinese civilization.

Part I of the volume consists of three essays on history and institutions. Hoyt Cleveland Tillman provides an overview of political and institutional developments that traces the evolution away from Jurchen tribal practices and toward Chinese imperial institutions. The Jurchen adapted a practical mixture of native and T'ang institutions inherited through Liao and Northern Sung institutional innovations. The Chin had some significant institutional differences from the Sung that arose largely from their Jurchen tribal heritage and the task confronting the ethnic minority determined to maintain its grasp on the reins of power. That consciousness of being a ruling minority notwithstanding, the Jurchen emperors deliberately expanded the civil service examination system to allow greater numbers of Han Chinese to enter the government. This expansion, especially from the last two decades of the twelfth century, played a major role in creating a critical mass of literati, some of whom excelled in the examinations and assumed cultural leadership during the Chin.

James T. C. Liu suggests major revisions in the way the Chin dynasty should be viewed in the larger historical context of conquest dynasties.

Although the Jurchen were the first people from the steppe region to cross the Yangtze River into South China, this fact has been ignored by historians, perhaps to enhance the historical significance of the later conquest by the Mongols, under whose supervision the official histories of the Sung, Liao, and Chin were compiled. The Jurchen did not attempt to conquer the South; they had more limited objectives, seeking at the time to rule through the Ch'i dynasty (1130–37) headed by Liu Yü (1073–1143). Although dismissed by later Chinese historians as a petty puppet regime, Liu Yü's government "secured the land and calmed the people" so successfully that his collaboration with the Jurchen paved the way for a bloodless transfer of power. The Jurchen might have achieved a complete conquest of China if they had realized the truth implemented so well by their descendants the Manchus in the seventeenth century: "No effective turncoats, no conquest." The ease with which the Jurchen unseated Liu Yü in their peaceful grasp of direct rule in North China meant that the Chinese government in Hangchow had little prospect for liberating the North. Nevertheless, the Jurchen were suspicious of turncoats and sometimes inflicted the cruelest punishments upon them. Such measures discouraged other Chinese from accepting similar roles in aiding the expansion of Jurchen power southward.

Tao Jing-shen explores how Chin patronage of local schools contributed to the revival of Confucian learning and the promotion of education. Based on a detailed scrutiny of essays written to commemorate the construction or repair of school buildings, Tao traces the development of local schools during the Chin, analyzes the nature of these schools, and assesses their influence on the culture of the period. The schools in question were "temple schools" (*miao-hsüeh*), which served as both schools and Confucian temples where statues or portraits of Confucius and his principal disciples were venerated. Professor Tao finds that the number of local schools either built or repaired during the Chin is actually greater than conventionally accepted estimates. Local schools were widespread enough both to continue the Northern Sung ideal of broadening educational opportunity and to promote Chinese literary and cultural values. The local officials' enthusiasm for these projects echoes through their essays. Moreover, the writers of these essays were convinced that Chin support for local education arose from the Jurchen emperors' aspirations to identify themselves with Chinese rulers of the past who were esteemed by Confucian literati.

Part II consists of three essays on religion and Confucian thought during the Chin. Two of the essays point to deep relationships between Chin, Sung, and Yüan Confucianism. Whereas Yoshikawa Kôjirô (1974) built his case for Su Shih's (1036–1101) near-total dominance of Chin literati culture largely on the culture of the civil service examinations,

Peter K. Bol has focused on the personal writings of leading intellectuals to demonstrate that they were indeed primarily committed to Su Shih's vision of literary culture (*wen*). That Northern Sung vision of culture rested on a philosophy of an integrated approach to various artistic and academic pursuits (like calligraphy, painting, poetry, prose composition, and historical writing) that would provide a broad base for the cultured literatus. Such major Chin literati as Chao Ping-wen engaged in these pursuits in accord with Su Shih's vision. Furthermore, having inherited Su Shih's criticism of Ch'eng I (1033–1107) as being too dogmatic and philosophically abstract, they were only cautiously receptive to the moral philosophy developed by various Tao-hsüeh Confucians. Although Ch'eng's focus on the *tao* and Su's on *wen* were in opposition during the Sung, Chin literati sought to ease the tension. Seeking to preserve Chinese culture in an era of militarism and foreign conquest, their efforts at harmonization set the tone for intellectual life until advocates of Confucian orthodoxy, grounded in Ch'eng I and Chu Hsi (1130–1200), gained such prominence in Peking by the 1350s that they could accentuate the tensions inherent in the approaches to *wen* and the *tao*. Professor Bol's thesis concentrates here on Chao Ping-wen.

Although Hoyt Cleveland Tillman agrees that Su Shih was an intellectual figurehead for Chin Confucians, he seeks to demonstrate that the degree of Su Shih's dominance needs to be qualified because Tao-hsüeh Confucianism became increasingly popular among Chin literati from around 1190 onward. Tillman thus dates the introduction and spread of Tao-hsüeh Confucianism in North China about forty-five years earlier than scholars conventionally have. The rising popularity of Tao-hsüeh Confucianism did not eclipse the allegiance of major Chin Confucians to Su Shih, but even they were attracted to it enough to praise those who dedicated themselves to propagating its writings and doctrines. Furthermore, the writings of these major literary figures, particularly Chao Ping-wen and Wang Jo-hsü, reveal some influence from Tao-hsüeh Confucian ideas and concerns. The overall direction of various intellectual developments appears to indicate that Tao-hsüeh Confucianism was beginning to gain ground at the expense of Su Shih's philosophy of culture—particularly in regard to understanding the *tao*, ethical cultivation, and the Confucian classics. These areas are particularly significant, because they were seen by Chu Hsi as crucial issues of contention with followers of Su Shih. In large part, the apparent differences between Bol's and Tillman's essays regarding the relative predominance of Su Shih's philosophy and the relative weight of Tao-hsüeh Confucian influences arise from the different issues or questions they are addressing.

Yao Tao-chung reminds the reader that Taoism and Buddhism under the Chin were far more pervasive than Confucianism, even among literati.

Professor Yao surveys the institutional relationship of Buddhism and Taoism to government and society under the Chin to relate the complexities of the ties of patronage and conflict. Much like other dynasties in China, the Chin exercised control over religious groups. And its impartial patronage of both Buddhism and Taoism provided an environment in which the two religions could flourish more harmoniously than during the succeeding Yüan period. A major development during the Chin was the movement toward unifying these two religions, along with Confucianism, into the "Three Teachings." Wang Che (1113–70) was the first person to use the term "Three Doctrines" (*san-chiao*) to name religious congregations. Hence, he sought to be impartial in his borrowing from the three religious traditions; given his emphasis on cultivation of the "inner elixir" of immortality, however, Wang Che's Ch'üan-chen ("Complete Perfection" or "Perfect Truth") movement was considered a Taoist sect—and is now known to have been the most popular of any religious group during the Chin and one of two Taoist sects to have survived to this day. Ch'üan-chen was one of the new Taoist sects that arose at least in part as a religious reaction to the cultural aftermath of the Jurchen conquest. It was, after all, the Taoists in Chin China, rather than those in the Southern Sung, who continued the tradition of compiling the Taoist canon.

In addition to contributing to the Tripitaka, Chin Buddhists also served as a vital link between Buddhism of earlier and later periods. Although long thought to have been lost, the Chin compilation of the Tripitaka was discovered in 1958 in the Yün-chü Temple near Peking and is now being reprinted. The very survival of the Ts'ao-tung sect of Ch'an Buddhism hinged on the master Hsing-hsiu (1166–1246), through whom all important later masters of this predominately northern school traced their lines of transmission. Although Hsing-hsiu lived most of his life under the Chin, it is revealing of the perspectives of later writers that he is usually presented as a figure of the Yüan era.

Part III includes four essays that relate aspects of literature and art to sociopolitical and cultural developments. Susan Bush addresses the nature of Chin literati from the vantage point of an art historian. In her survey of five paintings that have not heretofore been studied as a group or related to the cultural context of the Chin, Dr. Bush provides additional evidence to support the view that by the end of the twelfth century culture was flourishing under the Chin. Including a major reattribution of one of the five paintings, her study explores the ties of the artists to bureaucratic organizations in order to address the questions whether an Academy of Painting existed and what the status of "professional" painters was under the Chin. Compared to their Northern and Southern Sung counterparts, Chin painters did not have the benefit of as much institutionally structured government support, but there also appears to have been less of a status differential between painters and scholars than was true during the Sung. The early Yüan inherited these characteristics from the Chin; moreover, the only models for the early Yüan court artists were Northern Sung styles preserved by Chin painters and collectors. As during the Yüan, the relatively small status differential between painters and scholars actually reflected a decline in the status of the literati during the Chin as compared to the Sung, but the Chin devaluation in status was accompanied by a proliferation of examination degrees.

The essay by Jin Qicong, former head of the Shenyang Center for Research on Jurchen and Manchu Languages and Cultures, provides the first major study in English of the literature of the Jurchen people. A direct descendant of the Ch'ien-lung emperor (r. 1736–95), Professor Jin writes with the double advantage of academic background and personal familiarity with the culture of this northeastern minority people. Having studied in Japan several decades ago, Professor Jin draws heavily from Japanese scholarship on Jurchen people and culture in his work. In his contribution to this volume Professor Jin analyzes the evolution of Jurchen literature from its oral beginnings to its written forms. Because of the sinicization policies of mid-twelfth-century Chin rulers and the greater utility of literary Chinese, Jurchen literature lived in increasing danger of extinction until it was revived in the 1160s by the Chin emperor Shih-tsung. Yet even his heir apparent did not know Jurchen well, for the prince's studies concentrated on literary Chinese. Shih-tsung's successors forsook his re-Jurchenization program in favor of the sinicization policies of his two predecessors. Still, Shih-tsung's work bore some fruit in later years. By the first decade of the thirteenth century, there were enough schools and examination degrees in Jurchen that a significant number of scholars wrote in Jurchen, but their compositions were virtually translations from Chinese. Professor Jin argues that even Jurchen writings in Chinese should nonetheless be considered Jurchen literature because they express Jurchen thoughts and emotions.

Wilt Idema's essay considers a literary genre addressed to upscale urban audiences including, but not limited to, literati. A musical medium designed for entertainment, the all-keys-and-modes (*chu-kung-tiao*) was a prosimetric form of storytelling that smilingly satirized exemplars of social mobility, especially students preparing for the civil service examinations. The genre arose in Kaifeng in the late eleventh century, along with the markedly increased visibility of students and growing importance of civil service examinations. Although popular in Hangchow and performed through most of the Yüan period, the zenith of the genre was reached under the Chin. Students continued to bear the principal brunt of its humor because the gap between their initial expectations and actual success left them open to ridicule. The authors of *chu-kung-tiao* were generally sympathetic toward students struggling for upward mobility; however, they characterized students as victims of circumstance and slaves to passion rather than as strong masters of their own fates and fortunes. Even when presenting the tale of a historic figure before his rise to eminence, authors satirized the upwardly mobile figure as totally controlled by circumstance. Another characteristic of the genre under the Chin is the pervasiveness of sexual themes and imagery, reflecting a relative freedom in this period from more orthodox Confucian mores. But Professor Idema finds that the lessons inherent in stories involving sex generally mirror conventional Confucian morality. A new element in Chinese literature that appears in this genre is contempt for rural life. In contrast to the bucolic idealizations of earlier writers, *chu-kung-tiao* authors focused on the unpleasantness of village life and the ignorance of country yokels—and the fun they poked at them is devoid of the sympathy that characterizes their satiric portrayal of students. In such ways, Professor Idema's detailed discussion of the genre enriches our understanding of literati society of the era.

Stephen West's study of a series of poems by Yüan Hao-wen on the death and disorder wrought by the Mongol conquest is also a study of a Confucian literatus' reaction to what he perceives as the death of culture. In his poems, Yüan wrote of the new cataclysm of the Central Plain, the inundation of the seat of traditional culture by an (in his eyes) uncivilized horde of barbarians. Lamentation was soon replaced, however, by a new sense of mission to chronicle and preserve the textual and cultural heritage of the Chin. Yüan's sense of urgency was certainly inspired by a belief that it was Chinese, not just Chin, culture that was in danger. His identification with Confucius himself as the inheritor and perpetuator of culture demonstrates not only the deep sense of commitment such literati felt as participants in an unbroken cultural process, but also the value that commitment held in the formation of self-identity.

Running through these essays, there is an assumption that synchronic and diachronic dimensions point together toward the Chin's place in Chinese cultural history. Chin Buddhism, for instance, may be viewed from either the ecumenism of the Northern Sung or the syncretism of the Ming. A similar dual perspective applies to Tao-hsüeh Confucianism under the Chin. On the one hand, focusing on the importance of a Tao-hsüeh anthology, the *Chu Ju ming-tao chi* (Writings for propagating the *tao*), brings to the fore the continuation of broader Southern Sung Tao-hsüeh orientations into the Chin and Yüan. In this case, the prominence of early Southern Sung Tao-hsüeh philosophers, especially Chang Chiu-ch'eng (1092–1159), whom Chu Hsi excised from the tradition, suggests a certain tension between Chu Hsi's delineation of Confucianism and their own. On the other hand, focusing retrospectively on the degree to which Chu Hsi did delimit Tao-hsüeh for later generations, we may reflect upon Tao-hsüeh under the Chin as a preparatory stage preceding the triumph of Chu Hsi's Confucianism under the Yüan. Each perspective has validity and helps to place the culture of the Chin era in Chinese cultural history. Both are crucial to understanding the contribution of the Chin literati in providing bridges between the T'ang-Sung past and the Yüan-Ming future.

We would concede that there is a strong historical bias to accept the conventional wisdom that the most important and impressive causeway of culture passed through Southern Sung. But we must ask ourselves how much this bias is a product of the predilections of later historians who could trace their own roots to that stream of thought. We must ask ourselves if it is historical perspective, created out of the desire of later historians, and ethnic and cultural prejudice that have viewed the shorter and more direct spans between the Chin and the Yüan with such disapprobation.

In spite of the emphasis here on intellectual, religious, artistic, and literary trends in the rise of southern cultural dominance over northern culture, we are not trying to be reductionistic. Other factors, such as material culture and population distribution, were of major significance. For instance, James T. C. Liu (1985) has demonstrated that the impact of the progression toward increased urbanization and intensive agriculture during the Sung, especially in the South, militated against continuing the northern legacy of the physically rigorous and martially minded exercise of polo. Polo played riding horseback across large fields as a form of military training gave way to kicking balls in alleys and courtyards. Although numerous Confucians articulated the dangers of polo playing and preferred riding in sedan chairs to riding on horses, they reflected the realities of the urban settings of their offices and the intensively cultivated fields that dominated their landscapes.

There are other important cultural topics that we would have liked to have included in this volume. We had planned to have additional essays on literary theory, classical studies, Buddhist ecumenism, and retrospective views of the Chin from the standpoint of later scholarship. Essays on some of these topics are now to be found elsewhere (for instance, Wixted 1990 on literary theory, originally one of the papers presented at the ACLS conference), or have proved too difficult to write because of the present state of Chin studies, but some discussion of these topics is included in the present essays.

Especially given the underdeveloped state of Chin cultural studies, the present collection of essays should prove to be adequate for a pioneering work and certainly for encouraging further research. With such diversity of coverage and so much that needs to be explored, the various contributors have addressed very different questions that might at times appear to be more exclusive, even unrelated, than is actually the case. Indeed, to acquire an overview of the Chin, each paper should be seen in the context of the whole project. Because of the state of the field, we do not pretend to have achieved an adequate integration of the Chin into Chinese cultural history, but these essays do mark a milestone in the development of Chin cultural studies. And enrichment of our understanding of culture under Chin rule is important to the more complete appreciation of Chinese cultural history—one major component of our global cultural heritage.

Notes

1. This view has a pronounced effect on literary and cultural history even today. See, for instance, Liu Shih-p'ei's (1937) essay on the dissimilarity between northern and southern literature.

2. His point is, this opening couplet must always be cited to please the examiners.

3. That is, someone is always left out, anyway.

I
Politics and Institutions

1

AN OVERVIEW OF CHIN HISTORY AND INSTITUTIONS

Hoyt Cleveland Tillman

Before exploring topics in the cultural history of China under Jurchen rule, there is a need for context. Politics had an impact on culture, and culture influenced politics; some of the same forces were at play in both. Denis Sinor (1990, 13) has summarized the core dilemma faced by various tribal peoples along China's Inner Asian frontier thus: "So the choice was really between living in 'honorable poverty'—at the mercy of nature and in fairly constant conflict with other nomad groups vying for the better pastures—or asking for 'admittance' into the civilized world, at the risk of losing one's national identity." Jurchen interaction with Chinese institutions is indicative of their attitudes and policies toward Chinese culture, and institutional changes are often more concrete and better documented than cultural interaction. Moreover, most available Chinese, Japanese, and Western scholarship on the Jurchen and the Chin focuses on sociopolitical and institutional history.[1] This paper, then, a brief survey of institutions, will serve to set the stage for the essays that follow in this volume, most of which concern cultural topics.

For centuries while in the forests of Manchuria, the Jurchen were a fragmented collection of tribes under the sway of numerous chieftains and shamans. Unified and coordinated, these tribal units produced horsepower that quickly carried the Jurchen to their conquest of the Khitan (Ch'i-tan) Liao dynasty and then the Chinese (Northern) Sung. Unlike earlier conquerors of China who rode in from the steppe, the Khitan and Jurchen arose in the forest belt of Northeast Asia. Pastoralists on the open steppe grasslands generally clustered in larger units than did the forest tribes, and it was perhaps for this reason that Khitan and Jurchen chiefs were quicker to appreciate the organizational strategies of the Chinese. Even before the conquest the Jurchen had begun to accommodate themselves to the Chinese system by adopting certain Chinese practices and by seeking political recognition or investiture from the partly sinicized Liao state. Later, after consolidating their power in North China, the Jurchen initially dealt with the Mongols in much the same way that Chinese regimes had brought steppe tribes into the Chinese political order as vassals. While the Khitan and Mongols were purely nomadic before seizing power in agrarian China, the Jurchen had long engaged in marginal agriculture in addition to hunting and fishing. Thus it is not surprising that the Jurchen adapted more quickly and more thoroughly to Chinese lifestyles and culture.

Although Chin rulers adopted traditional Chinese political institutions to establish and administer an extensive agrarian empire, elements of Jurchen tribal organization and lifestyle persisted through the century of their dominance in North China. Jurchen ethnic interests necessitated some adjustments to centralized bureaucratic institutions. Thus, despite the trend toward absorption of elements of the Chinese system, the Chin's would remain a mixed system of relatively pluralistic and polyethnic character. It was polyethnic because it encompassed peoples as various as the Chinese, the Khitan, the Tanguts (T'ang-ku), the Po-hai, the Koreans, and the Turkish T'ieh-le (although the interaction between the Jurchen rulers and the Chinese majority remains the focus of our interest). Much of Chin history follows the general pattern of other polyethnic states wherein ethnicity was a factor in determining sociopolitical status and legal administration (Franke 1987).

The successive periods of Chin institutional history reflect different stages of the Chin's adoption of Chinese institutions. The first, predynastic period dates from the early eleventh century, when the Jurchen began to receive some official recognition from the Khitan Liao dynasty, and ends in 1115, when the Jurchen proclaimed their own independent imperial dynasty. The most widely accepted periodization for the dynastic phase is Yao Ts'ung-wu's (1971) tripartite division based on the change in location of the principal capital: from 1115 to 1153 the Chin capital was at Shang-ching (the Upper Capital, southeast of modern Harbin); from 1153 to 1214, at Yenching (the Central Capital or Chung-ching, modern Peking); and from 1214 to 1234, at Pien-ching (the Southern Capital, modern Kaifeng). Although an approximation, Yao's divisions represent more than a convenient scheme based on the geography of the Jurchen empire. While in Manchuria, the Jurchen court remained in its native habitat and cultural setting. After its transfer to Peking, the court, culturally transplanted to a Chinese environment, found itself increasingly alienated from Jurchen tribesmen and Jurchen ways. With its retreat to Kaifeng, the Jurchen court moved further into China—and further into the Central Plain, cradle of Chinese civilization.

During the predynastic period—that is, before 1115—the process of Jurchen utilization of Chinese institutions was slow and sporadic. Although Chinese accounts write of Jurchen envoys to the Sui and T'ang courts, this early contact with the Chinese apparently made little impact on the Jurchen. In the early tenth century the Khitan Liao achieved considerable success pacifying a number of Jurchen tribes by moving them into the Liaotung area of southern Manchuria and subsequently forbidding these "civilized" Jurchen from having contact with the "wild" Jurchen to the north (SCPM 3.1b–2a; Franke 1975, 122–26; Chao Ming-ch'i 1987; Yang Mao-sheng 1989). Around this time, too, Han-p'u (early 10th cent.) took what could be seen as the first step toward rationalization of institutions among the wild Jurchen when he eliminated the tradition of revenge by initiating compensatory payments to the victims of crimes. Unchecked vendetta among patrilineal clans made central coordination and organization of men and resources impossible, so the substitution was crucial to developing political and administrative control of their empire (CS 1.2; Franke 1981, 218–19; and 1989, 388–89).

By the early eleventh century, another wild Jurchen chieftain, Shih-lu of the Wan-yen clan, began to impose regulations on his tribesmen and thereby gained a minor title from the Liao. His son Wu-ku-nai (1021–74) brought several tribes under strict enough control—and brought order enough to one part of the Liao frontier—that the Liao rewarded him with the office of "military commissioner of the wild Jurchen tribes" (*sheng Nüchen pu-tsu chieh-tu shih*). Although he sought to maintain his independence, Wu-ku-nai won considerable trust from the Liao by handing over to them several of the unruly Jurchen chieftains he had defeated. Besides gifts of armor and weapons, which helped to augment the cohesion of the Wan-yen tribe and its growing dominance over other tribes, contact with the Liao provided the tribe access to knowledge of governmental organization. Like other tribal groups who eventually challenged Chinese dynasties, the Jurchen were thus first incorporated into the Chinese order in the status of vassals. Wu-ku-nai selected his second son, Ho-li-po (1039–92), as his successor and bestowed the title chancellor of state (*kuo-hsiang*) on his third son, P'o-la-shu (1042–94) (CS 1.3–7, 11; Franke 1978a, 418–22, 428). Such actions enhanced the consolidation of power by providing structures for the resolution of personal conflicts between tribesmen and struggles for succession to the leadership within the Wan-yen clan itself.

Ho-li-po (r. 1074–92) requested aid from the Liao in his campaigns to expand his power over other Jurchen chieftains. Relations with the Liao were entrusted to P'o-la-shu, who acquired considerable understanding of the Liao government through direct dialogue with Liao officials.

P'o-la-shu succeeded briefly to the office of military commissioner (*chieh-tu shih*); and with his death the title passed on to the next brother, Ying-ko (r. 1094–1103).

It was under Ying-ko, in around 1100, that the Wan-yen clan's expansion finally ran into conflict with the Liao, when a chieftain named A-shu fled to the Liao for protection from Ying-ko's forces. The Liao ordered a cease to the attack, but Ying-ko had earlier told his men to ignore such an order should it be sent down. After the town under siege fell, the Liao sent another military commissioner to order Ying-ko to return the town to A-shu and make compensation for those killed. To avoid this retreat, Ying-ko distracted the Liao by ordering tribes along the so-called falcon roads to rebel, simultaneously having a friendly military commissioner report to the Liao that Ying-ko alone could reopen the roads. (So valued were falcons for hunting that the Liao had routinely demanded the birds as the chief tribute item submitted by the Jurchen; hence, the roads along which the tribute was brought to the Liao were called "falcon roads.") Thereupon the Liao ordered Ying-ko to reopen the roads, and subsequently dropped the complaint against his seizure of the town and rewarded him for reopening the roads. After he had suppressed several other rebel tribes the Liao had failed to defeat, Ying-ko was given a personal audience with the Liao emperor and the title *shih-hsiang*, a military office carrying the rank of chief councilor.

In addition to winning the Liao's recognition of his increased strength, Ying-ko made significant changes in tribal rules that eventually elevated his position. He consolidated institutional power within the Jurchen homeland by initiating the use of tablets to authenticate his orders to tribal heads and by forbidding anyone else to use such tablets or to designate himself general chief of the tribes (*tu-pu chang*) (CS 1.11–16; Franke 1978a, 428–35).

Jurchen tribes were organized into a sociopolitical-military structure called *meng-an mou-k'o*. Each division, or *meng-an* (the Jurchen word for "one thousand"), was headed by a hereditary leader known in Chinese as a *ch'ien-hu*, or battalion commander. Within each of these divisions were a number of clan units, each headed by a *mou-k'o*, whom the Chinese referred to as a *pai-hu*, or company commander. These clan leaders participated in tribal councils held in open fields where members, their faces painted black with soot, sat in a circle and discussed important issues currently under consideration. Council members aired their views of alternative courses of action, and from them the *meng-an* leader ultimately made his selection and laid his plans. The agreements reached, the council members washed their faces, then feasted and drank heavily together (Franke 1990, 418). The Jurchen lacked the elaboration of status differentials inherent in Chinese rituals; moreover, the chiefs shared much of the frugal life of ordinary warriors. In short, besides relatively semi-egalitarian customs and free discussions, the Jurchen decision-making process was customarily more decentralized compared to what generally prevailed in the Chinese imperial model.

To strengthen the power of the Wan-yen clan and the cohesion among the Jurchen against the Liao, A-ku-ta (who was to become Chin T'ai-tsu, r. 1115–23) entrusted leadership of larger units of tribesmen to selected "chiefs," *po-chi-lieh* or *po-chin*. Although these two titles were synonymous in Jurchen and encompassed a large range in terms of number of households, the titles became more specific and more clearly defined in Chinese translation: a clan head was called a *po-chin*; the leader of several clans was called a *hu-lu*, or marshal. The title *po-chi-lieh* could refer to any level of tribal chief, but often it referred to a chief at the higher levels. The designated heir to the Jurchen leader was given major responsibilities, and other members of the Wan-yen clan manned high positions.[2]

With this revised organization, A-ku-ta was able to take the title of khan, or supreme chief (*tu po-chi-lieh*), in 1113 and to proclaim the establishment of the Chin dynasty two years later. His predecessor, Wu-ya-shu (r. 1103–13), had pacified the Korean border area and forced the Koreans to acknowledge Jurchen dominance. But it was the Khitan against whom the Jurchen, as vassals of the Liao, bore their major grievances. Liao envoys, for example, had customarily demanded Jurchen girls for bed partners and sometimes took married Jurchen women forcibly to bed for the night (Franke 1990, 415). Believing that Khitan strength was declining, A-ku-ta wanted the Liao to respect Jurchen customs and Jurchen power. After a devastating attack against the Liao, he demanded investiture as emperor, surrender of territory, and other concessions from the Liao. When the Liao emperor refused to treat him as a superior and concede to all of his demands, A-ku-ta proceeded to destroy the Liao. In donning imperial robes and adopting Chinese titles for his tribal chiefs, A-ku-ta heeded the advice of men like Yang P'u (Yang P'o, early 11th cent.) and Han Ch'i-hsien (1082–1146), who had earned *chin-shih* degrees in the Liao civil service examinations (*SCPM* 3.8b–12b; Franke 1975, 149–66; Mikami 1972, 65–72). Such decisions to follow the imperial model and listen to imperial bureaucrats meant that the basic tribal customs with their overlay of Chinese institutions were beginning to be transformed into closer approximations of the bureaucratic system of imperial China.

During the first period of the Chin state the Wan-yen clan further consolidated its power among the Jurchen tribes and extended its control to Chinese who formerly had been subjects of the Liao or the Northern Sung. Jurchen who had earlier been forced to settle in Liao territory and had acculturated surely provided a bridge for their more wild cousins arriving from the forests of Manchuria. Although Jurchen tribal practices predominated, structures of power began to change. A-ku-ta gradually allowed the introduction of Chinese court rituals that interjected status differentials between the emperor and various levels of officials. Wu-ch'i-mai (Chin T'ai-tsung, r. 1123–35) approved a suggestion in 1126 to set up a Chinese-style bureaucracy, and the stratum of chiefs (*po-chi-lieh*) was abolished in 1134. As the former chiefs were transformed into a more conventional nobility and integrated into the Chinese imperial system, the semi-egalitarian aspect of the old tribal customs began to wane and the influence of the hierarchical order of the Chinese imperial tradition waxed. Chinese honorary titles, as well as the *yin* protection system by which relatives were placed into office without undergoing the rigors of the civil service examinations, served to promote Jurchen nobles within the imperial system. The members of the imperial lineage of the Wan-yen clan consequently dominated the government and could treat even important officials like personal slaves. Jurchen nobles serving in bureaucratic offices likewise took advantage of the legacy of certain tribal customs to handle local affairs independently and punished their subordinates freely (*TK* 327.2571; *SCPM* 3.6b; Franke 1975, 141). Moreover, the *meng-an mou-k'o* remained independent and separate communities of Jurchen farmer-warriors or herder-warriors in scattered military garrisons. They remained the backbone of the garrison system; however, as the system's heads were hereditary, differences in wealth and status among its members became progressively pronounced, and its military effectiveness declined (Tao Jing-shen 1976, 48; Chang Po-ch'üan 1984, 300–301).

The pacification of large Chinese populations led the Jurchen to follow the example of the Liao, who had set up a dual system with a Southern Administration (*nan-mien*) to deal with Chinese affairs in predominately Han areas. Chinese aristocratic families (great households dating back to the T'ang era) from the area around modern Peking had never been incorporated into the Sung, so they served the early Chin as easily as they had the Liao (Wang Ming-sun 1981, 38–41, 63–125; Li Hsi-hou 1985). The Jurchen ruler set up a Bureau of Military Affairs (*shu-mi yüan*) in 1122 to oversee the Chinese area (Li Han 1989). At the end of the 1130s effective control of the Chinese population was shifted from the Bureau of Military Affairs to a mobile branch (*hsing-t'ai*) of the Department of State Affairs (*shang-shu sheng*). This branch administration was abandoned in 1150, opening the way for the Jurchen ruler to assume direct rule over the Chinese population. Still, a mixed system of administration continued, and the numbers of Jurchen in North China increased significantly as they migrated with the government to Peking.

Violent political changes during the late 1140s also paved the way toward significant shifts away from the polity and cultural environment of the early Chin. During the 1140s tensions grew between friends of the Sung literatus Ts'ai Sung-nien (1107–59) on the one side, and the aristocratic descendants of northern Liao scholar-officials led by T'ien Ch'üeh (d. 1147) on the other. Taking advantage of these tensions, Hsi-tsung (r. 1135–50) declared T'ien's group a dangerous faction and executed T'ien and forty-seven other officials (Tao Jing-shen 1981a, 985–86). As these executions demonstrate, the Jurchen did not honor the convention of exempting officials from beatings and other corporal punishment; the Chin bureaucracy was thus more brutalized than either the T'ang or the Sung. Although the Jurchen probably meant to use this purge to intimidate Chinese officials in general, it was a benchmark in the decline of the aristocratic northern families and the rise of individuals from areas once controlled by the native Chinese Sung dynasty. A bloody struggle within the Jurchen elite also resulted in the Chin's moving closer to a more centralized and bureaucratic system, for many tribal leaders were killed in the wake of the coup that cut down Hsi-tsung. The usurper, Liang, prince of Hai-ling (r. 1150–61), felt he had to kill many of the tribal leaders who had served the fallen emperor—including at least seventy-two of A-ku-ta's sons and grandsons. In the absence of fixed rules of inheritance such as the Chinese had, all of these clan leaders were a direct threat to the new ruler. Moving the capital out of the Jurchen homeland to Peking, the prince of Hai-ling continued Hsi-tsung's reforms, significantly expanding borrowing from Chinese ritual, fiscal, legal, and administrative systems. The midcentury reforms led the Chin to conform more closely to the Chinese models.[3] Despite his penchant for violence, Hai-ling's reign marked a watershed in the progression toward Chinese political institutions, and later Chin rulers benefited from his institutional changes.

After the overthrow of Hai-ling in 1161 and the conclusion of a peace treaty in early 1165 brought an end to the war the prince had begun with the Southern Sung, the level of violence abated. Although Hai-ling had sought to purge A-ku-ta's grandsons, Wan-yen Wu-lu (1123–89) escaped with the help of his wife, Wu-lin-ta (d. 1154), a gifted strategist. During Hai-ling's abortive invasion of the South in 1161, Wu-lu staged a coup and became the new emperor. As Shih-tsung (r. 1161–89), Wu-lu was such a successful ruler that his Chinese subjects referred to him as a "miniature Yao or Shun," thus comparing him with the sage-kings of early antiquity (CS 8.204; Liu Su-yung 1987). With the coming of peace, the cumulation of institutional changes finally produced an environment of political stability and cultural revival. "High Chin" began in the mid-1160s.

While the capital was in Peking, the Chin government came to resemble that of any traditional Chinese imperial dynasty. By 1156, the top of the administrative structure was streamlined to include the Department of

State Affairs alone. This organ, with its traditional six ministries or boards, was in charge of general administration. The director (*ling*) of the Department of State Affairs, the grand councilors (*ch'eng-hsiang*), manager of government affairs (*p'ing-chang cheng-shih*), and participant in determining governmental matters (*ts'an-chih cheng-shih*) were the leading executive officials. The Sung divided executive functions of these officials in such a manner that no one controlled the others, but the Chin placed the director of the Department of State Affairs above all other leading executive officials. To supervise other officials and review public petitions, the Jurchen established a Censorate (*yü-shih t'ai*) but made it more exclusively an imperial instrument than it had traditionally been among the Han Chinese (Wang Shih-lien 1989; Chiang Sung-yen 1989). As a regime of military occupation, the Jurchen paid special attention to the army. The top military office was sometimes the Bureau of Military Affairs and at other times the Chief Military Command (*tu yüan-shuai fu*). Heads of these organs had more direct command over the army than their counterparts under the Sung. This streamlined tripartite structure of civil administration, Censorate, and army—along with the enhanced status given to the army (compared to the Sung's)—served to concentrate power at the top. The Yüan and later dynasties essentially continued this streamlined system devised by the Chin.

Some Chin offices were significantly different from the T'ang and Sung. The Palace Inspectorate-general (*tien-ch'ien tu tien-chien ssu*) was in charge of the emperor's personal armies in the capitals and palaces. The Palace Inspectorate-general and the Court Ceremonial Institute (*hsüan-hui yüan*) replaced many of the courts (*ssu*) that had managed affairs for the imperial family in the T'ang structure. The Court of Imperial Sacrifices (*t'ai-ch'ang ssu*) and the Court of Judicial Review (*ta-li ssu*), as well as a couple of other courts on a temporary basis, did function under the Chin, but they were placed under the Department of State Affairs. In contrast to its Sung counterpart, which was abolished in the eleventh century, the Chin Court Ceremonial Institute was a strong organization. Among the many suboffices under its supervision were the Palace Gates Service (*kung-wei chü*) and the Palace Domestic Service (*nei-shih chü*), which oversaw the eunuchs serving at various palaces. The Palace Inspectorate-general generally appears to have reported directly to the throne instead of to the director of the Department of State Affairs—an indication of special status that reflects the dominance of Jurchen nobles and customs in the imperial household administration. Under the Palace Inspectorate-general, the Palace Attendants Service (*chin-shih chü*) was headed by a superintendent (*t'i-tien*) or a commissioner (*shih*). Although these heads held only the fifth rank, their actual importance resembled a grand councilor's because as Jurchen nobles they were close to the emperor and trusted by him. After the Mongols forced the central government to move to Kaifeng in 1214, the heads of the Palace Attendants Service gained even more political influence (*KCC* 7.70, 78).

The Directorate of Palace Registers (or Accounts) (*kung-chi chien*), which was also under the Palace Inspectorate-general, supervised palace slave households or "controlled families" (*chien-hu*). These households, once of free-commoner or even noble status, had been reduced to the status of slaves. Households already of slave status before their members were commandeered by the imperial clan to labor in its workshops were called "government families" (*kuan-hu*) and were placed under the Directorate of Imperial Treasury (*t'ai-fu chien*). Slaves belonging to private families outside of the imperial clan were called *nu-pei hu*, "slave families." Such distinctions of categories of households had existed during the T'ang, but not the Sung. According to the official *Chin History* (*Chin shih*), slaves owned by the government in 1183 were divided into several categories. There were 1,345,967 slaves and 4,812,669 commoners in the *meng-an mou-k'o* system; hence, 22 percent of the men in the system were slaves. The Imperial Clan General (*tsung-shih chiang-chün ssu*) in the capital was staffed by 27,808 slaves and 982 nobles; hence, 97 percent were slaves. Together, the Tangut and T'ieh-le tribes from the northwestern frontier totaled 18,081 slaves and 119,463 commoners; hence, 13 percent were slaves (*CS* 46.1034 and 47.1064). During the struggle with the Liao in the first quarter of the twelfth century, the Jurchen emancipated many of the slaves who had served the Khitan ruling group; moreover, at the end of the century Chin emperors, in order to increase tax revenues, freed large numbers of families who had been donated to Buddhist monasteries. There were also provisions for slaves to buy back their freedom (Liu Ch'ing 1987). Still, the large numbers of imperial slaves, in addition to the numbers of slaves owned by private families and monasteries, suggest a much higher percentage of slaves per capita under the Chin than under the Sung or most other dynasties in China. This larger number of slaves was probably due to the Jurchen custom by which slavery was an accepted penalty for criminal offenses and personal debts. Chin law generally gave slave owners much more power over their slaves and was much harsher on slaves than T'ang law had been (Yeh Ch'ien-chao 1972, 150–51, 233; Franke 1989, 401). Although the percentage of slaves per capita was exceptionally high during the Chin, the Chin state still followed the Chinese practice of using compulsory laborers and hired laborers for water conservancy and other public works projects. Moreover, the Chin was more successful and less discriminatory than the Liao or the Yüan in the implementation of labor services (Chan Hok-lam 1992).

The Chin law code of 1202 represented the culmination of a century of slow evolution toward the adoption of Chinese law. Judging from the still-extant sections of the Chin code, roughly half of the statutory ordinances were copied from the T'ang code. Earlier tribal customs that had sanctioned unnecessarily cruel corporal punishments were mollified, and the remaining punishments were standardized as fixed penalties for particular offenses. Among those ordinances in the 1202 code that involved changes in, or additions to, the T'ang code, many reflected the economic developments of the intervening centuries: illicit gains were assessed in these sections of the code in monetary terms rather than in commodity equivalents. The authority of officials and family elders was further strengthened by the Chin code. Penalties for both neglecting one's duties and endangering the state were increased, but punishment for beating a disobedient son to death was reduced to one and a half years of penal servitude. Jurchen tribal custom contradicted and prevailed over Chinese traditional law in such areas as extending corporal punishment to government officials or allowing a son to inherit property and set up a separate household while his father was still alive. The polyethnic character of the state and the differences between ethnic customs were also addressed. For instance, Jurchen could continue to practice both elopement ("free stealing" of brides) and levirate (marrying widows of paternal relatives, with the exception of one's own mother). Recognizing that Chinese tradition regarded such marriages as incest, the Chin prohibited succession by levirate to Chinese subjects. A few elements of Sung legal practice were incorporated, such as providing a court of appeal to anyone who came to the capital and beat a designated drum located outside the administrative offices in the capital, thereby calling attention to his or her supplication. In the main, the Chin code was a mixture of updated provisions from the T'ang code and non-Chinese customs. As such, it was easily adopted by the Mongols until they abrogated it in 1271, but the Mongols' Yüan code was never as comprehensive a code as the Chin's (Franke 1981; 1989, 387–403; Yeh Ch'ien-chao 1972).

Like the T'ang and Sung dynasties, the Chin divided all officials into nine ranks, each of which was further subdivided. Chin civil and military officials were also classified into forty-two grades of prestige titles (*san-kuan*), similar to the *chi-lu chieh* system of titles in the Sung. But these Sung titles were linked to salary and, in the Chin case, the prestige titles were not (except in the instance of the highest prestige title). For example, some state monopoly agents (*chien-tang kuan*) were given third-rank *san-kuan* titles but remained district magistrates (*CS* 54.1198, 58.1340). The Chin practice of bestowing prestige titles without any link to salary paralleled the dynasty's handling of the examination system: degrees were conferred and offices bestowed in such numbers that both were somewhat devalued.

By the 1180s the Chin had embraced the Sung practice of expanding the examinations to serve as a means of massive recruitment—and on a scale, moreover, that apparently surpassed that of the Sung. Degrees were awarded by the Chin readily, for often one out of every three or four candidates passed (CS 51.1139, 1144). Although the Chin ruled a much smaller population, they handed out almost as many degrees per year as the Sung did. By around the year 1200, the Chin also had as many civil officials (12,700) for their portion of China as the Northern Sung had had in 1046 for the whole of China. In 1193 the Chin had 11,499 officials on the rolls (of whom 4,705 were Jurchen), and by 1207 the number had mushroomed to 47,000—in contrast to the less than 20,000 officials employed by the Southern Sung at that time (CS 55.1216; Tao Jing-shen 1976, 60–67, 92; Chaffee 1985, 27; Thomas H. C. Lee 1985, 148). Perhaps so many degrees and posts were bestowed to pacify the Chinese population without having to curtail the numbers of Jurchen in major offices. Hsi-tsung had proclaimed, and Hsüan-tsung (r. 1213–24) reiterated, that all bureaucratic offices were open in principle to all ethnic groups (CS 4.84–85 and 14.302, 306; HTK 51.3250). As Liu Ch'i (1203–50) observed, however, the Chin actually reserved many of the top posts for Jurchen nobles (KCC 12.137).

Civil service examinations under the Chin were first given in 1123. After the conquest of the Northern Sung, the Chin instituted a dual system of examinations: one was a literary examination on poetry and rhymed prose (*tz'u-fu*), which tested knowledge of the literary tradition and ability to write in a good style; the other was an examination on the meaning of the classics (*ching-i*) (Chao Tung-hui 1989). The Liao and most reigns of the Northern Sung had employed the former, but Wang An-shih (1021–86) had opted for essays on the meaning of the classics and on contemporary policy issues (*ts'e-lun*) because he felt that poetic composition did not offer a relevant standard for judging the quality of potential public servants. The poetry examination was reintroduced in 1127 and consistently attracted more candidates than the classics examination throughout the Southern Sung (Chaffee 1985, 71). Under the early Chin, "northerners" from the areas around Peking and Liaoning that had formerly been ruled by the Liao concentrated primarily on the literary examination, while "southerners" from territory formerly held by the Sung were tested on the classics. This dual system was abolished in the early 1150s in favor of a single literary examination, but the examination on the classics was reinstituted in 1188. Even then, the literary examination continued to attract the vast majority of candidates (CS 51.1130–36, 1144–45; Yü Chieh and Yü Kuang-tu 1989, 237–43). The classics examination during the Chin (as during the T'ang) focused on exegetics instead of philosophical exposition (which was developing during the Southern Sung), and it included not only the Five Classics (the *Changes, Rites, Poetry, Documents,* and *Spring* and *Autumn Annals*), but also the *Analects*, the *Mencius*, the *Book of Filial Piety*, Yang Hsiung's *Fa-yen*, and Lao-tzu's *Tao-te ching*.

Although only sixty to seventy degrees were conferred at each palace examination held between 1151 and 1182, approximately five hundred degrees were awarded each time between 1185 and 1194. From 1197 onward, even higher numbers of candidates occasionally received degrees. These increased numbers of degree holders resulted from deliberate imperial policy. In 1164 Shih-tsung ordered that less attention be given to quotas in order that candidates might be judged according to their qualifications. After deciding that still far too few candidates were being passed, Shih-tsung abolished the quota system in 1183. Some officials complained that too many degrees were being awarded, but later Chin emperors imposed very few restraints (*CS* 51.1135–45). Even though it is difficult to estimate with certainty the total number of degrees conferred, a major expansion of the degree-holding literati certainly took place and continued after the mid-1180s. Thus, as Peter Bol (1983, 9) has noted, the Chin literati became a "critical mass" after the mid-1180s. The palace examinations were the major route to the higher rungs of the bureaucratic ladder for Chinese.

The Jurchen did not depend on the examination system for access to bureaucratic office. Jurchen nobles and relatives of officials did not need to climb the examination ladder because they were appointed directly to office through the protection (*yin*) system. This privilege of bringing relatives of high officials into government service was a common feature of Chinese dynasties, but it took on special meaning in protecting the status of ethnic groups like the Jurchen that established conquest dynasties. Chin Shih-tsung did institute a *chin-shih* examination in Jurchen in 1173, but apparently only about twenty-eight degrees were usually awarded at each examination held once every three years (*CS* 51:1133–46). Such examinations were designed primarily to recruit non-elite Jurchen tribesmen and promote the Jurchen language.

In the area of education, the Chin attempted not only to preserve Jurchen culture and status but also to promote learning more generally. Under the Directorate for Education (*kuo-tzu chien*) founded in 1152, there was initially only the School for the Sons of the State (*kuo-tzu hsüeh*), but the National University (*t'ai-hsüeh*) was added in 1166 and a special Jurchen School for the Sons of the State (*Nü-chen kuo-tzu hsüeh*) in 1173. Accepting students recommended by prefectural officials as well as failed *chin-shih* candidates and descendants of officials of the fifth rank or higher, the National University was less exclusive than the Schools for Sons of the State and thus particularly important in the expansion of educational opportunities (*CS* 51.1131–33). Schools outside the capitals were administered by educational intendants (*t'i-chü hsüeh-shih kuan*), who functioned under the supervision of local prefectural officials and the Ministry of Rites. Sometimes there were also separate schools for Jurchen in the prefectures. Shih-tsung greatly expanded the school system: seventeen provincial schools to handle one thousand students were ordered in 1176; and eighty-four schools with a total enrollment of 1,755 students were decreed in 1189 (*CS* 51.1131, 1133; Bol 1983, 4–5).

Taoist and Buddhist monks, priests, and nuns were also required to take examinations under the Ministry of Rites. Candidates wishing to become Buddhist monks had to read four passages from the *Avataṁsaka-sūtra* (*Hua-yen ching*) and another four passages from other sutras. For each of these eight sections there were two paragraphs, each with four problem passages of one hundred characters; hence, the candidate had to read a total of 6,400 characters. Examinations for nuns covered about one-quarter as many passages (*CS* 55.1234). Such examinations were probably very difficult, especially during the reign of Chang-tsung (r. 1190–1208), when only one out of eighty would-be monks were passed (Yü Chieh and Yü Kuang-tu 1989, 266). But larger numbers of people often became monks and nuns through special imperial dispensations. Important temples and monasteries that had won imperial favor were often granted titles through the Ministry of Rites. There was also a state-appointed hierarchy of religious functionaries to help supervise religious organizations. In the case of Buddhism, there was a state preceptor (*kuo-shih*) in the capital, a director of monks (*seng-lu*) at the prefectural level, and lesser directors at the subprefectural and county levels (*TCKC* 36.275–76). The Chin was following the conventional Chinese practice here of using institutional checks on religious organizations, for religion sometimes served as the medium for rebellion. Numerous uprisings against the Chin did arise among different ethnic groups, especially the Khitan and Chinese (Liu Suyung 1987; Chang Po-ch'üan 1981, 189–200; Aubin 1987; Wang Hung-chih 1987a). But the Chin appears to have been largely successful in managing religious groups. Some uprisings led by monks did occur, as in the case of Chih-chiu (d. ca. 1172) (*CS* 88.1961). Yet no religious sect as a whole engaged in extensive, covert anti-Jurchen action, as the Five Pecks of Rice Taoists had against the native Han dynasty during the second century, or as the White Lotus Society would do against the Mongols during the fourteenth century.

Religious organizations were also under the scrutiny of governors (*tsung-kuan*), who controlled all but five of the nineteen routes (*lu*, predecessors of the provinces). These remaining five were administered directly from the capitals. The governors or heads of the area commands (*tsung-kuan fu*) were essentially military figures, but they had broader powers than the regional officials of the Sung. The Chin governors, who were responsible for a range of functions that were divided into separate offices under the Sung, were rather similar to the military commissioners of the T'ang. Military administrative divisions served the need of the Jurchen for garrisons to control the larger Chinese population. Below the Chin governors and their area commands, the structure of prefectures and districts more closely resembled that of the Sung; however, there appears to have been somewhat more direct involvement of the center in local affairs. For instance, the Court of National Granaries (*ssu-nung ssu*) and its predecessor, the Court of Agricultural Advisors (*ch'üan-nung shih ssu*), appear to have reached from the capital down to the local level in promoting agriculture. Whereas this function was merely added to the other responsibilities of the Sung local official, the Chin created an independent office for it (*CS* 55.1243). The governors also had power over the *meng-an mou-k'o* as well as over various non-Jurchen tribal peoples whose separate administrative units paralleled the Jurchen military system.

Although during the conquest of the Liao and Northern Sung some non-Jurchen military and administrative units were treated as part of the *meng-an mou-k'o* system, the Chin excluded non-Jurchen from the system in 1140; the wars that ensued after 1206, however, forced the Chin to drop this prohibition (*CS* 46.1032; Tao Jing-shen 1976, 46, 90). This failure of the Chin to utilize Han Chinese military forces until the dynasty was already hard-pressed by the Mongols is probably one major reason why the Chin failed to unify China. Reluctance to use Chinese in the military reveals a deep-seated uneasiness about the large native population over which the Jurchen ruled, and such tension also suggests a counterforce against the overall trend toward Chinese culture and institutions.

The difficulty of evaluating Chin institutions is compounded by the fact that only part of the Peking period may be characterized as "High Chin," a period of normalcy, peace, and prosperity. Essentially, "High Chin" is an apt designation for only the approximately forty years following the 1165 peace treaty with the Southern Sung. Adopted institutions functioned reasonably well, and school and examination systems expanded rapidly to produce large numbers of officials and literati. But from the early thirteenth century onward, the Mongols attacked from the north, while the Southern Sung remained a threat from the south. By 1214 the Jurchen had lost the northern half of their empire and were forced to retreat to Kaifeng, where the embattled Chin lingered for two decades more. The functioning of the institutions became more irregular and ad hoc in the constant presence of military emergencies. After the "southern crossing" of 1214, for instance, clerks (*li*) on both the local and central levels gained unprecedented power and were often promoted faster than regular holders of the *chin-shih* degree (*CS* 51.1130, 115.2531; *KCC* 7.71–73, 76–77). Such irregularities contributed to the Chinese literati's decline in loyalty toward the Chin during the last decades of Jurchen rule.

Overall, beyond the obvious movement toward the adoption and adaptation of Chinese institutions, there are other parts of the institutional story that will be used here to summarize what institutional history can suggest about cultural trends. Although the Chin had an examination system from the 1120s onward and employed some former Sung officials, the environment during the first half of the twelfth century was not conducive to Sung learning. For advice about Chinese politics and policy, the Jurchen relied mostly on "northerners," members of aristocratic families from the former Liao area around Peking who were culturally linked to the T'ang. Northerners generally were receptive to neither Sung Confucianism nor former Sung subjects. Yü-wen Hsü-chung (1080–1146) and Kao Shih-t'an (d. 1146), for instance, were tried and executed in a literary inquisition because of books from the South that were found their possession, their lingering loyalty to the Sung, and their condescending manner toward the Chin officials with whom they served (*CS* 79.1791–92). The purge of 1147 fell particularly hard on these "northerners": forty-eight leading officials among them were executed for comprising a dangerous faction. Changes in the examination system after 1150 provided more opportunities for political advancement to "southerners" from areas formerly ruled by the Northern Sung.

The transition evinced by the move away from T'ang and Liao political culture and toward the Sung was mirrored in an institutional decision made by Chang-tsung. After years of debate beginning in 1194, Chang-tsung decided in 1202 to overturn the early Chin judgment that the dynasty had gained legitimacy from the T'ang through the Liao. He changed the symbolic ruling element of the dynasty to Earth in order to signify that the Chin was succeeding the Northern Sung, whose ruling element was Fire. Such emphatic attention after 1194 to the theme of the legitimate succession of dynasties reflects an enhanced consciousness of the need to locate the Chin in the Chinese cultural and political tradition. The reasoning behind the change also reveals a shift in cultural judgment to adopt Sung models: Chang-tsung's decision in effect recognized the legitimacy of the Northern Sung and its political culture—and thus by implication gave official sanction to Sung Confucianism. When Hsüan-tsung (r. 1213–24) let Chang-tsung's decision stand after the issue had come up for debate again in 1214, the intellectual rationalization in defense of Chang-tsung's decision was, in part, based on Ou-yang Hsiu's (1007–72) reading of the *Kung-yang* tradition: Confucian virtues and political unification were the criteria for legitimacy. This doctrine of Sung Confucianism supplemented the Han and T'ang criterion of the Five Elements or Powers (*wu-hsing*). As Chan Hok-lam (1984 and 1987) has shown, the debaters manipulated the Chinese political tradition skillfully. Emperor Chang-tsung also reflected and further enhanced the increasing vogue of Sung culture when he modeled his calligraphy on the distinctive style of Sung Hui-tsung (r. 1100–1125) and when he tried to assemble an art collection that would rival those of his Northern Sung predecessors (Toyama 1957).

Thus, besides the progression toward greater acceptance of Chinese institutions and values in general, the Chin showed signs of moving away from earlier T'ang models inherited through the Liao and toward the political culture of the Sung. This trend, which can be observed in political institutions, will also become evident in our discussions of literati values and religious practices.

Notes

1. Besides the sources noted in the narrative text, I especially benefited from Chan Hok-lam's (1984, 51–74) chapter on the historical setting, Mikami Tsugio's (1970 and 1973) surveys of sociopolitical institutions, and Charles Hucker's (1985, 55–57) outline of Chin government; I have followed Hucker's translations of official titles in all except a few instances (where his translation is supplied as an alternative to mine). Special notice should also be given to Yang Shu-fan's (1983) study of central government systems in the Liao and Chin. Good historical introductions to the Jurchen and their native culture are found in Sun Chin-chi et al. 1987 and Sun 1989, Sung Te-chin 1988, and Wang K'o-pin 1989. For an earlier, shorter version of this paper included in a Chinese essay published in Japan, see T'ien Hao (Hoyt Tillman) and Yü Tsung-hsien 1989.

2. *CS* 55.1215–16; *TK* 327.2571; *HTK* 51.3250; Mikami 1972 and 1984; Chang Po-ch'üan 1984, 48–51; and Li T'ang's (1978) biography of T'ai-tsu.

3. Franke 1989, 393–94, 402; Tao Jing-shen 1970, 123–28; Wang Hung-chih 1987a; Ts'ui Wen-yin 1987; Chao Tung-hui 1987; and Chao Yung-ch'un 1991.

2

THE JURCHEN-SUNG CONFRONTATION: SOME OVERLOOKED POINTS

James T. C. Liu

While I was conducting research for my book (1988) on the restoration process at the beginning of the Southern Sung, various points arose regarding the confrontation between the Sung and the Jurchen Chin empires. The paucity of literature in the field is a major impediment to a detailed investigation of these points. Some information, however, especially on the Sung side, makes it possible to sketch in broad sweeps and meaningful trends that have implications for later periods but have so far escaped the attention of historians. Even the discussion here of the Sung government is relevant because of the light it sheds on the Chin regime's relations with its major rival.

The Jurchen were the first steppe or pastoral-nomadic nationality in Chinese history to cross the Yangtze. In fact, they drove southward of that great river in two directions, east and west. Only one other attempt of this kind had ever been made, and it represented a decisive turning point in an enduring north-south division of Chinese culture (Lei Hai-tsung 1934–35, 531; and James T. C. Liu 1964). According to the Chinese historical account, Fu Chien (339–85) of the Former Ch'in (351–94) had pushed southward in 383 with his conglomeration of Turkish cavalry, Mongolian horsemen, and Chinese infantry, reaching as far as Fei-shui in the Huai River valley. One skeptical modern scholar suggests that Fu Chien suffered no great defeat, nor that the battle there was spectacular (Rogers 1968a and 1968b). Nonetheless, neither Fu Chien nor any other invaders from the northern borderlands had ever set their eyes on the Yangtze until the Jurchen poured over it in the early twelfth century.

Both the Sung and the Chin dynastic histories refrain from commenting on the significance of the Jurchen crossing. It makes one wonder whether the editors of these official histories brushed it aside to reserve the honor for their Mongolian masters who united the whole of China. If such were the case, this bit of understated historiography has certainly worked. Few historians have given full credit to the Jurchen for their military success.

In defense of conventional historiography, one could argue that the Jurchen penetrations below the Yangtze lack significance because they did not lead to conquest or even long occupation. These thrusts were, strictly speaking, neither invasions nor even campaigns, but rather expeditions with limited objectives. One expedition went after the Sung pretender to the throne who later became Emperor Kao-tsung (r. 1127–62). This column raced through Nanking, Soochow, Hangchow, the eastern Chekiang coast, Ningpo, and finally to the waters beyond. The Chinese court was able to escape captivity only by setting sail; this was the first time in history that a Chinese ruler had resorted to the open sea to evade an enemy. The other expedition turned westward from Nanking into the Kiangsi area to pursue Empress Dowager Meng—the only other symbol likely to unite attempts at restoring the Sung—as far as the central Kiangsi hinterlands. This expedition also failed.

There seem to be three interrelated reasons why the Jurchen did not attempt to occupy the South. First, they simply lacked the manpower. They had seized the North largely by what in modern times would be called a blitzkrieg. At this time they simply did not have the wherewithal to occupy all of China. Second, they did not have a logistic base near enough to supply the southward advance. Third, they saw no advantage in taking more territory. The idea of unifying all of the cultivated land and its sedentary population in China belonged primarily to the political traditions of the Han Chinese. The Jurchen, with their steppe background, did not share this value with the Chinese and apparently perceived diminishing returns from further expansion southward. Their task at hand was to return to North China and stabilize that area as a base for power and influence that would allow them to demand tribute from weaker peripheral states.

In attaining this Jurchen goal, the puppet regime of Liu Yü (1073–1143) played a crucial role in the Yellow River valley. His state of Ch'i was originally created in 1130 to fill the vacuum that the Jurchen withdrawal had left, but it was abolished in 1137 after Liu's joint campaign with the Jurchen against the Southern Sung failed. While historians have generally dismissed his dynasty as a puppet regime, it would perhaps be more appropriate to describe it as a collaborationist, or "turncoat," regime—not only in the figurative sense of English idiom, but also in vivid historical fact. Many who served in this regime actually took off their former Sung-style clothing and put on the costume of the Jurchen. Some double-faced opportunists, not sure which way the prevailing winds might blow, kept sets of both in readiness, changing dress at a moment's notice (*HNYL* 38.560, 51.912, and 129.2093). There was even one case of a three-time turncoat. Chang Chung-yen (mid-12th cent.), originally a Sung general stationed near the Szechwan border, surrendered with his brother to the Jurchen, served the new master in the Shensi area, became a Sung official again when the Jurchen agreed in a peace treaty to give the area back to the South, but on Jurchen demand was soon returned to serve the Jurchen once more (*CS* 79.1789–91). Thus, the term "turncoat" aptly designates such a regime as well as its officials.

The conventional explanation for the abolition of the Liu Yü regime was given by the Jurchen themselves. The Jurchen claimed that they were dissatisfied with its failure to provide promised supplies and services, and with its lack of military vigor. Regarding the first allegation, there is no evidence one way or the other. The second allegation is doubtful. At this time the Jurchen army itself used ethnic Han Chinese: some, officers who had surrendered to them and, many, soldiers they had drafted from the Hopei and Honan areas. These Han Chinese were apparently not eager to attack the Sung, so Liu Yü's army was certainly not alone to blame. Thus, the Jurchen explanation for abolishing Liu's regime was more an excuse than a straight truth. More importantly, the Jurchen denied Liu Yü due credit for his civil administration. In any event, their explanation was, at most, only half the story. The other half, hardly mentioned, had to do with civilian administration. It was this turncoat regime that cleared up the remaining pockets of resistance to the Jurchen in the North. Liu Yü organized the administrative machinery needed to implement the declared law-and-order policy of "securing the land and calming the citizens" (*pao-ching an-min*, the same expression used in Japanese-occupied China during World War II). Seeking further to project ancient Chinese ideals, Liu Yü attempted to reduce the land tax to one-tenth of the harvest. The plan did not work, and he had to increase other forms of taxation. Nevertheless, he put the broken pieces of North China together, and the Jurchen took it back without losing anything (*SCPM* 181.1–4, 12–14; and *HTCTC* 119.3158–59).

Biased historical assertions notwithstanding, Liu Yü had not done poorly at all, for he had paved the way to a smooth Jurchen takeover. With the administrative foundation reestablished, however, his services were no longer required. In the wake of what amounted to a bloodless reconquest of North China, the Jurchen established a provincial government by temporarily instituting a coalition government in which the four leading officials represented, in a sense, the four major ethnic groups of the area. The coalition included one former Sung official, one former Khitan official, one Jurchen, and one native of the Yen region immediately below the line of the Great Wall (*WCL* 3.4; *HTCTC* 119.3159; Mikami 1970, 476–78).

Another role played by the Liu Yü regime was as a contributing factor to the Southern Sung court's decision to seek peace with the Jurchen. From the outset, the southern court paid Liu's dynasty high respect. The Southern Sung occasionally addressed his regime by the dynastic title of "the Great Ch'i" (*HNYL* 49.873). The official reason for this ostensibly was to avoid antagonizing his Jurchen masters. But there were two pressing and realistic reasons for not offending Liu Yü himself: fear that he would raise troops to augment the Jurchen ranks in times of attack, and a secret desire that former Sung officials under his aegis would return their allegiance to the Sung dynastic family. The fear was well founded; the secret desire was not. In 1136 Liu Yü persuaded the Jurchen to launch a joint campaign in the Huai River valley. It was only after this invasion that the Sung began to criticize Liu Yü openly and vehemently. While a few officials and smaller army units under Liu did defect to the South, the situation was critically fluid and eventually underwent a catastrophic turn in the reverse direction. An influential Sung general, Li Ch'iung, fled with thirty thousand of his men to the Ch'i banner in 1137. Later, when Ch'i had been abrogated, he served under the Chin marshal Wan-yen Tsung-pi (d. 1148) (*SSHP* 188.735; *CS* 79.1781–83). Li's desertion shocked the southern court so much that it banished its hawkish chief councilor and moved the imperial headquarters back to Hangchow from Nanking. Official state policy shifted toward peace negotiations, and the few notable victories scored by Sung forces did not alter this new course.

Since the Jurchen and Liu Yü did not succeed in overrunning the Huai valley or the banks of the Yangtze, why did the Southern Sung court sue for a humiliating peace? To answer this puzzling question, historians have conventionally blamed either the supposedly irresolute emperor Kao-tsung and his allegedly treacherous chief councilor Ch'in Kuei (1090–1155), in particular, or the scholar-officials who were presumably addicted to the comfortable lifestyle available south of the Yangtze, in general.[1] Such explanations do not take into account a rather vital dimension: the realization, if not rude awakening, that the North had become conclusively unrecoverable. The Sung court had engaged in secret communications with some of Liu Yü's high officials, including his chief councilor Chang Hsiao-ch'un, in hopes of undermining the ruler of Ch'i (*WCL* 2.10–17; Umehara 1983, 347). The fact that none of them expressed a desire to defect must have been quite disheartening. The depression was deepened by Li Ch'iung's defection. Finally, the ease with which the Jurchen unseated Liu Yü and smoothly took direct institutional control confirmed the Sung's worst fear—the North, both turncoats and citizenry, were firmly under enemy control and lost forever. Confronted with these facts, the Sung court surely had difficulty finding a compelling reason to keep the war going.

The Jurchen confrontation with the attendant wars, defections, and peace negotiations had long-range effects on the Southern Sung government. The southern court's equivocal attitude toward the Liu Yü regime led to an ambivalent policy toward bandits and the military that contrasts radically with that of the Northern Sung.[2] The southern mode of accommodation began with the turncoats, for they were always assured of a welcome back into the fold without any questions about the morality of their previous actions. At the same time, Liu Yü raised troops, and the southern court had no recourse but to do the same. In the South neither conscription nor recruitment appeared to work effectively. The best soldiers were those with combat experience, and the only supply of that commodity was in the brigades of bandits. Thus, the southern government adopted a policy of "call to pacification" (*chao-an*) toward the bandits, giving them the public choice of risking annihilation at the hands of Sung armies or becoming regular army units themselves with due status, rank, and provisions. This stick-and-carrot proposition effectively both depressed the number of bandits and correspondingly increased the numerical strength of the army. Such accommodation had a costly demoralizing effect, however, as testified by a popular saying: "In order to get high rank in the army, just kill people, set fires, and then accept the call to pacification" (*SJIS* 15.750).

The accommodative mode, by no means limited to military matters, stemmed from the court and permeated the entire bureaucracy. Emperor Kao-tsung attributed the restoration of the empire, a supreme success of the greatest magnitude, to what he called "the soft approach" (*jou-tao*, the same characters, incidentally, are used in the name of the Japanese art of self-defense, judo) (*HNYL* 157.2553 and 159.2583).[3] This accommodative approach accentuated bureaucratic anomalies by attempting to whitewash them or rationalize them away. For example, glossing over bureaucratic inconsistencies was praised as "rolling them in harmony" (*yüan-jung*); soliciting favors was called "touching base" (*chao-ying*); and covering up irregularities was known as "filling in the gaps" (*mi-feng*).

In practicing the accommodative mode, Southern Sung emperors, beginning with Kao-tsung himself, became highly bureaucratized. This was particularly evident in the ways they dealt with honest officials who presented critical opinions in line with their duty as "opinion officials." Emperors often listened to criticism with ostensible grace (and without taking any corrective action), praised the critic for frankness, and asked him to compose a detailed exposition of the specific differences between his views and those of the party under attack. Thereupon, the emperor used the usual bureaucratic delaying tactics: ordering an investigation, asking for further opinions, or moving the critic up the bureaucratic ladder to a higher position where he no longer had the function of a censorial official (James T. C. Liu 1970 and 1974, 337). These sophisticated devices of accommodative politics caused widespread disillusionment, despair, and demoralization among the scholar-officials.

Reaction to the Jurchen confrontation was also a factor in the the rise of the "neo" Confucianism, but most standard discussions overlook this connection. Many Confucians were emotionally devastated by circumstances of the times. To them, the fall of the Northern Sung was tragic; the degeneration beforehand that had led to it was terrible; the Jurchen occupation of the North and the peace the southern court made with the Jurchen was humiliating; the scholar-officials who had become turncoats were shameful; the ineffectual armies and mealymouthed bureaucrats at home were disgraceful. What did intellectuals see as the common denominator in these ugly realities? The cause in every case clearly appeared to be a lack of morality.

Patriotic Confucian intellectuals of various philosophical persuasions were driven toward the same inescapable conclusion: moral rejuvenation was the prerequisite to cultural preservation, national security, and the eventual recovery of the Central Plain and of North China. Differences among them could be viewed in terms of a number of traditional polarities on which various schools placed their respective emphases. Some intellectuals based themselves on moral principle but quickly turned to such practical matters as defense. Ch'en Liang (1143–94) anchored his suggestions regarding the military firmly in moral principles, calling for the ruler to cultivate humaneness and for officials to do their proper moral duty (Tillman 1982, 79). Other intellectuals maintained active interests in both moral philosophy and national security. Chang Shih (1133–80), for example, the son of a prestigious scholar-general, practically identified moral principle with the needs of defense when he remarked, "To teach the Confucian *tao* and to consolidate the hearts of men is really the single most important item in erecting defenses and safeguarding the state." When he served as military commissioner in the middle Yangtze region, he wrote to Chu Hsi (1130–1200), "I give my exclusive attention to the fundamental matter of consolidating the hearts of men in order to induce people to set their minds on respecting the sovereign and supporting their superiors. This will definitely make defenses strong and assure future victory in battle" (*CKC* 30.6; *LSSI* 7.13). Such statements provide evidence that Chang might have been better known to men of the Sung for such sociopolitical ideas than for his philosophical dicta. Lastly, still other intellectuals, notably Chu Hsi and some of his disciples, moved upward from moral principle to metaphysical theory as the most fundamental of all things; yet they never entirely neglected practical issues.

Chu Hsi provided a metaphysical foundation for Confucianism, for he believed that without this foundation Confucian principles could not endure. Indeed, the confrontation with the Jurchen clearly demonstrated the sad decline of Confucian principles. Chu and his colleagues stood firmly for defense initiatives and the recovery of the North, but against the humiliating peace and shameful surrender to the Jurchen enemy. It is only reasonable to conclude that the general patriotic response of intellectuals to the extraordinary disaster of the Jurchen confrontation figured prominently in the dedicated search for, and deep commitment to, the profound body of knowledge that some have called "neo" Confucianism. Regrettably, most works on Confucianism tend simply to neglect this Jurchen confrontation, as if the history of ideas somehow unfolded by an inner logic, within a vacuum devoid of the military and political issues that were at the time threatening the very basis of cultural survival.

The Jurchen military expedition that forced Kao-tsung to escape by sea helped shape the conventional Chinese attitude toward the ocean. It was the Jurchen, too, who forced Kao-tsung to site the Southern Sung capital at Lin-an (Hangchow), practically on the coast. And this capital located near the seaboard instead of near the center of the agricultural plain—a case unique in Chinese history—continued to convey negative images. From that time onward the Chinese had a politically negative attitude toward the oceans that bordered them—far more negative than might be explained by the customary disinclination of an agrarian empire. I do not mean to suggest that Chinese attitudes before the Sung were very positive, but rather that in their traditional orientation toward Inner Asia the Chinese gave much less attention to the sea. Events during the Sung forced the Chinese to focus on the sea, and in primarily negative ways. It might seem that the development of a strong Sung navy contradicts this thesis. But that navy was primarily a river fleet rather than an ocean-going one. Similarly, ocean navigation for commercial purposes by men from southeastern coastal cities is only a partial exception to this pattern, for Sung international trade probably relied more on the passage of foreign ships than Chinese. Our concern, at any rate, is with political-cultural, not commercial, attitudes. The history of the Jurchen-Sung conflict provides further explanations for these negative images of the sea. The initial alliance between the Northern Sung and the Jurchen had been concluded at sea (*SSPM* 53.539–40). The treaty served to finish the Khitan empire, but it also sealed the fate of the Northern Sung. In the minds of the Southern Sung people, the sea came to be associated with this unhappy memory. No Southern Sung men were proud of Kao-tsung's escape out to sea, and few ever made reference to it. This contrasts sharply with the colorful legends that came to be built up around his midnight flight across the Yangtze when supernatural powers sent a flying horse to ferry him across—a horse that was discovered, after the emperor's safe arrival on the other shore, to be made of mud. This legend, so popular in vernacular literature, still finds a place in modern dictionaries (e.g., *Tz'u-yüan* 3:1759). At the end of the Southern Sung the infant pretender to the throne was drowned at sea to avoid capture by the Mongols, it was said, so as not to repeat the unspeakable humiliations his ancestors had suffered at the hands of the Jurchen. The sea, it seemed, compounded tragedy.

The Jurchen probably had some misgivings of their own about the sea. Not only were they frustrated by the ocean when they could not catch Kao-tsung, but a later proposal for an attack on the South via a sea route off the coast of Chekiang never materialized. On the contrary, the Southern Sung claimed a minor victory by landing naval forces behind Jurchen lines in Hai-chou (in present-day northern Kiangsu, near the Shantung border) (*SS* 370.11499–501; Umehara 1983, 182). Throughout extant Chin records, the word "sea" seldom appears.

Jurchen dealings with "turncoats" provide insight into why the Jurchen failed to go on to conquer the whole of China as the Mongols would over a century later. The Jurchen lacked a policy intelligent enough to make use of native Han Chinese in what, for the lack of better wording, might be called the "turncoat hypothesis." The Jurchen successfully used Liu Yü and other turncoats to stabilize the North, but when they abrogated Liu Yü's regime they created an image of themselves that was self-defeating. Having seen how Liu had been used and then discarded, relatively few Han Chinese would wish to serve as new turncoats to aid the Jurchen expansion.

The dreadful case of Shih I-sheng (d. 1159), in particular, discouraged many potential turncoats. A fugitive scholar from Sung China where personal misconduct had gotten him into trouble, Shih became a high official at the Jurchen court. Later dispatched as deputy envoy on a mission to the southern court, he allegedly leaked word that the Jurchen would attack again. On his return he was accused of treason and put to death by boiling (*CS* 79.1786–87; *TCKC* 28.2; *CSCS* 4.8; Umehara 1983, 242). Surely the story of this atrocity would have had a chilling effect on anyone who might have wanted to go over to the Jurchen side.

The case of the separatist rebellion of Wu Hsi in Szechwan in 1206 shows conclusively that the Jurchen government had little political appeal left for the native Han population. Wu Hsi came from a family that had provided the Sung with leading generals who had served in the Szechwan area for three generations. After proclaiming himself king, Wu Hsi contacted the Jurchen court, ready to accept investiture from it and a military alliance. He thought that subordinates who had lived long under his family's patronage and influence would support his venture. To his surprise, few did so, and those only as a formality to gain time. After eight months, Wu Hsi was assassinated by a group of his subordinates, and the Sung was able to put a swift end to the abortive rebellion before the Jurchen had had time to take advantage of it (SSPM 83.925–34).

In contrast, the Mongol conquest of China involved careful planning and was won not simply by undue reliance on military power alone. To begin with, they had run a stable administration in North China employing thousands of turncoats for some forty years prior to their attack on the Southern Sung. They already understood that a snowballing number of surrenders would prove far more effective than their own mounted horsemen. A pivotal event in the Mongol conquest involved a certain Liu Cheng, on whose advice Sung military strategy had often depended. After his defection to the Mongols, he offered the crucial opinion that the key to the conquest lay in Lü Wen-te (d. 1271), the commanding general of Hsiang-yang, a vital point in Sung defenses. Later on, when Wen-te's younger brother Lü Wen-huan (d. 1292?) assumed command, the defenses at Hsiang-yang were no longer as strong as they had been. After two years of siege, the younger Lü not only surrendered but also joined Liu Cheng to plan future campaigns. They were able to persuade many Sung officials and officers in the army and navy in the Huai valley to join them as turncoats, helped by the fact that many of these men were either relatives or former subordinates of the Lü family (James T. C. Liu 1977). The Mongol conquest of the Southern Sung did not proceed from north to south, but from west to east. They sailed from the mid-Yangtze to its lower reaches, greatly aided by former Sung naval forces that had surrendered.[4] The conquest was as smooth a military operation as the turncoats could politically make it. Before these key defectors triggered a chain reaction, the Southern Sung had stood against the Mongol world-conquerors for forty years—an impressive record in the Eurasian context.

The turncoat hypothesis of conquest dynasties applies equally well, if not better, to later periods of Chinese history. The Manchus were of Jurchen descent and initially called themselves the "Latter Chin." If not for Hung Ch'eng-ch'ou (1593–1665), Wu San-kuei (1612–78), and other turncoat generals who did much of the planning and fighting and who exercised considerable political pressure, the Manchu conquest of all of China would have been much more difficult to achieve. The same hypothesis is relevant to the Japanese military occupation of China during World War II. On the Soviet-Manchurian border in 1940–41, the Soviet side had Mongolian forces in addition to their own. But on the Japanese side the Manchukuo army, Japanese trained, did not seem employable or, at least, did not seem as good as the troops of Liu Yü under the Jurchen. In other parts of occupied China, the turncoat troops were comparable. Some Japanese scholars in the 1930s, either voluntarily supporting the military or subsidized by such affiliated agencies as the South Manchuria Railway Company, researched conquest dynasties in Chinese history in the hope of providing some precedent or historical support for the perpetuation of Japan's expansion on the continent. Nevertheless, they did not seem to see, or have the courage to say aloud, the principle of decisive importance: no effective turncoats, no conquest.

In conclusion, looking at the Jurchen confrontation with the Sung in the larger context of Chinese history has highlighted the impact of that conflict on the course of Chinese history and on such popular attitudes as the politically negative bias toward the sea. This overview has also illustrated how problematic historical assessments of the Jurchen and their place in Chinese history have sometimes been. Summarizing various points that have been overlooked by earlier historians has brought forward a "turncoat hypothesis." The Jurchen were far more effective in using turncoats than earlier would-be conquerors, such as Fu Chien, had been. When they removed Liu Yü's regime, the Jurchen first opted for a coalition government in North China that reflected the polyethnic forces there. But ethnic tensions soon came to the fore. From the late 1140s through the 1150s the Jurchen executed a number of prominent Han Chinese who had served them as officials. Gradually, Han Chinese were also excluded from any national military role—until Mongol invasions compelled the Chin to reinstitute Han armies. Thus, ethnic tensions hampered long-term policy formation and prevented the Chin from fashioning a more successful turncoat policy. The Mongols, at least during their conquest phase, pursued a more open policy toward turncoats and used Han Chinese military units more efficiently. The result was the first foreign conquest of all of China. The second foreign conquest of all of China came with Manchu horsemen in the seventeenth century, and their banner system incorporated Han Chinese military units even more effectively than the Mongols had. Compared to the Jurchen and the Mongols, the Manchu elite was more clever in presenting a Chinese cultural face to the Han Chinese; moreover, the Manchus were not as sidetracked by nativistic movements as the Jurchen and Mongols had been. Apparently, the Manchu rulers had learned effective lessons from their Jurchen ancestors.[5]

Notes

1. Even though no evidence has ever been found, Ch'in Kuei has been accused of high treason in both historical writings and popular literature. I have suggested (1984) that while Ch'in Kuei had no direct contacts with

the Jurchen, he knew about their disposition through a cousin in the Liu Yü regime.

2. For a study of the Northern Sung army, see Lo Ch'iu-ch'ing 1957 and Wang Tseng-yü 1983, 127–255.

3. Sung Kao-tsung consciously emulated the successful restoration of the Han emperor Kuang-wu (r. 25–57), who also used the "soft approach" (*HHS* 1B.68–69).

4. History thus repeated what had happened once before in 280, as lamentingly portrayed in the poem by Liu Yü-hsi (772–842):

> The multi-decked ships of Admiral Wang Chün set sail from I-chou downstream;
> The kingly air of Chin-ling gently folded and faded away.

See *T'ang-shih san-pai-shou*, no. 202. On Admiral Wang Chün (206–85), see *CSH* 42.1207–17.

5. A personal recollection about Pu-yi (1906–67), the last Manchu emperor (r. 1908–12) and the nominal head of Manchukuo (1932–45), illustrates this legacy and the Manchu elite's appreciation of Chinese turncoats. I served as historical assistant at the International Military Tribunal for the Far East (IMTFE), better known perhaps as the "Tokyo Trials" of Japan's war leaders. The Soviet authorities, who had custody of Pu-yi at the time, brought him to Tokyo to testify as a witness to Japanese aggression in Manchuria. A Japanese defense attorney, cross-examining him, asked whether his ancestors, in founding the Manchu empire, had committed aggression against the rest of China. The question came as a great surprise. The prosecuting attorneys, none too familiar with Chinese history, stared blankly at the court without attempting to object to the question as irrelevant and immaterial. But Pu-yi calmly replied, "That was different. My ancestors were invited to go in by the Ming dynasty." Evidently, the ex-emperor had received appropriate instruction in history as a child. The Japanese defense attorney, apparently not briefed with a view to historical depth or technicalities, looked puzzled and did not challenge Pu-yi's response. What transpired in the courtroom that day was reported in Japanese newspapers the next, but without detail or comment. This exchange at the Tokyo Trials acknowledged that early history had been relived in the recent past; yet few present at the occasion had the historical background to appreciate it. It also simply, but clearly, demonstrates the importance of realizing connective linkages between diverse historical events.

3

PUBLIC SCHOOLS IN THE CHIN DYNASTY

Tao Jing-shen

Among the writings collected in the anthologies *Chin-wen tsui* (Anthology of Chin essays) and *Chin-wen ya* (Anthology of fine Chin essays) are a number of essays concerning "temple schools" (*miao-hsüeh*). A temple school was a combination school and Confucian temple, where an image or portrait of Confucius, together with portraits of his chief disciples, was worshiped. Most of the essayists praise the Chin rulers, including the despot Hai-ling (r. 1150–61), for promoting civil rule and taking an interest in the construction or repair of schools. One essay reads:

> There are schools even in the villages in our country. Like [the trees of] a forest, schools spread over our land. The teachings of benevolence, righteousness, and morality and the practical application of the classics are so brilliantly carried out that we are [now] on a par with the Three Dynasties of antiquity. (*SYSK* 23.4b)

Most of these essays were written for the occasion of a school's opening or reopening after the completion of repairs. The essays were dedicated to the schools and inscribed on stone steles that were to be kept in them. The writers do not describe in detail the organization and operation of the schools; their main concern is rather the establishment or repair of them and the contributions made by local officials, schoolteachers, and others involved in the construction projects. There is information about neither primary education nor the selection of students to be enrolled in these higher-level schools. In contrast to the educational system of the Southern Sung, there were almost no private schools (*shu-yüan*) in North China during the Chin period; it was the primary task of the public schools, apparently, to prepare students for participation in the civil service examinations.

Despite their limited scope, we can learn something about public schools under the Chin from the essays in the *Chin-wen tsui* and *Chin-wen ya* as well as the *Chin shih*. In this paper, I will attempt to use these sources to trace the development of public schools during the Chin period, to analyze the nature of the schools, and to assess their influence on Chin culture. But because the essays deal mostly with regional schools, the focus will necessarily be on these schools rather than the state institutions of the capital.

In 609 a Confucian temple and a temple dedicated to the Duke of Chou were built on the campus of the National University in Ch'ang-an (*CTS* 24.916). Around that time, too, the government ordered all prefectures and counties to build schools. Shortly afterward, Emperor T'ai-tsung (r. 627–49) stopped the worship of the Duke of Chou in the schools (*CTS* 139A.4941; *TS* 15.373), and in 630 he initiated an ambitious project to build Confucian temples in all prefectures and counties of the empire (*TS* 15.373). In 669 Emperor Kao-tsung (r. 650–83) reiterated that all schools should install images of Confucius for students to worship (*SWCY* 3.40b), and twice in the Northern Sung the government ordered that all prefectures and counties build schools.[1] It is important to note that when Fan Chung-yen (989–1052) called for the establishment of public schools, his aim was to replace the civil service examination system with a school system. As a step toward the realization of this goal, the government ordered that students be enrolled for three hundred days before taking the civil service exams. This was meant to establish a link between the examination system and the schools, such that the schools would become the main channel for government recruitment of scholar-officials (Lü Ssu-mien 1982, 1089–90). Although the Northern Sung reforms failed to meet the goal set by Fan, a large number of schools were built for the education of potential candidates for government positions and to indoctrinate the people at large (Thomas H. C. Lee 1977, 45; and 1985). The "prefectural school" at Chi described in Ou-yang Hsiu's essay (*OYWC* 39.297–98) is, in actual fact, a temple school. And centuries later, in the Ming dynasty, Ch'iu Chün stated that since the Ch'ing-li era of the Sung, all schools had been built as temple schools (*CFTC* 117.3835). Thus, there is reason to believe that most of the local public schools, if not all, were temple schools.

According to Tuan Ch'eng-chi, a literatus of the late Chin, since T'ang times all prefectures and counties had built schools and in every school Confucius was worshiped (*CWY* 8.8a–8b). A few Confucian temples were probably too small to be used as schools. Tso Yung states, "In recent times in big prefectural cities [*fu*] schools have been established, but in small prefectures and counties there are only Confucian temples"—which had not been repaired (*CWT* 38.4b). Shih Cho points out that in the county of Ch'ang-tzu, Shansi, there was previously a Confucian temple with a single hall, which naturally could not have served as a school (*CWT* 39.18a). Some Chin writers report that when the Northern Sung fell, a number of temple schools were destroyed and that when these institutions were rebuilt, they functioned only as Confucian temples, the parts that had been schools left unrestored (Meng Hsien-ch'eng 1980, 214). In the cases of a few writers, it is not clear whether the Confucian temples they mention were also schools, or whether the schools they mention were temple schools. For example, a few prefectural and county schools described by Yüan Hao-wen (1190–1257) were actually temple schools, but the titles of his essays concerning them do not indicate this (*CWT* 15.10b, 12a–12b). A survey of seventy-three essays concerning fifty-eight schools in Chin times indicates that most Chin schools were temple schools. Of these fifty-eight schools, we have information about only two that is insufficient to determine whether there were temples in them.[2] It would be safe to say that over 95 percent of all schools in the Chin were temple schools. The geographical locations and textual sources for the existence of the schools are summarized in table 1.

Many of the Chin essays report that when the Jurchen conquered North China a number of schools were destroyed. Although warfare and military activity prevented many schools from being repaired, almost all the Chin emperors seem to have paid attention to the maintenance of public schools. In 1129, two years after the capture of the Sung capital, the Jurchen army was ordered not to disturb the birthplace of Confucius (*KS* 3.18a). Even as early as the T'ien-hui reign of T'ai-tsung (1123–35), several hundred students flocked to the prefectural school at Ting in Hopei to study under Hu Li, a prominent scholar. It is said that a large number of students from that school who subsequently passed the *chin-shih* examinations shared a common literary style inherited from Hu (*CS* 125.2721).

During the reign of Hai-ling, the National Academy (*kuo-tzu chien*) was established with an enrollment of two hundred, and all regional Confucian temples were ordered repaired (*CWT* 34.4b–5a, 35.11b, 40.17a). Furthermore, the emperor ordered all newly appointed officials to visit the local Confucian temple, before any other temple, on arriving at their assigned posts (*KS* 3.19a). Emperor Shih-tsung (r. 1161–89) expanded the school system at the capital by establishing a School for the Sons of the State (*kuo-tzu hsüeh*), a University (*kuo-tzu t'ai-hsüeh*), and a School for the Jurchen Sons of the State (*Nü-chen kuo-tzu-hsüeh*). The University alone had an enrollment of four hundred (Mao Wen 1936, 28–29), and in 1193 the six capital schools had a combined enrollment of 795 (*CS* 10.229). In 1176, moreover, seventeen Chinese schools were established at the *fu* level, and twenty-two Jurchen schools, in which the Jurchen language was taught, at the regional level (*CS* 51.1131–32). Despite the efforts made by Hai-ling and Shih-tsung to repair and build schools, the overall number of schools seems not to have been large, and their enrollments were small.

When Emperor Chang-tsung ascended the throne in 1190, a group of officials sent up a memorial requesting that more schools be established and that, among other things, the "three grades" (*san-she*) system of Wang An-shih be restored at the National University. The officials were called together to discuss the matter at a meeting held in the Secretariat, but most proposals were rejected. In the final memorial submitted by Teng Yen and others, it was pointed out that although there were defects in the school systems of the T'ang and Sung, there were still eight thousand students in the T'ang state schools and five thousand in the two state schools of the Northern Sung capital alone. During the Chin dynasty, however, the National University had an enrollment of only 160, and some of the major regional schools (the *fu* schools) had as few as ten students each. The combined enrollment of all the schools was only one thousand. The authors of the memorial suggested the establishment of prefectural schools with full-time professors and monthly examinations by mandate. Schools producing large numbers of successful exam candidates would be rewarded. School examination scores would be divided into three categories: schools whose students most often obtained grades in the uppermost category would be rewarded, and students who consistently failed to test in the upper categories or whose behavior was not up to standard would be dismissed. This, concluded the officials, would be the right way to recruit qualified officials.

The emperor accepted their suggestions and increased student quotas for the prefectural schools in proportion to the number of households in their respective areas. In 1189, eight schools at the *fu* level were added to the seventeen already in operation, and sixty prefectural schools were established. In 1201 the emperor reiterated the court's wish to establish Confucian schools all over the state, and allocated government funds liberally to subsidize building in localities where resources were insufficient for repair or construction of prefectural schools. As to county schools, the government made it clear that wherever local officials and populations wished to establish schools, they would be permitted to do so if they could raise the necessary resources in their respective localities (*CWT* 14.1a, 40.1b). Each of these schools had one professor who had taken the civil service examinations five times (without passing) or who held a *chin-shih* degree but was over fifty years of age (and therefore too old to embark on an official career). The enrollment quotas for these schools are summarized in table 2 (*CS* 51.1131–33).

Table 1
Geographical Locations of and Textual Sources for Fifty-eight Chin Schools

Shansi

Ch'ü-wo	曲沃	*CWT* 11, 14
Pao-te-chou*	保德州	*CWT* 12, 39
Fen-chou	汾州	*CWT* 13
Hsiang-ling*	襄陵	*CWT* 14, *CWY* 8
Shou-yang	壽陽	*CWT* 15
Kuan-shih	冠氏	*CWT* 15
Kao-p'ing	高平	*CWT* 31
Nan-kung	南宮	*CWT* 31
Ch'ang-tzu	長子	*CWT* 39
Wan-ch'üan	萬全	*CWT* 33
T'ai-yüan-fu	太原府	*CWT* 38
Ying-chou	應州	*CWT* 39
Lu-chou	潞州	*CWT* 39
Ying-yang-chen	穎陽鎮	*CWT* 58
Tse-chou	澤州	*CWT* 42
Huo-chou	霍州	*CWT* 42
Hsin-chou	忻州	*CWT* 58
Yang-ch'eng	陽城	*CWT* 58
Ling-ch'uan	陵川	*CWT* 58
Liao-chou	遼州	*SYSK* 21
Wen-hsi	聞喜	*SYSK* 23

Hopei

Ch'ü-chou	曲周	*CWT* 14
Hsing-t'ang	行唐	*CWT* 14
Chao-chou	趙州	*CWT* 15
Chi-chou*	冀州	*CWT* 33, 38
Ta-ch'eng	大城	*CWT* 33
Ch'ing-ho	清河	*CWT* 34
Wei	威	*CWT* 34
Cho-chou	涿州	*CWT* 36
Chi-tse*	雞澤	*CWT* 39, *PCS* 128
Ch'ing-feng	清豐	*CWT* 40

Table 1, cont'd.

Fei-hsiang*	肥鄉	CWT 40
Yü-yang	漁陽	CWY 8
Chen-ting-fu	真定府	CWY 10, CTFC 45

Shantung

Chi-yang*	濟陽	CWT 11, 39
Fu-shan	福山	CWT 11
Po-chou	博州	CWT 15
T'ai-an-chou	泰安州	CWT 24, 37
Yen-chou*	兗州	CWT 33
Wen-teng	文登	CWT 35
Chang-ch'iu	章邱	CWT 36
Ch'ü-fu	曲阜	CWY 8
Ch'i-hsia*	棲下	CWY 8
Tung-p'ing-fu	東平府	CWY 9

Honan

Yü-chou*	裕州	CWT 13
Shang-shui	商水	CWT 13
Chia*	郟	CWT 14
Chang-te-fu*	彰德府	CWT 33
Hsin-hsiang	新鄉	CWT 34
Teng-chou*	鄧州	CWT 35
Ti-chou	棣州	CWT 35
Hsia-i	夏邑	CWT 38
Hsü-chou	許州	CWT 39
Yeh*	葉	CWY 9
Chün-chou	鈞州	PCS 128

Shensi

Ching-chao-fu	京兆府	CWT 34, CSTP 158, 159
Sui-te-chou*	綏德州	CWT 39, 40
Ho-chung-fu	河中府	CWY 8

*Schools built during the Chin.

Table 2
Enrollments of Chin Schools[3]

Type of Schools	Number of Schools	Enrollment
Fu	25	920
Prefectural, including defense command (chieh-chen)	39	630
Defense-prefectural (fang-yü chou)	21	250
Total	85	1,800

It should be noted that the twenty-five *fu* and sixty prefectural schools for Chinese students were not necessarily actually built at the time they were "established." Most of the schools were probably already in existence and were simply selected by the government to form part of what was intended to be a well-balanced and well-organized school system. The *Chin shih* provides names for forty-five out of the eighty-five schools, and information about eleven of these forty-five is available in the seventy-three essays. Of these, probably only one, the school of Po-chou in Shantung, was built in 1189.[4] In terms of geographical distribution, a number of the forty-five schools were established in Manchuria and the western border areas of Shensi and Kansu.

When the government established the school system in 1189, it seems that the smaller *tz'u-shih* prefectures were excluded. In 1201 Emperor Chang-tsung issued an edict requiring these prefectures to build schools (*CS* 12.267). A good example of one is that at Sui-te, Shansi, which was promoted to the status of *tz'u-shih* prefecture in 1182; the school was built there in 1199 (*CWT* 40.2b). Other *tz'u-shih* prefectures in Shansi alone that were known to have schools, according to the seventy-three essays, include Tse (*CWT* 42.12b–14a), Pao-te (39.23a–24a), and Hsin (58.8b). In addition to the upper-level schools, a number of county schools must have been built during the reigns of emperors Shih-tsung and Chang-tsung. As mentioned above, the government encouraged the people to build schools although it was unable to allocate funds for these schools. Examples of county schools built during this period are: Chi-yang, Shantung (*CWT* 39.17b–18b); Fei-hsiang, Hopei (40.1a–2a); Chia, Honan (14.1a–2a); and Hsiang-ling, Shansi (14.9a–10b). It is surprising to read in a short essay by Li Chün-min that a Confucian temple, which seems also to have been a school, was built in the garrison town (*chen*) of Ying-yang, Shansi (*CWT* 58.8b).

It is impossible to determine exactly how many schools existed in Chin times due to the limited nature of the sources. It seems that by the Ch'ing dynasty there were schools in almost all the prefectures and counties of North China. Exceptions are found only in the border areas, such as the northern portions of Shansi and Hopei. Extant Sung and Yüan gazetteers indicate that already in Southern Sung times every prefecture and county in southeastern China had a public school of its own. The information concerning schools in the Ch'ing provincial gazetteer for Chekiang (*Che-chiang t'ung-chih*) is consistent in this respect, probably because the Ch'ing compilers, like their predecessors, made use of all available local gazetteers. It seems that the compilers of provincial gazetteers for North China worked in a similar fashion, though the quality of provincial gazetteers varies somewhat.[5] A preliminary study of the *Ta Ming I-t'ung-chih* (General gazetteer of the Great Ming) and the provincial gazetteers for Shansi, Hopei, Shantung, and Honan, all of which were compiled in the Ch'ing period, yields some interesting figures—although it should be emphasized that this is only a sketchy and preliminary attempt, and that the compilers of the Ch'ing gazetteers had detailed and more complete sources only for Yüan and later times. In many cases the compilers of the four provincial gazetters arbitrarily fix the date of the construction of a school in a certain locality, when the school actually may have been built some time earlier. They might remark that a school was built in the Yüan period, for example, on an "old site" or that it was moved from an "old site" to a new location. In such cases, I would regard the school in question as having been built before the Yüan. In other cases, the compilers note that the time of a particular school's construction is simply "unknown." In such cases, I would not regard the school in question—if no mention of it is found prior to the Ming—as having been built before the Yüan, although such a possibility naturally exists.

A large number of prefectures and counties were established after the Chin dynasty, mostly during the Ming and Ch'ing periods, and there were a good number of changes in place-names as well. Here we will consider only places mentioned in the four provincial gazetteers that have also been identified with place-names in the *Chin shih*, disregarding prefectures and counties that were established in post-Chin times and a few that are mentioned in the *Chin shih* but have not been identified with Ch'ing place-names. Of the 113 *fu*, prefectures, and counties included in the *Shan-hsi t'ung-chih*, for example, 106 can be identified with names in the *Chin shih*. There were 39 schools built in Shansi in Sung times or earlier, including 1 built in the Han dynasty, 5 in the T'ang, 2 in the Five Dynasties, and 1 in the Liao. During the Chin, 14 new schools were established. Local populations also carried out construction and repair projects on 14 of the 39 schools during the Chin. On the basis of the data thus far, 53 of the 106 designated Chin localities had schools. In addition, there is a group of 17

Table 3
Schools in North China during the Chin[6]

	Shansi	Hopei	Shantung	Honan	Total
Total number of places	113	153	118	113	497
Number of places identified in the Chin shih	106	139	100	100	445
Number of schools built before the Chin	39	38	48	28	153
Number of schools built during the Chin	14	15	15	16	60
Number of schools repaired during the Chin	14	11	15	2	42
Number of schools possibly existing during the Chin	17	21	12	12	62
Total number of schools during the Chin (excluding number of schools possibly existing during the Chin)	70	74	75	56	275
Percentage of localities with schools during the Chin	66%	53%	75%	56%	62%

schools whose original construction dates are unknown, but most of which were in existence in the Yüan period. Among these 17, probably as many as 14 were already in existence during the Chin period. If we add these 17 schools to the above-mentioned 53, the number of schools existing in the Chin period reaches 70. And if we assume that there was only one school in each designated place, then 66 per cent of all *fu*, prefectures, and counties in Chin dynasty China had schools.

I have made similar studies of the sections on schools in the *Chi-fu t'ung-chih*, *Shan-tung t'ung-chih*, and *Ho-nan t'ung-chih*. The results are shown in table 3. From these figures we know that many more schools existed in Chin times than those attested to in the *Chin shih* and other primary sources. And while a considerable number of schools were built in Sung and Chin China, we still cannot state that there were schools in all, or even almost all, prefectures and counties.

In terms of geographical distribution of the schools, Shantung and Hopei apparently had more schools than Shansi and Honan. In the Northern Sung period, however, Shantung already had more schools than any of the other three provinces. It is surprising that the area where the smallest number of schools was built during the Sung and Chin periods should be Honan. Kaifeng was the capital of the Northern Sung, and also of the Chin from 1215 to 1234; we can hardly explain the lack of school construction there as failure on the part of local officials to execute central government orders. But it is possible that the section on schools in the *Ho-nan t'ung-chih* is inferior to that in other gazetteers. For example, we know that one of the sixty prefectural schools established in 1189 was built in Huai-ch'ing-fu (called Huai-chou in Chin times), yet the *Ho-nan t'ung-chih* wrongly indicates that the school was built there only in Yüan times (*HNTC* 42.19a).[7]

Among the four provincial gazetteers, the *Chi-fu t'ung-chih* contains more details than the others and includes more essays on schools. In most cases it records exactly when the schools were built or repaired. Of the new schools built in Chin times, 5 were built before 1161; 6 were constructed during the reigns of emperors Shih-tsung and Chang-tsung, from 1161 to 1208; 1 school was built after 1208; and the time of construction of 2 other schools is unknown. The repairs are distributed as follows: 4 projects in the early period, before 1161; 8 in the middle period, from 1161 to 1208; none in the later period, after 1208; and 6 at unknown times. According to the *Shan-hsi t'ung-chih*, most new schools (11) were built during the middle period, a few (4) in the early period, and only 1 in the later period. As to the number of repairs, there were 10 projects in the early period, 16 in the middle period, and only 1 in the later period, with the time of 2 repair projects unknown. We can conclude, then, that in Hopei and Shansi most new construction and repair work was carried out in the middle period. This corresponds with our findings in the primary sources. Among the 13 new schools built in the Chin dynasty, 6, according to the seventy-three essays, were constructed during the middle period.[8] The educational policy that caused most schools to be built or repaired during the reigns of Shih-tsung and Chang-tsung attests to the traditional claim that the Ta-ting (1161–89) and Ming-ch'ang (1190–96) eras marked the period of highest development in Chin culture. Since Shansi and Hopei were lost to the Mongols in 1215, naturally very few construction projects were found in those areas after that date. Yet according to the primary sources, 5 new schools were erected in Honan and Shantung between 1208 and 1234, when the Chin was in the process of decline. This indicates that the Chin central government and its local officials continued to give attention to education even in times of peril.⁹

Another conclusion we can draw is that the combined enrollment figure should be far greater than the reported 1,800, which represents only the number of students in upper-level schools. Although lower-level schools had very small student bodies, education was considerably widespread. The student quotas set in 1189 seem to have been maintained long after that time. According to Yüan Hao-wen's essay on the prefectural school in Tung-p'ing, Shantung, the enrollment of that school still stood at sixty in the late Chin; and at that time the school had an additional fifteen students, descendants of Confucius who were under the instruction of the well-known scholar Wang P'an (1202–93) (CWY 9.12a–12b).

Following the reorganization of the school system in 1176 and its subsequent expansion in 1189, the government increased the number of *chin-shih* to be recruited from the civil service examinations (CS 51.1138). During the reign of Emperor Chang-tsung, the government raised quotas for recipients of *chin-shih* degrees (CS 9.217), and in 1193 quotas for *chin-shih* degrees were again increased (CS 10.231). In 1201 the number of *chin-shih* to be enlisted was fixed at six hundred (CS 11.252). Certainly there is a link between the improvement in the number of schools and quality of education, and the increase in candidates recruited from those schools.

The sources tell us little about either the curriculum or the organization of the regional schools. Each school had one superintendent (*t'i-chü*) and one professor (*chiao-shou*). The curriculum of the state schools in the capital included the Nine Classics, seventeen histories, and three philosophies (*Lao-tzu, Hsün-tzu,* and *Yang-tzu*) (CS 51.1131–32). The classics and histories were taught in translation at the Jurchen schools (CS 51.1133).

Students' composition requirements at the state schools in the capital included one essay, one *fu* (rhyme-prose), and one poem every three days. Every three months an examination on essays, *fu*, and poetry was administered. The five students receiving the highest grades were sent to the Ministry of Rites for official appointments. Students had one day off in every ten and were given holidays on festival days. There were punishments for students whose behavior violated school regulations and dismissal for those whose coursework was not satisfactory (CS 51.1132).

As a general practice in the Sung dynasty, regional schools were supported by the income from land assigned to them as "school land" (*hsüeh-t'ien*). Some local officials used government funds to buy this land. For example, when Wang Tseng (978–1038) was prefect of Yün-chou (Tung-p'ing in Chin times) in present-day Shantung, he purchased at least two hundred *ch'ing* of land for the regional school (CWY 9.12a). Hai-ling ordered that all land previously owned by schools in Sung times but later confiscated by local governments in the chaos of war should be returned to the schools (*CWT* 34.3b, 35.11b). Students in institutions supported by the central government apparently received better treatment than those in county schools. In 1196 the government promulgated a law "supporting the schools and educating the students" that assigned sixty *mou* of state land—complete with tenant farmers—to each regional school student, and 108 *mou* to each University student. A regional student received only thirty piculs of millet annually, but a University student received all that was harvested from the land assigned to him (*CS* 11.257).

Several more observations can be made from the seventy-three essays. First of all, there is appreciation of the fact that the Chin rulers favored Chinese culture in general and were interested in the development of the school system in particular. A typical essay reads: "Having responded to the will of Heaven and followed the wish of the people, our dynasty occupied China. Following military accomplishments, the rule of civilization flourished. The court therefore ordered that schools be repaired and that the expenses be covered by local government funds" (*CWT* 38.6a). Another writer points out: "Now peace has been maintained for a long time, and the imperial court respects the teachings of the Duke of Chou and of Confucius, and establishes schools to educate gifted people" (*CWT* 13.8b).

Several writers praise Emperor Shih-tsung for promoting Chinese culture by building schools. In their writings we can discern recognition and approval of Shih-tsung's efforts to establish the practice of Chinese ceremonies and music at the Chin court, as well as his espousal of Chinese cultural values in order to achieve good governance in the Chinese style. One writer by the name of Mao Hui, choosing to ignore Shih-tsung's measures to preserve Jurchen values as well, claims that the literary developments of the Ta-ting era were so brilliant that the period could be compared with the Three Dynasties, the golden age of antiquity, and that it certainly surpassed both the Han and the T'ang (*CWT* 39.8a). P'ang Yün describes Emperor Chang-tsung's efforts to build schools in similarly favorable terms:

> Now that the percipient Son of Heaven is above us, His Majesty considers respect for [the teachings of] Confucianism and the promotion of civilization as [his] primary concern and the way to attain good rule. In the first year of the T'ai-ho era [1201], the emperor promulgated to all under Heaven that in whatever prefectures did not have temple schools, the local officials should build them and that in the counties schools could be established by scholars and commoners. (*CWT* 40.1b)

Yüan Hao-wen describes the development of Chinese literary culture in these words:

> Civil rule has attained harmony, and the sound of [students] reciting the classics can be heard from the county to the private schools. In the Shang-tang and Kao-p'ing regions, scholars often carry the classics with them while tending their fields.... From this fact one may know [what achievements the government has made in] the education of the people and the nurture of good customs. (*CWT* 15.13a)

This claim represents the second characteristic of the essays on schools: that is, these writers obviously felt that the Chin rulers were trying to identify themselves with the good rulers of China's past. One writes that in ancient times there were good officials who effected the spread of education and Chinese culture to barbarian lands. Nowadays, he contends, officials such as the new prefect of Sui-te establish schools, stimulate the morale of scholars, and assume responsibility for developing the Son of Heaven's educational system so that the people will be able to understand the virtues of traditional Chinese education (*CWT* 40.3a). Another writer praises the measures taken by Chang-tsung to build regional schools and writes that he expects to see the Confucian Way spread far to the four directions (*CWT* 10.17b). Li Chün-min wrote these two lines in the early Chin:

> For twenty years this land has been left thorny;
> But one day it suddenly witnesses the Chinese way.
> (*CWT* 31.10a)

Yüan Hao-wen states that the schools formed the foundation of traditional Chinese culture because they represented the Confucian Way and trained scholars who would employ the Way in assisting the rule of their own state and foreign lands (*CWT* 15.11b–12a).

A third observation from the essays is that many local officials were enthusiastic about building schools. Although some writers point out that a few local officials did not regard the establishment of new schools to be an important responsibility of local administration, others did worry about poor maintenance of the temple schools and made efforts to repair or rebuild them. Still others initiated the work of building, which was eventually completed by their successors. There seems to have been a pattern to such endeavors: local officials first enlisted the assistance of local scholars and wealthy citizens, who in turn supported the construction projects by raising funds. Chinese and Jurchen officials, local notables and commoners often collaborated in building the schools. A typical example of such a project is the construction of the temple school in the county of Chang-ch'iu, Shantung. According to an essay written by Chiang Kuo-ch'i in the sixteenth year of the Ta-ting period (1176), the county's old Confucian temple was destroyed in the wars. One day the county magistrate summoned the local scholar-officials and told them that it was the responsibility of Confucian scholars to "attack" Buddhism and Taoism. Buddhist and Taoist temples were flourishing and were magnificently built, while Confucius, whose merit had been recognized for myriad generations, did not receive the degree of worship accorded either Buddhism or Taoism. This, declared the magistrate, made the followers of Confucianism little less than criminals. He donated his own salary to the construction project, and the local people cooperated with him in restoring the old temple (CWT 36.8a–8b). Another case is found in Hsiang-ling, Shansi, where local officials persisted for some forty years in their efforts to build a Confucian temple. The work was completed in 1209, but only after the local magistrate set an example by donating his salary to the project. This led the county's scholars to follow suit by making their own donations, and they were followed by wine merchants and other private citizens (CWT 14.9b–10a). In a few cases the poor also made contributions by organizing free labor for the actual construction of the schools (SYSK 23.3b).

A number of Jurchen officials also participated in the process of rebuilding the school system. They did this partly because they were obliged, as local officials, to carry out the government's plans and projects, and partly because they took a personal interest in the work. In one example from the early Chin, a top Jurchen official took part in the planning and construction of a new school in Ching-chao (now Sian), Shensi (CWT 34.5a). Much later, two high-ranking Jurchen officials were involved in the rebuilding of another *fu*-level school in Shensi. They appointed two Jurchen scholars to serve as the school's superintendents, and another as professor (CWT 41.13a–13b). It should be noted that these Jurchen educators were posted to a Chinese school; Jurchen schools had been abolished in Shensi in 1197 (CS 51.1134).[10]

A final point worth noting in regard to the characteristics of Chin public schools is the schools' considerable influence on government recruitment of literati for officialdom. One example of an old school that continued to produce successful and well-known scholar-officials through the years is the prefectural school of Tung-p'ing, Shantung, which was built in T'ang times. In the Sung, as mentioned, when Wang Tseng was appointed prefect of Tung-p'ing, he used his influence as former prime minister to purchase two hundred *ch'ing* of land for the school. Afterward, a handful of prominent scholar-official families maintained a tradition of learning there down to the Chin period. During the Chin the success of three prime ministers who had been educated there, Chang Wan-kung, Hou Chih, and Kao Lin, brought further renown to the school (*CWT* 9.12a–12b).

The *fu* school of Ching-chao also produced a number of scholar-officials. It was a sizable school when built in 1103, but it was almost completely destroyed less than a century later during the Jurchen campaigns. The Chin deputy prefect, Han Hsi-fu, lamented the lack of a school in Ching-chao and discussed the matter with the prefect, Wan-yen Hu-nü. The two started a reconstruction project, and the new school was completed within a year. On two lists of names of successful candidates graduated from this school, there are at least nineteen natives of the prefecture and forty-three non-natives from all over the Chin empire.[11] Among those who passed the *chin-shih* examinations between 1135 and 1218, Feng Pi (*CS* 110), Li Hsien-fu (*CS* 110), Chia I (*CS* 90), Li Chung-lüeh (*CS* 96), Chang Pang-hsien (*CS* 123), and Li Hsien-ch'eng (*CS* 126) had their careers recorded in the *Chin shih*. The two Li brothers also made contributions in the field of literature, as did Chao Ssu-wen, Liu Kuang-ch'ien, Feng Ch'en, Chang Chü, and P'ang Han, biographical sketches of whom are found in the *Chung-chou chi* (Anthology of the Central Plain). The large number of refugees who apparently fled west to the Kuan-chung area after the fall of Yenching to the Mongols in 1215 (*CWT* 41.13a) might account for the high percentage of non-native graduates. Nonetheless, there were some who had moved west even before 1215: Feng Pi from Chen-ting, Hopei, and Chia I from T'ung-chou, Kiangsu. This suggests that there was a certain degree of movement among people in Chin times.

Another example of the interest in education during the Chin is found in the story of the *fu* school of Taiyuan, Shansi. According to an essay written by Chao Feng, the school in Taiyuan was destroyed during the war in the early twelfth century. When Yeh-lü Tzu-jang was appointed prefect in 1131, he ordered minor repairs made to the school. In the 1150s, Wan-yen Tsung-hsien became prefect, and he also ordered repairs. When Chang Ta-chieh was appointed prefect in 1191, he lamented the poor condition of the buildings: "This does not live up to the court's intention to promote civic culture!" He started a new construction project that resulted in a much larger temple school with the addition of a library. In the same year seven of the school's students passed the *chin-shih* examination, and one of them, Wang Tse, attained the highest ranking of *chuang-yüan*. In his previous appointment as military prefect of Heng-hai, Chang Ta-chieh had earlier initiated construction of a temple school; moreover, in 1185 one student from that school, Hsü Wei, had also taken first place in the *chin-shih* examination (*CWT* 38.13a–14b). Another example is found at the county school of Chi-tse, Hopei. The inscription on the back of the stele there, dated 1212, lists the names of the officials who initiated construction of the temple school and all those who were in one way or another involved in the project. After the county magistrate completed the work, his own brother Kao Ch'ung and his son Kao K'o-chiu both acquired *chin-shih* degrees. The rolls record the names of a number of other degree holders who were also presumably graduates of the school, as well as the names of all who contributed toward the construction of specific parts of the buildings or the sculpture that was displayed in them—names and details that testify again to the coordinated efforts made by the local citizenry and administration for the promotion of education (*PCS* 128.8a–10b).

In conclusion, education served as the foundation of culture because, as one essayist aptly puts it, "all affairs concerning ceremonies and music [*li-yüeh*], politics and law are related to education" (*CWT* 34.2b). From the early years of the Chin dynasty, it seems that almost all its rulers were committed to the maintenance and development of the school system they had inherited from the Northern Sung. They repeatedly issued orders for the construction of schools throughout the empire, introduced measures to appropriate funds for the building projects, and attempted to reorganize the school system for the purposes of upgrading the quality as well as increasing the number of the schools. Their ultimate goal was to produce educated and talented officials who would serve in the government bureaucracy. But the spread of education to every corner of the land also had the effect of bringing literary refinement (*wen-ya*) to the people who inhabited it; it "penetrated all the prefectures and distant towns, where people in high mountains and deep valleys were stimulated by [its] virtues," and this was achieved by the temple schools (*CTFC* 45.19a). Indeed, in many cases, spontaneous efforts were made by people of different economic classes or social standing to collaborate toward the completion of a construction project. Moreover, the balanced school system provided even people in frontier regions with the opportunity to train for official careers as well as to contribute to Chin culture. The ultimate contribution of the widespread school system during the Chin era was the promotion of Chinese literary and cultural values. In the judgment of many Chinese at that time, the cultural achievements of the Chin eventually reached the level attained by any of the exemplary dynasties in the history of the Chinese tradition.

Notes

1. In 1044, during the Ch'ing-li reform, Fan Chung-yen caused the issuance of an imperial edict to that effect. When the new party again

assumed power in 1102, Emperor Hui-tsung decided that schools should be built all over the empire, creating a system that would eventually replace the civil service examinations as the most important channel for official recruitment. See SS 11.217, 155.3613, 19.364.

2. There are also four essays on schools in *CWT* 13, *CWT* 43, *CWT* 58, and *CWY* 1 with information insufficient to determine, for example, whether the schools were temple schools, whether they were newly constructed or simply restored, when the construction was completed. The essay in *CWT* 58, written by an unknown author, concerns a temple school. Among the fifty-eight schools, only those in Huo-chou and Fu-shan were, perhaps, not temple schools; in both cases the information in the essays is too scant to allow us to determine the nature of the schools with certainty.

3. According to *STTC* 89.2703, the school in Tung-ch'ang-fu or Po-chou was built during the Yüan-feng reign of the Northern Sung. The school built in 1189 could still be a new one, however. In *CS* 51.1154 n. 6, the modern editors of the history, citing *CS* 25, write that they suspect that at this time Chang-te was still a military prefecture (*chün*), not a *fu*. But Chia K'uei's essay in *CWT* 33.3b–4b clearly indicates that Chang-te was a *fu*.

4. For the number of schools in Sung times, cf. Chaffee 1985, 75, table 10. His Southern Sung total of 161 is surprisingly small in comparison to my figure of 275 for the Chin in North China. As indicated above, all prefectures and counties in the southeast had public schools in Southern Sung times. (I have not counted the numbers from prefecture to prefecture.) Chaffee's small estimate probably stems from his exclusive use of the *Ta Ming I-t'ung-chih*, which I do not regard as a reliable source.

5. Cf. Mao Wen 1936, 32–34. The figures for *fu* schools and students have been revised according to Shih Kuo-ch'i's studies. It should be noted that Mao Wen's figure for the combined enrollment of all schools, including some 2,200 Jurchen students, is 5,000. He makes the mistake, however, of adding 1,800 students who enrolled in the twenty-five *fu* schools established in 1189 to the 1,000 who were enrolled in the seventeen already-existing *fu* schools. Actually, the 1189 figure includes the enrollments of only eight additional schools, not of the twenty-five additional schools. There were simply not so many *fu* in Chin times. Moreover, I have not been able to find the sources attesting to the 2,200 Jurchen students whom Mao thinks were enrolled in Jurchen schools in 1189.

6. I have not included schools in Manchuria, Shensi, and parts of Anhwei and Kiangsu in this study. Because the Chin *lu* (circuit) does not correspond to the Ch'ing province, some of the unidentified places are outside the Ch'ing provincial jurisdictions. For example, Ho-chung-fu, where an upper-level school was established in 1189, was not under the jurisdiction of Shansi in Ch'ing times and is therefore not included among

the Shansi schools in this study. Similarly, a number of places that were in Honan in Chin times were in Anhwei in the Ch'ing dynasty. The largest number of new administrative divisions were established in Hopei between the Yüan and Ch'ing periods, and that is why so many places there have not been identified with their Chin dynasty antecedents. I have compared the dates of school construction in the primary sources (CS and the seventy-three essays) with those in the four local gazetteers and have corrected a few mistakes in the latter.

7. There are a few more errors in the Ch'ing gazetteers that can be corrected by comparing the dates of school construction there recorded with those in the primary sources. Examples are:

(1) Yü-chou, Honan. According to Chao Ping-wen's essay on the school here, it was repaired in the late Chin. But *HNTC* 42. 27b records that the school was built in Ming times.
(2) Wan-ch'üan, Shansi. According to the essay written by Chang Pang-yen, the temple school at Wan-ch'üan was repaired during the T'ai-ho reign. But *CFTC* 116.3819 records that the school was built in Ming times.
(3) Liao-chou, Shansi. According to *SHTC* 36.735, the date of the establishment of the school there could only be traced to Yüan times. But according to *SYSK* 21, it was already in existence in the Chin period.

The small number of repairs reportedly done in Honan during the Chin is also doubtful.

8. See table 1 above for the new schools. They were "newly created" (*ch'uang-chien*) instead of "newly built" (*hsin-chien*). Actually, the school in Tung-p'ing, Shantung, was completely rebuilt in the Chin and probably should be regarded as a new school.

9. These are schools in Chi-tse, Hopei; Ch'i-hsia, Shantung; Teng-chou, Yü-chou, and Yeh, Honan.

10. Other examples of Jurchen officials' involvement in the building of schools can be found in *PCS* 128.2a–6a; *CWT* 13.17a; *CWT* 35.12a; *CFTC* 45.18b; *PCS* 128.9b; *CFTC* 114.3699.

11. The first list, "Chin-shih t'i-ming chi" (Record of the names of *chin-shih*), can be found in *CSTP* 158.23b–24a. The second list, "Kai-chien t'i-ming pei" (Names of *chin-shih* from the reestablished school) can be found in *CSTP* 159.1a–3b and in *CWT* 42.2b–3b (without the commentaries included in *CSTP*).

II

Religion and Thought

4

CONFUCIANISM UNDER THE CHIN AND THE IMPACT OF SUNG CONFUCIAN TAO-HSÜEH

Hoyt Cleveland Tillman

According to traditional Chinese scholarship, Chinese intellectuals living under Jurchen Chin rule in North China were not cognizant of major intellectual developments in the South under the Southern Sung and did not read the works of Chu Hsi (1130–1200) until Mongol conquerors brought the Southern Sung Confucian Chao Fu (ca. 1206–ca. 1299) captive to the North in 1235. The cornerstone of this view was laid in the official *Yüan History* (YS 189.4314). In the present essay I will set forth evidence for questioning and revising this interpretation. A recent article (T'ien Hao [Tillman] 1988) on the introduction of Sung Confucianism into the Chin has already persuaded some scholars in East Asia to begin rethinking this issue.[1] A fuller exposition of Chin Confucianism will be set forth here for a broader Western audience. But first, more needs to be said about the conventional view.

China's premier intellectual history, the *Sung Yüan hsüeh-an* (Record of the Sung and Yüan Confucian schools of thought), displays a partisan bias against northern culture of the Chin period. In his editorial comments in the *Sung Yüan hsüeh-an*, Ch'üan Tsu-wang (1705–55) portrayed the Chin as a dark age. After the Jurchen conquest of the Yellow River valley, the remnant of the Sung dynasty fled southward, and "all scholarly traditions migrated with it." In the North there were "no scholars," and "for a century there was no system of thought." Only in the last years of the Chin did scholars like Chao Ping-wen (1159–1232) emerge; still, Ch'üan Tsu-wang alleged that Chao was merely "a Buddhist at heart," parading in Confucian clothing, a man whose open embrace of heterodox Buddhism was inhibited only by his fear of censure from those within the Confucian tradition. Two Chin intellectuals, Liu Ts'ung-i (1181–1224) and Sung Chiu-chia (d. 1234), were heroic enough to criticize Buddhism; but their writings soon vanished, so these scholars "were nothing more than points of light in the darkness" (*SYHA* 100.1879). The editors of the *Sung Yüan hsüeh-an* relegated the one chapter covering Chin intellectuals to the status of a brief introduction (*lüeh*) in order to belittle Chin intellectuals as being outside the Confucian tradition. Ridiculing the vulgar things said by someone like Li Ch'un-fu (P'ing-shan, 1175–1231), who was allegedly mired in Ch'an Buddhist heterodoxy, would, in the eyes of the editors, promote even greater respect for Confucian orthodoxy: "If there were no crazy and weird points of view, there would be nothing against which to measure the brightness of the sun" (*SYHA* 100.1873). This traditional interpretation has dominated contemporary studies and has been accepted by many of the most eminent scholars in China and the West.

Since the mid-1970s, a few scholars have made minor, but significant, qualifications to the traditional interpretation. In a pioneering essay, Yoshikawa Kôjirô (1974) explored the northern transmission of Chu Hsi's Confucianism. What Yoshikawa characterized as an "iron curtain" between the Chin and the Southern Sung was apparently porous enough to allow some books to be traded or smuggled into Chin territory in spite of stringent prohibitions by both regimes against books crossing the border, even at official trade stations. The prohibition would have been particularly strict in the case of Chu Hsi's writings, Yoshikawa reasoned, for they would have been seen by Sung authorities as equivalent to state secrets. Yet Wang Jo-hsü (1174–1243) had access to some of Chu Hsi's commentaries on the *Analects* and the *Mencius*, and Li Ch'un-fu quoted some of Chu Hsi's philosophical writings. Both of these Chin thinkers cited Chu Hsi simply to refute his arguments, according to Yoshikawa. The North was not receptive to Chu Hsi because the intellectual milieu was dominated by a school of thought centered in Su Shih (Tung-p'o, 1036–1101). Su Shih's tradition was a rival to the one that Chu Hsi followed. The civil service examination system under the Chin emphasized the composition of highly stylized poetry that militated against the expression of philosophical ideas; therefore, the institutional environment was also a major obstacle to the introduction of Chu Hsi's ideas into the North. Yoshikawa concluded that Chu Hsi's reputation, but not his thought, had reached the Chin. In a similar vein, in the mid-1980s Yao Ta-li (1983, 217–19) and Chang Po-ch'üan (1985, 136–37) noted that a few Chin literati had maintained an interest in the writings of Ch'eng Hao (1032–85) and Ch'eng I (1033–1107). Nonetheless, these scholars still emphasized Su Shih's overwhelming influence and the popular trend to merge Confucianism with Taoism and Buddhism.

In the West, the prevailing version of the conventional view comes from Wing-tsit Chan. He surmises: "Chu Hsi was certainly known in the Chin. However, if we are to follow the *Yüan History* and emphasize 'the learning of Ch'eng-Chu,' that is, the Ch'eng-Chu teaching as a systematic school of thought and an intellectual lineage, this did not exist in the Chin. In this respect, the Yüan almost began in a vacuum, which Chao Fu filled" (Chan 1982, 199–200). Professor Chan thus rationalizes and clarifies the crux of the traditional interpretation.

Reading Chin materials has raised in my mind questions about the traditional interpretation and doubts about the limits of recent scholarly qualifications to that interpretation. Should we be searching Chin texts for more specific indicators (e.g., terms and concepts) of particular Sung Confucian schools? Were there trends and directions developing in the intellectual milieu that by some "inner logic" were moving Chinese intellectuals—even while under Jurchen rule—progressively toward receptivity to, and even acceptance of, some of the principal viewpoints that we associate with Chu Hsi and his group? Are we utilizing the most appropriate lens when we use either "Neo-Confucianism" or "the Ch'eng-Chu teaching as a systematic school of thought and an intellectual lineage"? Would some other term from the documents themselves—a term such as "Tao-hsüeh" (a fellowship or community for learning the Confucian Way)—bring the vital aspects of Confucian thought under the Chin into focus? I have elsewhere (Tillman 1992a and 1992b) elaborated on "Tao-hsüeh" as a term, as a fellowship, and as a tradition in the Sung. My hypothesis here is this: although only a small percentage of Chin texts are extant, those extant materials contain enough evidence to demonstrate that my questions should be answered in the affirmative and that the traditional interpretation should be fundamentally revised.

Recognition and Dating of Tao-hsüeh in the Chin

To document that Tao-hsüeh under the Chin belonged to the same tradition as under the Sung and that it had flourished several decades before the Mongols brought Chao Fu to North China in 1235, this section first turns to Li Ch'un-fu. Two of Li Ch'un-fu's foremost contemporaries explicitly claimed that his book addressed the Tao-hsüeh tradition. Li Ch'un-fu's major work was the *Ming-tao chi shuo* (Discussions on writings for propagating the *tao*), which was designed to be an answer to an anthology of Tao-hsüeh writings compiled in the Southern Sung.[2] Observing that Li read extensively from all traditions, Yüan Hao-wen (1190–1257) commented:

> After becoming thirty, he emphasized the reading of Buddhist books and was able to grasp all of their subtle and profound points. He also collected Tao-hsüeh books and read them. He wrote a book [the

Ming-tao chi shuo] to unify the Three Teachings. Thus, he discussed points raised by Ch'eng I, Chang Tsai [1020–77], and Chu Hsi and did not neglect giving attention to the smallest of points where he disagreed. He regretted that he had not been born in the same era as they so that he could have debated with them. (CCC 4.219)

Besides presenting Li Ch'un-fu as a serious collector of Tao-hsüeh books, Yüan Hao-wen here clearly identified Tao-hsüeh as a tradition begun in the Northern Sung by such people as Ch'eng I and Chang Tsai and continued in the Southern Sung by Chu Hsi. This consciousness of Tao-hsüeh as an intellectual tradition rooted in the thought of Ch'eng I and his contemporaries was also reflected in the preface Yeh-lü Ch'u-ts'ai (1189–1243) wrote to Li's *Ming-tao chi shuo*: "Left of the Yangtze"— by which he meant the Southern Sung— "Tao-hsüeh is rooted in the thought of Ch'eng I and his brother, and more than ten major philosophers there are in harmony with them" (*MTCS*, p. 51).

Did Li Ch'un-fu also demonstrate an awareness that Tao-hsüeh was a special intellectual lineage? In combating what he saw as determinism in Chang Tsai's theory of *ch'i* (psychophysical or vital energy), Li Ch'un-fu claimed that if Chang Tsai's position were true, "then Confucian teachings [*ming-chiao*] need not be treasured and Tao-hsüeh need not be transmitted" (*MTCS* 2.86, no. 31). In other words, Chang's deterministic views would allegedly reduce Confucian ethical practice to self-imposed bondage or restraint. More to our point, Li Ch'un-fu was here making a distinction between Tao-hsüeh and earlier Confucian teachings, but at the same time associating them with one another. He also had a view of the *tao* that was similar to that of Tao-hsüeh, in that he claimed the *tao* had not been transmitted for some fifteen centuries after the death of Mencius (ca. 371–289 B.C.) until its revival by Chou Tun-i (1017–73) and the Ch'eng brothers during the Northern Sung.

Other of Li Ch'un-fu's comments further illustrate his awareness of Tao-hsüeh as an intellectual lineage distinct from those established or continued by other Sung Confucians. In his preface to *Ming-tao chi shuo* Li listed major Sung thinkers, juxtaposing Wang An-shih (1021–86) and his son with the Su brothers. Following this, Tao-hsüeh philosophers were classed by "generation": first, Chou Tun-i , Ssu-ma Kuang (1019–86), Chang Tsai, and Ch'eng I; second, Hsieh Liang-tso (1050–1103), Liu An-shih (1048–1125), Yang Shih (1053–1135), and Chang Chiu-ch'eng (1092–1159); and last, Lü Tsu-ch'ien (1137–81), Chang Shih (1133–80), and Chu Hsi. Furthermore, Li Ch'un-fu was aware that there had been a significant increase in the popularity of the Tao-hsüeh school as a result of the writings of this last generation (*MTCS*, pp. 55–56). His concluding section is more explicit. Listing the doctrines of Tao-hsüeh with which he agreed, Li praised these philosophers (whose attacks on Buddhism had elsewhere provoked his criticism): "They continue the transmission of the lost teaching of the immemorial past; they establish the complete teachings of their one school. Other Confucians of the Sung dynasty were not their equal. The Confucians of the Han and T'ang were likewise not their equal. Soon they will be galloping neck and neck with Mencius" (MTCS 5.195, no. 217). Thus, Li Ch'un-fu judged Tao-hsüeh to be a singular lineage and a distinctly Confucian tradition.

Li Ch'un-fu also presented Tao-hsüeh thinkers as having inherited ideas from earlier generations within the school. In two of the eight sections on Chu Hsi's statements, for example, Li passed over Chu Hsi to attack Ch'eng I instead (MTCS 5.188–90, nos. 210–11). In a third case, he explicitly charged that Chu Hsi was "limited to the views of Ch'eng I on [the subject of] ethical cultivation" (MTCS 5.191, no. 213). Such passages imply that Li knew not only that Chu Hsi was in Ch'eng I's intellectual lineage but also that the linkage was in a sense direct, rather than a mere function of Chu Hsi's place in the chain of descent through a series of teachers.

Although Li's arrangement was essentially chronological and reflected that of the *Chu Ju ming-tao chi*, this Southern Sung anthology did not include Chu Hsi's generation. The *Chu Ju ming-tao chi* was compiled between 1158 and 1168 by an unspecified person who was almost certainly one of Chang Chiu-ch'eng's students (Ch'en Lai 1986). The fact that few texts from the Southern Sung were available in the North during the Chin enhances the importance of this anthology. The arrangement and coverage therein indicates a conception of Tao-hsüeh and the succession and transmission of the *tao* broader than that Chu Hsi developed in the mid-1170s. For instance, the anthology presented Chang as the culmination of Tao-hsüeh in his day; hence, it is not surprising that Chang Chiu-ch'eng was a significant figure in Chin discussions of Tao-hsüeh. Comparison of Li Ch'un-fu's work with the *Chu Ju ming-tao chi* demonstrates that Li decided on his own to include Chu's generation and to conclude with Chu Hsi. Taken together, these various characteristics of Li's work suggest that for him Tao-hsüeh had reached its culmination with Chu Hsi's synthesis and definition of the tradition. Li, after all, did proclaim in his preface, "How fortunate I am to be able to see the discussions of these philosophers! I know that the teachings of the ancient sages have not died out and that the great *tao* is at the point of coming together" (MTCS, p. 56).

Another example of Li Ch'un-fu's awareness of Tao-hsüeh as a school of thought indicates that he could even use this awareness to make a clever argument against a point he disliked. In answering Chang Tsai's statement that the Lao Tan from whom Confucius—according to the *Shih chi* (Historical records) of Ssu-ma Ch'ien (ca. 145–90 B.C.)—inquired about rituals was not the Lao-tzu of Taoism, Li Ch'un-fu accused Chang Tsai of "intending to do damage to Tao-hsüeh" (*MTCS* 2.90, no. 34). At face value, this accusation would appear to indicate that Li placed Chang Tsai outside the Tao-hsüeh tradition. Li might even be seen as using the term "Tao-hsüeh" to refer to Taoism—as had sometimes been done in the late Northern Sung. But seen in the larger context of Li's book, this was definitely not his intent. The unstated step in his reasoning apparently ran like this: Tao-hsüeh masters, most notably Ch'eng I, sought to translate the meaning or spirit of ancient rituals into terms or forms that were appropriate to Sung times; hence, like Lao-tzu, they understood the essence of propriety and could dispense with what was not essential. If this line of reasoning were accepted, Chang Tsai could be seen as going counter to his own school in belittling Lao-tzu's understanding of propriety. Thus, Li was seeking to reduce Chang Tsai's argument to absurdity. Li Ch'un-fu associated himself primarily with Buddhism, so it might be more appropriate to turn our attention to one who regarded himself as a champion of Confucianism—Chao Ping-wen.

Chao Ping-wen was regarded by Chin intellectuals as "leader of our culture" (*ISWC* 38.9a; *FSWC* preface, 6a). They also saw Chao as seeking to imitate Han Yü (768–824) in transmitting the *tao* from antiquity (*CCC* 3.152–53; *ISWC* 17.6b; *KCC* 9.106). In an essay on human nature, Chao Ping-wen subscribed to the doctrine that the early Tao-hsüeh masters had not only recovered the transmission of the *tao*, but also advanced new insights into how cultivation must begin in the mind-and-heart before the feelings or emotions were aroused:

> After the death of Mencius, his transmission [of the *tao*] was not continued. Only Chou and Ch'eng, the two masters, reconnected with the severed tradition of learning from early antiquity and made manifest the inner mysteries of the ancient sages by teaching people to seek before the feelings of pleasure and anger, sorrow and joy had yet been expressed in order to be fearful and watchful over oneself when others cannot see or hear what one is doing. Being essentials for entering into the *tao*, these teachings are what previous sages never realized and are indeed most excellent. (*FSWC* 1.3b)

The disciples of Chou Tun-i and the Ch'engs were, according to Chao, so proud of their masters' achievement that they relegated Han Yü, Ou-yang Hsiu (1007–72), and other Confucians to the status of not knowing the *tao*. Chao Ping-wen insisted that there were merely different levels of understanding the *tao*; furthermore, due to a neglect of practicality and a bias toward abstractness in discussing human nature, there was a "blindness" in Tao-hsüeh that inclined it unconsciously toward Taoism and Buddhism. Ironically, this was precisely the inclination that students of Tao-hsüeh accused the Su family of having: "Someone asked: 'How do you deal with the lack of purity both in the learning of Han Yü and Ou-yang Hsiu, which erred in being shallow, and in the learning of the Su family, which erred in being adulterated?' I replied: 'Ou-yang and the Sus were experts on changes in statecraft; but when it comes to its [the *tao*'s] constancy, one ought to return to Chou and Ch'eng'" (*FSWC* 1.3b–4a).

Praising Chou and Ch'eng specifically for regaining the transmission of the *tao* that had been lost after Mencius, the paragraph's context justifies understanding the "it" (of "its constancy") to refer to the *tao*. In spite of his being appropriately associated with Su learning as well as his having reservations about the impact of Tao-hsüeh on governmental and daily affairs, Chao here conceded a particular advantage to Tao-hsüeh when it came to understanding the *tao*. This was an issue of utmost importance to Tao-hsüeh thinkers.

Chao Ping-wen wrote a laudatory preface for a Chin anthology of Tao-hsüeh writings, the *Tao-hsüeh fa-yüan* (Expressing sources of Tao-hsüeh), compiled by Fu Ch'i (late 12th cent.) and several friends. Although this anthology itself is apparently no longer extant, its name may still serve as evidence that scholars were compiling and publishing Tao-hsüeh writings under the Chin. From Chao's preface, which was preserved in his collected works, we know that Chang Chiu-ch'eng figured prominently in the anthology (as he did in Li Ch'un-fu's *Ming-tao chi shuo* and Wang Jo-hsü's commentaries)—perhaps because of the importance accorded him in the *Chu Ju ming-tao chi*. Thus, Fu Ch'i and his friends had access and were receptive to Tao-hsüeh philosophers from the Southern Sung. Because Li's work and Wang's commentaries cited a considerable range of Tao-hsüeh thinkers from both Northern and Southern Sung, we could infer that Fu Ch'i probably included others, in addition to Chang Chiu-ch'eng, who were not specifically named in Chao's preface. In contrast to Chao Ping-wen's essay on human nature and the reservations voiced in it, his preface to this anthology extolled the usefulness of Tao-hsüeh writings in both the daily praxis of personal cultivation and the extension of knowledge. When he heard that Fu Ch'i and his friends had studied Chang Chiu-ch'eng's explanations of key concepts of the Confucian sages and were disseminating them far and wide, Chao Ping-wen professed "to being so happy that he was unable to sleep." Moreover, he recommended that everyone—even monks, Taoists, and ordinary folks—read Fu Ch'i's anthology (*FSWC* 15.3a–4a).

Wang Jo-hsü's postface to the *Tao-hsüeh fa-yüan* provides much more detail about the book's presentation of Tao-hsüeh, as well as his own response to it. If this is indeed the same book for which Chao Ping-wen wrote his preface, it is significant that the two foremost Confucian scholars of the North wrote introductory pieces for it. If it is a similar but different anthology, there was more than one such effort, to which we have extant reference, to popularize Tao-hsüeh under the Chin. Wang began his postface:

> Han Yü's *Yüan-tao* [Essentials of the *tao*] said, "After the death of Mencius, his transmission [of the *tao*] was not continued." This statement is quite accurate. A person of integrity would not consider it excessive. The *tao* of the sages could be handed down through myriad generations and continue to exist. Mencius died and there was no transmission of it. Why? The reason is, stupid ones could not understand it, perverse ones destroyed it, muddled and impure ones discarded it, and no true Confucians were able to continue it; therefore, although it did exist, it almost perished. From the time of the Ch'in and Han dynasties, it daily became weaker. Those who mastered the classics stayed in the peripheral realm of word-and-sentence commentaries, while those who handled governmental affairs fell into self-centered quests for merit, reputation, wealth, and passion. When they came to discussing the *tao*, they were all engaged in groundless speculation and never reached [its] practical use for society. It appeared to be rather similar [to the *tao*], but it had lost the genuineness of the *tao*. Their fragmented and empty talk was not unified by any central thread. Can their weakness be fully expressed in words? Therefore, scholars read many books and debated as eloquently as a river flowing from the heavens, but they could not escape being mediocre Confucians. They possessed special characteristics that surpassed others' and noble reputations that were esteemed in society; yet because they were a little lacking in their understanding of the *tao*, they unexpectedly ended up doing evil. The reason was simply that they were not one with the public-oriented and completely just *tao*. Han Yü certainly knew how to talk, but what he attained also never reached the profound and subtle level, so as a result, the learning of Mencius was actually never transmitted. (*HNIL* 44.7a–8a)

Thus, Wang Jo-hsü embraced Tao-hsüeh's evaluation of the failures of Confucians after the death of Mencius.

The Sung marked a return to the *tao* that had long been lost, Wang continued:

> From the time the Sung Confucians clearly explained profound ideas, caused early antiquity's almost severed transmission of learning to be restored and continued afresh, established for the first time the concept of the extension of knowledge through the investigation of things [chih-chih ko-wu], and expended great energy to clarify the difference between Heaven's principle [t'ien-li] and human desires [jen-yü], they began at the most mundane and reached the most pure or profound; all of these are truths that earlier people never perceived. Thereupon, ordinary people all of a sudden realized what to do. Their [the Tao-hsüeh masters'] philosophy is as trustworthy as a weighing balance or a compass. How could their contribution to our *tao* possibly be regarded as superficial? (HNIL 44.8a)

Wang's focus on such themes as the extension of knowledge through the investigation of things, the clear distinction between Heaven's principle (order or pattern) and human desires, the transition from routine affairs to more philosophical subjects clearly suggests Tao-hsüeh, and such themes are particularly prominent in the writings of Ch'eng I and Chu Hsi. These concepts, Wang argued, were major contributions to the understanding of the Confucian *tao*.

After commenting on the spreading influence of Tao-hsüeh under the Chin, Wang proceeded to praise those who were taking a lead in propagating this tradition:

> Now, the various gentlemen [meeting] in the provincial courtyard have exerted their utmost effort especially and announced impassionedly that they have taken the revival of this [Confucian] culture of ours to be their own responsibility. Furthermore, they want to share this [work] with those who do not yet know of it; and for this reason, this book is being published with enthusiasm. Scholars who examine and use it will certainly learn something. If they are clear about methods for cultivating the mind-and-heart [hsin-shu], and if their orientation becomes correctly set, and if they proceed along this course, it will not be difficult to reach even the realm of sagehood—just like water from the [Yellow] River's source flowing unceasingly eastward toward the sea and dispersing into the sea before it stops. Ah, can it [i.e., the benefits of studying this book] be measured! I am happy you are taking on this cause as your commitment, and I praise your delight in a good thing and your concern [to share it] with the people. I am glad to announce you to the world; therefore, I am making this general statement to append to your book. (HNIL 44.8a–8b)

Like Chao Ping-wen's preface, this postface is an unqualified endorsement of Tao-hsüeh and an expression of belief that it would, or should, spread widely under the Chin. It is, of course, customary for prefaces and postfaces to be laudatory, but the substance of the praise by Wang Jo-hsü and Chao Ping-wen is still noteworthy.

Elsewhere, Wang Jo-hsü even claimed that many scholars were using Tao-hsüeh as the measure of one another's learning: "In recent times, various Confucian scholars have been using Tao-hsüeh to gauge who is more learned" (HNIL 25.6b). In another reference to Tao-hsüeh, he encouraged District Magistrate Chang Ku-ying (Chung-chieh, chin-shih of 1209, KCC 4.42) to concentrate on it. He further urged this young official to be fond of, and to delight in, Tao-hsüeh. In an earlier letter to Wang Jo-hsü, Chang had set forth some thoughts about Tao-hsüeh. Unfortunately, Chang's letter has been lost, and its contents are thus unknown, but we do know that Wang Jo-hsü approved of the apparently positive things Chang said about Tao-hsüeh, for he replied: "What you wrote about Tao-hsüeh is the basic duty of Confucians" (HNIL 44.6a–7a). Wang Jo-hsü also wrote positively about other Tao-hsüeh masters. On one occasion he remarked that Chu Hsi was the best of the commentators on the *Analects* (HNIL 3.2a).

There are also diffuse references in other Chin texts to various scholars' favorable orientation toward Tao-hsüeh. For example, in his preface to the collected works of Liu Chi (chin-shih of 1151), Li Ch'un-fu praised Liu Chi: "He liked Buddhism very much and at the same time had a deep understanding of 'the learning of human nature and principle' [hsing-li hsüeh]. His every single word and sentence contained profound meaning" (CCC 2.78). Chou Ang (d. 1211) and his nephew Chou Ssu-ming (d. 1211) both had profound knowledge of "the learning of moral principles" (i-li hsüeh) and esteemed Ch'eng I and Shao Yung (1011–77). Chou Ssu-ming even proclaimed, "One cannot be a true Confucian unless one's study extends to Shao Yung and Ch'eng I" (CCC 4.166–67). The *Sung Yüan hsüeh-an* (100.1881) does not mention Chou Ssu-ming's esteem for Shao Yung and Ch'eng I, for such reverence would have countered the biased thesis of the editors. Another friend of Tao-hsüeh, Ma Chiu-ch'ou (1174–1232), was a classical scholar whose interests ranged from the *Book of Changes* and the *Spring and Autumn Annals* to Shao Yung's *Book of the August Ultimate* (*Huang-chi shu*) (CS 126.2740). In short, there is substantial indication that many intellectuals under the Chin had a positive interest in Tao-hsüeh and recognized it as a distinct intellectual tradition.

There are also some clues for dating the spread of Tao-hsüeh from Southern Sung China into Chin territory. In his postface to the *Tao-hsüeh fa-yüan*, Wang Jo-hsü indicated that the Chin had been at peace for a long time and that during the past three years Tao-hsüeh had begun to spread more widely through the North:

Our country has been at peace for a long time. The use of the classics to select men for public office has particularly encouraged scholars to grasp the good points brought forth in various discussions in order to seek the truth of ethical principles and not simply concentrate on passing down notes to the commentaries. What has been opened up is very impressive. But this perspective from the [Chu Ju] ming-tao [chi] is not yet very prevalent. During the past three or so years, this transmission has begun to spread more widely. Those who are fond of good things have come more and more to hear of it and to delight in it [i.e., Tao-hsüeh]. (HNIL 44.8a–8b)

At the latest, Wang Jo-hsü could have been referring to sometime before 1204 when the Southern Sung under the leadership of Han T'o-chou (1152–1207) began the raids on Chin territory that would escalate into a full-scale war by 1206. His remark about a "long" period of peace might well push the date back before 1192, when the Chin began building large fortifications and making repeated punitive strikes into Mongol territory. In either case, one would also have to subtract the three years Wang mentioned to get back to the approximate time when Tao-hsüeh began to spread more widely under the Chin. His data would suggest sometime in the 1190s and probably quite early in that decade.

A date in the early 1190s is compatible with evidence from Li Ch'un-fu's *Ming-tao chi shuo*. In this work, completed in 1218, Li wrote: "Ch'eng I's teachings have already penetrated into the North from East of the River [i.e., the lower Yangtze region of the Southern Sung]. Talented scholars from the elite families are convinced by it. Even I have been playing with it for almost thirty years" (*MTCS* 5.179, no. 202). By this calculation, we would again arrive at a date of approximately 1190.

What about the survival of a possible remnant of the Tao-hsüeh fellowship in North China after the fall of the Sung in 1127? It is reasonable to assume that Tao-hsüeh had not totally disappeared in the North. Extant evidence is extremely fragmentary and problematic, however. For example, Ch'eng Hao's cultural legacy in Tse-chou, Shansi, where he had served as district magistrate, was reportedly not completely severed. As a youth, Li Chün-min (1176–after 1256) inherited that local legacy and later dedicated himself to teaching Tao-hsüeh there; Li thus contributed to a revival of Ch'eng Hao's learning in the early Yüan (*Chuang-ching chi* preface, 3a–4a, 11a–11b; Yao Ta-li 1983, 217–18). But such retrospective claims, which might have been influenced by Tao-hsüeh's popularity during the Yüan, fail to provide details regarding the generational links through the Chin. An even bleaker picture is presented in other sources.

Most leading Northern Sung literati families had fled southward in the wake of the Jurchen conquest, and now that "only a few literati families were left in the region," the less distinguished began to rise to prominence (*MSTW* 12; trans. Makino 1983, 2). Hsü Yu-jen (1287–1364) asserted that during the early Chin, Confucian "learning and culture became well-nigh extinct" (*CHCC* 32.2a; trans. Makino 1983, 4). Furthermore, Northern Sung Tao-hsüeh had flourished primarily in places, such as Loyang, long regarded as centers of culture and learning. The fact that during the Chin known Tao-hsüeh scholars did not hail from those areas, but from new centers of intellectual life, adds weight to the case for a lapse in the fellowship's continuity. Even though it perhaps survived in its base areas, extant records point to new areas and new developments almost six decades after the fall of the Northern Sung. Moreover, the *Chu Ju ming-tao chi*, the anthology compiled in the South in the 1160s, played a significant role in this revival. Thus, the nature of extant sources concerning Tao-hsüeh leaves us no choice except to focus on this latter half of the Chin dynasty.

What intellectual orientations prevailed during the first half of the Chin? Although there were diverse Buddhist, Taoist, and Confucian trends, it seems that someone like T'an Ch'u-tuan (or T'an Yü, 1123–85) might be most representative. A copy of his collected works, the *Shui-yün chi* (original preface dated 1187), is preserved in the rare book collection of the Peking Library. Although found in the collection of Taoist sacred writings (*Tao-tsang* 798), the *Shui-yün chi* is not included in two major Ch'ing dynasty collections: the *Ssu-k'u ch'üan-shu* (Complete library of the four treasures), or the *Chiu Chin-jen chi* (Collected writings of nine Chin personages). Given the fact that most Chin literati works are no longer extant, one might take the low visibility of the *Shui-yün chi* as one basis for regarding it as typical. Being attracted to the most popular religious movement of the era adds to T'an's representativeness. Ch'u-tuan was the personal name bestowed on him by Wang Che (1113–70), founder of the Ch'üan-chen ("Complete Perfection" or "Perfect Truth") sect of Taoism. T'an was one of the earliest of Wang's seven disciples in this new Chin sect, but he never achieved the religious influence or government patronage accorded to some of the seven. Also characteristically Chin, he was a poet and loved to wax poetic about scenery. He did occasionally talk about Buddhism and mentioned Confucius and Mencius, as well as the notion of the "Three Teachings." Still, his writings evidence little concern for the major political issues of the day or for the Confucian classics. What he valued was "entering the gate of Ch'üan-chen" (*SYC* 1.7b, 1.9a, 1.17a, 2.1b, 2.13a, 2.15b–16a, 3.3a–3b, 3.6a–6b, 3.7a–7b, 3.14b, 3.20a–20b). Ch'üan-chen remained popular throughout the Chin; Confucianism regained some of its conventional influence only during the second half of the dynasty.

Confucianism—and very likely Tao-hsüeh itself—was widespread enough that Li Ch'un-fu's 1218 work evoked condemnation for his criticism of certain ideas and attitudes of the Tao-hsüeh masters. Even his friends sought to stifle him. Liu Ts'ung-i, Sung Chiu-chia, and Wang Jo-hsü rebuked him for his zeal for Buddhism; Liu Ts'ung-i and Chao Ping-wen, moreover, blocked the publication of his collected works (CCC 6.286; Yoshikawa 1974, 1252–53). It appears reasonable to credit Tao-hsüeh attitudes for much of the hostility toward Li Ch'un-fu: Tao-hsüeh men often condemned Buddhism more vigorously than other Confucians did; furthermore, Li had concentrated almost all of his own criticism against Tao-hsüeh Confucians. Wang Jo-hsü and Chao Ping-wen expressed reservations about the tendency within Tao-hsüeh toward intolerance of other views. Thus, it is somewhat surprising to find them joining in a move to limit the free expression of one of their personal friends. Their uneasiness about Tao-hsüeh Confucians' penchant for excluding other Confucians from knowing the *tao* should *not*, in the light of their actions against Li, be mistaken for a wider liberalism, for their own tolerance apparently did not encompass other literati with more pronounced Buddhist inclinations.

In his denunciation of such hostility toward Li Ch'un-fu and Buddhism, Yeh-lü Ch'u-ts'ai explicitly blamed the spread of Tao-hsüeh Confucianism in both the Southern Sung and the Chin. Writing near the end of the Chin in a preface to the *Ming-tao chi shuo*, Yeh-lü Ch'u-ts'ai proclaimed:

> Li Ch'un-fu grasped the subtle mysteries of the teachings of the three sages [Confucius, Lao-tzu, and the Buddha] on principle and human nature, but in the final analysis his basic orientation was toward Buddhism and nothing else. Left of the Yangtze [i.e., among the Southern Sung] Tao-hsüeh is rooted in the thought of Ch'eng I and his brother, and more than ten major philosophers there are in harmony with them.... I had earlier read the *Ming-tao chi* and became distraught and dissatisfied. I wanted to write a book to correct its wild mistakes but did not have the time to do so. Moreover, Li Ch'un-fu forged ahead and wrote one. I will just write a preface to his work in order to prescribe medicine and use acupuncture needles to cure the serious illness of those Left of the Yangtze as well as those scholars from the Central Plain [i.e., North China] who have this same illness. (*MTCS*, pp. 51, 53–54)

To summarize our findings thus far, Tao-hsüeh was introduced into North China from the Southern Sung by around 1190, propagated by scholars like the editors of the *Tao-hsüeh fa-yüan* who took this task as their mission, encouraged by such leading intellectuals as Chao Ping-wen and Wang Jo-hsü, and spread to such an extent that it apparently contributed to the hostile reaction against Li Ch'un-fu's critical remarks about Tao-hsüeh masters.

Chin Confucians' Agreements and Disagreements with Tao-hsüeh

Major Chin thinkers are usually perceived simply to have been opposed to Chu Hsi and Tao-hsüeh; therefore, we should examine their areas of agreement as well as disagreement with Tao-hsüeh. In his thirty poems on poetry completed in 1217, Yüan Hao-wen sought to establish an orthodox succession of poets on the basis of definite standards (such as decorum, sincerity, and clarity of expression) in order to distinguish the pure and impure within the poetic tradition.[3] This agenda in his literary theory is analogous to the concept of the *tao-t'ung* (a succession of sages and masters who realized the complete *tao*), which was of great importance to the Tao-hsüeh school in the Sung and Yüan periods. As already demonstrated, Chao Ping-wen, Wang Jo-hsü, and Li Ch'un-fu accepted this proposition that the *tao* had been eclipsed since the death of Mencius, until the Ch'engs and other early Tao-hsüeh masters recovered the transmission of the *tao*. Hence, the thought of all four major literati reveals this trace of a Tao-hsüeh perspective. But we need to explore the texts of such individuals in greater depth.

Li Ch'un-fu

Li Ch'un-fu made a convenient summary of areas of agreement with Tao-hsüeh. In the concluding section to the *Ming-tao chi shuo*, he wrote:

> The differences of opinion between myself and these scholars are contained in entirety in the above sections of this volume. With the exception of these sections, everything that is contained in the *Ming-tao chi* and all that these gentlemen have written—commentaries on the *Book of Changes*, the *Book of Poetry*, the *Book of Documents*, the *Doctrine of the Mean*, the *Great Learning*, the *Spring and Autumn Annals*, the *Analects*, the *Mencius*, and the *Book of Filial Piety*—teach the purification of human desires and the clarification of Heaven's principle, the eradication of hegemonic practices and assistance to the kingly way, the exposition of teachings regarding the mind-and-heart [*hsin-hsüeh*] beyond the confines of language and literature, as well as the practice of ethical training in the midst of daily affairs and chores. In their nurture of human nature they regard sincerity [*ch'eng*] as the basis; in their cultivation of the self, they take seriousness [*ching*] as the entrance. The great *tao* is sought from the good; sagehood is arrived at from learning.... Is it not proper to say that they are heroes? If a scholar with determination to study the *tao* will first read the books of these gentlemen, he will begin to realize that

I have labored to understand their hearts and minds. If he who reads my book uses it as a pretext to belittle the writings of these gentlemen, he will truly be doing the equivalent of throwing away jade because of a speck of impurity, or giving up eating because of choking on a burnt piece. He will be not only making me an offense to these gentlemen but also betraying my expectations of him as a scholar. (*MTCS* 5.195, no. 217)

Thus, Li professed to respect a considerable range of Tao-hsüeh concepts, even if his primary commitment was to Buddhism.

Bartholomew Tsui has put forth the thesis that Li Ch'un-fu was not a Buddhist partisan, but rather an independent believer in the oneness of the Three Teachings. (Other modern scholars have emphasized Li's identification with, and defense of, Buddhism.)[4] Arguing that Li achieved a unique synthesis in which the truths of Buddhism, Taoism, and Confucianism became one, Tsui outlines philosophical equivalencies that Li claimed among the Three Teachings. In terms of the structure of the absolute, Lao-tzu spoke of "constant nonbeing" (*ch'ang-wu*) and "constant being" (*ch'ang-yu*), the Buddhists spoke of "absolute void" (*chen-k'ung*) and "wonderful existence" (*miao-yu*), and the *Book of Changes* spoke of the "physical" (*hsing-erh-hsia*) and the "metaphysical" or the "non-empirical" that is above or transcends determinate form (*hsing-erh-shang*). These were, Li insisted, merely different names for the same essential truth. On the one hand, Tsui admits that Li Ch'un-fu's philosophy mirrored the Mahâyâna Buddhism of his day: human nature was the Buddha-nature, and mind was identical with the Buddhist Absolute. Moreover, Li used this philosophy as the interpretative principle to be applied to the native traditions of China. On the other hand, crediting him with having sincere motives and true belief in the identity of the Three Teachings, Tsui presents Li's theory for harmonizing the three sages as being comprehensive and unprecedented in scope (Tsui 1980, 1–11). Whether or not one would agree with all the individual points Bartholomew Tsui makes, his core thesis—that Li Ch'un-fu was a harmonizer of the Three Teachings instead of a narrow partisan of Buddhism—appears, after reading Li's book, to be quite plausible. A subsequent study of syncretism during the Ming dynasty also calls special attention to the influence of Li's *Ming-tao chi shuo* in popularizing the unity of the Three Teachings (Langlois and Sun 1983, 114–19, 137).

Li Ch'un-fu's generally sophisticated work was marred by flaws that would impede serious consideration by Confucians, however. Although he does quote the *Analects*, his presentation of Confucius' thought (other than the comment on the similarity of human natures at birth) was based essentially on the *Book of Changes* and supplemented by statements attributed to Confucius in the *Chuang-tzu* (*MTCS* 2.98, no. 43; 2.103, no. 50; 3.114, no. 70; 4.147, no. 142; 5.208–9, no. M8). Taking comments ascribed to Confucius by Chuang-tzu at face value and treating them as of equal value to those in the *Analects* would have been objectionable to Confucian scholars. Li also weakened his efforts at harmonization by the derogatory remarks he sometimes voiced about Tao-hsüeh masters, as when he likened Ch'eng I to a frog in a well looking up at the sky (*MTCS* 4.143, no. 129). The *Kuei-ch'ien chih* recorded what are probably Li's most extreme remarks of this kind (*KKC* 1.7–9, 9.105–6). Such comments so scandalized more orthodox Confucians that they would, as in the case of the editors of the *Sung Yüan hsüeh-an*, treat his thought only in caricature. His two inscriptions of 1220 and 1222 for the Shao-lin Monastery in Honan were far more partisan than his book of 1218. Although these later inscriptions might have arisen from either a desire to please his hosts or a reaction to Confucian criticisms of his effort to harmonize the Three Teachings, they were prominently embedded in the public record, in stone, at one of the most famous Ch'an monasteries in all of China (*KCC* 1.7–9).[5]

With his grounding in Buddhist philosophy, Li Ch'un-fu did not regard Tao-hsüeh masters as excessively abstract or inadequately practical, but he did object to their tendency to dismiss those outside their school as being ignorant of the *tao*. The Tao-hsüeh Confucians' more abstract philosophizing had affinities with Buddhist metaphysics; furthermore, these direct borrowings from Buddhism, as Li insisted on putting it, brought the profundity of Confucius into view and revealed the essential oneness of Confucianism, Taoism, and Buddhism. Tao-hsüeh Confucians erred, however, in not only attempting to deny their philosophical debts to Buddhism, but also slandering Buddhists and Taoists. More than half of his *Ming-tao chi shuo* consisted of point-by-point refutations of accusations that various Tao-hsüeh Confucians had made against Buddhism and Taoism. Another large percentage of the passages contained corrections to delineations of Tao-hsüeh concepts, such as human nature (*hsing*), mind-and-heart (*hsin*), equilibrium (*chung*), and harmony (*ho*).

Irrespective of the degree of Li Ch'un-fu's partisanship, his *Ming-tao chi shuo* can be seen as having had a number of benefits for the development of Tao-hsüeh in the late Chin. Aside from passages in which he spoke positively about Tao-hsüeh, his work brought to the attention of an audience broader than just Confucians 217 quotations from leading Tao-hsüeh masters of both the Southern and Northern Sung. Demonstrating a considerable affinity between the ideas of Tao-hsüeh proponents and those of Buddhists and Taoists, Li Ch'un-fu probably enhanced receptivity to Tao-hsüeh Confucianism within these two groups. Apparently, his interests in Tao-hsüeh arose from a sense that if its hostility to Buddhism and Taoism could be purged, this version of Confucianism had more potential than earlier Confucianism for finding common ground with his Mahâyâna Buddhism. In his preface, for example, Li displayed excitement that he lived at a time when he could read the discussions of Tao-hsüeh philosophers and know that the *tao* was at the point of coming together (*MTCS*, p. 56). At the very least, he interjected some Tao-hsüeh content into Chin discussions of human nature, mind, equilibrium, harmony, and the quest for sagehood. Focusing on such themes promoted a dialogue through which Chu Hsi's philosophy could be more easily disseminated. In this regard, one should also note that Li Ch'un-fu gave a more positive presentation of Chu Hsi than he did of the Ch'engs.

Chao Ping-wen

When Chao Ping-wen decided to seek the leadership role among Confucians, he set aside all of his writings on Taoism and Buddhism (*KCC* 1.6, 9.106) and sent them to the master of Shao-lin Monastery, who had them printed as a separate collection (Bush and Mair 1977–78, 37, 50 nn. 29 and 32). Despite Chao's interaction with Buddhism, Yüan Hao-wen presented him as responsible for defending Confucianism in a time of cultural crisis. In his tomb inscription, Yüan Hao-wen eulogized Chao for his analysis of moral principles and for taking personal responsibility for upholding humaneness (or benevolence) and integrity (*jen-i*), morality (*tao-te*), and human nature and destiny (*hsing-ming*). Chao's discussion of *tao-te* and *hsing-ming* was not inhibited by his observation (*FSWC* 1.2a) that the ancient sages rarely discussed these theories and that it was Sung Confucians alone who had enhanced the importance of these concepts. According to Yüan, Chao Ping-wen organized his own collected short writings to begin with substantial essays on such concepts as equilibrium, harmony, and sincerity (from the *Great Learning* and the *Doctrine of the Mean*) in order to imitate Han Yü's exposition on recovering the *tao* (*CCC* 3.152–53; *ISWC* 17.1b–2a, 6a–6b). Liu Ch'i presented the arrangement of Chao's writings as consciously continuing the model of Ou-yang Hsiu, as well as that of Han Yü (*KCC* 9.106). These Chin literati thus implied that like Tao-hsüeh masters, Chao Ping-wen perceived himself to be transmitting Confucian teachings from antiquity.

In Chao Ping-wen's six essays on concepts from the *Doctrine of the Mean* and the *Great Learning*, he explained the concepts in such philosophical terms of Tao-hsüeh as *t'ien-li* (Heaven's principles), *t'ien-tao* (the Way of Heaven), *li* (principle, pattern), *hsing-erh-shang* (the metaphysical), and *hsing-erh-hsia* (the physical). His major points in these essays were also in unison with exponents of Tao-hsüeh. First, although one's human nature was Heaven's principle and originally good, one easily became blocked by human desires, so it was difficult to recover Heaven's principle within oneself. One could become good and recover Heaven's principle through the process of study and the extension of knowledge (*FSWC* 1.2b–3b). Second, like Chu Hsi and Lü Tsu-ch'ien in their *Chin-ssu lü* (Reflections on things at hand), Chao Ping-wen believed that Confucianism was profound but that one had to begin with moral cultivation in the midst of everyday affairs in order to reach that profundity. He wrote: "Although Confucius' learning is like Heaven, one must still start from what is near at hand. Since this is so, where should one begin? I reply, being watchful over one's behavior while one is alone" (*FSWC* 1.4a–5a). Third, Chao likewise felt that people were confused by a comment in the *Analects* that the disciples never heard Confucius talk of human nature and the *tao* of Heaven. Confucius so successfully communicated his teachings in terms of daily affairs, Chao insisted, that his own disciples failed to notice that he actually discussed nothing except human nature and the *tao* of Heaven. They did not realize that the Master had taught them such profound things, because Confucius had not employed lofty and abstract language. In his essay on equilibrium, Chao also specifically approved of, and elaborated on, Ch'eng I's proposition that "human nature and the *tao* of Heaven are equilibrium" (*FSWC* 1.5a–8a). Fourth, *ch'eng* meant more than "sincerity," or even consistently harboring no depravity or self-deception, for *ch'eng* enabled one's virtue to participate in Heaven's transformation and nourishment of all things (*FSWC* 1.8b–10a).

Chao Ping-wen's historical essays expound traditional Confucian virtues of humaneness and integrity (*i*) but also resonate with the historiography of Chu Hsi. First, Chao Ping-wen's elaboration of integrity centered on making sure that both governmental principles and regulations were correct; moreover, without humaneness, a dynasty was not truly legitimate and could not last for many generations (*FSWC* 14.1a–1b, 2b).

Second, although he recognized the Northern Sung as legitimate and although he played an active role in the Chin debates on dynastic succession on the side that advocated seeing the Chin as the successor to the Northern Sung, Chao displayed no cultural ties to his ethnic brothers in the Southern Sung when he castigated them as "barbarians of the Huai River" (*FSWC* 10.7a–7b) and "barbarians of the islands" (18.5a). He talked of "the Great Chin receiving the Mandate [of Heaven to rule]" (18.4b) and praised Chang-tsung for adopting Earth as the official element in succession from the Sung in order to strengthen "the legitimate succession of the Central Plain" (10.9a). Chao Ping-wen apparently had no doubts about the legitimacy of the Chin dynasty, in spite of its foreign origins, and assumed that it was proper to serve this conquest dynasty (Chang Po-ch'üan 1985, 138;

Tao Jing-shen 1981a, 987, 989). His attention to the question of dynastic legitimacy and succession paralleled the heightened importance of this concept in Sung learning and Tao-hsüeh.

Third, Chao Ping-wen's concept of loyalty affected his writing of history. He quoted with approval the condemnation that Ou-yang Hsiu had leveled against officials since the third century: "From the time of the Wei and Chin onward, all officials who have facilitated the transfer of the mandate to rule can be criticized; one could say they had divided loyalties toward their original dynasties" (*FSWC* 14.8b). Loyalty was centered on the position, not the person, of the emperor. Similarly, Chao demanded that proper titles be accorded to the last two rulers of the Wei, who had been degraded by those deposing them. His only regret about Liu Pei (162–223) was that he had proclaimed himself emperor while Han Hsien-ti (181–234, r. 189–220) was still alive; and he could not sanction Chu-ko Tan's (d. 258) loyal uprising to protect the house of Wei because Chu-ko Tan had raised troops without imperial approval (*FSWC* 14.9a–9b, 11b). Chao's heightened sensitivity to questions of loyalty and the position of the ruler was in harmony with the new ideals of the Sung Confucians, including Chu Hsi (Tillman 1982, 78–79, 204, 206–9, 269 n. 28; Schneider 1980, 76–77).

Fourth, in contrast to such major Northern Sung historians as Ssu-ma Kuang, Chao Ping-wen had an exalted view of Liu Pei and the Shu-Han, but a condescending view of Ts'ao Ts'ao (155–220). Chao Ping-wen reiterated how Ts'ao Ts'ao had hideously usurped the power of the Han throne, murdered even his own officials, and, without any regard for the *tao*, invaded other sovereigns' territories (*FSWC* 14.3a, 8a–9a). Liu Pei, by contrast, had been able to transform the peripheral state of Shu into the legitimate successor of the Han dynasty because of his virtue, his loyalty to the Han, and his dedication to promoting the commonweal (*FSWC* 14.2b, 10a–12b). Chao Ping-wen's disagreement with Ssu-ma Kuang's judgment concerning the legitimacy of the Wei versus the Shu-Han was in unison with the prominent view that Chu Hsi presented in the revision he directed of Ssu-ma Kuang's history. This well-known judgment, enshrined in Chu Hsi's "general principles" (*TCKM* 3a–4a, 8a) for the monumental *Tzu-chih t'ung-chien kang-mu* (Outline and details of the *Comprehensive Mirror for Aid in Government*), might have been known to Chao Ping-wen, although he did not specifically cite it. If he had been aware that in the late 1190s Chu Hsi had reluctantly demoted the Shu-Han to the status of a dynasty that had "begun to attain the legitimate succession but afterwards failed to attain it" (*CTYL* 105.4189–90), Chao might have taken Chu to task. Chu Hsi's subsequent view, revised toward the end of his life, has generally been overlooked by modern historians, so we can hardly fault Chao for not taking note of it.

Fifth, Chao Ping-wen selected Chu-ko Liang (181–234) as his principal hero from the Three Kingdoms period. This selection—and particularly the grounds for it—implicitly demonstrated important agreement with Tao-hsüeh masters rather than with either Su Shih or Li Ch'un-fu. Chao Ping-wen did not share Su Shih's unusually high regard for Hsün Yü (163–212) (*FSWC* 14.9a). Li Ch'un-fu, as a young man with stunning upward mobility in the bureaucracy, had compared himself to Chu-ko Liang (*KCC* 1.6). Years later, he bemoaned the fact that he did not have the position or resources to defeat invaders along the Yellow River the way Chou Yü (175–210) had defeated Ts'ao Ts'ao at Red Cliffs along the Yangtze (*CCC* 4.220). This shift of attention away from Chu-ko Liang, who had also been a major participant in setting up the victory at Red Cliffs, and toward Chou Yü, as well as the respective grounds for comparison, implies that Li Ch'un-fu was concerned with Chu-ko Liang as a successful general and advisor rather than as an exemplar of Confucian virtues. This was evident in Li's condemnation of Ch'eng I's appraisal of Chu-ko Liang, whom Ch'eng had upheld for not seeking personal benefit and thus being able, without violating Mencius' injunction against killing innocent people, to wage war against unrighteous rulers (*ECC* 1:68). Li retorted:

> Ch'eng I's unswerving purpose was to regard Chu-ko Liang as having obtained the true teachings of Confucius, but when he said these words, it was really too extreme! Chu-ko Liang compared himself to Kuan Chung [d. 645 B.C.] and Yüeh I [3d cent. B.C.] [*SKC* 35.911]. Could he really have been a disciple of Confucius and Mencius? These words of Ch'eng I's are certainly ones that will bring calamity to all living beings and endanger the states of various kings and princes. (*MTCS* 3.119–20, no. 84)

Because Kuan Chung and Yüeh I had become symbols of Realpolitik, Chao was able to point easily to an apparent contradiction in Ch'eng I's use of Chu-ko Liang as a model for Confucian ethics.

Chao Ping-wen lauded Chu-ko Liang as one worthy to join with Liu Pei in turning the peripheral state of Shu into a commonweal intended to be the legitimate successor of the Han empire. He praised the way the dying Liu Pei entrusted the heir apparent and even the throne to Chu-ko Liang as revealing a degree of the Confucian virtue of sincerity that had not been seen since the golden age of the Three Dynasties (Hsia, Shang, and Chou) in early antiquity:

> This is what the ancients called causing one's intent to be sincere and having no self-deception. The Three Dynasties and the earlier sages

used rectified minds-and-hearts and sincere wills to govern the world and family, and there was nothing that was not accomplished. Looking into Liu Pei's intent in entrusting everything to Chu-ko Liang, [one can see that] this is a case of having a mind-and-heart to share the empire, and with this, one sees this [kind of] mind-and-heart again for the first time since the Three Dynasties. The virtue of King T'ang [r. ca. 1766–1754 B.C.] of the Shang dynasty and his chief minister I Yin [d. ca. 1740 B.C., to whom T'ang entrusted his heir, T'ai-chia] does not exceed that of Liu Pei and Chu-ko Liang. (FSWC 14.11b)

Chao Ping-wen further likened Chu-ko Liang's repeated capture and release of the rebel chieftain Meng Huo (fl. 220s) to the deeds of Shun. Instead of attacking the barbarian Miao people, this sage-king of early antiquity danced with his weapons to display his *tao* and win their submission. Chu-ko Liang's actions likewise possessed the *tao*, for he sought the submission of the chieftain's mind-and-heart (FSWC 14.12a–12b; SKC 35.921).

Only Chu-ko Liang's premature death prevented the full fruition of his virtue from becoming manifest in deeds, particularly in setting up a new order for a unified empire. Chao Ping-wen quoted with approval Wang T'ung's (584–617) evaluation: "If Chu-ko Liang had not died, rites and ceremonies [*li*] and music [*yüeh*] would have been restored" (FSWC 14.12b). In essence, Wang T'ung and, in turn, Chao Ping-wen were claiming that Chu-ko Liang would have actualized the proper operation of the *tao*, for Confucius had proclaimed, "When the *tao* prevails in the world, rites and music as well as punitive expeditions issue from the Son of Heaven" (*Analects* 16/2). Chao Ping-wen's high opinion of Chu-ko Liang as a statesman of extraordinary Confucian virtue who sought to implement the true teachings of Confucius was in accord not only with Ch'eng I's opinion but also with Chu Hsi's as well (ECC 1:68, 4:1234–35, 1244–45; CTYL 136.5191–202). During the Sung dynasty those who praised Chu-ko Liang were, of course, not restricted to members of the Tao-hsüeh fellowship, but they were generally far more enthusiastic about Chu-ko Liang and the Shu-Han than were such major leaders of Sung learning as Ssu-ma Kuang, Wang An-shih, and Su Shih. More importantly, members of the fellowship were particularly noted for basing their evaluations of Chu-ko Liang on exemplary Confucian virtues, and Chao utilized the same standard.

Sixth, Chao Ping-wen's penchant for moralizing made him critical of the major historians of imperial China for their failure to conform adequately to the historiography of the *Spring and Autumn Annals*. According to tradition, Confucius had personally edited this history of his native state of Lu and its relations with other states in order to pass veiled ethical judgments on officials and thus frighten later generations into doing what was right. Although much of later historical writing in China was imbued with this "praise and blame" approach to evaluating actions and actors, Tao-hsüeh Confucians often judged the monumental standard histories to be inadequately rigorous in following the example of the *Annals*. Similarly, Chao Ping-wen asked, "Why were the historians from Ssu-ma Ch'ien and Pan Ku [32–92] onward so vacillating and lacking in historiographical methods?" (*FSWC* 14.8b, also 8a–10a). He then made a considerable number of criticisms about the way the official histories had been organized, as well as the titles they bestowed on particular individuals. The operative principle behind his suggested revisions was to make it much clearer to perpetuators of evil that their deeds would be unflinchingly censured in the historical record. The basic orientation that Chao Ping-wen demonstrated in suggesting revisions of the standard histories was in harmony with Chu Hsi's purpose in directing the compilation of the *Tzu-chih t'ung-chien kang-mu* to rectify Ssu-ma Kuang's historical judgments. Chao Ping-wen's philosophical discourse and moralistically oriented historiography were largely going in a direction comparable to Chu Hsi's.

In summary, Chao Ping-wen judged Tao-hsüeh Confucians to have a poor grasp of practical governance; moreover, their speculative philosophizing was the source of both their strength and their weakness. With their fondness for discussing what was abstract and remote, Tao-hsüeh masters tended to consider concrete and practical aspects of the *tao* to be extraneous. With such concentration on the profundity of Confucian teachings, Chao Ping-wen warned, one easily lost sight of the fact that one must begin with the practical matters of daily personal cultivation; without being aware of it, one would stray into Buddhism and Taoism. Disciples of the Tao-hsüeh masters became so proud of their understanding of the profundity of the *tao* that they dismissed other Confucians as being ignorant of the *tao* (*FSWC* 1.3b–4b). But Chao Ping-wen is the primary figure in Peter Bol's essay in this volume, so I will presently give greater attention to Wang Jo-hsü's life and thought.

Wang Jo-hsü

Wang Jo-hsü was mentioned only once in passing in the *Sung Yüan hsüeh-an* (100.1882), but he was the last major Confucian thinker of the Chin and perhaps the one who dealt most effectively with the *problématique* of Confucian values.[6] In contrast to Chao Ping-wen, Wang Jo-hsü did not talk much about Buddhism and Taoism; moreover, his writings are largely "disputations" on points and passages in the classics, histories, and collections of belles lettres. This suggests that he focused on setting the cultural record straight for Confucians.

Wang Jo-hsü's commitment to the Confucian tradition was instilled in him by relatives and friends when he was still a youth in the area around Chen-ting (near modern Shih-chia-chuang in Hopei province). Maternal uncle Chou Ang, who took charge of Wang's education upon his father's death, was a Confucian scholar-official of considerable renown (CCC 4.166–67; CS 126.2730). Chou Ang himself had been tutored by Ch'u Ch'eng-liang (chin-shih of 1124), a follower of Su Shih's intellectual legacy (CCC 4.166).

Wang's Confucian consciousness was further reinforced by Chou Ang's fraternal nephew, Chou Ssu-ming. This young friend of Wang's was famous for his ability to discuss ideas, his understanding of integrity, and his discussions of human nature and principle (HNIL 45.4b–5a; CCC 4.167). Chou Ssu-ming, along with Wang Ch'üan (chin-shih of 1208), also numbered among Li Ch'un-fu's valued friends (KCC 2.13–14). But Li's fascination with Buddhism was apparently not transmitted through them to Wang Jo-hsü. During their drinking parties, Wang reportedly could use as few as three sentences to respond to, and silence, the eloquent and usually persuasive Li (CCC 6.286). All three of these close friends were junior to Wang Jo-hsü but died much earlier (HNIL 43.1a–1b; CCC 4.167; KCC 2.13). The deaths of Chou Ang and Chou Ssu-ming in particular must have had a poignant impact on Wang—they committed suicide after the Mongols broke through the walls of the town they were defending.

Such early loss of friends and relatives, especially in the wake of the even earlier death of his father, seems to have enhanced Wang Jo-hsü's sense of mission. Linkage of some of these personal losses to the ever-increasing threat of savage conquest by the Mongols would have augmented Wang's responsibility as the survivor to organize the Confucian tradition in an effort to preserve it. Chu Hsi had similarly been orphaned as an adolescent, passed the chin-shih examination at an early age, and survived his two closest friends by almost two decades. Although Wang did not synthesize and define the Confucian tradition to the degree that Chu Hsi did, these two survivors produced, in the face of perceived cultural crises, the most extensive and encompassing approaches to the Confucian tradition in the North and the South.

Wang Jo-hsü personally experienced life in the city of Kaifeng under Mongol siege and witnessed the surrender of the city to the Mongols in 1233. Before the Chin emperor, Ai-tsung (r. 1224–34), fled eastward out of the city, Wang, as a member of the Han-lin Academy, had been engaged in the emperor's efforts at stirring up popular support to resist the Mongols. Soon after the emperor fled, the commander left in charge of the city's defense, Ts'ui Li (d. 1234), slaughtered whatever civil officials remained who openly dared resist his orders; he then surrendered the city to the Mongols (CS 115.2525–30). Before the enemy actually occupied Kaifeng, a pack of Ts'ui Li's henchmen attempted to pressure Wang Jo-hsü into writing an inscription for a stele praising Ts'ui's meritorious virtue. Confiding to Yüan Hao-wen, Wang expressed his preference to die rather than write such an inscription, for if he wrote it, his "name and integrity would be used to sweep the ground and would be held up to ridicule by future generations" (ISWC 19.3b–4a). With Yüan's advice, Wang was able to calmly and steadfastly refuse to write in praise of Ts'ui's virtue. Although he reportedly did edit a straightforward account of Ts'ui's actions allegedly written by Yüan Hao-wen, the stele was never erected because Ts'ui was soon slain by a subordinate and the Mongols subsequently plundered Kaifeng (CS 115.2529, 126.2727–28).[7] Some of Yüan Hao-wen's prose and poetry vividly depict the physical destruction and cultural disorientation encountered by the city's survivors (West 1986, 199–210; Chao T'ing-p'eng 1987).

Dressed in commoner's clothing, Wang managed to flee to his home in Chen-ting and thereby escape death or forced tenure of office under the Mongols. Already about sixty years of age, he spent the remaining decade of his life as quietly as possible in the villages near Chen-ting, until he finally took advantage of an opportunity to realize a long-cherished wish to climb Mt. T'ai, near the center of Shantung province. Delighting in the scenery and reverent in manner, Wang forgot his fatigue until he sat down to rest on a large rock and there mused that his ambitions would be fulfilled if his life were to end on the sacred mountain. His traveling companions thought that he was merely dozing, but they soon discovered that he had indeed expired resting peacefully on the rock (ISWC 19.1a; CS 126.2727–28).

This pilgrimage to Mt. T'ai was a symbolically appropriate end for Wang Jo-hsü. T'ai was the sacred peak closest to the ancient home of Confucius and one that the Sage had enjoyed climbing. According to legend, the early death of Confucius' favorite disciple Yen Hui (521–490 B.C.) resulted from exertions suffered during a trip made with the Master up Mt. T'ai. Yen Hui strained so hard to see the details of a scene in the distant state of Wu south of the Yangtze that Confucius was describing to him that his body began at that point to deteriorate rapidly and his life ended soon thereafter (LH 4.56–57; trans. Forke 1962, 2:242–43). Confucius wept over Yen Hui; this disciple was to become the favorite of Sung Tao-hsüeh scholars, who saw him as a model for all students of the Sage's teachings. Wang Jo-hsü, self-consciously taking his stand with Confucius, had also labored to see the details of the Confucian legacy, and he was perplexed by what he perceived south of the Yangtze. Unlike Yen Hui's dedication to the teachings of Confucius, however, Wang's has been generally ignored by later generations.

Almost prefiguring this eclipse of Wang from Confucian view, his traveling companions bore his body down Mt. T'ai and placed it in a Taoist temple until it could be transported to Chen-ting for burial. The temporary lodging of Wang's corpse in the temple was no doubt a mere convenience, but in the context of historical analogy, it can be seen to have symbolic and ironic significance. As evident in his decision to risk death rather than praise the tyrannical Ts'ui Li, Wang was acutely concerned with how later generations would evaluate him. But his labors to write disputations on problematic points within Confucian traditions, his avoidance of Buddhism and Taoism, and his reverent pilgrimage to Mt. T'ai did not win him any significant notice from the editors of the *Sung Yüan hsüeh-an*. If he had been more in accord with Ch'eng I and Chu Hsi's interpretation of Confucianism, the editors might have treated him differently.

Yoshikawa regarded Wang Jo-hsü's commentaries as written simply in refutation of those of Chu Hsi and other Tao-hsüeh masters, but this is not a fair representation. Although he took issue with Chu Hsi over the interpretation of some passages, Wang also accorded with Chu Hsi's views in other passages; moreover, in his discriminations on the classics he mostly censured the views of the traditional scholiasts, especially Cheng Hsüan (127–200). In his discussions of major historians, like Ssu-ma Ch'ien, Wang could become excessive in his criticism, even nit-picking; however, he usually remained a fair critic and was able to point out places where previous historians had been inconsistent. Holding Su Shih's to be the model for prose style and venerating Tu Fu (712–70) in the realm of poetry, Wang Jo-hsü consistently opposed highly crafted and overly refined writing. Despite occasional bias, he possessed such a broad range of learning that the editors of the *Ssu-k'u ch'üan-shu tsung-mu* concluded that there was no one better grounded in classical and historical studies during the Chin and Yüan periods (*SKTM* 166.1422). Yüan Hao-wen had earlier lamented that with the death of Wang Jo-hsü there was no one left to pass reasoned judgment in such diverse fields as classical and historical studies, belles lettres, and the evaluation of historical personalities (*CCC* 6.286).

By writing in the form of commentary, Wang Jo-hsü was calling on passages and personages of the traditional canon to bestow cultural legitimacy on the views he held. In his disputations on the classics, histories, and belles lettres, he spanned the whole tradition of Confucian scholarship and implicitly established a line of transmission down to himself. In his disputations on the classics, in particular, he tended not to address larger philosophical issues but to focus on points of detail that could be adjudicated on the basis of context and the meanings of words.

Wang displayed this methodological penchant for the exegetical approach when as a youth he opted to take the *chin-shih* examination on the classics, rather than the far more popular literary examination. Exegetical methodology would remain the hallmark of Wang's writings throughout his long life. The prevalence of this penchant in his historical, literary, and classical studies suggests (as observed in Bol 1983) that his primary purpose was to establish his own ability to judge these corpora of the cultural tradition.

Wang Jo-hsü's agenda should not be reduced to an effort simply to prove how right his literary judgments were. Although he modestly claimed to be writing only for the youngsters in his own clan, the implication of his extensive and highly technical work was that if he and his method were widely accepted, there would be a way out of the predicament of his day. There was a need both for assurance as to the place of one's own culture in the mainstream of Chinese tradition and for confidence in the survival of that culture in the face of the destructive Mongol conquest.

The first of two standards for his judgments was explicitly human feelings (*jen-ch'ing*). In his preface to his comments on the *Analects*, Wang wrote: "Why not reason along the lines of human feelings and take centering on the *tao* as the standard?" (*HNIL* 3.1a). At the beginning of his general discussion he returned to this theme:

> The words of the Sage were nothing more than human feelings; this is why [the *Analects*] is clear, easy to understand, centered on the mean, and enduring. If scholars are too excessive when they seek his meaning, their expositions, however beautiful, will lose his original message—is this of any value? Now regarding the Master's statements about human nature and the *tao* of Heaven, Tzu-kung [520–ca. 450 B.C.] himself said that he had never heard of them; however, all Sung Confucians regard him as having heard. (*HNIL* 3.2a–2b)

Commenting on the Five Classics, Wang Jo-hsü again held forth human feelings as the standard for judging the reasonableness of interpretations—even in the case of the *Spring and Autumn Annals*. Even though the *Annals* had customarily been read as veiled and obscure political commentary, he asserted that it was simply "a book of human feelings" (*HNIL* 1.3b). Wang's focus on human feelings, instead of human nature, was significant. It was traditionally one's view of human nature that was seen as the touchstone of one's orientation to other Confucian issues. The centrality of the doctrine of human nature applied to members of the Tao-hsüeh fellowship.

The second of Wang's principles for judgment was to be reasonable and follow the middle path. According to Wang, traditional Han and T'ang commentators did not attain the meaning of the *Analects* because they held too tightly to the language of the individual passages. Sung commentators went to extremes in grasping at meaning that transcended the language of the text. The problem lay in the fact that Confucius' meaning was not completely expressed in language yet was not to be found outside of language. On the one hand, Sung Confucians did have merit in achieving levels of explication never reached by earlier Confucians: in analyzing the contradiction between integrity (*i*) and utility (*li*); in clarifying the subtlety of the methods of cultivating the mind-and-heart; and in explaining with relative accuracy and clarity the thought of Confucius. On the other hand, Sung Confucians were more open to criticism than earlier commentators: when their analysis was excessively profound; when their adulation and criticism were overdrawn; when they sought hidden messages in every sentence; and when they sought to link all affairs, great or small, to major philosophical concepts. Even though all were generally applicable to Sung Confucians, Wang cited good and bad points that appear particularly directed toward Tao-hsüeh Confucianism (*HNIL* 3.1a–2a).

Wang Jo-hsü quoted a Southern Sung Confucian, Yeh Shih (1150–1223), to summarize his own criticism:

> Scholars of recent times think they must talk of human nature and must definitely know destiny. All link their discussions to the Six Classics and the writings of Confucius. Using beautiful rhetoric and subtle, mysterious language, they confuse others by giving [them] no way to comprehend, but they themselves have never understood clearly the reality of the sages and worthy statesmen. The shallowness of earlier generations [Han and T'ang commentators] lay in their not seeking for meaning in the *hsin* [mind-and-heart]. The mysteriousness of recent generations lay in their not stopping at the *hsin*. Not seeking in the *hsin* and also not stopping with the *hsin*—neither attains the meaning of the sages and worthy statesmen. (*HNIL* 3.1a–2a)

Thus, Wang's own evaluations of earlier commentators placed him somewhere between the philosophical scholars of the Sung and the traditional, more philologically oriented scholars of the Han and T'ang.

Wang Jo-hsü had a complex evaluation of Chu Hsi as a commentator. The reason he focused on Chu Hsi's comments about the *Analects* was that he considered Chu's work to be the most comprehensive and the most suitable, so he wanted to concentrate on those points where Chu Hsi was "not lucid or not yet penetrating" (*HNIL* 3.2a). Yet he could also chide Chu Hsi for being too literal or narrow-minded (*HNIL* 4.2a) and for being too manipulative (4.5a) in explaining the *Analects*. Even though he regarded Chu Hsi as the best overall commentator on the *Analects*, he also judged him to have been affected by the errors of both the old commentators of the Han and T'ang and the new commentators of the Sung.

Although he criticized Sung Confucians for being too profound (*shen*) and too speculative or lofty (*kao*) in their commentaries, Wang Jo-hsüeh also spoke in Tao-hsüeh terms of a "set principle" (*ting-li*) (HNIL 30.3a). On occasion he also used the philosophical concept of *t'ien-li* (Heaven's principle).

> Although the Sage [Confucius] himself had no mind-and-heart for fame and advantage, he often used fame and advantage to lure people toward goodness in order to cause them to go from human desires and to know Heaven's principle; therefore, ordinary and even below-average people could all have hope of achieving goodness. This is the completeness of the way the Sage taught people. For example, he said, "Do not be concerned that people do not know of you; strive energetically to do things and you will become known" [*Analects* 1/16]. This is using [people's] desire for fame to lead them to seek real virtue. Hsieh Liang-tso, however, remarked, "This still involves the idea of seeking to be known and thus is not the Sage's best discussion." Tzu-chang [503–ca. 450 B.C.] asked about studying in order to get a government salary, and the Master taught him in terms of the *tao* of obtaining a salary [*Analects* 2/18]. This was accurately using profit to cause him to think about what is right. (*HNIL* 3.2b–3a)

The two passages quoted from the *Analects* are often interpreted and translated differently from the way Wang read them (e.g., Wing-tsit Chan 1963a, 22, 24). Despite using the philosophical concept of Heaven's principle, this passage introduces two themes on which Wang expressed disagreement with Tao-hsüeh.

These two points of difference were set forth even more clearly in two other passages from Wang's writings. First, in explaining Mencius' phrase "accepting injures *lien* [honesty and frugality]," Ch'eng I had talked in terms of accepting a gift only if it came from a friend and only if one needed the item for one's own use. Wang Jo-hsü dismissed this consideration of prior possession and brought the issue back into focus: "Mencius' meaning was restricted to focusing on what is right" (*HNIL* 8.2a).

Second, in discussing the possibility, which Mencius (7A/30) raised, that the five hegemons of the Eastern Chou period might have "borrowed [benevolence and integrity] for a long time without returning [or relinquishing these virtues]," Wang Jo-hsü put forth a particular interpretation and contrasted it to that of Chu Hsi:

I think the five hegemons were people who temporarily borrowed benevolence and integrity but then relinquished these virtues. If they had borrowed but were to practice these virtues for a long time, they would certainly not be doing it casually. Who could then say these virtues were not their own? Possessing is related not to borrowing, but to not relinquishing. These works of Mencius were designed to help people to be good and opened up a way for them to reform themselves. His use of this to teach later generations is extraordinarily good. But Chu Hsi says, "Even if they borrow or pretend all their lives, they will still not know that these virtues are really not their own." And he also says, "Although they might borrow these virtues for a long time, in the end these virtues would still not be their own." These statements are very unreasonable. All of the people of the world cannot be of superior character. The gentleman uses many methods to teach people. The important thing is simply to get them to orient themselves toward the good. Therefore, whether extending benefit to lure them to do it or forcing them to do it, a gentleman would adopt either method because he considers the results to be the same. If it were really as Master Chu says—unless one was a sagely Yao or Shun, everything one did would be in vain and without benefit—who could make progress in becoming good? (*HNIL* 8.3a–3b)

Wang points here to an alleged contradiction in rigid views of means and ends: Ch'eng I could be distracted from the basic ethical question or goal; and Chu Hsi could make the quest for sagehood, and even ethical cultivation, essentially impossible for anyone who was not already a sage. To Wang, one should be flexible about the means used to reach the ethical goal of getting people to conform to what is right.

Although Wang Jo-hsü advocated flexibility regarding the means to attain Confucian goals, his criticism of historical personalities displays an intensely moralistic historiography. Wang wrote scoffingly: "In discussing Ts'ao Ts'ao's usurpation of the Han, Ssu-ma Kuang was of the opinion that he did not seize power from the Han, but from the hands of bandits [like Tung Cho, d. 192]. The offense of this mistaken judgment cannot be purged in a myriad of generations" (*HNIL* 30.3a, also 27.7b–8b). Wang Jo-hsü's evaluation of Liu Pei demonstrated that his sense of moral outrage surpassed that of Chao Ping-wen. Although Wang praised Liu Pei's humane and generous character, he chose to focus on an incident that Chao Ping-wen had bypassed in seeking a model ruler from the Three Kingdoms period. Liu Pei had, out of personal malice over a disrespectful remark, killed Chang Yü (d. ca. 218), whose most serious offense was saying privately that the Liu family had exhausted its fortunes—that is, its mandate to rule—and that there would be a change of dynasties soon (*SKC* 42.1021). When Chu-ko Liang requested an explanation of Chang Yü's crime, Liu Pei could come up with no better answer than comparing Chang Yü to a flower growing in the doorway that had to be removed for being in the way. Lamenting this killing of a man for no valid reason, Wang concluded that Liu Pei "in doing this was actually no different from Ts'ao Ts'ao" (*HNIL* 26.1b–2a).

Wang also stood apart from most Confucians in his debunking of the rulers of the early Han, especially Han Kao-tsu (r. 206–195 B.C.). He enumerated the mistakes of Kao-tsu: his unfilial lack of concern for his father being held captive and threatened by Hsiang Yü (d. 202 B.C.); his haughty disregard for some of his other relatives; and his unfounded suspicions and contrived ill-treatment of even his most loyal advisors and commanders (*HNIL* 25.6b–7b). Wang criticized such Tao-hsüeh scholars as Chang Shih for praising Han Kao-tsu as humane and generous, but Chu Hsi himself had similarly debunked the Han ruler's character and behavior. Wang's criticisms of historical personalities were more severe than those of most Confucians; however, he did not necessarily exceed Chu Hsi in this regard. For instance, Chu Hsi derided the character and deeds of T'ang T'ai-tsung (r. 627–49) (Tillman 1982, 145–50), but Wang praised the T'ang ruler's edicts as "generous and enlightened" (*HNIL* 26.4a–4b).

Like his interpretations of the classics, Wang Jo-hsü's historical writings combined elements of moral didacticism and pragmatic judgment. He took Yeh Shih to task for his statement that "Han Wu-ti [r. 141–87 B.C.] did things poorly his whole life, but as he approached death he did everything right." In fact, one of the major acts Wu-ti ordered as he faced death was the execution of the mother of the son whom he was setting up as his successor to the throne. The rationale offered was that her death would prevent the young emperor from being dominated by a strong empress dowager who might threaten the Han imperial line the way Han Kao-tsu's empress had done. Han Wu-ti boasted about his brilliant foresight, and the official historian too praised him as sagely, adding that Wu-ti routinely took this precaution after one of his wives had borne a child. Wang Jo-hsü reacted, on the one hand, with moral revulsion: "I think Wu-ti rebelled against Heaven's principles and destroyed human feelings." On the other hand, he condemned Wu-ti's judgment as "not only inhumane but also unwise." He detailed the rather obvious effect that such an extreme policy would have—as it later did have in the case of the imperial family of the To-pa Wei dynasty—on the willingness of the women in the palace chambers to bear children and, consequently, on the continuity of the imperial line. With such evidence, he chided Yeh Shih: "Who could possibly project Wu-ti as a model?" (*HNIL* 25.8a–11a). This fixation on having models to guide behavior was shared by both pragmatic and moralistic Confucians, even though they differed on the models to be adopted. And this concern for models brought together many of Wang Jo-hsü's moralistic and prudential judgments on historical personalities. These two strains of thought, as Confucian polarities of virtue and achievement or integrity and utility, were also evident in Chu Hsi's thought, although he gave even greater priority to moralistic considerations.

Out of loyalty to the Chin, neither Wang Jo-hsü nor Yüan Hao-wen, the two most prominent Chin intellectuals to survive the dynasty, served the Mongols. It was Sung Confucians who made service to one dynasty alone a cornerstone of the concept of loyalty (Wang Gung-wu 1962). Wang Jo-hsü reiterated the importance of the Confucian rites or ceremonies between sovereign and subject; moreover, he held up Han Yü and Ou-yang Hsiu as models of the loyal official (*HNIL* 25.10a, 29.4b and 5a, 31.1a). He criticized emperors during the imperial period for lacking the degree of concern for the people that was evident in such rulers of the ancient Three Dynasties as King T'ang of the Shang dynasty and King Wu of the Chou (*HNIL* 26.9b–10a, 27.10a–10b), but such criticism is not inconsistent with elevating the position or the office of the emperor. Respect for the position of the ruler could demand, as Wang Jo-hsü did, that one should not conceal one's ruler's faults even while praising his benevolent deeds. Wang censured Han Yü for flattering his ruler, and Ssu-ma Kuang for asserting that Sung T'ai-tsung was a sage (*HNIL* 26.8b–9a). This insistence on remonstrating one's ruler for his shortcomings was also a hallmark of Chu Hsi's behavior and ideal of loyalty (Tillman 1982, 204–9).

In summary, Wang Jo-hsü generally criticized Tao-hsüeh Confucians for being too abstractly philosophical and too inadequate in dealing with practical matters and moral cultivation. He faulted the Sung commentators (especially Tao-hsüeh commentators) for being too profound, too lofty, and too generous in trying to explain the classics. Ch'eng I's and Chu Hsi's restricted views of appropriate means resulted at times, Wang argued, in their losing sight of ethical goals and turning moral cultivation into an impossible and useless ordeal. This concern for moral cultivation was behind his rebuke of Tao-hsüeh scholars for being too liberal in their evaluations of historical personalities like Han Kao-tsu; the question of suitable ethical and political models was at stake. His practicality and common sense led him to chastise Ch'eng I for the extremely harsh statement that a widow's starving to death was a trivial matter in comparison with her forfeiting her chastity by remarrying.[8]

Still, Wang Jo-hsü's discussions of Heaven's principle, his own investigation of things to extend his knowledge, his direct approach to the classics to grasp their larger ethical meaning for self and society, as well as his mixture of moral didacticism and practicality, taken together, lend considerable substantiation to his praise of Tao-hsüeh Confucians in his postface to the *Tao-hsüeh fa-yüan*. The major purpose here is not to prove that Wang had greater affinity with Tao-hsüeh than with some other school, but rather to show that he was consciously engaged in the world of Confucian discourse.

Tao-hsüeh and the Question of Su Shih's Legacy in the Chin

The Chin made poetic compositions (*lü-fu*) the most important section of the civil service examinations, a step that has been seen as a reflection of the widespread popularity of Su Shih's writings and thought during the Chin dynasty. Besides arguing for the place of poetic compositions in the examinations, Su regarded poetry and literary creativity as the means to attain the *tao*. Su valued *wen* (belles lettres, especially as expressions of cultural patterns) and criticized Ch'eng I's more philosophical approach to the *tao*. It was upon the political culture of the *lü-fu* examinations that Yoshikawa Kôjirô (1974, 1254–57) built his argument: the Chin was dominated by Su Shih and unreceptive to Chu Hsi. I will start, as Yoshikawa did, with the civil service examinations, but I will point to a markedly different conclusion.[9]

During the reign of Shih-tsung, poetic compositions were technically and artistically excellent; however, after the beginning of the thirteenth century, "examination papers steadily worsened. It seems that officials merely followed strict regulations. Passing papers, shabby and hackneyed, merely conformed to specified requirements. Anything in the least unusual would ensure failure. Thus literary style greatly declined" (*CS* 110.2427; trans. Wixted 1982, 9). By grading solely on formalistic conventions of style, most scholar-officials presiding over the examinations contributed to the decline in literary quality. In addition to passing unusually high percentages of papers, the Chin state also enforced cultural rigidity, as when, for instance, Chao Ping-wen was temporarily demoted two ranks for passing an examinee who had violated convention by using the same rhyme word more than once in a poetic composition (*CS* 110.2427).

The *Chin History* editors' condemnation of late Chin *wen* reflected a judgment made by leading intellectuals of the late Chin. Although complaints about the declining quality of culture and education are often set conventions, some leading Chin intellectuals believed a significant decline in *wen* had begun after the middle of the first decade of the thirteenth century.[10] The rising disorder in the late Chin and the rigidity of grading criteria for the examinations lend credence to their perception. Whether or not the decline of *wen* evinced in the examinations and more widely was actual fact, the responses made to the perceived decline have real relevance to any discussion of intellectual trends.

Seeking to reform the civil service examinations, leading Chin scholar-officials initiated what Yoshikawa characterized as an "ancient learning" (*ku-hsüeh*) movement. Around 1214, Chao Ping-wen, Li Ch'un-fu, and Yang Yün-i (1170–1228) began advocating a broader and more practical examination curriculum so that literary considerations would not be so crucial. This "movement" might best be understood as an effort by scholar-officials to bring their understanding of the *ku-wen* (ancient or classical writing style) tradition from the Northern Sung to bear on the current problems of the Chin examination culture. Chao, Yang, and Li did reportedly have some positive influence on the quality of writing in the examinations (*KCC* 7.8a–10b). But although this protest was made by the best writers of the day, it is by no means certain that they won the support of a majority of the intelligentsia; in any event, they failed to change the practice of either the bureaucracy or their colleagues among the examiners. And since the movement took place during the final, declining phase of the Chin, when it was caught between Mongol and Southern Sung armies, it had little chance of succeeding.

If the excellent quality of literary compositions during the late twelfth century is accepted as proof of Su Shih's influence, what does the subsequent decline imply? On the one hand, concern over the impact that rigid grading of poetic compositions was having on literary style and the quality of the civil service selection process is strong evidence that Su Shih's philosophy maintained considerable influence. On the other hand, the *ku-hsüeh* movement of the Chin suggests a departure from the philosophical convictions of Su Shih. Instead of championing a return to the late twelfth-century approximation of Su Shih's views on *wen*, the leaders advocated a major reduction in the weight given to literary composition and a corresponding increase in the value assigned to intellectual content and practical learning. The modern scholar Kuo Shao-yü (1961, 250–58) has observed a similar priority of scholarship over original expression and substance over style in poetic expression in a "school" of critical theory headed by Chao Ping-wen and Wang Jo-hsü.

What this swing toward greater emphasis on substance and intellectual content both demonstrated and further portended might be seen in an apparently parallel evolution that took place in the *ku-wen* movement during the Northern Sung. Ou-yang Hsiu's *ku-wen* movement had developed in three distinct directions by the next generation: Wang An-shih's institutional orientation; the Ch'engs' philosophical *tao* and ethics; and Su

Shih's cultural approach to self-cultivation (Tillman 1982; Bol 1982 and 1992). The present essay seeks to draw attention to the evolution *within* the transmission from Ou-yang, through Su, to Su's successors. In his quest for deeper purpose and function, Su Shih felt compelled to address philosophical questions regarding the relationship between *wen* and the *tao* that had not impinged on Ou-yang Hsiu a generation earlier. Su Shih's personally chosen successors, the Four Masters—Ch'in Kuan (1049–1100), Chang Lei (1054–1114), Ch'ao Pu-chih (1053–1110), and Huang T'ing-chien (1045–1105)—had to be even more specific about the relationship between *wen* and the *tao*. In the process, they generally took a more practical, and ultimately narrower, view of *wen*. Concerns about ethical values and intellectual inquiry loomed larger in the minds of these Four Masters than in Su Shih's. In this evolution there appears to be an "inner logic" arising from the conviction within the movement that *wen* should express ideas clearly.

Thus, embedded within the movement there seems to have been an operative assumption about *wen* that implicitly favored a quest for the higher idea that *wen* was supposed to be conveying and eventually a narrower and more functional perception of *wen*. Hence, a concern for the *tao* appears logically almost certain to triumph over or to be superior to *wen* itself. As this became evident, the specialists on the philosophical approach to the *tao*—that is, the Tao-hsüeh Confucians—had a real advantage in proclaiming the superiority of their concepts for understanding the *tao*. The Chin intellectuals who championed substance over style and intellectual content over creative expression were generally among the most prominent of those who had in the earlier period written excellent poetic compositions. Thus, these Chin literati were apparently making a transition comparable to that within the *ku-wen* movement of the Northern Sung.

As *ku-hsüeh* advocates focused their concerns on questions of larger meaning, the intellectual milieu became more conducive to Tao-hsüeh; nevertheless, the progression was more complex than a simple transition from a decline of *wen*, to the *ku-hsüeh* movement, and then to Tao-hsüeh. The introduction of Tao-hsüeh around 1190 predated the *ku-hsüeh* movement and even the decline of *wen*. The growing currency of Tao-hsüeh among a broad range of scholars, including those below the level of the few giants whose literary collections are extant, probably contributed to the decline of *wen*. The *tao* became for them an even greater focus, and few individuals indeed could both philosophize and engage in belles lettres well. The spread of Tao-hsüeh in the Southern Sung had a similar impact on the belles lettres of most scholars within the fellowship and reached such a point that even Chu Hsi on several occasions during the 1190s lamented the decline in good writing (*CTYL* 109.4292, 4297–4301; Shuen-fu Lin 1978, 8–9, 47–48). It is hence reasonable to associate the general decline in *wen* with the growing popularity of Tao-hsüeh. The emphasis on intellectual content instead of poetic style among spokesmen for *ku-hsüeh* already indicated affinity with, and perhaps even some influence from, Tao-hsüeh.

The explanatory model here proposed is one of interaction between literary trends and broader intellectual currents that led increasingly to substantial orientations toward Tao-hsüeh. I am *not* suggesting that Su Shih's influence was eclipsed or that Chin literati ceased to pursue a variety of literary arts. Yet there are signs that Su's dominance among Chin literati was weakening just as some of them were becoming attracted to Tao-hsüeh.

A few Chinese literati under the Chin even evidenced conscious choice in regard to this process of transcending *wen* to focus on the *tao*. Chao Ping-wen expressed the opinion that although the Su family was better at dealing with changes in practical governance, one should study the Ch'eng brothers and Chou Tun-i to understand the constancy of the *tao* (*FSWC* 1.4a). Wang Yü (1204–36) wanted to join the style of *ku-wen* writers, particularly Han Yü and Liu Tsung-yüan (773–819), with the principles of Tao-hsüeh masters, especially the Ch'engs and Chang Tsai (*SYHA* 100.1882; *CS* 126.2735–36).

All three leading Chin intellectuals also criticized Su Shih's views. Despite his admiration for Su Shih's poetry, Wang Jo-hsü complained that Su's comments on the classics "did not reach the level of a pedestrian follower of the school of the two Ch'engs" (*HNIL* 31.3a). In the process of citing as erroneous some of Su Shih's specific explanations of the *Mencius*, Wang Jo-hsü remarked, "Master Su comes close to not understanding anything and does not have to be considered" (*HNIL* 8.3b–4a)! Su also "could be said to use words to destroy meaning" (*HNIL* 8.4a). Sharing some of the faults of the Sung commentators, Su could err in being too "lofty" in explaining what Confucius meant (*HNIL* 5.5a–5b). Wang pronounced an even more more sweeping judgment: "Master Su's eight essays on the *Analects* and the *Mencius* are comparatively a little better [than Ssu-ma Kuang's ten-some essays questioning Mencius' views]. Su himself feels that he is not far from the sages; but on close scrutiny, I conclude that all [of his essays] have also lost the sages' original points" (*HNIL* 8.1b).

In addition to belittling Mencius, Su Shih had erred in denying King Wu's status as a sage while elevating the likes of Hsün Yü to the level of close disciple of Confucius (*HNIL* 8.3b–5a, 30.2b–3a). Similarly, although Chao Ping-wen did not explicitly cite Su Shih's well-known appraisal of

Hsün Yü, he implicitly discredited Su's view by explaining Hsün Yü's loyalty as allegiance to Ts'ao Ts'ao rather than to the Han dynasty (*FSWC* 14.9a). Although praising Su Shih for being better at practical governance than Chou Tun-i or the Ch'engs were, Chao also implicitly charged that the Su family was more involved with Buddhism and Taoism (*FSWC* 1.3b–4a, 7b). Li Ch'un-fu questioned Su Shih's separation of human nature from that with which we are endowed by Heaven (*MTCS* 5.200–202, no. M2).

Yüan Hao-wen's judgment of 1217 is of particular importance because in Su Shih's philosophy, creativity was the principal mark of being one with the *tao*. Although he admired Su's poetry and genius, Yüan Hao-wen was still ambivalent, especially about Su's too conscious striving to be novel (*ISWC* 11.5b–6a; trans. Wixted 1982, poems 22 and 26). Yüan Hao-wen's implicit disparagement of Su Shih's relation to the *tao* was independently reinforced by Wang Jo-hsü's and Chao Ping-wen's evaluations of Su Shih as being good at governance and poetry rather than at understanding the Confucian *tao*.

I would not assert that such substantial criticism by major intellectuals under the Chin refutes the generally accepted view that Chin intellectuals belonged essentially to Su Shih's school of thought. Such criticism should, however, raise questions enough to qualify Yoshikawa Kôjirô's statement (1974, 1246) that Su Shih "was the spirit [*kami*] of civilization in the Chin dynasty." Against the backdrop of criticism leveled against Su Shih one should, at the very least, disallow the critiques of Tao-hsüeh Confucians in denying or neglecting their affinities with Tao-hsüeh.

In Conclusion: A Characterization of Chin Confucians

What are we to conclude about the many Chinese intellectuals under the Chin dynasty who were not totally dominated by Su Shih's learning? How are the ones who were not Taoists or Buddhists to be characterized? On the most general level, they were simply Confucians in a sense that cuts across lines or schools of thought within Confucianism. Even the *Sung Yüan hsüeh-an* in its curt biographical abstracts, which largely passed over any discussion of their actual ideas, included some details that implicitly reveal that most of these intellectuals were men of traditional Confucian virtues who strove in difficult circumstances to be both loyal and humane officials (*SYHA* 100.1879–83; also *CS* 110.2421–29 and 2434–35, 126.2733–43). They studied belles lettres and the Confucian classics to improve themselves as persons as well as to pass the civil service examinations. Continuing to venerate Confucius, they participated in rites at temples including the one maintained by his descendants at Ch'ü-fu, where in 1190 the Chin rebuilt the K'uei-wen-ko (Great Pavilion of the Constellation of

Scholars), which still stands as a magnificent monument to official sponsorship of the state cult of Confucius under the Chin. Chin imperial steles are found behind the K'uei-wen-ko along with steles from the T'ang, Sung, Yüan, Ming, and Ch'ing dynasties. A special stele dating from the Chin also marks the Apricot Pavilion, where Confucius once taught his students underneath the shade of an apricot tree.

Chinese intellectuals under the Chin also had affinities with T'ang Confucianism in the areas of classical commentaries, the art of governance, and princely education. Although critical of Han and T'ang commentators for having focused on words and phrases so narrowly that they lost the basic meaning of the classics, Wang Jo-hsü and Chao Ping-wen still recognized their value: Wang's careful scrutiny and exposition of language in his own writings reflected the imprint of Han and T'ang scholarship. The influence of T'ang models was more pronounced in Chao's and Wang's writings on practical governance and princely education. Both men drew heavily on T'ang sources in their discussions of the duties of the ruler and in their construction of models for the ruler to follow. Chao Ping-wen edited a digest of the major T'ang work on the art of government, the *Chen-kuan cheng-yao* (Essence of government during T'ang T'ai-tsung's reign). Moreover, in conjunction with Yang Yün-i, he wrote a handbook modeled on the T'ang work. Yüan Hao-wen followed with a similar work (Franke 1982, 179). But even in their commentaries and theories of governance, intellectuals under the Chin were more than simply T'ang Confucians.

Confucians under the Chin were also scholars of Sung learning. In their study of and writings on the classics, they sought the larger meaning of the classics to apply to their own lives and society; furthermore, they approached the classics directly, as well as through commentaries. Although Wang Jo-hsü and Chao Ping-wen were critical of all Sung commentators, they also shared Li Ch'un-fu's praise of Sung scholars for recovering much of the more basic and profound meaning of the sages. Their criticism of Sung Confucians essentially did not leave the boundaries of Sung learning—a fact of which Wang Jo-hsü was evidently aware when he quoted Yeh Shih to summarize his own critique of Sung commentators. In the area of statecraft, they shared the particular Sung conception of loyalty with its enhanced attention to the position of the emperor, the question of legitimate succession of dynasties, and the standard of service to one dynasty alone. During the early thirteenth century, the Jurchen rulers officially reversed dynastic policy to claim their place in the line of legitimate succession from the Northern Sung—and thus recognized the legitimacy of the Northern Sung. This was intellectually justified on the grounds of the political thought of Ou-yang Hsiu, a principal founder of Sung learning. The implicit sanction that the Jurchen court thereby extended to Sung learning was mirrored in other actions, such as Chang-tsung's efforts to copy Hui-tsung's calligraphy and to acquire works of art formerly in the imperial collection of the Northern Sung.

The *chin-shih* examinations of the second half of the Chin dynasty were dominated by candidates from areas once ruled by the Northern Sung, and this appears to have been a major factor in the flourishing of Sung learning among scholars. Their families likely preserved some legacy of education from the Sung. Both the dominant place of poetry in the examinations and the exceptional quality of the poetic compositions written as part of the examinations during the last part of the twelfth century and the opening years of the thirteenth suggest that Su Shih's poetics, and probably his philosophy as well, enjoyed special popularity. Characterizations of Chin civilization during this period as dominated by Su Shih, the "spirit" of that civilization, certainly are largely valid. But even during the zenith of Su Shih's dominance, there are signs of the introduction and spread of a rival school of Confucian thought—Tao-hsüeh.

Testimony by Wang Jo-hsü, Chao Ping-wen, and Li Ch'un-fu, in addition to other evidence, substantiates the claim that Tao-hsüeh Confucianism was introduced around 1190 from the Southern Sung and that it won the allegiance of a considerable number of intellectuals in the North. Although it is logical to assume that the fellowship did not disappear in North China with the demise of the Northern Sung, extant sources provide almost no evidence of Tao-hsüeh in the North until the second half of the Chin dynasty. In terms of the writings that were quoted and the thinkers who were discussed, this Tao-hsüeh community or fellowship was receptive to both Northern and Southern Sung Tao-hsüeh philosophers. "Fellowship" here should not be taken to imply that development under the Chin reached the same levels as under the Southern Sung or the Yüan. Still, the weight of the evidence—particularly given the paucity of extant Chin sources—for the quality and volume of Tao-hsüeh Confucian thought and influence suggests that a far more widespread and significant development of Tao-hsüeh Confucianism took place under the Chin than has been conventionally realized. Such individuals as Fu Ch'i and other compilers of the *Tao-hsüeh fa-yüan* made a special commitment to study and propagate the learning of the Tao-hsüeh masters, and their efforts were encouraged, even cheered, by Wang Jo-hsü and Chao Ping-wen. Both of these leading Confucians of the period, as well as Li Ch'un-fu, indicated that many of the more gifted young men among the scholar-official class were attracted to this fellowship. Even Li Ch'un-fu is known to have studied Tao-hsüeh texts for almost thirty years before writing the *Ming-tao chi shuo* in 1218. By this reckoning, he began reading Tao-hsüeh writings around 1190, a date that is consistent with that given by Wang Jo-hsü and compatible with other evidence for dating the introduction and spread of Tao-hsüeh. Hence, the Tao-hsüeh tradition began to flourish in North China at least a decade before Chao Fu was born and over four decades before he reportedly introduced Chu Hsi's version of Tao-hsüeh to the North.

Chao Ping-wen, Wang Jo-hsü, and Li Ch'un-fu individually expressed various areas of agreement with Tao-hsüeh Confucianism in general as well as with particular Tao-hsüeh philosophers. These individually proclaimed affinities share a basic acceptance of a number of Tao-hsüeh positions: the eclipse of the *tao* after the death of Mencius and the particular role of early Tao-hsüeh masters in reviving the transmission of the *tao*; the concept of Heaven's principle; ethical cultivation in daily affairs with special emphasis on the mind-and-heart; and the extension of knowledge through the investigation of things. In their revisions of the historical judgments made by Sung and earlier historians, Chao Ping-wen's and Wang Jo-hsü's historiography drew on the "praise and blame" methodology of the *Spring and Autumn Annals* and was in essential accord with Chu Hsi's moral didacticism. Chao Ping-wen and Li Ch'un-fu further demonstrated appreciation for Tao-hsüeh Confucians' contributions to understanding of the concepts of human nature, sincerity, equilibrium, and harmony, as well as the physical and the metaphysical. Even points on which they had reservations must have enhanced the North's awareness of Tao-hsüeh ideas and initiated a dialogue into which even more Tao-hsüeh could be introduced later, after the Mongol conquest had destroyed what Yoshikawa characterized as the "iron curtain" between the Chin and the Southern Sung. At the very least, Tao-hsüeh Confucianism was already having an impact on the thought and writing of these three leading intellectuals of the period.

By the thirteenth century, there were signs that Tao-hsüeh was having an impact on other areas of Chin culture and militating against Su Shih's influence. A hallmark of the Su school was its embrace (relative to Tao-hsüeh) of intellectual pluralism or toleration and its resistance to moral didacticism. In addition to the rigorous ethical judgments in Wang Jo-hsü's and Chao Ping-wen's historical essays, the hostile reaction to Li Ch'un-fu's *Ming-tao chi shuo* of 1218 suggests that Tao-hsüeh was beginning to alter the intellectual climate. This hostility from Confucians was provoked by Li's critical, and sometimes intemperate, remarks about Tao-hsüeh masters. Even Chao Ping-wen, who was both Li's friend and a relatively tolerant individual, acted to block publication of Li's collected writings on the grounds that they were too Buddhistic.

Another sign of the impact of Tao-hsüeh Confucianism is intertwined with the apparent decline in the importance of *wen* during the last three decades of the Chin. From sometime during the first decade of the thirteenth century, the quality of poetic compositions in the civil service examinations had been declining markedly, while the examiners had begun grading on the basis of rigid stylistic criteria. Scholars were thus paying less attention to poetry and especially to Su Shih's philosophy in which *wen* and poetic creativity were essential to oneness with the *tao*. The solution posed by the leaders of the *ku-hsüeh* movement from about 1214 onward did not return to Su Shih's philosophical position. Instead, it advocated decreasing attention to poetic composition and increasing emphasis on scholarly content and practical learning. The writings of Chao Ping-wen, Wang Jo-hsü, Li Ch'un-fu, and Yüan Hao-wen displayed a similar emphasis on scholarship over original expression and on substance over style in poetic composition. These developments in the area of *wen* during the Chin have parallels in the evolution of the *ku-wen* movement during the Northern Sung, when even Su Shih's chosen successors defined *wen* in narrower and more functional terms than Su Shih had.

The evolution of the *ku-wen* movement and its parallels to Chin developments provide grounds for suggesting that there was an "inner logic," which we can observe within the *ku-wen* movement's turning toward a quest for higher meaning (i.e., the *tao*) and toward a more narrowly functional conception of *wen* in relation to the *tao*. In the Sung, this inner logic worked to the advantage of Tao-hsüeh and facilitated the devaluation of Su Shih to the status of a merely great writer. Critical remarks leveled against Su Shih's views—by Chao Ping-wen, Wang Jo-hsü, and Yüan Hao-wen—suggest that leading intellectuals in the late Chin likewise had their doubts about his understanding of the *tao* in spite of their respect for his belles lettres and practical views on governance. In turning to the Tao-hsüeh masters for explication of the *tao*, Chao, Wang, and others in effect demonstrated a major victory for Tao-hsüeh Confucianism, for that school regarded the *tao* as the most central issue in its contention with Su Shih's way of thinking. In his expressed desire to join the literary style of *ku-wen* writers with the ethical and philosophical principles of Tao-hsüeh masters, Wang Yü perhaps consciously reflected the symbolic transformation of *ku-wen* leaders into mere literary giants and the philosophical evolution away from *ku-wen* toward Tao-hsüeh.

In addition to "inner logic" in the realm of intellectual trends, there were external pressures that inclined intellectuals in the late Chin toward Tao-hsüeh. Competition from other ideologies and movements, particularly the flourishing Ch'üan-chen sect of Taoism, surely enhanced the need of Confucians to seek a fundamental truth that would allow them to contend with Ch'üan-chen and to win back some of the many literati who had joined that sect to preserve native Chinese culture in the wake of the Jurchen conquest. Tao-hsüeh dogma about the *tao* and its transmission provided such fundamental assurance and authority. During the last three decades of the Chin, the ever-increasing encroachments on North China by the Southern Sung and the Mongols produced a climate of cultural crisis and a sense of doom—most notably after the Mongols' bloody conquest of much of North China in 1214. Fear of the Mongols' ferocious destructiveness surely heightened the felt need for clarity about orientations and certainty about values. Tao-hsüeh Confucianism provided grounds for such certainty. In the thirteenth century in the Southern Sung, the growing concern for ideological unity and cultural confidence, in large part due to the Mongol threat, led the government to swing from hostility to receptivity toward Tao-hsüeh (James T. C. Liu 1973, 502–3; and 1988, 147–48). It is not unreasonable to assume that a sense of doom and cultural crisis made Tao-hsüeh a more attractive haven to a larger number of scholars than might have otherwise been the case. Bringing the rise and flow of Tao-hsüeh Confucianism into sharp focus should not be taken to imply that it was an irrepressible tide sweeping all along with it, but the strength of this current may be seen in its influence on even the major intellectuals who stood outside the fellowship.

The impact of Tao-hsüeh and their own affinities with it notwithstanding, leading intellectuals in the North still criticized Tao-hsüeh Confucianism. The thrust of their criticisms claimed that Tao-hsüeh Confucians were too philosophically abstract, too inadequately attuned to moral cultivation and practical matters of governance, and too rigid and unaccommodating in dealing with other schools of thought. Similar criticisms can also be found even in the writings of Lü Tsu-ch'ien and Chu Hsi (Tillman 1982, 56–67, 115–16, 180–81, 202, 213–14; 1992a, chaps. 4 and 5). Thus, it was possible to make such criticisms of Tao-hsüeh and yet still identify oneself with the fellowship or even be one of its leading figures. In the cases of Chao Ping-wen and Wang Jo-hsü, however, intellectual ties to other components of Confucianism (and in Li Ch'un-fu's case to Buddhism) were strong enough to inhibit them from going beyond the encouragement they extended to the spread of Tao-hsüeh and the acceptance they demonstrated of some of its major ideas. Their Confucianism was broad enough to embrace much of Tao-hsüeh but too broad to be confined to that camp. Yet the overall direction of their intellectual evolution was apparently beginning to move away from Su's philosophy and toward Tao-hsüeh. The relative intellectual diversity and pluralism of the Chin makes the detectable drift toward Tao-hsüeh Confucianism even more significant. To explore a major Confucian *problématique* between Su's philosophy and Tao-hsüeh, the diversity of the Chin intellectual milieu has been necessarily simplified here, setting aside the flourishing Buddhist and Taoist alternatives.

The reservations that Chin intellectuals expressed in reference to Tao-hsüeh also point toward the character of Chu Hsi's Confucianism under the Yüan dynasty. Recent research on Chu Hsi's school of Confucianism in the Yüan period has shown that compared to Chu Hsi, the Yüan Confucians placed more emphasis on practical affairs and ethical cultivation than on speculative philosophy or metaphysics, and were more open to intellectual accommodation.[11] These characteristics correspond precisely with the principal reservations of Chin intellectuals in respect to Tao-hsüeh, that is to say, the changes they would have liked to see. Yüan followers of Chu Hsi apparently had a pronounced sense of commitment to the transmission of the *tao* and the salvation of civilization in the face of the Mongol barbarism that they perceived. This strong sense of commitment was also characteristic of the self-image of Confucians under the Chin, some of whom even pictured themselves and those they admired as Confucian cultural heroes.[12]

These parallels between Chin Confucianism and the changes in the Chu Hsi school of thought between the Sung and the Yüan raise the possibility that Confucianism, and especially Tao-hsüeh, under the Chin might have had some influence on the way Chu Hsi's thought was perceived and received during the Yüan dynasty. Recognizing such influence would not negate the importance of the Southern Sung background, the Yüan milieu, or Chao Fu's contribution in further popularizing Chu Hsi's thought. The excitement over Chao Fu might largely be explained by thinking of him in terms of an "apostle" with more direct and complete knowledge of Chu Hsi's teachings than had earlier been available during the Chin. But Chao Fu would probably not have had such a dramatic impact without the preparatory context of the Tao-hsüeh fellowship in North China.

We should at least have reservations about continuing to portray northerners under the early Yüan as struck by the "new revelation" brought by Chao Fu from the Southern Sung, that the classics had personal meaning in their own lives and were not simply texts of antique learning. Chinese in the North under the Chin had long been aware of this central doctrine. It might be true that Hsü Heng (1209–81) was the key that turned Chu Hsi's Yüan followers toward practical matters and personal cultivation and away from metaphysics, but what forged the key, and from what metal was it made? The flow of Southern Sung Tao-hsüeh into Chin Confucianism and the changes leading intellectuals under the Chin wanted to see in Tao-hsüeh Confucianism provide a basis for suggesting that Hsü Heng's key might well have had some gold (Chin) in it.

Notes

1. This article has circulated in China since early 1984 and was published in 1988 under my Chinese name, T'ien Hao. Before writing that

essay, I had discussions with scholars in Peking, some of whom dismissed my project because they held on to the conventional outlook of the *Sung Yüan hsüeh-an*. In 1982, for instance, the chairman of the philosophy department at People's University told me that there were no Confucians under the Chin because they had all fled to serve the Southern Sung. But Professor Teng Kuang-ming urged me to publish my findings in Chinese in order to draw the attention of China's scholars to an issue too long overlooked. And after reading a draft of the article, Professor Ch'iu Han-sheng expressed regrets that the Chin had been passed over in his *Sung Ming li-hsüeh shih* (Ch'iu 1984). Ts'ai Mei-piao (1988, 141–42) has written very briefly of Wang Jo-hsü's and Chao Ping-wen's roles in a revival of Confucian studies and the Ch'eng-Chu school. At the 1991 Liao-Chin conference held in Tatung, Shansi, Shih Tao-kang specifically cited my 1988 essay in his paper on relations between Confucians and the Ch'üan-chen Taoists; Tung K'o-ch'ang spoke about the Confucianization of Chin governance; Mu Hung-li focused on the influence of Confucianism on Jurchen culture; and Fan Shou-k'un discussed patronage of Confucian temples. More attention is now also being given to Confucianism under the Liao by scholars such as Meng Ku-t'o-li (1991) and Miao P'o (1991).

2. The undated (Ming) manuscript copy of Li Chun-fu's *Ming-tao chi-shuo* once in the rare book collection of the former Peiping Library is now in the Library of Congress, Washington, D.C.; only a microfilm of the manuscript remains in the Peking Library. The work is in five *chüan* and there are no page numbers on the microfilm copy; hence, citation is awkward. I have therefore cited the page numbers from the photolithograph edition published in Taipei (number 45 of the Chung-kuo tzu-hsüeh ming-chu chi-ch'eng series). In addition, I have noted the passage numbers assigned by Bartholomew Pui-ming Tsui in his 1982 dissertation, which contains the only complete English translation of the work. *Chüan* numbers and passage numbers do not apply to the prefaces found on pp. 51–56 of the Taiwan edition. I am very thankful to Dr. Tsui, now at the Chinese University of Hong Kong, for sharing with me the second half of his dissertation containing his translation. English excerpts from *MTCS* in the present essay are amalgams of his translation and my own (made before I had learned of Dr. Tsui's). The *Chu Ju ming-tao chi* itself (discussed below) can be found in the rare book collections of the Peking and Shanghai libraries; the Harvard-Yenching Library also has a microfilm of the printed edition owned by the Shanghai Library.

3. *ISWC* 11.3b–6b, 14.8b, 36.16b–19a; trans. Wixted 1982, poems 1, 5, 7, 11, 13, 23, and pp. 235–38, 243–44.

4. See especially Takeo 1929; Kubota 1931, 557–86; Nogami 1953, 209–20; Yoshikawa 1974, 1249–54; Jan Yün-hua 1976 and 1979.

5. Jan Yün-hua (1979, 169) offers these two possible reasons for Li's more partisan statements in the Shao-lin inscriptions and gives a date of 1230 for them; Yoshikawa (1974, 1251) gives dates of 1220 and 1222.

6. My understanding of Wang Jo-hsü has been enriched by Stephen H. West's unpublished translations of some of Wang's writings.

7. This account has come under question in recent years; see Wu T'ien-jen 1987.

8. This passage appears in the last pages of the *CCJC* edition of *HNC* (32.4b–5a) but is not to be found in the SPTK edition. See also Tao Jing-shen 1981a, 992. For Ch'eng I's comment, see *ECC* 1:301; for a defense of Ch'eng I, see Wing-tsit Chan 1986, 4.

9. Although Yoshikawa's perception may be taken as an interpretative baseline, his view is problematic for reasons beyond those central to my argument as presented in the text. First, although Chin scholars clearly admired Su Shih for his belles lettres, it is more difficult to establish that they were fully committed to his total philosophy of culture. In demonstrating Su's cultural dominance during the Chin, it would be better to focus on the writings of the principal literary giants, as Peter Bol does, rather than on the culture of the examination system, as Yoshikawa did. Second, the *lü-fu* tradition was not founded on Su alone, but had a broad historical grounding. Should we assume, therefore, that the *lü-fu* examinations indicate the primacy of Su's influence? Citing the *lü-fu* as evidence of Su's impact on the examination curriculum, for instance, runs directly counter to Liu Ch'i's observation (*KCC* 8.80) that the *lü-fu* examiners were hostile to Su Shih; however, Liu Ch'i's bitterness and frustrations with the examinations complicate the reliability of his perhaps self-serving account. For a study of Su's views on literati temperaments, see Huang Ming-fen 1985.

10. Besides those I will mention in the text, see Wang Yü's lament on the literary decline in *SYHA* 100.1881–82 and Yüan Hao-wen's in *YISCC* 2.157 and 7.346 (trans. Wixted 1982, 30 and 52).

11. See the articles by Tu Wei-ming, Wm. Theodore de Bary, and Wing-tsit Chan in Chan Hok-lam and de Bary 1982. See also Yao Ta-li 1983; Ch'en Kao-hua 1976; and Hsiao Kung-ch'in 1985.

12. *SYHA* 100.1880–82, especially Sung Chiu-chia, Lei Yüan (1186–1231), Chang Chüeh (late Chin era), and Wang Yü. Li Ch'un-fu (*MTCS* 5.194–96, no. 217) called Tao-hsüeh philosophers heroes. Yüan Hao-wen (*CCC* 4.220) said that people regarded Li Ch'un-fu and Lei Yüan as heroes. Yüan Hao-wen's poetic criticism also paid special attention to the heroic tradition that he associated with North China.

5

CHAO PING-WEN (1159–1232): FOUNDATIONS FOR LITERATI LEARNING

Peter K. Bol

Why Chao Ping-wen?

During the last forty years of Chin, beginning late in Shih-tsung's reign (1161–89) and continuing to the end of the dynasty in 1234, through both the good years of Chang-tsung's reign (1190–1208) and the troubled years of military losses to the Mongols and the usurpation of imperial authority by generals, literati (*shih*) culture flourished. More men engaged in literati pursuits then than ever before in the Chin, and more and better literary and scholarly works were written. Han literati culture and the fortunes of the Jurchen's polity, which many Han literati served but which few of them greatly influenced, seemed to have separated. What was the character of this flourishing culture of the Han elite? Why did literati become involved in it? What meaning did it have for them? What historical significance should we attach to it?

Chao Ping-wen died in 1232. He had been a central figure in this cultural revival, which took place in a narrow segment of Chinese society during a very short period of Chinese history, in a state on the periphery of Han wealth and power. Yet his case has some bearing on how we think about the Chinese past, particularly the intellectual history of the literati during the later imperial period. Chao provided many literati with a model of intellectual engagement, cultural accomplishment, and political success. And he can provide us with one interpretation of the nature and meaning of the late Chin revival of literati culture.

This inquiry is organized around *wen* and *tao* as two categories of intellectual concern and activity. Yüan Hao-wen (1190–1257), the great historian of Chin literati culture, used them to place Chao in intellectual-historical context and define his influence on Chin literati. Chao himself wrote on how literati should understand and practice both. And we can use them to relate Chao and the intellectual revival he helped bring about to the intellectual history of Sung and the post-Chin dynasties.

In Chin, as in Sung, *wen* and *tao* could be taken both broadly and narrowly. Taken most inclusively, *wen* meant the cumulative tradition of writings (the classics, histories, philosophers, and belles lettres) as the legacy of civilization. The textual tradition was the basis for literati learning because it was seen as the source of models for a sociopolitical order in which civil (*wen*) interests ranked above military interests. The textual tradition was the repository source of institutions and values. Men schooled in the textual tradition would be able, it was commonly thought, to secure the state. Taken more narrowly, *wen* was individual cultural accomplishment: literary prose and poetry, calligraphy and (sometimes) painting. These were the means by which individuals manifested their learning and character to others. In Chin, as in Sung, an examination system testing literary composition was the institutional mechanism by which learning from the textual tradition, government service, and individual talent and accomplishment were related. *Tao*, taken broadly, could mean that which impelled and organized the universe of Heaven-and-earth and the ten thousand things. In *tao* literati saw the possibility of universal values, for the ultimate source of creation and the process that enabled things to function together harmoniously were generally presumed to contain guides for human social conduct. When *tao* was understood narrowly, as doctrine or the Way, it usually meant the one real moral way according to which man should proceed in the effort to establish harmony and integration in human society. But just as literati spoke of an individual's *wen*—the ability to write well, the literary and artistic output of an individual, and the style or voice that marked his work—so did they speak of a man's guiding values, his way of acting, or his philosophy as his *tao*. *Wen* and *tao* were categories of thought and action of a particular period and culture. They could be taken as separate subjects, just as we treat philosophy and literature as different subjects men can study. But in Chin, as in Sung, it was common for literati who were concerned with values to treat them as the two parts that together constituted the whole of learning. Taken as two parts of a whole, they suggested tensions that transcended time and place: between culture and nature, writing and thought, the literary and the philosophical, and individual creativity and holistic universals.

Chao Ping-wen's intellectual endeavors were understood by his contemporaries in terms of *wen* and *tao*. I shall argue that we ought to understand Chao and the late Chin intellectual revival as involving both *wen* and *tao;* to take one without the other is to miss half the story and to ignore what men like Yüan Hao-wen thought was important. To some extent this approach is at odds with current ideas about Chinese intellectual history. We readily grant that what a man writes about *tao* bears directly on his role in the search for values during his times; we often treat his literary prose and poetry and what he has to say about the practice of *wen* as normal, even insignificant, literary activity. In short, we do not easily see how activities that are subsumed under the category *wen* can be as important to the kinds of questions intellectual history asks as activities that aim at establishing an understanding of *tao*.

It is not hard to see how it has come about that we prefer to use ideas about *tao* to trace intellectual change. It is common for modern descriptions of Sung intellectual history to proceed from the account found in the *Sung Yüan hsüeh-an* (Record of Sung and Yüan Confucian schools of thought), which appears to have drawn its account from Chu Hsi (1130–1200). Chu Hsi saw himself as part of a new intellectual movement among literati, called Tao-hsüeh by many at the time. He explained the origins of this movement in a narrow manner, arguing that in the eleventh century Chou Tun-i (1017–73) had understood the *tao* of the sages, which no one had understood since Mencius. After Chou he placed the brothers Ch'eng Hao (1032–85) and Ch'eng I (1033–1107) and their uncle Chang Tsai (1020–77); they had followers and the followers had followers, so that Chu himself was able to become part of the line of direct transmission. By *tao* Chu understood the moral way the sages acted and the natural foundation that made moral values real. But Chu Hsi also had a broader historical view, and this is reflected by those treated in the first four chapters of the *Sung Yüan hsüeh-an*. Chu credited others with contributing to the rise of true learning by turning attention toward the *tao* of the sages without having entirely understood it themselves. Thus, he praised Fan Chung-yen (989–1052), Hu Yüan (993–1059), Sun Fu (992–1057), Shih Chieh (1005–45), and Ou-yang Hsiu (1007–72) for having helped set the stage for Chou Tun-i and the Ch'engs (*CTYL* 129.4948–54). In Chu's eyes, once the *tao* had been recovered, those who spoke about values but failed to adopt the correct understanding of *tao* were perversely misguided. He (and the *Sung Yüan hsüeh-an*) treated Wang An-shih (1021–86) and Su Shih (1036–1101) as examples of men who had threatened true understanding by accepting Buddhist and Taoist ideas.

We tend to assume that later men, if they did not subscribe fully to the internal history of Tao-hsüeh, still conceived of "Confucian" thinking about values along the lines set out by Tao-hsüeh. But if we go back to the eleventh century, to the men Chu included in his "broader" historical view, we can see that there had been an alternative mode of discussing literati values and intellectual tradition. Viewed from the situation of their own times, Ou-yang Hsiu and the others are best understood in terms of the revival of a literature of moral commitment known as *ku-wen*, "ancient-style prose," which opposed the approach to reading and literary composition that was dominant in their day. For these men, changing the way literati engaged in *wen*—learning from the textual tradition and composing their own works—was a means of changing the intellectual orientation and values of the literati. In general those in Chu's "narrow" history had given up on the idea of literary change as a means of changing literati values, turning instead to the problem of establishing a philosophical foundation for ethics in the self-dependent processes of Heaven-and-earth. Clearly, asking how men had contributed to the correct philosophical understanding of *tao* as a means of tracing intellectual change works best when discussions of *tao* are the dominant mode for debates over values. But since men then believed that literary activity was central to learning and realizing enduring values, a narrow concern with philosophical inquiry may lead us to overlook ways of thinking about values and "cultivating the self" that were not articulated in terms of philosophical issues.[1]

We should not, however, simply treat all that is *wen* as an alternative to Tao-hsüeh. Those whom we associate with the eleventh-century *ku-wen* movement, while treating the study of texts and literary composition as the central activities of learning, set themselves apart from contemporary practice by insisting that those who learned from the textual tradition and composed texts themselves should seek to apprehend *tao*. In the style of Han Yü of T'ang they believed in the possibility of a unity of *wen* and *tao*. Thus, for example, we find some speaking of "this *wen* of ours" and "this *tao* of ours" (*ssu wen, ssu tao*) as a single normative tradition of texts and ideas, which began with the sage-kings of antiquity and which they would seek to continue in their own writing. Such formulations generally treated *tao* as primary but, because they also treated *tao* as something that could not be fully known, continued to treat *wen* as the only means men had of coming to understand the values of the cultural tradition and making them known to others. This was very different from what Chu Hsi had in mind, and he objected to such attitudes that mistakenly gave *wen* parity with *tao* (*CTYL* 139.5309). Seeing the textual tradition as nothing more than a vehicle for ideas has an alluring simplicity. Not all literati supposed that this was the case. For some it was because *wen* and *tao* were independent of each other that effort was necessary to keep them together.

Chu Hsi saw one true line of intellectual development, but others saw a set of intellectual alternatives originating in the eleventh century. This is illustrated by an entry in Ch'en Shan's *Men-shih hsin-hua* (New remarks from a man of independent mind), a book of comments and reading notes from early Southern Sung that gives particular attention to Northern Sung literati culture. It is of particular interest because the author, whose sympathies may have been with the Wang An-shih school (*SKTM* 1:1093), uses different styles of *wen* to sort out intellectual culture. The passage begins with an idea from the introduction to the literary biographies in the *New T'ang History*: literature underwent three successive transformations (*pien*) in the course of T'ang, with Han Yü representing its ultimate transformation into the "model for a unifying king."[2] In this case the successive transformations result in coexisting variations.

> In T'ang, *wen-chang* [underwent] three transformations. Our dynasty's *wen-chang* has also [undergone] three transformations: [by] the duke of Ching [Wang An-shih] with classical studies, [Su] Tung-p'o with opinion, and Mr. Ch'eng with innate morality. In essence, each of the three established his own school without borrowing from the others. But none of their later followers avoided going astray. Although this is a fault [that results from] an entire age practicing [the mode of one school], it was really something caused by the situation of the time. To the present, everyone who learns *wen* chases his shadows and barks at his sounds; there has never been a consensus. In truth, they have not seen what the men of the past really cared about. This always makes me sigh. (*MSHH* 5.6a)

This identification of schools of thought as literary traditions had much to do with the fact that literati education was seen by many as examination education, and examinations required literary composition. But if it was possible to see intellectual choices as literary choices at a time when the teachings of Su Shih, Wang An-shih, and Ch'eng I were still being transmitted by followers of followers, it is not hard to imagine that Chin literati, who had to work to reestablish a connection to eleventh-century schools from texts, could also see intellectual alternatives as literary variations.

The literary perspective on intellectual history, and the role of literature in literati thinking about *tao*, has been given little attention. We tend to see men who made their names through cultural accomplishment as "mere" literary men or "men of culture" (*wen-jen*), as they were seen by those who sought to define moral doctrine. Yet before and after Sung, literary ability remained important. It was tested in the examinations, nurtured in the schools, and admired in the individual. The world of literature and art was an integral part of the culture of the literati. Sung "literati of culture" (*wen-shih*) and Ming "men of culture" were not ignored in their own times. The Chin intellectual revival differs from the Tao-hsüeh movement of Southern Sung in part because men like Chao, cognizant of the emergence of Tao-hsüeh, continued to believe that *wen* played a vital role in the search for values.

Yüan Hao-wen on Chao Ping-wen

The categories *wen* and *tao* provided Yüan Hao-wen with a framework for understanding the nature of Chao Ping-wen's intellectual leadership. Yüan's assessment, in his funerary biography of Chao, cannot be taken lightly; he was well versed in the history and literati culture of Chin and his *Collection from the Central Regions* (*Chung-chou chi*) is the most important literary anthology and work of private historiography for the Chin period.

The center of Yüan's biography is an account of Chao Ping-wen's political career. Yüan traces Chao's rise through a succession of everhigher offices, but he also shows that Chao's political success did not translate into real influence over major policy decisions. After receiving the *chin-shih* degree in 1185, Chao served three terms in local government: once as a subprefectural registrar and twice as a subprefect. He was noticed, for after mourning his father's death he was recommended for promotion and appointed to the staff of a fiscal intendant. Then, after mourning for his mother, he was recommended for promotion to a court office with responsibility for preparing state documents, a post traditionally given to promising officials of scholarly attainments. But Yüan tells us nothing about Chao's early work in local government. We do learn that his service at court ended in a temporary setback: he was dismissed for colluding with other Han officials in urging the dismissal of the prime minister. This did not keep Chao from speaking out on policy, once he was recalled to court in 1200. During the first decade of the thirteenth century, as a drafting official in the Han-lin Academy, Chao prepared a position paper on defenses against the Mongols. His advice was not followed, and he was sent out to serve as a prefect. Yüan Hao-wen writes that he was a good prefect, quelling banditry and organizing famine relief. The next time he was recalled to court, between 1210 and 1213, he stayed, holding a succession of ever-higher posts. To his death in 1232, Chao held offices befitting a great scholar: Han-lin academician and minister of rites. He tried to influence policy. In 1213, when the court, having submitted to Mongol demands, was deciding what to do next, Chao advised moving the capital to Shantung, rerouting the Yellow River to a strategically advantageous channel, and bolstering local resistance by enfeoffing imperial clansmen. Under the sway of a military strongman, the court moved to Kaifeng instead and made no move to divide its power further. In 1218, as director of the examinations, Chao tried to shift examination standards away from the technicalities of style toward greater concern with content. He was demoted and temporarily retired. Restored to rank and recalled by the emperor on the grounds that he needed a man with Chao's ability in *wen-chang*, Chao tried to instruct Hsüan-tsung (r. 1213–24) in the correct approach to taxation, jurisprudence, and national defense. When Ai-tsung (r. 1224–34) came to the throne, Chao tried to persuade him to learn from the histories and classics and, together with Yang Yün-i, prepared treatises (now lost) to provide the emperor with correct models. We do not know how much the emperor did or could absorb, or if he really wanted to learn anything; power at court remained in the hands of leading Jurchen aristocrats, men with little interest in giving Han officials a real say in political decisions (*ISWC* 17.2a–5a; and *CS* 110.2426–48).

Although a high-ranking official, Chao had little effect on Chin institutions and matters of state. We may speculate that the court kept Chao in a leading position because he was influential among the Han literati, who, thanks to the expansion of the examination system, had become a major interest group in the Chin government. Indeed, it is clear that Yüan Hao-wen uses his biography to argue that Chao's true historical importance lay in his influence over literati values. The biography begins with a section on *wen*, from T'ang through Chin, and ends with a discussion of *tao*. Chao, we are told, revived *wen* and restored the transmission of *tao*. The opening section is translated here.

> In T'ang, *wen* [underwent] three transformations. During the five dynasties [that followed], it reached the nadir of decline. From the five dynasties to Liao and Sung, and from Liao and Sung to our dynasty, the fall and rise of *wen* can be examined. Sung had [tests on] ancient-style prose [*ku-wen*], poetry, and the classics [in the examinations]. Liu [K'ai], Mu [Hsiu], Ou[-yang Hsiu], and Su [Shih] attacked customary learning with the strength of a hundred and twice the results. But although they began in T'ien-sheng [1023–31], it was not until Yüan-yu [1086–93] that T'ang *wen* truly recovered. [*Wen*,] which seemed right and was neither empty nor useless, again reappeared at the end [of the Sung dynasty] during Cheng-ho and Hsüan-ho [1111–25]. As for Liao—it treated examinations as the epitome of Ju [Confucian] learning; borrowing and plagiarizing, piecing together and mending, [Liao *wen*] declined below even [that of] the five dynasties. T'ang *wen* was lifeless and defeated; the energy of the North was lost and no one had any idea how to restore it.
>
> [Our] dynasty at first followed the traditions of Liao and Sung in using poetry and the classics to choose from among the literati [*shih*]. Selection officials regarded those taking part [in the examinations] as

the most worthy. Wherever the path to glory lay, men raced against each other there. The commentaries [on the classics they studied for the examination] were pale imitations of [Wang An-shih of] Chin-ling; their rhyme schemes [in poetry] were faint reflections of Liu [?] and Cheng [?]. But once they had claimed high rank and grasped a fat salary, they never had any interest in becoming comprehensive Ju in classical [studies] or famous writers in *wen*. T'ang and Sung schools of *wen* were not properly transmitted until Ts'ai [Kuei (d. 1174), who followed the traditions of his father, the chief minister Ts'ai Sung-nien (1107–59)] ... and had direct contact with the spirit and style [*feng-liu*] of Yü-wen [Hsü-chung (1080–1146)] of Chi-yang and Wu [Chi (1090–1142), prefect of] Shen-chou [both of whom were educated in late Sung]. Then the several Ju were able to harmonize with him.

So it is that in the hundred years after Sung and the three hundred years since the beginning of Liao, [only these men] can be called heroic *shih*: Transmitter of Documents Tang [Huai-ying (1134–1211)] Shih-chieh; Han-lin [Drafter] Wang [T'ing-yün (1156–1202)] Tzu-tuan; Finance Commissioner Chou [Ang (1143–1211)] Te-ch'ing; Minister of Rites Yang [Yün-i (1178–1228)] Chih-mei; [Prefect of] Yen-chou Wang [Jo-hsü (1174–1243)] Ts'ung-chih; Secretary of the Right Li [Ch'un-fu (1175–1231)] Chih-ch'un; and Censor Lei [Yüan (1190–1231)] Hsi-yen. As for one neither mired in custom nor beguiled by profit, a noble man who made the learning [that explains] morality, ethics, human nature, and the common good his responsibility, who was immersed in the Six Classics and at home in the hundred schools, who from youth to maturity to old age did not cease in his delight or growth until his death—there is only one man: our Hsien-hsien [Chao Ping-wen]. (*ISWC* 17.1a–2a)

We shall take the points in Yüan's account in reverse order. We learn that Chao Ping-wen, known by his studio name, Hsien-hsien ("Effortless," from Chuang-tzu's statement that "the greatest knowing is effortless"), devoted himself to understanding values throughout his life and immersed himself in the great texts of antiquity. He was the most important figure in a larger group of Han literati who held office under the Jurchen and led the intellectual revival of late Chin. These men reestablished continuity with T'ang and Sung *wen* while living in a state where men treated learning merely as a means of getting ahead. In short, they turned from Liao to Sung tradition and, in the manner of Sung *ku-wen* authors and Han Yü of T'ang, struggled to restore *wen* to its proper role as the way literati maintained a shared commitment to ideals. The state of *wen* is a sign of the state of the literati because, Yüan suggests, the examination system sets a common standard for *wen*. But the revival of *wen*, and the revival of literati spirit, was accomplished when men attacked the examination standards and found their models in the past.

Yüan follows this introduction with his account of Chao's political career, at the end of which he notes Chao's writings. Chao wrote commentaries on the *Book of Changes*, *Doctrine of the Mean*, *Wen Chung-tzu*, *Chuang-tzu*, *Lieh-tzu*, *Analects*, *Mencius*, and the writings of Yang Hsiung. He notes also that Chao edited his own literary collections, from which he excised material pertaining to Buddhism and Taoism (on the grounds that while their ideas were worth reflecting upon, their doctrines were harmful). Finally, he assesses Chao's achievements in prose (his essays are predominantly concerned with moral principles), in poetry (his poems in five-character lines recall Juan Chi and T'ao Yüan-ming), and in calligraphy (his cursive script is outstanding) (*ISWC* 17.5b–6a).

Chao's accomplishments in literary prose, poetry, and calligraphy were intrinsic to the revival of *wen* discussed in the introductory section of the biography. The philosophical texts on which Chao chose to write commentaries were central to his vision of the cultural tradition and were also part of the revival of *wen*. But they cross over into the realm of thinking about *tao*. Indeed, with the exception of the *Chuang-tzu* and the *Lieh-tzu*, these are the texts many eleventh-century literati had treated as works representing both "This Culture of Ours" and "This Way of Ours." This implies that Chao's role in the revival of *wen* can also be seen in terms of *tao*. Indeed, Yüan closes the biography by arguing that Chao had restored the transmission of *tao* in Chin.

> For the transmission of *tao*, one man is enough; but when *tao* is broadened, it is not the achievement of one man alone. In T'ang, Han [Yü] Ch'ang-li and in Sung, Ou-yang [Hsiu] were great Ju [Confucians] who determined whether *tao* would be ignored or revived. [But in T'ang] there were also Huang-fu [Shih] and Chang [Chi], and [in Sung] there were also Tseng [Kung] and Su [Shih]. Only after these several men came to the aid [of Han and Ou-yang] did the purveyors of lesser doctrines cease disputing. The gentleman [Chao Ping-wen] was entirely sincere, pleasant, and easygoing. In his relations with others he did not arrogantly set himself apart. He led the alliance of Our *tao* for forty years without ever relying on his great fame for authority. He served the courts of five emperors and [attained] the rank of minister of a department while maintaining himself in the style of a poor literatus, without the least concern for wealth and honor. He was born in the North in the midst of saddled

horses; without a basis in instruction or progress through teaching, he restored the lost enterprise of sage learning and practiced that which custom had forsaken. In the regions where he sped, there was not one man to appreciate him. This [is why] literature and calligraphy were secondary affairs for the gentleman. How could it be that men should know the value of that which merely cost daily effort without knowing that they should value his *tao*? Huan T'an [of Han] said [in the *Hsin-lun*], "People despise what is near and admire what is far. They saw for themselves Yang [Hsiung] Tzu-yün's salary, position, and appearance, none of which could move the people, so they scorned his writings" [trans. Pokora 1975, 173, *mod. auct.*]. If they were to reread what was praised by the wise and good, it is certain they would be transmitted. T'an's words are still true today. Thus, does not such a man as the gentleman [Chao Ping-wen] depend on something as well? (*ISWC* 17.6b–7a)

Chao had single-handedly restored the transmission of *tao*, Yüan claimed, but whether his efforts would be further extended and *tao* broadened would depend on whether the literati were willing to value the *tao* that lay behind his *wen*.

For Yüan, who lived to see the end of Chin, Chao's cultural role was of greater importance than his political career and loyalty to Chin. He saw Chao much as he saw himself: one whose greatest loyalty was to the cultural tradition (Huang Shih-chien 1981). From a later perspective, however, Yüan's account is striking because it uses the paradigm of the *ku-wen* movements of Han Yü or Ou-yang Hsiu to define Chao's historical role. This explains, I think, why the biography begins with *wen* and ends with *tao*, treats the two as independent traditions, and presents Chao as the man who brought them into conjunction. Perhaps if Chin had defeated the Mongols and the Jurchen elite had transformed themselves along the lines envisioned by the Han literati of Chin, we would see Chao as another Han Yü or Ou-yang Hsiu. Certainly the intellectual revival Chao helped bring about did survive the fall of Chin, in large part because Yüan Hao-wen and others worked to keep it alive in the confusing decades after 1234. But Yüan's hopes for Chao's reputation seem to have been misplaced. We usually assume that, in the intellectual history of Yüan and Ming China at least, the idea of being another Ou-yang Hsiu was overshadowed by the desire to be another Chu Hsi and that the framework men used to understand intellectual change was provided by Tao-hsüeh.

Yüan's decision to go back to the pre–Tao-hsüeh era to find a framework for describing intellectual change is appropriate to the Chin case. But it is also somewhat misleading. Chao Ping-wen's own writings do not simply repeat *ku-wen* themes of the Ou-yang Hsiu generation. It is apparent from Chao's work, although not from the biography, that Chao was well aware of the emergence of Tao-hsüeh and the roles ascribed to Chou Tun-i and the Ch'engs therein. I would suggest that Chao, as a leader of the late Chin intellectual revival, is of particular interest because he sought to establish connections to Northern Sung thinking about *wen* and *tao* that appeared in the aftermath of the failure of the *ku-wen* consensus. From Chao we stand to learn what these categories were coming to mean in literati thinking about values. And this, in turn, leads to conclusions about what "literati learning" was becoming, what Northern Sung literati contributed to that understanding of intellectual culture in later imperial China.

Chao Ping-wen and Literati Independence

Chao Ping-wen's collected writings support Yüan Hao-wen's conclusion that Chao concerned himself with reviving *wen* and *tao*. In essays, letters, prefaces, and other writings Chao sought to define for the literati the correct "practice" of *wen*, as literary composition, and *tao*, as moral conduct. He spoke of eleventh-century examples and teachings, taking Su Shih as a model for the practice of *wen* on the one hand, and Ch'eng I as a theorist of moral universals on the other. In both cases he also recognized cumulative traditions, and, while taking the goal as individual practice, he stressed that literature (and calligraphy) and moral theory were cumulative historical traditions. Chao typically accounted for his efforts to define standards in these areas by referring to a general moral malaise among the literati. He saw a signal lack of integrity on their part. In politics, for example, he complained that literati pandered to the interests of the powerful in order to advance their own careers; they lacked a vision of the true purpose of government. As Chao put it, "They did not know the larger structure [*ta t'i*]" and were unwilling to withdraw in protest (*FSWC* 14.16a). In their social conduct their desires guided them; they did not cultivate their ethical characters (*FSWC* 13.18a). In literary learning they merely memorized texts and imitated the forms required by the examinations; they did not learn how to express their own selves authentically (*FSWC* 19.7b).

It is fair to say, I think, that in the twelfth and thirteenth centuries, for men who looked back to Northern Sung literati models, *wen* and *tao* were the most obviously available means for addressing questions of literati values because they were the most important categories of learning (*hsüeh*). But it is striking that in both cases Chao is concerned with the cultivation of individual character and integrity. This was not the only way of thinking about literati values. Wang An-shih and Ssu-ma Kuang (1019–

86), in spite of their profound political differences, had been alike in defining literati values and learning with reference to their ideas about the institutional systems they believed would secure the common good. Moreover, both had found a basis for their views in the textual tradition and ideas about *tao* as universal process. Thus, Chao Ping-wen's use of *wen* and *tao* to explain how individuals could cultivate themselves needs to be explained.

I think we can find a general explanation by examining what Chao had to say to Chin literati about their relation to political institutions. A set of six undated historical essays speaks directly to this issue. As Chang Po-ch'üan (1985, 135–36) has argued, the essays use issues from political history as analogies for the Chin situation. They represent a pessimistic assessment of the possibility for institutional improvements in the workings of political authority. This assessment leads, I believe, to conclusions about what literati could reasonably expect to accomplish. The thesis of the introductory "General Discussion" is, Chao argues, as true as it is banal. The principles that enable men to establish political order are three: substantial rather than superficial customs, correct rather than deviant talent, and sparing use of taxation and the military. The survival of the polity depends upon "benevolence," but that is not within man's control. From the perspective of Sung political theory this last claim is unusual, not commonplace. Sung literati assumed that the survival of the state was entirely within human control. In contrast, Chao's position is this: literati should act as best as they can and exercise their political responsibilities in the least harmful manner; but whether the state survives will depend upon whether Heaven endows the barbarian rulers with the necessary benevolence. Literati should not aspire to lofty political goals or heroic action. As Chao explains at the end of this introduction, he has refused to glorify heroic individuals in the essays to follow because heroism leads to crisis and war. The only common political goal literati can afford to have, he concludes, is "preserving life" (*FSWC* 14.1a–3a).

Chao's second essay, "On Western Han," elaborates his position. Literati in government should not try to improve the situation by promoting grand schemes to restructure political authority. Western Han history, Chao argues, teaches that those who try to increase central authority at the expense of regional power, in the hope of unifying and rationalizing the political system, destroy what has already been accomplished (*FSWC* 14.3a–5b). Here Chao engages one of the most sensitive political problems of the Jurchen dynasty. Chin was quite decentralized relative to Sung and, in spite of efforts at the center to establish a centralized system managed by civil officials along the lines of those of Chinese dynasties, the tension between the imperial court at the center and military aristocrats with regional power bases was never fully resolved. Although Han literati were allied with central, civil interests, Chao argues that they must resist the temptation to disturb the existing balance of power in an effort to make the center paramount. Chao's belief that literati should work within the structure of authority as it exists is also evident in his discussion of Eastern Han. Literati gain little by a principled refusal to cooperate when various non-bureaucratic elements usurp imperial authority. They must cooperate with "evil men" if they wish to ameliorate the problems evil men have created (FSWC 14.5b–8a). Chao himself continued to serve at court during the military usurpations of the 1210s and the troubled years of Hsüan-tsung's reign. These essays may be seen as self-justification, or his actions may be taken as acceptance of his own conclusions.

The notion of cooperating with "evil men" can, perhaps, be read as a reference to cooperating with the Jurchen in general. In any case, the next essay deals with the problem of political loyalty. History faults only those who transfer allegiance at the moment of dynastic change, Chao argues; those born later are part of the new order and have no choice but to accept its authority (FSWC 14.8a–10a). This point is extended in the fifth essay. The provenance of the rulers does not matter; the question is the nature of their political values, not whether they are Han. Chao goes even further, asserting that all states with rulers who "have in mind the interests of all under Heaven" can rightfully be called "Han," for " 'Han' means treating all under Heaven as a public trust." This, Chao argues, is the meaning of the ancient saying, "When the barbarians enter China, they are to be treated as Chinese." The analogy to Chin is clear: if the Jurchen accept responsibility for the common good, literati need feel no shame in serving them. But, Chao adds, such rulers depend on ministers who know how to "secure the ruler, order the people, shift the style, and change the customs" (FSWC 14.10a–12b).

The final essay, on T'ang history, suggests that Chao, who tried to tutor the last two Jurchen rulers, was pessimistic about the possibility of transforming rulers. The problem with the rulers is that they are rulers, they "like grandiosity and enjoy [military] achievement." Literati who serve in government cannot depend on rulers for guidance, Chao warns; they should follow Mencius' dictum to "value the people first and the altars of the state next." They should see institutions as a means of serving the common good. Instead of trying to perfect institutions and, in the manner of Wang An-shih, recast the present order to match the model of antiquity, literati should accept the blending of past and present institutions that exists at the moment (FSWC 14.12b–14b).

Chao's historical essays speak to the relationship between Han literati and Jurchen power. Chao urges literati to cooperate with those in power, to set aside the idea of large-scale institutional reform, to work within the system, and thus to "preserve life." Chao recognizes that political institutions are controlled by men who cannot be counted upon to see all under Heaven as a public trust. Thus, serving the system itself, holding office and carrying out instructions, is not adequate for those who wish to be truly responsible. Chao puts the literati in a difficult position. Devotion to the interests of the powerful is wrong, but a principled refusal to cooperate is also wrong. Literati cannot rely on the system to know how to act; yet they must act within the system. Chao leaves it up to literati as individuals to determine what is moral according to the situation.

But how are literati to cultivate the personal integrity necessary to being part of the political order without becoming subordinate to it? Chao's answer is simple: if literati learn in the correct manner—that is, if they practice *wen* and *tao* in the correct manner—they will cultivate the ability to act morally even in the most difficult and compromising situations. Through learning literati can find a basis for moral independence and autonomy. If Chao had little hope of changing the political system or transforming Jurchen power holders, he seems to have had some hope that the literati could be persuaded to transform themselves into morally responsible men. This was a fairly practical strategy. In contrast to other Han officials, many of whom had gained posts in the civil administration on the basis of their earlier service in the military or clerical bureaucracy, literati gained office through achievements in learning. They were, therefore, the group in the Chin elite most open to persuasion. The late Chin intellectual revival that took place during Chao's lifetime signaled the success of this strategy.

We find an indication of the direction Chao's efforts took and a mark of his success in the preface to his literary collection, written in 1123 by Chao's friend and fellow official Yang Yün-i. Yang's categories are the familiar *wen* and *tao*, but he also treats *li* (principle) and the Ju doctrine of Confucius and Mencius as the basis of learning and *wen*.

> Ju [the Confucian view] makes for correct learning. If it is not pure in Ju, it is not learning. *Li* [principle] makes *wen* correct. If it is not rooted in *li*, it is not *wen*. From Wei and Chin on, those who learned did not investigate the teachings of Confucius and Mencius, and became mired in different starting points [of Buddhism and Taoism]; they did not find a basis in the doctrines of benevolence and righteousness, but esteemed empty talk. Superior men have faulted this. Today Minister of Rites Chao is truly the leader of the alliance of This Culture of Ours.... [These writings of his] are all [composed in] the language of benevolence and righteousness. It appears he has been able to achieve this because his learning unfailingly returns to Confucius and Mencius while different starting points do not adulterate it. What is called the correctness of Ju and the correctness of *li*

is completely realized here. All those who learn will ... know what to follow. ... He has served our *tao* well. (*FSWC* preface)

Taken literally, this preface can mislead us on two counts. First, it presents Chao as a champion of a Confucian orthodoxy. Chao Ping-wen himself encouraged this view of his work: he edited out of his collection all pieces he thought were tinged by Taoist and Buddhist influences (yet he allowed them to be published by a monastery). Second, it implies a perfect integration of *wen* and *tao*, in which writing serves only to transmit moral principles. Read in this manner, Chao fits neatly into Sung Tao-hsüeh tradition, although somewhat too much weight is given to *wen* in his writings.

In fact, Chao's own writings make the problem of learning much more complex. He avoids fusing *wen* and *tao*, treating them instead as two separate disciplines. Our task in the following pages shall be to resurrect that difference, only then asking how and why Chao makes them compatible.

Wen as a Literati Practice

In various writings Chao Ping-wen articulates a general theory of the practice of prose, poetry, and calligraphy. Two kinds of relationships are at its center: between the individual and his works, and between the individual who writes and the cumulative tradition of writing. Quite correctly, Chao points out that his views are based on those of the men of the past. In fact, the position he adopts was defined in the eleventh century by Su Shih and his circle. Chao's debt to Su is evident in his frequent use of Su's words and ideas, although he treats Ou-yang Hsiu as the great Sung model. What Chao has to say about *wen* has little to do with moral doctrine, but it does reveal a possible connection between the practice of *wen* and literati values.

Chao used Tang Huai-ying as a model for other Chin literati. In a stele inscription for Tang's grave (*FSWC* 11.16b–18b) and in an introduction to Tang's literary collection (*FSWC* 15.1a–1b), Chao asserts that Tang obtained the "correct artery," or simply the "correctness," of the "men of the past" (*ku-jen*) in his own literature and calligraphy. Thus, although Tang was one of several men at the time famous for prose and poetry, he was the first in Chin to recognize and continue the correct tradition. This tradition of *wen* began in antiquity and was revived during the major later dynasties in manners appropriate to the times. The literature and calligraphy of the pre-Ch'in period was inimitable, but in the Han dynasty there was writing that enabled men to see the source of the *tao*. In T'ang, Han Yü's writing gave men a sense of the vastness of the whole, and in Sung, Ou-yang Hsiu's encouraged readers to persevere. All these works represented "the correctness of *wen-chang*" and commanded the attention and respect of men, just as the greatest calligraphy can make viewers feel reverent. Chao stresses Tang's mastery of the technical skills necessary to continue the normative tradition. He was equally adept in prose, poetry, and calligraphy: "The men of the past made reputations for only one art. Tang alone had them all. He can be called complete." The normative tradition is not a narrow doctrinal tradition, however. Tang was learned in "the doctrines of Ju, Taoism, Buddhism, and the many masters and hundred schools." His work realized the larger purpose of *wen*—to inspire and move men to a concern with values, without making the inculcation of values its goal. On the other hand, Tang did not make composing good *wen* his goal, either. The stele inscription begins with the claim, borrowed from Su Shih's "Preface to *The First Collection from the Journey South*" ("*Nan-hsing ch'ien-chi hsü*"), that "in *wen-chang* true skill lies not in being able to do it but in being unable not to do it. True unusualness lies not in forcing it to be unusual but in it being impossible for it not to be so" (*FSWC* 11.16b–18b). Tang's technical skill, mastery of diverse genres of expression, and revival of the true artery of the past were all achievements subordinate to his effort to give apt expression to what he had in mind.

The idea that *wen* expresses what the author has in mind is an essential aspect of good *wen*, that is, *wen* that continues the true line of tradition into the present. In his preface to Tang's literary collection Chao elaborates on this. Here again his principal points are drawn from Su Shih's descriptions of his own practice.

> In *wen*, the intent [*i*] is the principal thing. Language is merely to get the intent across. The men of the past did not esteem empty elaboration. They chose their words according to the situation only to manifest what their own hearts wanted to say. When there was something their hearts were unable to say but they were able to manifest in *wen*, this too was the perfection of *wen*. Water provides an analogy: when it is not moving, it is still; when splashing up against rocks and whirling around pools—turbulent, a dragon hovering; calming, a phoenix pressing—the thousand variations and ten thousand transformations cannot be exhausted. This is the most perfect *wen* in the world. (*FSWC* 15.1a)

The idea here is that good *wen* expresses the individual mind's responses to changing circumstances. As circumstances vary, so will the mode and form of expression vary. There is something constant—water is always water, and water can always return to stillness—but its manifestations are diverse. This is also a statement of fundamental values for literati. They should be able to respond to change and manifest their minds in diverse ways without losing their own voices or integrity. The work will then reveal the true character of the man. Tang's *wen-chang*, Chao continues, "is like he is as a man" (*ju ch'i wei jen*). Chao holds that Ou-yang Hsiu illustrated these ideas and Tang "apprehended the correct [approach to *wen*] through the *wen* of Ou-yang" (*FSWC* 15.1b). Perhaps we can say that Tang the man is the "one" and his compositions are the "many"; his one voice is capable of a multiplicity of expressions.

The idea that cultural accomplishment in prose, poetry, and calligraphy[3] ought to manifest the character of the author and demonstrate that he is capable of responding to change is an idea about how literati ought to be. Tang was versed in many doctrines, yet instead of writing to promote a particular doctrine, he responded personally to specific situations through *wen*.

But how, precisely, does one get to the point of having the voice or self that can maintain its integrity while responding variously? At this point it is tempting to shift from Chao's discussion of practicing *wen* to his account of *tao*, in expectation of finding a theory about cultivating the self that is capable of responding to change. But Chao does not make this connection. We do find an answer, however, in a long letter to Li Ching. We learn from the letter that Li had sent a number of poems that carefully avoided any sign of influence from "the men of the past," thus to ensure that the poems would be "authentic" expressions of himself. Criticizing this desire to be free of tradition, Chao offered himself as an example and argued that the individual voice is formed through synthesizing the accomplishments of the past. Here, too, Chao draws on ideas from the Su circle about the synthesis of tradition. The passage begins with the important supposition that men have given characters (*hsing*, often translated as "human nature"), which correspond to some degree with their literary choices.

> I have said that the men of the past each apprehended one aspect of poetry, and generally it was the semblance of his own character. For example, T'ao Yüan-ming, Hsieh Ling-yün, Wei Ying-wu, Wang Wei, Liu Tsung-yüan, and Po Chü-i apprehended blandness [*ch'ung-tan*]; Chiang Yen, Pao Chao, Li Po, and Li Ho apprehended loftiness [*ch'iao-chün*]; Meng Chiao and Chia Tao further apprehended the quality of anxiety in withdrawal [*yu-yu pu-p'ing chih ch'i*]. As for Old Tu Fu—he can be said to have combined these. Tu Fu, however, understood that poetry was poetry; he had yet to understand how what was not poetry could be poetry. But Han Yü let ancient-style prose spread till it overflowed and became poetry; then the variations of past and present were realized. Li Po was stronger in language than in structure [*li*];[4] Po Chü-i was stronger in structure

than in language. Su Shih further combined into a unity Li Po's unbridled quality [*hao*] and Po Chü-i's structure. Thus, we look on past men from a superior vantage, but we cannot dismiss past men.

You go too far when you hold that T'ang and Sung poets, at their best, avoided the vulgar but in fact lacked elegant correctness [*feng-ya*, typical of the verse in the *Book of Poetry*]. What is called "being close to elegant correctness" does not mean sticking exactly to a single rule like Chin and [Liu-]Sung litterateurs [*tz'u-jen*]. As for saying that Liu Tsung-yüan stayed close to the ancient while Han Yü transformed the ancient—this is Li Ch'un-fu's mistake of treating the consequence as the cause; such is not my view. To think that poetry at the level of Li Po and Tu Fu is inadequate is as perverse and foolish as [saying that good] painting [must] reach what is without form and [good] hearing reach what is without sound. This is so for calligraphy as well.

In establishing your intent and using language, you do not imitate a single word of past men. This is the sublime achievement of poets. But one still enters [the sublime] from the midst of the past men. An analogy would be plucking a lute without learning from a score, measuring things without using a scale, or building things without using line and mark but instead singly following your own mind. Even if you did it all your life, you would not accomplish anything worthwhile.

Therefore, in doing prose one should learn from the Six Classics, Tso Ch'iu-ming, Chuang Chou, Ssu-ma Ch'ien, Chia I, Liu Hsiang, Yang Hsiung, and Han Yü. In doing poetry one should learn from the *Book of Poetry,* "Li sao," "Nineteen Old Poems," and on down to Li Po and Tu Fu. In calligraphy one should learn from the [inscriptions on] bronze and stone of the Three Eras, Wang Hsi-chih, Ou-yang Hsün, Yü Shih-nan, Yen Chen-ch'ing, and Liu Kung-ch'üan. Completely apprehend what the various men were strongest in and then, excelling, form your own voice [*tzu ch'eng i chia*]. Do not aim only to learn from past men, do not aim only to reject past men. Since the beginning of writing, no one has ever rejected past men and established himself independently. (*FSWC* 19.2b–4a)

Irrespective of one's personal character, one must master the tradition, making choices only about what to adopt from the variety of the past. On one level this is a matter of formal techniques. One learns the "language use" of past poets, calligraphers, and prose writers. On another level, however, this involves acquiring the ideas and attitudes of the past writers as men. *Wen* is not merely an "art" (*i*).

But this poem was [the result of] human skill in constructing phrases; past men were right to call such [merely] one art. As for the intent of poetry and prose—they should take illuminating the kingly way and aiding transformation through education as the principal things. The Six Classics are my teacher. Can you refer to this as "one art"? (*FSWC* 19.4a)

Having raised the issue of a socially responsible, intellectual role for poetry and prose (promoting good rulership and inculcating values in the people), Chao now proceeds to describe his own synthesis.

Chia I, Tung Chung-shu, Ssu-ma Ch'ien, Yang Hsiung, Han Yü, Ou-yang Hsiu, and Ssu-ma Kuang—theirs is the prose of great Ju. I am still unable to learn from them. Liang Su, P'ei Hsiu, Ch'ao Chiung, and Chang Shang-ying—theirs is the prose of duties and principles [*ming-li chih wen*]. I learn from them. Li Po, Tu Fu, and Su Shih—theirs is the writing of litterateurs. I learn from their language, but not their intent. T'ao Yüan-ming and Po Chü-i—theirs is the poetry of lofty literati, and I learn from their intent but not their language. (*FSWC* 19.4a–4b)

Chao's personal synthesis was constructed after studying the wider range of writings he noted in the passage above. The core of values he subscribes to is not easy to label. In prose, instead of identifying with the defenders of Ju moral-political ideals, he follows less well-known T'ang and Sung men who sought to integrate Ju, Buddhist, and (to a lesser extent) Taoist ideas. In poetry he aims to combine the very different approaches to language of Li, Tu, and Su and the ideas of T'ao Yüan-ming, famed for renouncing the world, and Po Chü-i, an example of engagement. Finding a voice in *wen* and cultivating a persona in life, Chao suggests, is a matter of bringing together tensions and contrasts.

But mastering past techniques and choosing among past ideas is not enough. Later in the letter Chao answers Li Ching's complaint that Li has been stuck in a brushwork technique and unable to accomplish "flying movement" (*fei-tung*). The subject is calligraphy at this point, but Chao uses the difference between learning technique and flying movement to propose a polarity between diligent, cumulative study and the kind of spontaneous, free-flowing responsiveness required for flying movement.

But the concealed brush tip [technique] is only one starting point for calligraphy. What we value is learning from past men in all aspects. Earlier men called this imitating calligraphic models; this was not doing whatever you pleased. Really accumulating strength over a long period, beginning with the regular style, is what previous men called being able to walk after you had learned to sit. Flying movement is the sublime [achievement] in the minds of our kind [*wu pei*]; it is not something you learn. If the common run of men can accumulate learning but are unable [to realize] flying movement, while our kind are able [to realize] flying movement but are unable to accumulate learning, we both fail by being one-sided. (*FSWC* 19.4b–5a)

Spontaneous, unself-conscious practice cannot be learned; yet it should be practiced only in the context of cumulative learning from the past. For Chao, as we saw in his account of Tang Huai-ying, the ability to respond spontaneously and flexibly to change—to respond with "flying movement"—is the greatest achievement. But as Chao's instructions to Li Ching suggest, the guarantee that those with this gift will be responsible in composing *wen* and acting as men is the result of forming themselves through synthetic, cumulative learning.

What conclusions may we draw from Chao's standards for good *wen*? Most immediately, his standards allow him to separate "our kind," those who have formed their characters and voices by drawing on the cultural tradition and respond to change, from their run-of-the-mill contemporaries, who are stuck imitating others. Li Ching is an interesting problem. He wishes to achieve a voice of his own but fails to learn from the past; he wants to be free and spontaneous but finds himself locked in by technique. He still has a way to go, but Chao encourages him to think of himself as one of "our kind." What makes "our kind" better? They are independent of one another, yet they share a common culture; they have their own individual voices, yet these are constructed from a shared repertoire; they have their own integrity, yet they are able to respond flexibly to change. Together they are a collection of different voices, yet each has cultivated his voice in the same manner and learned the history, sound, and meaning of all the other voices. They should be able to harmonize with each other—at the very least they will be able to "know" each other—even if they live in a world where few can carry a tune. And they are able to put what they know into practice, sounding differently according to the circumstance, but never losing their true voices. As Chao presents it, learning to practice *wen* is a form of literati self-cultivation, in the sense that it is a means of establishing an individuated self within a shared culture. The practice of *wen* provides a vehicle for manifesting the integrity of that self in an inconstant world. But if this is so, why does Chao find it necessary to treat *tao* as a separate practice?

Realizing the Tao as a Literati Practice

Chao Ping-wen's literary collection begins with a set of essays on the theme of what he calls "doing *tao*" (*wei tao*), "practicing *tao*" (*hsing tao*), or "cultivating *tao*" (*hsiu tao*). As these terms suggest, the essays are about the kind of action that realizes *tao*. Although these essays include an understanding of *tao* as universal natural process, they treat what Chao calls the "teaching" (*chiao*) that men should follow to be true to *tao* in social action. In his "Inscription for the Subprefectural School at Yen," Chao places his understanding of *chiao* in context. It is for the literati and it entails learning: "Literati rise through learning, and the people submit to their transformative [influence]." It comes from the Ju tradition: "This learning begins with attaining knowledge and investigating things, rectifying the mind and making the will sincere, [all] to the point of ordering the state and pacifying the world. Below, even to the techniques of *tao* and *yin* and *yang*, norms and rules, and war and agriculture—all are uniformly based on Ju." Finally, it relates action and knowledge by supposing that men innately possess that which enables them to be ethical: "I have said that all men have the mind [for knowing] the good and the ability to be good [*liang hsin liang neng*], it is merely that they have not yet had the means to develop it." And further,

> All that with which Heaven endows men is the same as [that with which it endows] sages and worthies. Those who have not avoided acting as villagers have simply been blinded by selfish desires. As human desires diminish ever more, Heaven's principle [*t'ien-li*] becomes ever brighter, and my mind becomes the mind of Heaven-and-earth, then benevolence will not be far off. (*FSWC* 13.16b–18a)[5]

These passages from the inscription show that Chao Ping-wen has adopted language from Sung Tao-hsüeh to discuss the "teaching." This was quite self-conscious; Chao uses the term "Tao-hsüeh" to refer to both the Sung school of moral philosophy and the activity of cultivating the innate ability to practice *tao*. The following passage from "An Explanation of the Nature, the Way, and the Teaching" indicates that he has drawn his ideas from the Ch'eng-Chu school of Tao-hsüeh. Earlier in the essay Chao has been discussing Mencius' claim that human nature is good and that all men possess the four hearts.

> "The great man is able not to lose the heart of a newborn babe" [*Mencius* 4B/12]. This is a case of following one's nature and putting it into practice; therefore, it is called *tao*. Human desires have domi-

nated for a long time. Is it not difficult to seek to recover the actuality of *t'ien-li* in a single day? Certainly one should devote [oneself] to learning in order to extend one's knowledge. First, [one should] become clear about the discrimination between the principled and the profitable so that each affair and every thing is obvious. When I have gone over this in my mind for a long time, *t'ien-li* will become ever brighter and the artificial will diminish ever more. I will then have come closer to reaching the realm of sages and worthies. Therefore, the sages cultivated *tao* [i.e., followed their hearts of innocence] to teach all under Heaven and cause them to curb human desire and preserve *t'ien-li*. Thus, cultivating *tao* is called *chiao* [teaching]. After Mencius it was not transmitted. Only the two masters Chou [Tun-i] and Ch'eng [I] restored the learning cut off for a thousand years, expressed the secrets of previous sages, and taught men to seek it before happiness and anger were expressed. (*FSWC* 1.3a–3b)

Nonetheless, does Chao's use of the language of Tao-hsüeh mean that he has accepted its philosophical system? He subscribes to the idea that learning is conducive to awareness of innate moral capability and shares a belief in the moral autonomy and responsibility of the individual. But his preference for syncretic moral thought in prose, noted in his letter to Li Ching, should make us cautious. Indeed, throughout these essays Chao maintains the view, stated in the first line of the first essay ("On the Origin of Teachings"), that *tao*, as a term for what is ultimately real, is beyond particularistic definition. "It refers inclusively to the marvelous substance [*miao-t'i*]" (*FSWC* 1.1a), and "it is without 'other' and without 'this,' without large and without small; it includes all things and comprehends the hundred schools. The sages did not regard *tao* as their own possession; did *tao* favor only the sages?" (*FSWC* 1.1a–1b). In the famous phrase "Many paths return to the same starting point," Chao finds confirmation for his belief that no single teaching can be exclusively correct: "*Tao* is only one, but there are different teachings," and it cannot be said that "the theories of Buddhists and Taoists are all wrong" (*FSWC* 1.7a). Different teachings take different versions of *tao* as the basis for practice: "There is the *tao* of the void and the *tao* of great centrality" (*FSWC* 1.7a). Although in these essays Chao argues that the best "teaching" for literati is "great centrality," there are other possibilities: "Now the *tao* of the pure void and quiet extinction cuts off society and departs from human relations; it is not directly concerned with human practice. One may practice it or not as one pleases. As for the great constants of ruler and minister, father and son, husband and wife, older and younger brother, and friend and friend— how can one depart from them for a single day?" (*FSWC* 1.8b). Because he aims to promote a teaching that takes social relations into account, this teaching is most useful. But this does not mean it is natural or absolute; Chao argues, for example, that taking the five virtues as universals is a Han idea of great utility, but not a cosmic given (*FSWC* 1.1b).

Chao rejects exclusive claims even within the bounds of Ju doctrine. For example, he sets aside the accusation, attributed by him to followers of Chou and Ch'eng, that the great *ku-wen* writers Han Yü and Ou-yang Hsiu "did not know *tao*," explaining that such critics overlooked the cumulative nature of thought. He also rebuts the charge that "Ou-yang's learning was too shallow and Su [Shih]'s learning too adulterated [by Buddhism and Taoism]" with the comment that "Ou[-yang] and Su were strongest in changes in regulating and aiding," while allowing that "for the constants, one of course should return to Chou and Ch'eng." And he argues that "Tao-hsüeh also erred in treating centrality as a [fixed] correct position and benevolence as the inherent nature; it drifted off into Buddhism and Taoism unconsciously, its error even worse than the commentary study [it opposed]" (*FSWC* 1.3a–4a).

In spite of these objections, Chao insists on the idea that men are innately endowed with *t'ien-li* and that practicing *tao* requires its cultivation through learning and ridding oneself of selfish desires. Thus, to determine Chao Ping-wen's approach to *tao* as practice, we must understand what he means by *t'ien-li*. In fact, Chao's essays do explain this innate moral capability of man. "Explanation of the Nature, the Way, and the Teaching" contains the following passage.

> The *Record of Rites* says, "Man comes into being and is quiescent. This is the nature of Heaven." It also says, "Centrality [*chung*] is the great basis of the world." This refers to the original substance of the nature. Before happiness, anger, sorrow, and joy are expressed, when there is not a single particle of the selfishness of human desire, it is purely *t'ien-li*. Therefore [the *Record*] says, "Heaven's decree is called the nature." (*FSWC* 1.2b)

Chao has given equal weight, perhaps priority, to the term *chung*; *t'ien-li* describes *chung* before any action has taken place. In "On the Origin of Teachings," he explains that the sage, as one who never deviates from his original nature in responding to events, "does not go outside of great centrality [*chung*]" (*FSWC* 1.1b). The equation of *t'ien-li* with *chung* is explicit in "Explanation of Centrality."

> Centrality is the correct *li* of all under Heaven.... Perfectly impartial and perfectly correct, without a single particle of human desire, it is not being biased in favor of a single thing. At this time [before

emotions are expressed], if we do not call it *chung*, how can we describe this *li*? When it is expressed in human relations and affairs, happiness does not go too far, and one is happy about what one should be happy about, ... angry about what one should be angry about. One is merely according with the *chung* innate to one's nature. (*FSWC* 1.6a–6b)

"How do I know," Chao continues in the same essay, "that this is *t'ien-li*?" He asserts that Heaven-and-earth function according the principle of *chung* and that this is apparent from the "harmony" (*ho*) of nature. It follows that man, as a creature of Heaven-and-earth, is endowed with *chung* and that "those who are able to cultivate it bring the blessing of harmony" to human society (*FSWC* 1.7a). In "Explanation on Constancy in Practice" ("Yung shuo"), Chao explains that to practice *chung*, and thus through impartiality and balance to keep all parts in a harmonious whole, requires "varying from the norm in responding to change." That is, the ability to be "constantly *chung*," or to "hit the mark all the time" (*shih chung*), and thus to follow one's nature and *t'ien-li* in practice, requires *ch'üan*: deviating from the constant in a measured response to changing circumstance. In other words, to remain centered and keep things in balance requires tilting to one side or the other as circumstances dictate rather than sticking to traditional norms (*FSWC* 1.10a–11a).

Put into practice, *t'ien-li* is the innate ability to judge partial interests from a standpoint of disinterestedness. Chao does not treat this disinterestedness as an attitude gained by willing oneself to believe in the unity of all things or the reality of a greater whole. His most lyrical account of his philosophical view, a Tao-hsüeh rendition of T'ao Yüan-ming's "The Return," makes it clear that he regards the disinterestedness of *chung* or *t'ien li* as a real faculty of the human being that is often obscured by selfish desire (*FSWC* 1.16a–17a). What is equally present or innate in the nature of every man is only this ability. Chao does not take the view that there is a universal moral nature constituted by the total sum of *li* or a set of ethical principles. *Chung*, as an ability, is the "one thing" all men possess. For Chao the five constant virtues can be defined only in terms of being true to *chung*, not as things or self-dependent principles in themselves (*FSWC* 1.1b). Similarly, he uses *chung* to explain some of the major philosophical concepts Tao-hsüeh thinkers used to understand man.

> But what the sages called *chung* was something to be accomplished. When spoken of in terms of substance, they called it "unmoving." In terms of the pure and single, they called it "[the heart of] the newborn babe." In terms of what is endowed, they called it the "nature." In terms of what all proceed through, they called it *tao*. In terms of

something to cultivate, they called it the "teaching." In terms of the not-changing, they called it the "constant." In terms of not-going-astray, they called it "integrity" [*ch'eng*]. (*FSWC* 1.8a)

It is fair to conclude, I think, that the idea of *chung* is at the center of Chao's understanding of practicing, cultivating, and "doing" *tao*.

By adopting the language of Tao-hsüeh while redefining concepts central to that school, Chao Ping-wen has made the enterprise of being moral far less exclusive. On one hand, it allows him to include Ou-yang Hsiu and Su Shih among those who "understood *tao*."[6] On the other hand, he can point out that Taoists and Buddhists also prize *chung*, even while they do not treat it in the context of social accomplishment (*FSWC* 1.7b). *Chung* makes moral action a matter of balancing and accommodating diverse interests from a standpoint of impartiality. The ethical course is determined in response to changing circumstance; it is situational and relative, proven by whether it furthers harmony in a world of conflicting interests. It fits well with the realities of politics, for it justifies accommodating partial interests. One who is moral by being *chung* does not find it necessary to demand that those in power transform themselves out of their self-interested state before he will cooperate. Good choices, Chao explains at one point, balance the demands of benevolence (all-embracing love) and righteousness (strict adherence to standards), and involve learning from both the sage-kings and later kings (*FSWC* 1.2a).

Although Chao adopts the language of Tao-hsüeh, his understanding of the universal moral capability of men is limited to the faculty of impartial judgment. The mind does not contain the sum of *li*; it provides a basis for moral autonomy without being a source of moral knowledge complete in itself. This is illustrated in Chao's essay "Explanation of Integrity," where he asks, "How does one practice *tao*?" His initial answer does seem to assume an internal source of moral knowledge to which men only need be true: "The means of practicing it is one thing; it is called 'integrity' [*ch'eng*]. Integrity is not deceiving oneself." But as this idea is developed, we find that integrity and not deceiving oneself are understood in external, social terms. Not deceiving oneself "begins from learning," a process defined as using the moral faculty to discriminate between righteousness and profit in affairs. Integrity is something acquired: "Broad learning, questioning, careful thought, clear discrimination, and diligent practice are how one learns this integrity." And the "completion" of integrity is a social achievement. One must develop the ability to be appropriate to the time, then become so without cease, and finally assist in transforming others. In the end, Chao concludes, only one who "completes himself and completes others is *ch'eng*" (*FSWC* 1.8a–10a).

This does not make the enterprise of *tao* irrelevant, however. Chao has argued that all men are innately capable of acting morally—in his terms. Individuals possess the ability to determine what is right according to the situation; they cannot blame their failures on the political environment. The basis for moral action is real. Yet because it is limited, it is also true that realizing the moral faculty in practice is not enough to make one a complete human being. For establishing a personal identity, literati cannot rely on the moral faculty. They must turn to the enterprise of *wen*.

Wen and Tao as the Two Sides of Literati Learning

In Chao Ping-wen's vision, realizing the common good required men who could participate in the political system while maintaining their independence. *Wen* and *tao*, as the two sides of literati learning, provided the grounds for that independence, as Chao explains practice in these two areas. The cultural tradition provides the individual with the resources and techniques to establish a personal identity through writing. Literati who do so—and the men active in the later Chin intellectual revival did so—gain identities that resonate with the Chinese past. Who they are cannot be adequately described by their careers as officials under the Jurchen rulers. Just as literati can establish a personal relation to the cultural tradition, so can they establish a personal connection to *tao* as universal, cosmic process. The innate moral faculty Chao speaks of is available to each person. Individuals can judge for themselves what is in the interest of the whole and how they can keep their balance in a world of change. Chao's literati are to serve in government, but they have a real alternative to taking the interests of rulers, the demands of the system, or their own private desires as guides.

Chao's explanations of the enterprises of *wen* and *tao* ask literati to see themselves as real participants in both the cultural tradition and Heaven-and-earth, as the two greater contexts in which the Chin order exists. Seen in this light, his political-historical essays, which oppose efforts to perfect the institutional system, appear to be aimed at persuading literati not to treat the dynasty as the only context in which they live. Seeing themselves as part of these two greater contexts encourages literati to view the dynasty as a passing phase. They should, as far as possible, use its institutions to further the common good, but they should not let themselves become adjuncts or servants of the institutions and the rulers.

Chao is not asking literati simply to imagine themselves as participants in the cultural tradition and Heaven-and-earth. He sets out the substantive ways of literary-artistic practice and moral cultivation through which men can demonstrate that they are true participants. Note, however, that the substantive ways he defines are processes. Chao explains how men can establish cultural identities and realize the moral faculty; he does not say what the individual identity should be or what the ethical choice for a given situation is. In his scheme of things there is a correct tradition of learning how to speak and act that all literati can have in common, but what they say and what they do will vary. Setting standards for the process of participating in *wen* and *tao* allows Chao to treat the two enterprises as the basis for the corporate identity of the literati, a particular group within the broader Chin political elite. Chao is concerned, I think, with finding the basis for literati identity that will not divide literati from each other.

Participation, in this case, is also possession. If *wen* and *tao* are things all literati can participate in, they are also things that make the literati as a group unique among other interest groups in the elite. Literati become spokesmen for the cultural tradition because they continue it in the present, and for moral universals because they realize them in practice. In their own eyes, at least, they can act as arbiters of Chinese civilization and serve as the source of legitimacy for those who wish to be seen as cultured and moral. The expansion of the examination system during Chao's lifetime, which brought increasing numbers of literati into government at the expense of other groups of Han officials, reminds us that Jurchen rulers were not averse to Chinese forms of legitimation.

Chao Ping-wen's reliance on Northern Sung literati sources to define the true tradition of participating in *wen* and *tao* suggests another perspective on his work. Han literati in Chin were well aware that there were literati in Southern Sung as well. They read their writings and discussed their intellectual concerns among themselves in the North. We may only speculate, lacking Chao's own words on this, that Chao, in addition to finding persuasive ideas and models in Northern Sung sources, believed that continuing Northern Sung approaches to *wen* and *tao* made Chin literati the equal of their Southern Sung contemporaries, who also justified their views as the continuation of Northern Sung ideas. In this view, *wen* and *tao* provided Chao with a means of defining both the legitimacy of Han literati in the Chin polity and the legitimacy of Chin literati in Chinese history.

The use of *wen* and *tao* to speak to questions of literati values, and the reliance on Northern Sung ideas to do so, has some implications for how we think about intellectual culture during Sung and later periods. Chao Ping-wen's writings illustrate a simple point. Tao-hsüeh captured the center of literati thinking about *tao*, but thinking about *tao* was only part of the intellectual culture of the literati. Chao recognized this and, looking back to Northern Sung, sought to understand how the philosophy of moral self-cultivation established by Ch'eng I and the ideas about literary and artistic practice developed by Su Shih and his circle could be made compatible as two sides of a larger whole. Making Ch'eng and Su compatible meant reducing each, although I think Ch'eng I's Tao-hsüeh ultimately suffered more than Su Shih's ideas about *wen*.[7]

As Chao shows, Su and Ch'eng can be accommodated in a single vision of literati learning that treats *wen* and *tao* as separate, but complementary, enterprises. Su, after all, saw cultural accomplishment as the best way literati could learn to bring *tao* into practice in responding to changing circumstances. Although he discussed philosophical issues in his commentaries on the classics, his greatest influence was felt among those who believed that prose, poetry, calligraphy, and painting could have real value. Similarly, Ch'eng had a place for the cultural tradition in moral self-cultivation, but he spoke most directly to men who sought a real foundation for ethics in the self. For Su, "ethical conduct" (*te-hsing*) was not of fundamental concern. He was certain that men could learn to act responsibly without having to rely on fixed ideas about good and bad—ideas that limited the individual's ability to respond to events flexibly and spontaneously. For Ch'eng, the "learning of literature" (*wen-hsüeh*) was not a priority. He believed that moral self-cultivation was furthered by learning from the sages through texts, but he held that literary and artistic pursuits distracted men from realizing their moral nature and were thus an obstacle to true learning. From the vantage of one bent on establishing the unity of literati learning and tradition, the different priorities of Su and Ch'eng, given that both were profoundly concerned with the individual's moral and intellectual independence, might appear as parts of a larger whole, even if a more historical reading of each position suggests that it was originally conceived to be sufficient in itself.

The difference between *wen* and *tao*, as Chao defines them, illuminates the kind of synthesis he envisioned and, indirectly, points to a enduring tension in literati values. Clearly, the "sources" of values are not the same for each enterprise. For *wen* the source is the cultural tradition, the body of texts, language, and ideas accumulated through history. The cultural tradition is available to all men, provided they make the great effort necessary to become broadly acquainted with it. It is outside the person but can be acquired and embodied by the person in practice, according to ability and inclination, through synthesis of the achievements of past men and past ages. The individual cultivates a voice, ideas, and interests that match his character yet develop it; Chao takes as a given that men are of different characters. The cultural tradition does not determine what a man should become in any specific sense; it allows a man to elaborate and refine his self into a more sophisticated and complex embodiment of the qualities perceived in past men. Chao may not listen to literati with shallow, narrow, and uncultivated voices, but he does not demand that cultivated voices sound the same; there is room for diversity.

Tao, however, is outside culture and history, although Chao insists that "teachings" on the practice of *tao* are historical. The "source" of values in practicing *tao* is a universal ability innate to all men: *chung*. The source of *chung* is Heaven-and-earth, of which man is a creature. *Chung* is accessible to all men who are willing to curb selfish desires and become aware of their ability to be impartial. All men are absolutely the same in this regard. The possibility of truly fair judgments, which take into account the real interests of all things as part of a whole, is grounded in the cosmos; it does not depend on culture to be so. Cultural sophistication does not make men *chung*. Being *chung*, however, does not make men cultured, either. Chao is uneasy with this; he repeatedly argues that the moral capability must be developed through cumulative study, although he does not explain why this should be so.

Literati learning thus has two foundations, equally real but fundamentally different: the historical tradition of China and the innate capability of man as a creature of Heaven-and-earth. Chao argues that both should be cultivated: the first to give form to the individual self, and the second to enable the individual to keep that self centered in social action. It is up to the individual to combine these two aspects of learning, to embody *wen* and *tao* and keep them alive and relevant in the present. Yüan Hao-wen asked readers to think of Chao Ping-wen in this way: as a man who had made "This *Wen* of Ours" and "Our *Tao*" his personal responsibility.

I would suggest that in Chao Ping-wen's understanding of *wen* as literary and artistic practice, and *tao* as the cultivation of the faculty of moral judgment we can derive essential elements of literati intellectual culture. First, Chao recognizes two great realms as sources of value: the cultural tradition and Heaven-and-earth. Second, he sees the literati as responsible for holding them together through their action as individuals. (This is not Tung Chung-shu's [ca. 179–ca. 104 B.C.] imperial Confucianism, in which the ruler has the ultimate responsibility for the unity of Heaven, earth, and man.) Third, we see that the aim of learning is to establish a foundation for the moral autonomy of the literati as a group in a broader society, with a shared intellectual identity. Like Su Shih and Ch'eng I, Chao accepts the inevitability of tension between political power and moral authority. The tension can be attributed in part to their particular political contexts—Chao as a Han under Jurchen rule and Su and Ch'eng as opponents of Wang An-shih's regime—but ultimately, I think, it is a consequence of believing that larger values are realized only through individual action. But within literati learning there is certainly an endemic tension between the kind of individuality and creativity necessary to the literary and artistic pursuits that mark participation in the cultural tradition and the commitment to the constant and holistic values that make it possible to be part of universal process. Chao Ping-wen was hardly the first to face these tensions, but he helps us understand how they became deeply rooted in literati learning.

Notes

1. There are some important exceptions to this. De Bary (1953) looks at the "broader" history of eleventh-century literati thought, notes the importance of political concerns, and includes a discussion of Wang An-shih. By calling these men Neo-Confucians, however, he leaves the distinction between them and those who figured in Chu Hsi's narrow view unclear. Tillman (1982 and 1992a) discusses the value of maintaining such distinctions in the analysis of Sung intellectual history.

2. See *TS* 201.5725–26, which probably draws the device from the late eighth-century literatus and intellectual Liang Su; see his preface to Li Han's collection in *CTW* 518.6a.

3. For the application of this view to calligraphy specifically, see Chao's "Inscription for the Hall for Treasuring Ink," *FSWC* 13.14b–16a.

4. *Li* is often translated as "principle" in philosophical writings. Here, however, Chao is referring to a traditional dichotomy in the analysis of literary writing, the dichotomy between language use (*tz'u* and, often, *wen*) and the structure or organization of the piece. His point is that both are involved in the expression of intent, but writers can depend on one more than the other.

5. Cf. *FSWC* 13.18a–20b.

6. Although the terminology is quite different, there are marked similarities between Chao's use of the idea of *chung* and Su Shih's treatment of the concept in his three-part essay of 1061 on the *Chung-yung*; see *STPC* 18.45–48, discussed in Bol 1982, 175–87.

7. Although I shall not attempt to demonstrate this here, it seems to me that Chao's treatment of *tao* is congruent with Su's ideas about *tao* (but not his language), while his account of *wen* contradicts Ch'eng's ideas about the value of *wen*. Even if this is so, however, the problem of explaining why Chao adopts the language and issues of Tao-hsüeh remains. I might note here that Chao takes Wang An-shih's ideas as yet another school of Sung literati thought but does not seek to accommodate it. His critique of Wang's learning (*FSWC* 1.2a, 4b) is drawn directly from Su Shih's writings, not Tao-hsüeh critiques; see Bol 1982, 204–10.

6

BUDDHISM AND TAOISM UNDER THE CHIN

Yao Tao-chung

Religion under the Chin dynasty has generally been neglected by scholars or regarded as a peripheral phenomenon of little significance because they have considered this conquest dynasty to be outside the mainstream of Chinese cultural history. But knowledge of Buddhism and Taoism during the Chin is not only necessary for an understanding of the development of these religions in China, it is also helpful in the study of other aspects of the Chinese intellectual and cultural traditions. And the most important aspect, perhaps, of these religions at this time is the trend of *san-chiao ho-i*, "unification of the Three Doctrines" (or "three religions," i.e., Taoism, Buddhism, and Confucianism), a trend that actually coincides with the last two thousand years of Chinese intellectual and religious history (Jen Chi-yü 1980, 4). Interest in harmonizing the Three Doctrines is first apparent as early as the Eastern Han and subsequently appears at different times with different emphases and under different names—names such as *san-chiao kuei-i*, "Three Doctrines leading to one," and *san-chiao t'ung-yüan*, "Three Doctrines, one origin." During the Northern Sung dynasty, the trend toward unification of the Three Doctrines was already conspicuous (P'an Kuei-ming 1983, 78–79; Ch'en Ping 1984, 20). After the fall of the Northern Sung, the trend continued into the Jurchen Chin dynasty, gaining even more strength, through the Yüan dynasty, and into the Ming, when it reached its zenith, as exemplified in the person of Lin Chao-en (1517–98), Master of the Three Doctrines (Berling 1980, 3; Han Ping-fang and Ma Hsi-sha 1984, 81; and P'an Kuei-ming 1983, 78–80).

It is a commonplace for Chinese to accept and follow the teachings and practices of all three religions, or to adopt any of the religions for different purposes. To understand how the three religions could and can exist side by side, we must study the history of this trend toward unification, and to do that we must consider the important role played by Chin dynasty Taoism and Buddhism. This essay will examine the development of Buddhism and Taoism during the Chin, their relations with the Jurchen rulers, and their influence in respect to other aspects of the Chinese intellectual and cultural tradition.

The Development of Buddhism under the Chin Dynasty

Chin Buddhism arose from several sources. Buddhism was first introduced to the Jurchen from Koryo (Korea) long before the founding of the Chin dynasty (Tao Jing-shen 1976, 10; Chung-kuo Fo-chiao hsieh-hui 1980, 95). A-ku-nai, brother of the founding ancestor of the first Jurchen Chin emperor, A-ku-ta (r. 1115–23), is known to have been very interested in Buddhism (*CS* 1.2; Tao Jing-shen 1976, 13). When the Jurchen conquered the Khitan Liao, the Chin took over its peoples and beliefs, including Buddhism, the state religion of the Liao. The most popular schools of Buddhism under the Liao were the Hua-yen, Tantric, Pure Land, and Disciplinary (Lü-tsung). These schools continued to flourish under the Chin, especially in what had once been Liao territory (Chung-kuo Fo-chiao hsieh-hui 1980, 91, 98–99). In contrast, the Ch'an school, which was popular in Northern Sung China, did not seem to exercise any great influence in the North under the Liao. Not until the Jurchen conquest of the Northern Sung did Ch'an begin to gain popularity in northern cities such as Peking (then called Yenching) and Shang-ching (near present-day Harbin). According to the *Sung-mo chi-wen* (Travel records of the pine and desert area) by Hung Hao (1088–1155), a Sung envoy detained by the Chin for fifteen years from 1129 to 1143, there were thirty-six large Buddhist monasteries in Peking, and all of them belonged to the Disciplinary school. Only after Ch'an monks from the South traveled to Peking were four Ch'an monasteries established there (*SMCW* 1.16a; Kenneth K. S. Ch'en 1964, 413). Hung Hao's observation, if accurate, would mean that the most popular school of Buddhism in Peking, which the Chin took over from the Liao, was the Disciplinary school. Hung's account also indicates that Ch'an gained some ground in Peking in the decade and a half after the fall of the Northern Sung. Since Ch'an had been popular in Northern Sung, we would expect that most monasteries located in former Northern Sung territory during the early years of the Chin would be Ch'an monasteries. Yet in at least one corner of what had been Northern Sung China, Lin-i county (in present-day southern Shantung), the Disciplinary school dominated. A stele dated 1144 records the existence of six Buddhist monasteries in Lin-i: five of the Disciplinary school and one of the Ch'an school. This monastery was *not* established as a result of the northward spread of the Ch'an sect, however. Originally a monastery of the Disciplinary school, it was later converted into a Ch'an monastery by edict of the Northern Sung emperor Chen-tsung (r. 993–1022), who ordered that each county in the empire turn one of its Disciplinary monasteries over to Ch'an (*CWT* 33.348).

There are two high points in the development of Buddhism during the Chin dynasty. The first occurred in 1142, the year Emperor Hsi-tsung's (r. 1135–50) first son was born (*CS* 4.78). To celebrate this joyful event, the emperor ordered a general amnesty and granted a general ordination of monks and nuns (*FTTT* 30.28a). Hung Hao, who personally witnessed the event, estimated that some three hundred thousand men and women took advantage of this opportunity to join the Buddhist clergy (*SMCW* 1.16a). According to another source, one hundred thousand people in Peking alone became monks or nuns of the Disciplinary school (*CWT* 55.580). Since most of the Buddhist monasteries in Peking in 1142 belonged to the Disciplinary school, it is no surprise that a large number of the monks and nuns ordained were affiliated with this school. Ch'an was another major beneficiary of the 1142 edict. According to the Buddhist chronological history *Fo-tsu li-tai t'ung-tsai*, Emperor Hsi-tsung summoned the Ch'an master Hai-hui (d. 1145) to the Chin capital at Shang-ching in 1142 and there built a monastery for him. During Hai-hui's obsequies three years later, the emperor and empress personally carried the master's ashes, and the emperor bestowed on Hai-hui an honorary posthumous title (*FTTT* 30.28a–28b). Although the Disciplinary was still the dominant Buddhist school around 1142, Ch'an was apparently catching up quickly.

The second high point in the development of Buddhism during the Chin occurred in 1162, during the early years of the reign of Emperor Shih-tsung (r. 1161–89), a period of constant warfare. The Jurchen armies fought with the Sung to the south and the Khitan to the north. In order to raise funds to cover military expenses, Emperor Shih-tsung issued an edict allowing those monasteries that had not yet received official temple titles to purchase them, and those persons who wished to join the priesthood to be ordained (*CWT* 35.373, 39.422). Numerous Buddhist and Taoist monasteries seized this opportunity to legitimize their monastic property, and the majority of the monasteries receiving official titles as a result of the 1162 edict were Ch'an monasteries. By the time of Emperor Shih-tsung's reign, Ch'an had clearly become the most popular of all Buddhist schools. Further evidence of this is the body of Chin dynasty source material concerning Buddhism written after 1162, most of which deals with the Ch'an school (*TCKC* 36.275).

Although the Ch'an school had split into five branches by the end of the T'ang dynasty, only two of the five, the Lin-chi and the Ts'ao-tung branches, were flourishing by the end of the Northern Sung dynasty. Both branches continued to develop under the Chin and the Southern Sung. The

Ts'ao-tung branch was popular in North China under the Chin and the Lin-chi branch in South China under the Southern Sung, although there were also followers of the Ts'ao-tung branch in the South and of the Lin-chi branch in the North. Scholars generally agree that the Ts'ao-tung branch of the Ch'an school has never been as popular as the Lin-chi branch (Chung-kuo Fo-chiao hsieh-hui 1980, 341). Yet during the Chin, especially during the late Chin, Ts'ao-tung was definitely the most important branch of the Ch'an school.

From about 1220 on, the abbots of Shao-lin Monastery on Mt. Sung in Honan, the center of Ch'an Buddhism, were all followers of the Ts'ao-tung branch of Ch'an, and for a period of five centuries almost all of the Shao-lin abbots were in the succession line of the single most important Ch'an master of the Chin dynasty, Hsing-hsiu (also known as Wan-sung-lao-jen, or "Old Man of the Ten Thousand Pines," 1166–1246) (Wen Yü-ch'eng 1981, 139; Nogami 1953, 199–200; and de Rachewiltz 1962b, 362 n. 27). All well-known Ts'ao-tung Buddhists of later times can be traced back, through the chain of his disciples, to Hsing-hsiu. Without him, the Ts'ao-tung branch of the Ch'an school might not have continued into the Ming or Ch'ing dynasties. Hsing-hsiu's prominent position is evident from the favor accorded him by the Chin emperor Chang-tsung (r. 1190–1208), who invited him to the inner palace to preach and asked him to take charge of several monasteries in Ta-tu (Peking) (*FTTT* 31.34a–34b; *CWT* 58.604). Many of Hsing-hsiu's disciples were similarly treated with respect by later rulers. Fu-yü (1203–75), one of Hsing-hsiu's disciples and once the abbot of Shao-lin Monastery, was highly respected by the Mongol ruler Khubilai Khan (Yüan Shih-tsu, r. 1260–98), who appointed him leader of all Buddhist schools (*CTL* 1.361a; Wen Yü-ch'eng 1981, 137). Yeh-lü Ch'u-ts'ai (1189–1243), a Confucian statesman who was once secretary to the Mongol conqueror Chinggis Khan (Yüan T'ai-tsu, 1167–1227) as well as secretary and later chief of the Secretariat under the Mongol ruler Ogödei (Yüan T'ai-tsung, r. 1229–41), was also a lay disciple of Hsing-hsiu's (de Rachewiltz 1962b, 189).

Although Hsing-hsiu officially belonged to the Ts'ao-tung branch of the Ch'an school, he included the views of other Ch'an branches in his teachings (*CJWC* 13.293–94; de Rachewiltz 1962b, 193; and Wen Yü-ch'eng 1981, 140–41). The fact that he wrote several books on Pure Land Buddhism indicates a profound level of interest in that school (Chung-kuo Fo-chiao hsieh-hui 1980, 99). Too, Hsing-hsiu instructed his disciples in Confucian as well as Buddhist doctrine. In his preface to Yeh-lü Ch'u-ts'ai's collected writings, Hsing-hsiu remarked that Yeh-lü Ch'u-ts'ai had learned from him the "illustrious formula" (*hsien-chüeh*) of his school, which taught people to forget about life and death and not to be affected by slander or flattery, sorrow or joy. In Hsing-hsiu's opinion, his "illustrious formula" was comparable to the teaching of the Confucian classic the *Great Learning*. To refute the popular notion that Buddhism could regulate only the individual mind but not the state, he pointed out that Yeh-lü Ch'u-ts'ai had rectified his mind, cultivated his person, regulated his family, and ordered the state and had thus also manifested the teaching of the *Great Learning* (CJWC first preface, 1–2). Hsing-hsiu studied Buddhism before he studied Confucianism, and he incorporated Confucian thought into Buddhist doctrine; his own teaching has therefore been described as "Confucian learning within the Ch'an school" (*Ch'an-men K'ung-hsüeh*) (Wen Yü-ch'eng 1981, 141). With his wide knowledge of Buddhism, Confucianism, and Taoism and his efforts to combine them, Hsing-hsiu was truly an important figure in the long history of the trend toward harmonization.

Yeh-lü Ch'u-ts'ai and Li Ch'un-fu (P'ing-shan, 1175–1231) both studied under Wan-sung Hsing-hsiu, and they were both once colleagues in the Han-lin Academy under the Chin government (Jan Yün-hua 1979, 169). As students of Hsing-hsiu's, they both advocated harmonization of the Three Doctrines. According to Igor de Rachewiltz (1962b, 209), "While Li Ch'un-fu's attempt to combine Confucianism and Taoism with Buddhism in a grandiose synthesis embracing and fusing diverse and complex teachings shows preeminently philosophical preoccupations, Yeh-lü Ch'u-ts'ai's synthesis was animated by a practical spirit." In describing and summarizing Yeh-lü Ch'u-ts'ai's beliefs and practices, de Rachewiltz (1962b, 215) coins the phrase "Buddhism for the substance; Confucianism for the functions" (*Fo-hsüeh wei t'i, Ju-hsüeh wei yung*)—a phrase that echoes to some extent Yeh-lü Ch'u-ts'ai's practice of "ruling the state with Confucianism and the mind with Buddhism" (Wen Yü-ch'eng 1981, 143; Chung-kuo Fo-chiao hsieh-hui 1980, 98; de Rachewiltz 1962b, 210). Confucian scholars accused Yeh-lü of "betraying Confucianism" and of having "forgotten his roots." But his own teacher, Hsing-hsiu, accused him of having "wronged Buddhism in order to favor Confucianism," and Yeh-lü had to write a letter to Hsing-hsiu defending himself (CJWC 13.294). Yeh-lü Ch'u-ts'ai did not really deserve criticism from either side, for he apparently adhered to both Confucianism and Buddhism. He tried to assert the equal importance of the Three Doctrines, although he tended to neglect Taoism in his discussions (de Rachewiltz 1962b, 210).

Whereas Yeh-lü Ch'u-ts'ai tried to maintain a neutral position between Confucianism and Buddhism, Li Ch'un-fu openly placed Buddhism in a position higher than that of either Taoism or Confucianism. He wrote: "When, studying, I arrived at Buddhism, there was nothing left to be studied. I know, therefore, that Buddha is the sage and that the [Chinese] sage is not a Buddha. There are Chinese books in the West [i.e., India], but there are no Western books in China" (*CSPC* 128.19a). Li Ch'un-fu not only asserted the superiority of Buddhism, he also refuted in writing Sung Confucian criticism and misunderstanding of Buddhism. These writings were collected by Yeh-lü Ch'u-ts'ai after Li's death in 1231 as *Ming-tao chi-shuo* (Discussions of writings for propagating the *tao*) (Jan Yün-hua 1979, 169). The fact that Li Ch'un-fu lived under the Chin government and that he had no connections with Sung Confucian scholars certainly made it easier for him to speak out against them. Yao Ta-li (1983, 219) has recently written that many Chin scholars who embraced Buddhist as well as Confucian doctrines were discontent with Sung Confucian criticism of Buddhism and that Li Ch'un-fu's refutations of such criticism were approved of and supported by those discontented Chin scholars.

Although the Ts'ao-tung branch of Ch'an Buddhism was the most important Buddhist sect in the second half of the Chin dynasty, it was not the only Ch'an school that flourished. The Lin-chi branch of Ch'an also had something of a following. During the Northern Sung the Lin-chi branch had split into two subbranches: the Huang-lung and the Yang-ch'i. Two of the better-known masters of the former subbranch were Ching-ju (d. 1141) and Tao-hsün (1087–1142). Tao-hsün was ordained under the Northern Sung. In 1135, several years after the fall of the dynasty, he was invited to head P'u-chao Monastery in Tsinan, Shantung, then controlled by the puppet state of Ch'i (1130–37). In 1141, when Ching-ju died, Tao-hsün was appointed to succeed him as abbot of Ling-yen Monastery in Tsinan. Unfortunately, Tao-hsün died shortly after his arrival at the monastery (*CWT* 55.577–79). The Yang-ch'i subbranch also continued into the Chin. The line of the Yang-ch'i master Yüan-kai (1132–95) of Ching-yen Monastery can be traced back to Fo-chien Hui-ch'in (1059–1117) (*CWT* 56.586), one of the three Yang-ch'i masters of the Northern Sung known as the "Three Fos" (the other two being Fo-kuo K'o-ch'in, 1063–1135, and Fo-yen Ch'ing-yüan, d. 1120) (Yin-hai 1972, 218–30). Lines of other Lin-chi Buddhists of the Chin dynasty can also be traced back to earlier masters of the branch.[1]

Other Buddhist schools flourished as well. The Disciplinary school dominated Chin Buddhism during the early years of the dynasty. Wu-chu (d. 1154) and Fa-lü (1099–1166) were two well-known masters of the school in Peking (Chung-kuo Fo-chiao hsieh-hui 1980, 99). It was Fa-lü who received the imperial order to ordain one hundred thousand monks and nuns in 1142 (*CWT* 55.580). The Disciplinary school continued to develop until the end of the Chin dynasty. The last important master of the school was Kuang-en (1195–1243), who is said to have ordained more than a thousand monks (Chung-kuo Fo-chiao hsieh-hui 1980, 99). The Hua-yen school, which enjoyed popularity in the Liao, was still thriving toward the end of the Chin dynasty. Hui-chi (1148–1226) of the Hua-yen school is said to have copied the entire *Avataṁsaka-sûtra* (*Hua-yen ching*) by hand and to have read many Buddhist works (*ISWC* 31.409). The Indian monk Su-t'o-shih-li, who came to China at the age of 85, is known to have been an expert on the *Hua-yen ching* (Chung-kuo Fo-chiao hsieh-hui 1980, 99). He is portrayed in the *Fo-tsu li-tai t'ung-tsai* as a 208-year-old master of incantation (*FTTT* 30.26b–27a). The Tantric school must also have flourished during the Chin, for most of the Chin dynasty stone inscriptions still extant in Fang-shan, Hopei, are related to the school. In the realm of Pure Land Buddhism, one of the best-known monks of the school was Tsu-lang (1149–1222), who served as abbot of several monasteries in Peking during Emperor Shih-tsung's reign. As noted, the famous Ts'ao-tung master Hsing-hsiu was also known for his works on Pure Land Buddhism (Chung-kuo Fo-chiao hsieh-hui 1980, 99).

In short, popular Buddhist schools of the Liao dynasty—the Disciplinary, Hua-yen, Pure Land, and Tantric—all survived through the Chin dynasty. With the Jurchen Chin conquest of the Northern Sung and its expansion into former Northern Sung territory where Ch'an Buddhism was popular, the Ch'an school quickly spread north into old Chin territory, and it eventually overshadowed all other Buddhist schools. The Ts'ao-tung Ch'an master Wan-sung Hsing-hsiu not only tried to combine the teachings of the five Ch'an branches into one, he also advocated harmonization of the Three Doctrines, linking Buddhism with Taoism and Confucianism. Following in Hsing-hsiu's footsteps, his disciples, such as Yeh-lü Ch'u-ts'ai and Li Ch'un-fu, promoted the unification of the Three Doctrines. This syncretic tendency is also evident in Taoist teachings of that time.

The Development of Taoism under the Chin Dynasty

There is a clear difference between the paths of development followed by Taoism and Buddhism during the Chin dynasty. While Chin Buddhism was an extension of Buddhism under the Liao and Northern Sung, without the addition of any new schools, Chin Taoism saw the emergence of several new sects that continued from the Northern Sung dynasty into the Chin. These sects are called "new" mainly because their founders had no formal connections with the Taoist sects formed in the past. Among the new sects were the T'ai-i (Grand Unity), Ta-tao (Great Way), and Ch'üan-chen (Complete Perfection).

Of these, the first to make an appearance was the T'ai-i sect, founded by Hsiao Pao-chen (d. 1166) in Honan in about 1138 (*YS* 202.4530; *HNIL* 42.217). T'ai-i sect leaders earned their reputations by demonstrating magical powers. It is said that when the first patriarch, Hsiao Pao-chen, treated his patients with secret amulets that he claimed an immortal had given to him, he never failed to effect a cure (Ch'en Yüan 1962, 112). The third patriarch, Hsiao Chih-ch'ung (1151–1216), is reported to have successfully exterminated a horde of locusts by using magical incantations (*HNIL* 42.219). In addition to their magical powers, some T'ai-i masters were also famous for their humanitarian deeds. The fourth patriarch, Hsiao Fu-tao (d. 1252), is reported to have sold all his belongings to pay for the collection and burial of human bones after the seizure of Wei-hui (present-day Chi-hsien, Honan) by the Mongol army in 1213 (*CCWC* 39.4b–5b). Hsiao Fu-tao survived the Mongol conquest and was later summoned to Khubilai Khan's residence to respond to inquiries about governance (*CCWC* 38.11b–13a). Thus, the T'ai-i sect thrived well into the Yüan dynasty but failed to outlive it.

The Ta-tao sect, known as the Chen Ta-tao (True Great Way) after Emperor Hsien-tsung (r. 1251–59) of the Yüan bestowed this title on the sect in 1254 (Ch'en Chih-ch'ao 1986, 18), was founded by Liu Te-jen (1122–80) in present-day Hopei. Legendary accounts tell us that one morning in 1142 Liu met an old man riding in an ox-drawn cart. The old man instructed him with passages from the *Tao-te ching*, whereupon Liu became a master of Taoist teachings and attracted many followers. Liu reconstructed what he learned from the old man into the following nine commandments (*SHSWC* 55.921–22):

1. Regard [other] things as [you regard] yourself. Do not have a malicious mind.
2. Be loyal to your lord, filial to your parents, and sincere toward other people. Do not use flowery expressions or bad language.
3. Do away with lewdness and maintain tranquillity.
4. Stay away from power and profit. Be at ease in poverty. Support yourself by working hard in the fields and spend only in measure to what you earn.
5. Do not play chess or [other] games. Do not rob or steal.
6. Do not drink wine or eat meat. For clothes and food, take only what you need. Do not be arrogant or boastful.
7. Empty your heart and weaken your ambition. Mask your brightness and be at one with the dust of the earth.[2]
8. Do not be violent or fierce. Humility in a position of honor makes that [position] still more brilliant.[3]
9. If you know what satisfaction is, you will not be humiliated. If you know when to stop, you will not be endangered.[4]

The above commandments—taken from the *Tao-te ching*, the *I ching*, and the corpus of traditional moral teachings—are a good example of the complex nature of Taoist beliefs.

In addition to the preceding commandments, Ta-tao disciples were enjoined not to beg for alms but to work in the fields to provide for their daily needs (*SHSWC* 55.921–22). When a member of the sect became ill, magical amulets (such as those widely used by the T'ai-i) were not employed; rather, the afflicted person would simply pray for himself until he recovered (Ch'en Yüan 1962, 86–87). That the Ta-tao sect did not employ amulets does not mean that it did not employ other forms of magical power. Liu Te-jen, the founder of the sect, was known for his exorcistic skills. It was said that when a certain person named Chao was haunted by the spirit of a fox, Liu exorcised the fox. Spontaneously the cemetery in the neighborhood began to burn, and the fox, howling, jumped into the fire and died. Thereafter, people revered Liu as a deity (*SHSWC* 55.922).

Like the T'ai-i, the Ta-tao sect left no writings of its own. Compared to the T'ai-i sect, there are fewer contemporary accounts of the Ta-tao from which we can draw reliable information. Because of this, very little is known about the lives of its patriarchs. We know only that its second patriarch, Ch'en Shih-cheng (d. 1194), is said to have had special powers of extrasensory perception; its third patriarch, Chang Hsin-chen (1164–1218), was a man of letters; its fourth patriarch, Mao Hsi-ts'ung (1186–1223), was able to survive the wars at the end of the Chin by applying the principle of "yielding" (Ch'en Yüan 1962, 89). According to Ch'en Chih-ch'ao's study (1986, 17–18), the Ta-tao sect was divided during the Mongol conquest into two branches; hence, there were two different fifth patriarchs at the end of the Chin era. Li Hsi-an (d. 1266) became patriarch in 1228 and received a Taoist robe from Emperor Hsien-tsung (then crown prince) in 1241. Despite this honor to the rival branch, the name of the other fifth partriarch, Li Hsi-ch'eng (1182–1259), is mentioned more often in historical records, and his seems to have been the main branch of the Ta-tao sect. Ta-tao became quite popular during the tenure of Li Hsi-ch'eng (Ch'en Yüan 1962, 89–91) and was still flourishing at the beginning of the fourteenth century, but it faded away soon afterwards.

Ch'üan-chen, historically the last of the three new Taoist sects, was the most popular.[5] It dominated the religious scene for about a century, overshadowing not only other Taoist sects but the Buddhist schools as well. The Ch'üan-chen sect was founded by Wang Che (Ch'ung-yang, 1113–70), a native of Shensi province. He was the scion of a well-to-do gentry family and so apparently received a standard classical education. When Wang reached adulthood, he entered the prefectural academy in Ching-chao (present-day Hsien-yang, Shensi) to study for the civil service examinations (*KSHY* 1.2b). Wang Che's attempts to enter officialdom through the examination system were not successful, and he is reported to have been an alcoholic for a good part of his life. Wang's life changed at the age of forty-eight, when he allegedly encountered two supernatural beings who instructed him in secret rituals (*KSHY* 1.3a). Soon afterwards, Wang became delirious. He deserted his family, dug himself a grave, which he named the "Tomb of the Living Dead," and lived in it for three years (*KSHY* 1.3b; *HYHC*, 19a). He then filled the tomb up and built himself a hut, which became his home for the next four years (*HYHC*, 19b–20a). In the summer of 1167, Wang Che suddenly burned his hut to the ground. As his neighbors were putting out the fire, he sang and danced around the conflagration. After that, Wang traveled to Shantung, where he founded several religious associations, all with the term *san-chiao*, "three teachings," in their titles (*KSHY* 1.5a–5b). While in Shantung, Wang gathered around himself a coterie of seven disciples, later known as the *Ch'üan-chen ch'i-tzu*, the "Seven Masters of the Complete Perfection Sect."[6]

It was through the talents and efforts of Wang Che's seven disciples that the Ch'üan-chen expanded rapidly to become a major religious sect. The development of the Ch'üan-chen sect reached its peak when Ch'iu Ch'u-chi (1148–1227) was patriarch. Ch'iu was summoned to the Mongol court in 1219 by Chinggis Khan to discuss ways of attaining immortality (*HYC* A.1a, B.3a–4a). The khan treated him with great respect and granted him and his clergy the privilege of exemption from tax and corvée (*HYC* B.4b, appendix 1b). When Ch'iu returned to China from the Mongol court, the sect experienced a dramatic growth in membership. Yüan Hao-wen observed that one-fifth of the population in North China were followers of Ch'üan-chen (*ISWC* 35.18a, 22b). It is possible, however, that a considerable portion of its new members joined the sect simply to take advantage of the privileges it could offer them.

The Ch'üan-chen sect is well known for its syncretic teachings. Wang Che is said to have instructed his followers to study the Confucian *Hsiao-ching*, the Buddhist *Pan-jo hsin-ching* (Heart sutra), as well as the Taoist *Tao-te ching* and *Ch'ing-ching ching* (Classic of tranquillity) (*CSTP* 158.44b; *KSHY* 1.8a).[7] The term *san-chiao* that appears in all the titles of the religious associations Wang Che established is another clear indication of Wang's intention to found a sect that would appeal to people of different religious preferences. The best summary of Wang Che's teachings is a short book entitled *Ch'ung-yang li-chiao shih-wu lun* (Fifteen discourses on the founding principles [of the Ch'üan-chen] sect by [Wang] Ch'ung-yang) (*TT* 989). The fifteen discourses are a group of simple, straightforward, but sometimes esoteric, teachings designed to instruct people in how to reach the Way: that is, by leaving home, undergoing a hard process of self-cultivation, and accumulating merit. The ultimate goal is to "enter the Way," to separate one's mind (spirit) from one's body (form), to let the body remain in the mundane world and the mind ascend to its heavenly dwelling. In the process of entering the Way, one was to try to avoid going to extremes, since keeping to the mean is the most effective and the least harmful way to attain success. Human emotions were to be controlled, and nature to be refined. A stoic life was necessary, because a life of luxury would not lead to the Way.

Such works by Wang Che testify that the ultimate goal of the members of the Ch'üan-chen sect was to reach the Way, that is, to attain immortality, a goal pursued by Taoists of other sects as well. Unlike some of the older Taoist sects, however, that practiced alchemy in their search for an orally ingested pill of immortality, the Ch'üan-chen sect sought immortality through cultivation of the "inner elixir." The "inner elixir" school of Taoism believed that the pill of immortality could be cultivated within one's body by means of meditation and moral perfection. This "inner elixir" school had become quite popular during the Northern Sung but had split into two branches with the Chin occupation of North China: the Ch'üan-chen sect carried on the "inner elixir" tradition in North China and became known as the "Northern School"; and its counterpart in Southern Sung China came to be referred to as the "Southern School." The two branches did not reunite until the Mongols unified China in 1279.

The new Taoist sects came into existence during the warfare and social upset of the Jurchen conquest of the Northern Sung, and they attained their maximum popularity only later, when the Mongols destroyed the Chin in the early thirteenth century. Although the three sects originated in different regions—the T'ai-i in Honan, the Ta-tao in Hopei, and the Ch'üan-chen in Shantung—they were all able to spread their teachings to other areas. They were also able to attract followers from all social strata. These new Taoist sects developed independently of one another, and each had its own set of teachings. While the T'ai-i is especially known for its use of magical amulets, the Ta-tao and the Ch'üan-chen showed little interest in them. Both the Ta-tao and Ch'üan-chen required their followers to adopt vegetarian diets and to live frugal lives. In an era of constant warfare, banditry, and famine, the high spiritual value placed on moderation and frugality must have had considerable appeal for the great numbers of people who really had no choice but to live simply. They could at least console themselves with the thought that through physical suffering and deprivation they were gaining spiritual merit. Of the three new Taoist sects to emerge during the Chin dynasty, only the Ch'üan-chen sect exists today.

Why is Ch'üan-chen the sole survivor of the three new sects? There are both intrinsic and extrinsic reasons. Intrinsically, the teachings of the T'ai-i and the Ta-tao sects were not as attractive as those of the Ch'üan-chen sect. There are two major traditions in Taoist religion: the *tan-ting* ("cinnabar and caldron," or alchemical) and the *fu-lu* ("talismans and incantations," or magical and ritual). While the magical and ritual tradition stressed devotional activities and the use of charms, talismans, and rituals, the alchemical tradition put great emphasis on the cultivation of pills of immortality. The pills can be further divided into two types, *wai-tan*, or "outer elixir" (i.e., pills compounded of chemicals, minerals, herbs, etc., and taken orally), and *nei-tan*, or "inner elixir" (i.e., pills cultivated within one's own body; immortality was achieved upon completion of the pill). Both "inner elixir" and "outer elixir" schools existed before the Sung. But whereas the "outer elixir" school was very popular before the Sung, the "inner elixir" school became more popular during the Sung, and the alchemical tradition was carried on almost solely by the "inner elixir" school. The Ch'üan-chen sect, with its emphasis on meditation and moral values, became the representative of the alchemical tradition and was at least equal to the Cheng-i ("Orthodox One," also known before the Yüan as the T'ien-shih, or "Celestial Master," sect), which represented the magical and ritual tradition. The T'ai-i sect, with its emphasis on magical powers, was very much in the magical and ritual tradition, but its teachings were not as elaborate as the Cheng-i sect's. The Ta-tao, with its emphasis on traditional moral values and tranquillity, shared some common ground with the Ch'üan-chen sect. Nevertheless, it did not really have anything to offer that Ch'üan-chen did not already offer, and this is probably why it was unable to compete with it. Since the Ta-tao sect did not stress either the use of amulets or the importance of cultivating the pill of immortality, it could not fit into either of the two major traditions of the time.

Extrinsically, neither the T'ai-i nor the Ta-tao experienced any rise in popularity that could be attributed to the ruling class. Chinggis Khan's granting of special privileges to Ch'iu Ch'u-chi and his followers, however, elevated the Ch'üan-chen sect to such a prominent position that neither the T'ai-i nor the Ta-tao could possibly compete with it. With no especially unusual qualities within and no special assistance without, it is not surprising that these two sects were much shorter-lived that the Ch'üan-chen.

Information concerning the traditional Taoist sects—the Celestial Master and Mao-shan sects—is very limited compared to the source material available on the new sects. The Celestial Master sect is the oldest and most important sect in the history of Taoism. The Mao-shan sect was founded on the practices of the Celestial Master sect but had adopted certain reform measures of its own. The Celestial Master sect was originally founded by Chang Tao-ling (ca. 34–156) in Szechwan, but his followers later centered the sect in the Dragon and Tiger Mountains of Kiangsi. The Mao-shan sect was named after its place of origin in the Mao Mountains of Kiangsu. While the Ch'an Buddhist schools were the major benefactors of the 1162 edict allowing the sale of temple titles to raise funds for military campaigns, some of the older Taoist monasteries also benefited (*SYTP* 21.10b, 45b). Most older Taoist temples in the Chin period appear to have belonged to the Celestial Master sect, although temples of the Mao-shan sect also existed (*CSPC* 127.4a–4b). Because they were based in South China, these two sects were geographically separated from their followers in Jurchen-occupied North China—the reason, perhaps, why they were overshadowed by the new Taoist sects within Chin territory. Ch'en Yüan (1962, 1) reports that of the stone inscriptions he has gathered concerning Chin and early Yüan Taoist sects, one-tenth pertain to the older sects, two-tenths to the Ta-tao and the T'ai-i, and seven-tenths to the Ch'üan-chen sect. If these inscriptions can be used as an index of popularity, the older Taoist sects were certainly less conspicuously favored.

The most important Taoist monastery in Chin China was T'ien-ch'ang Monastery in Peking, which enjoyed close ties with the ruling house. Although the monastery was first built in the T'ang dynasty, it does not seem to have been well known until after the Chin dynasty moved its capital to Peking in 1153.[8] In 1167, an imperial edict ordered the temple rebuilt. The funds required for this construction project, which amounted to millions of cash, were raised exclusively by selling palace furnishings and movable property; it was therefore reported that the reconstruction did not cost the people anything (*KKPC*, 20). When the restoration was completed in 1174, the emperor ordered a Taoist ceremony three days and three nights long to be held in celebration.

The restored temple housed the traditional Taoist pantheon headed by the Triad of the Three Pures, and Yen Te-yüan (1094–1189) was appointed its abbot (*KKPC*, 18–19; Ta-t'ung shih po-wu-kuan 1978, 4). In 1186 Emperor Shih-tsung named Sun Ming-tao abbot, granted twenty million cash to the monastery, and built a facility on a mountain nearby where members of the monastery could work at refining cinnabar pills (*KKPC*, 22). In 1190, while Sun Ming-tao was still abbot of T'ien-ch'ang, the mother of Emperor Chang-tsung fell ill. When no medicine would cure her, a *chiao* sacrifice[9] was ordered and was held at T'ien-ch'ang Monastery over a period of seven days and seven nights, with Sun Ming-tao and two government officials presiding over the ceremony. Shortly after the *chiao* sacrifice, the empress dowager recovered from her illness (*KKPC*, 26–30). The Chin ruling house thereupon made T'ien-ch'ang the "imperial" monastery, and the imperial family thereafter usually called on T'ien-ch'ang when it needed a sacrifice performed; it was to T'ien-ch'ang that the imperial family came on important occasions, joyful or sorrowful, to offer thanks or to pray for help. Since the monastery belonged to the Celestial Master sect, it might seem logical to speculate, therefore, that the Chin court treated the Celestial Master as the leading sect of the Taoist religion.

Other records reveal, however, that no single sect was authorized to take precedent over any others during the Chin and that the Jurchen rulers' patronage of Taoism was not limited to the traditional sects; the Chin emperors were also interested in the masters of the new sects. Emperor Hsi-tsung summoned Hsiao Pao-chen, founder of the T'ai-i sect, to his court in 1148 (Ch'en Yüan 1962, 112–13). Emperor Shih-tsung summoned Wang Ch'u-i (1142–1217) of the Ch'üan-chen sect to the capital and housed him at T'ien-ch'ang Monastery in 1187 (*HYHC* 37B.4; *KSHY* 2.33b). Ch'iu Ch'u-chi, another prominent member of the Ch'üan-chen sect, was also summoned to the capital and housed at T'ien-ch'ang in the spring of 1188 (*PCC* 3.6a–7a). At the beginning of his reign, Emperor Chang-tsung summoned Hou Yüan-hsien (1162–1230) of the T'ai-i sect to T'ien-ch'ang Monastery (*HNIL* 42.219–20). In 1197 he also summoned Wang Ch'u-i to the monastery and went there in person to meet him (*YKC* 1.1a–1b). Imperial orders were also issued appointing masters of the new Taoist sects to serve as abbots, and ordering performance of *chiao* sacrifices at various Taoist monasteries (*CTC* 5.3a–3b; *ISWC* 31.417).

The fact that masters of different sects were housed alike at T'ien-ch'ang Monastery suggests that the ruling house did not try to draw any sharp distinctions between one Taoist sect and another. Nor is there any evidence that the various sects vied with each other for power or imperial favor. Imperial patronage of Taoist monks did bother some Buddhist monks. When Emperor Shih-tsung invited Wang Ch'u-i to the capital in 1187, it is reported, jealous Buddhist monks bribed a court official to tell the emperor that Wang should be tested with poisoned wine to see if he was truly a Taoist "immortal." The emperor thought this a good idea and gave Wang three cups of poisoned wine as an offering. Wang drank it all with no ill effects (*CTC* 5.2a–3a; *KSHY* 2.33a–33b). The Buddhist monks (if this incident ever actually occurred) probably acted out of fear of losing the emperor's favor. Their fear was unnecessary, however, because the imperial favor bestowed on the Buddhists was, as we will see, certainly no less than that granted the Taoists.

The Chin Court's Attitude toward Buddhism and Taoism

Chin religious policies can be roughly divided into two categories: those that were helpful and those that were harmful to the development of Buddhism and Taoism. The most common pro-religious measure taken at the official level was a ruler's patronage of well-known religious figures. There were several reasons for this rapport between rulers and religious leaders. Personal interest in a religion sometimes led an emperor to meet with spiritual masters. For example, the emperor Shih-tsung's summoning Wang Ch'u-i and Ch'iu Ch'u-chi to the capital seems to have been motivated in part by a desire to learn Taoist methods of personal cultivation (*HYHC* 37a–37b; *KSHY* 2.33b; *PCC* 3.6a–7b; *CWT* 41.441). The empress of T'ai-tsung (r. 1123–35) built the Buddhist monk Hai-hui a monastery in Yenching (Chung-kuo Fo-chiao hsieh-hui 1980, 95). In 1142 Emperor Hsi-tsung invited Hai-hui to Shang-ching and ordered construction of Ta Ch'u-ch'ing Monastery, which Hai-hui would head (*FTTT* 30.28a). Empress Chen-i (name in religion, T'ung-hui Yüan-ming, 1094–1161), mother of the future emperor Shih-tsung (r. 1161–89), became a nun in 1145, ten years after she was widowed. When her son assumed the post of *liu-shou* (governor) of the Eastern Capital in Liaoning in 1155 (Chang Po-ch'üan 1984, 183), Chen-i also moved to the Eastern Capital and there spent more than three hundred thousand cash building the Ta Ch'ing-an Ch'an Temple. She served as its first abbess. When the empress died in the spring of 1161, her son built a pagoda and had a stele erected commemorating her devotion. After becoming emperor later that year, Shih-tsung further expanded Ch'ing-an Temple to honor the memory of his mother (Tsou Pao-k'u 1984).[10] In 1162, when construction of Ta-ch'ing Monastery was completed in the new capital at Peking, Emperor Shih-tsung summoned the Ch'an master I to be its first abbot. Shih-tsung also ordered Prince Yen to bestow on the monastery twenty thousand cash and twenty *ch'ing* (a *ch'ing* is equivalent to about 15.14 acres) of productive land (*FTTT* 30.30a). In 1168 Master I was summoned to the Eastern Capital to take charge of Ch'ing-an Ch'an Temple (*FTTT* 30.32a).[11] In 1180, when Ch'i-yin Ch'an Monastery was built by imperial edict in the Yang-shan (now known as the Western Hills), outside Peking, Master I was named its first abbot. More land was bestowed and ten thousand monks ordained to celebrate the founding of the monastery (*FTTT* 30.33b). Emperor Chang-tsung summoned the Ch'an master Hsing-hsiu to his court in 1193 and received him with the highest respect. After listening to the Buddhist teachings, Chang-tsung personally offered Hsing-hsiu a gift of embroidered silk; furthermore, imperial consorts and kinsmen also presented the monk with valuable gifts (*FTTT* 30.34a). In 1197 Hsing-hsiu was appointed head of Ch'i-yin Ch'an Monastery (*FTTT* 30.34b; Jan Yün-hua 1982, 377). Even after the Mongol takeover of North China, Hsing-hsiu continued to be favored by the rulers of the Yüan dynasty (*CWT* 58.604; *TTPN* 25.190a).

Imperial patronage was also a political act that could be used to win the support of a religious group. One common method for winning such support was to pay personal visits to the monasteries of both religions. Imperial visits were usually accompanied by imperial gifts. In 1186, for example, Emperor Shih-tsung visited the newly completed Hsiang-shan Monastery near Peking and bestowed on it the name Ta Yung-an. He also made the monastery a present of two thousand *mou* of rice fields (6.6 *mou* are equivalent to one acre), seven thousand chestnut trees, and twenty thousand cash (*CS* 8.192). On the first day of the seventh month in 1197, Chang-tsung visited T'ien-ch'ang Temple, where a *chiao* sacrifice was being held.

> During this stay at the monastery, the emperor also met with Wang Ch'u-i. On the third day of the seventh month, [Wang] was summoned. The emperor granted him a seat and asked about the *Ch'ing-ching ching*, and Master [Wang] explained it. Next, the emperor asked about affairs concerning expeditions to the north. The master answered that it [i.e., the war] would stop in the year *wu-wu* [1198], which later indeed turned out as predicted. Afterwards, the emperor inquired about affairs of the Ch'üan-chen sect, and the master answered each and every question. The emperor was deeply impressed and praised him. The master stayed until dark and then left. The following day the emperor granted him a purple robe and the title "T'i-hsüan ta-shih" [Great Master Embodying the Mystery]. The emperor also sent a retainer to deliver an edict granting him the choice of living in either Hsiu-chen or Ch'ung-fu Monastery. Also, every month the emperor would give him a food allowance of two hundred strings of cash. (*YKC* 1.1a–1b)

Chang-tsung's questions to Wang Ch'u-i concerning matters of war—and the rich rewards he bestowed on the Taoist master for his imparted wisdom—suggest that the ruler believed the Taoist master had the ability to predict future events.

Imperial patronage was not gratuitous. Monasteries and religious leaders were frequently asked by the court to perform religious sacrifices for the sake of the imperial family. For example, in 1190 Emperor Chang-tsung ordered T'ien-ch'ang Monastery to hold a *chiao* sacrifice for his mother (*KKPC*, 26a). In 1201, Chang-tsung, then aged thirty-four and still without offspring, had a *chiao* sacrifice performed at T'ai-ch'ing Monastery to pray for a son (*HNIL* 42.218). The sacrifice appears to have worked: Chang-tsung's consort gave birth to a son, the prince T'e-lin, the following year. Another *chiao* sacrifice was ordered to be held at Hsüan-chen Monastery to pray for the prince's good fortune. Unfortunately, this time the sacrifice did not bring long-lasting results: the prince died at the age of two (*CS* 64.1528–29).

Another gesture of imperial patronage with political implications was the welcoming and housing of the Sandalwood Buddha (Chan-t'an-Fo). The Sandalwood Buddha, the holiest and most venerable relic in China, was said to have come to China from India through East Turkestan, the same route over which Buddhism was introduced into China. This Buddha was regarded as a palladium of Buddhism and as such was protected by state authorities (Franke 1978b, 73–74). After the Northern Sung fell in 1127, the statue was moved to Peking, where it was housed at Sheng-an Monastery from 1131 to 1143. In 1143 it was moved to Shang-ching and there was housed at Ta Ch'u-ch'ing Monastery, which Hsi-tsung had built for Hai-hui. After staying in Shang-ching for twenty years, the Sandalwood Buddha was returned to Peking and housed in the inner palace until it caught fire in 1217. The Buddha was then moved back to Sheng-an Monastery (HLC 9.377–82). Possession of the Sandalwood Buddha was significant for both the Jurchen Chin and the Buddhist sects in North China. Since according to tradition, the statue came only to a country whose ruler possessed the Way, the image's presence in North China signified the legitimacy of the Chin (CKL 17.248). The presence of the Sandalwood Buddha in Jurchen-occupied North China also made the Buddhists in the North, rather than those under the Southern Sung, the legitimate carriers of the Buddhist tradition (Franke 1978b, 73–74).

The selling of monk certificates and official monastic name tablets benefited both the government and the Buddhist and Taoist schools. The practice of selling certificates did not originally exist in Chin China (SMCW 1.16a–16b). The Chin probably learned it from the Sung, which was known for its sale of certificates (Kenneth K. S. Ch'en 1956; and 1964, 391–92). The first Chin emperor to approve the practice was Shih-tsung. In need of funds to cover military expenses, Shih-tsung issued an edict in 1162 allowing all the monasteries in the empire that were not officially registered or that lacked official monastic name tablets to contribute money to the government in exchange for the tablets (CWT 35.373, 39.422; CSTP 156.14a). The same edict also allowed the sale of monk certificates, purple robes, and honorific religious titles (CS 50.1124–25). Many monasteries became legitimate as a result of the 1162 edict, and many Buddhist and Taoist monks, as well as nuns, were ordained. And the popularity of Buddhism and Taoism reached unprecedented heights during the Chin dynasty.

Three years after issuing this edict, when the Chin dynasty was no longer at war, Shih-tsung ordered the sale of certificates stopped (CS 50.1125). But it appears that the sale of certificates, titles, and name tablets had been firmly established as a feasible revenue-raising practice that would be used by other Chin emperors after Shih-tsung. Chang-tsung adopted the practice in 1197 to raise military funds and again, one year later, to generate relief funds for the Western Capital, then plagued by famine (CS 10.241, 50.1125). More monk certificates, honorific religious titles, and official monastic name tablets were sold in 1207 when the Chin engaged in war with the Southern Sung and bad harvests caused by drought and locusts brought famine to the Shantung area (CS 95.2105). The sale of titles was subsequently continued under emperors Wei-shao (r.

1209–13) and Hsüan-tsung (r. 1213–24) (*SYTP* 23.46a; *CS* 13.295, 14.319, 50.1126).

Most official monastic name tablets were sold for cash, but some were sold for grain. The prices for tablets sold during Shih-tsung's reign ranged between three thousand and one hundred thousand cash.[12] In addition, many monastic posts were up for sale in the Chin (*CS* 14.319, 46.1030). The prices of those posts varied according to their importance. In 1216, for example, seventy *tan* (133.3 pounds) of grain would buy the post of master of ceremonies for thirty months, and ten *tan* of grain, superintendent of a monastery for a year (*CS* 50.1126). This sale of monk certificates and monastic posts has been cited as one factor leading to the decline of the traditional Buddhist schools and the rise of the new religious sects, such as the Buddhist Ch'an sect led by Hsing-hsiu and the Taoist Ch'üan-chen sect led by Wang Che (Nogami 1953, 240).

The Jurchen Chin took the same steps many other dynasties had and would to control organized religion. First, all important monastic appointments were made by the state. The *Ta Chin-kuo chih* (A record of the great Chin kingdom) states that the highest-placed Buddhist monk at the capital was called "state preceptor" (*kuo-shih*). The state preceptor wore a robe of pure red and was as exalted as a tutor to the emperor. He might be summoned to court to explain sutras to the emperor, and sometimes the emperor would even bow to him. At the local level, the religious officials overseeing the affairs of Buddhist clergy in a prefecture were known as "directors of monks" (*seng-lu*) and "vice-directors of monks" (*seng-cheng*), and they wore purple robes. These positions were filled by monks of high prestige. Each term was limited to three years; after three years, new directors and vice-directors were appointed. Disputes within a religious community were usually settled by the director of monks. Below the prefectural level, there were also directors of monks at the subprefectural (*tu-kang*) and at the county (*wei-na*) levels. The director of monks for a county had the authority to handle litigation that did not result in any punishment more severe than flogging. Litigation entailing heavier sentence was redirected to higher authorities. Similar appointments were given to Taoists. The prefectural director of Taoist clergy was titled *tao-lu*, and the vice-director *tao-cheng*. They were reappointed every three years (*TCKC* 36.275–76).

Second, while the court itself often bestowed money and gifts on monasteries and built monasteries to house famous Buddhist monks or Taoist priests, the Chin government prohibited individuals from using private funds to build monasteries. For example, it is reported that in the third month of the fourteenth year of the Ta-ting era (1174) Shih-tsung visited T'ien-ch'ang Monastery, which had been rebuilt by the court at a cost of millions of cash (*KKPC* 18a–20a). One month later, the emperor told his ministers: "I have heard that the masses, praying for blessings, have often built Buddhist temples. Although regulations have been made to prohibit this, there are still many violations. The regulations should be explicated; they do not allow the masses to waste money" (CS 7.161). Apparently, the emperor's wish was not successfully carried out, because another edict was issued in 1178 prohibiting the construction of Buddhist and Taoist monasteries by the masses (CS 7.170). These bans on private construction probably represent an attempt to control the growth of Buddhism and Taoism and to protect officially registered monasteries. The difficulty of enforcing the 1178 edict is evident in a later report concerning a privately built monastery that would have been condemned had it not been for the fact that the authorities could not bear to destroy the statue of Buddha housed there (CSTP 157.1a–2b).

Third, while the Chin rulers had from time to time issued edicts allowing ordination or the sale of monk certificates, they could not tolerate unapproved ordinations. Measures were taken by Emperor T'ai-tsung as early as 1130 to prohibit private ordination of monks and nuns (CS 3.61). And in 1185 Shih-tsung issued an edict specifically prohibiting farmers and the sons of officials from evading taxes and corvée by becoming Buddhist monks or Taoist priests (CS 46.1035). Fearing the harmful effects private ordinations might have on agricultural production, Chang-tsung too issued an edict banning them (CS 46.1035).

Prohibition of unauthorized ordination was meant to stop opportunists from using religion to escape taxes; it could stop only the poor, however, because the rich could afford to buy the monk certificates that allowed them exemption from taxes. Many of those who were ordained during the Chin dynasty wanted not to be priests but to purchase tax shelters. Many others who genuinely wanted to be priests could not be ordained for lack of funds to buy the necessary certificates.

There was a channel open to pious devotees who wished to be ordained but did not want to wait for a specially granted quota or could not afford to purchase monk certificates. They could become monks or priests or nuns by passing an examination on certain Buddhist or Taoist scriptures.[13] The examinations were not just for the poor; the wealthy could also enter the priesthood by examination (CWT 56.585; PHKS 12.107a). After ordination, a monk could take additional examinations to advance in the monastic ranks (CWT 55.580). These examinations fell under the jurisdiction of the Board of Rites, as did all Buddhist and Taoist affairs throughout the Chin dynasty. The examinations were held once every three years, and each time only eighty candidates were ordained. If a candidate passed the examination, he received a certificate from the examiner and his name was reported to the authorities; when a monk or priest died, the certificate was returned to the Board of Rites, where it was destroyed (CS 55.1234). It is not clear whether eighty was the number of ordinations allowed each county, each prefecture, or the entire empire. Nor is it clear whether the eighty ordinations were divided equally among Buddhist monks, Buddhist nuns, Taoist priests, and Taoist nuns, or whether each of the four groups had a quota of eighty. In any event, the number of persons ordained by examination appears to have been very small compared to the number ordained by special imperial favor. In 1196 Chang-tsung issued an edict allowing all older Buddhist or Taoist masters to ordain two to three disciples each, and all ordained priests over the age of forty to ordain one disciple each (CS 10.239). It apparently was not very easy to be officially ordained in the Chin, even when the various channels were open.

Fourth, there were also periods during which certain sects were proscribed. Although there is no clear evidence that any particular religious school, as a single, unified organization, used religion as a guise while engaging in anti-Jurchen activities, there are reports of revolts led by Buddhist monks during the Chin dynasty. The monk Chih-chiu, for example, believed that he had a mission to overthrow the Chin government. He therefore led a revolt in 1171, which the Chin army suppressed, killing more than 450 people in the process (CS 88.1961, 7.160). The monk Fa-t'ung of the Eastern Capital (Liao-yang) used magical methods to incite a mob but was put down by government troops (CS 6.130). Given the large numbers of ordained Buddhist monks and Taoist priests during the Chin, it should come as no surprise that some of them were anxious for power (KCC 6.66). Also, given that some Buddhist monks did revolt during Shih-tsung's reign—even though they by no means represented all the Buddhists in the Chin—it is understandable that when Chang-tsung assumed the throne after Shih-tsung's death in 1189, he would be on his guard against organized religion and would ban several new religious sects. Toward the end of 1190, for instance, he banned the Ch'üan-chen and Wu-hsing-p'i-lu sects on the grounds of their having "deluded the masses and disoriented the people" (CS 9.216).[14] Yüan Hao-wen wrote that the Ch'üan-chen sect was banned because Chang-tsung suspected that it might be insurrectionary (ISWC 35.17b). Chang-tsung's suspicion of the Ch'üan-chen sect was probably unfounded, because there is simply no evidence that the Ch'üan-chen sect ever engaged in any anti-Jurchen activities. The fact that Chang-tsung summoned the Ch'üan-chen Taoist Wang Ch'u-i to the capital in 1197 and treated him with great respect suggests that the ban did not hinder the growth of the sect. Whatever suspicions Chang-tsung had about this sect in 1190 had been forgotten by 1197.

In another unfriendly gesture toward religion, Chang-tsung issued an edict in the early months of 1191 forbidding Buddhist monks, Buddhist nuns, and Taoist priests to enter the homes of imperial kinsmen or high officials (CS 9.217)—an edict that could be construed as a deliberate effort to downgrade the prestige and social status of the clergy. But although it was Chang-tsung who made the ultimate decisions, it appears that his religious policies were often influenced by his ministers. For instance, a memorial was presented to Chang-tsung in 1192 stating that Buddhists and Taoists did not salute their parents and that such behavior should not be tolerated. Citing an edict issued during the T'ang dynasty ordering Buddhist and Taoist religious to salute their parents, the memorial suggested that Chang-tsung reinstate this order; and Chang-tsung consented to do so (CS 9.221).

Chang-tsung was not the only Chin emperor to maintain that the social status of monks and priests should be lower than that of the imperial family and high officials. Upon learning that his chief ministers Chang Hao and Chang Hui had tried to keep the monk Fa-pao from moving away from the capital, Emperor Hai-ling summoned his high officials to court in 1155 and reprimanded them:

> [I] have heard that each time you go to the monastery, the monk Fa-pao sits in the center and you ministers sit at his side. I dislike this very much. The Buddha was originally the prince of a small kingdom. He was able to discard wealth and rank easily and thus became the Buddha. Nowadays, people respect [the Buddha because they] hope for happiness and profit. This is all wrong. Moreover, those who have become monks are often failed *hsiu-ts'ai* [i.e., beginning-level scholars] and idlers of the marketplace. They have no sufficient means to make a living and therefore have become monks. Comparing statuses, they have decided that civil and military officials cannot be treated as their own equals in terms of etiquette or proprieties. Old ladies of the villages, anticipating death, often have confidence in it and believe in it [i.e., Buddhism]. Yet you imitate such [behavior] and disgrace the status of chief minister. (CS 83.1861)

The two chief ministers were each dealt twenty blows, and the monk Fa-pao, who was charged with self-importance, received two hundred (CS 83.1861, 5.103–4). Hai-ling also issued an order in the eleventh month of the first year of the Cheng-lung era (1156) banning the "welcoming Buddha" ceremony held on the eighth day of the second month each year (CS 5.107). Perhaps, after viewing the Buddhist festival, he jealously felt that the Buddha received greater respect and more support from the people than he did. Banning the Buddhist festival certainly would have made him feel that he was the ultimate ruler of the country and that no one, not even the Buddha, could overshadow his presence.[15]

Hai-ling's lack of consideration for organized religion can also be seen in two other measures of his that were unfavorable toward Buddhism and Taoism. In 1156 Hai-ling ordered his officials to seize all land belonging to Buddhist and Taoist clergy in the prefectures of Ta-hsing (the area of modern Peking) and P'ing-chou (present-day Lu-lung, Hopei), along with other underdeveloped or improperly occupied land, so that the property could be granted to the households of Jurchen *meng-an* ("heads of a thousand men," i.e., battalion commanders) and *mou-k'o* ("heads of a hundred men," i.e., company commanders) who had relocated in the two prefectures (CS 47.1044). This was a case of sacrificing the interests of one social group to satisfy the needs of another, politically more important ethnic group. After the harvest of 1157 had been destroyed by locusts in many areas, the emperor ordered the leveling of Ch'u-ch'ing Monastery (built by Emperor Hsi-tsung in 1142 for the monk Hai-hui), along with many old, ruined palaces and various large residences, so that the land could be used for farming (CS 5.108).[16] Although Hai-ling had a very good reason for this expropriation, it is clear that for him the interests of religious groups were of low priority.

Even Shih-tsung, the emperor who made quite a few friendly gestures toward Buddhism and Taoism, more than once expressed his doubts about the value of either religion. For example, in 1179 he told his ministers:

> People often become followers of Buddhism and Taoism to seek happiness. In my early years, I was also deluded by them, but I soon became aware of the wrongness of it. Moreover, Heaven establishes a ruler to have him govern the people. It would be very difficult for [a ruler] who strolls about for pleasure and is remiss in his duties to [rule successfully simply by] praying for happiness and depending on luck. [But] if he could indeed nourish the people with love, he would suit the mind of Heaven above and be repaid with happiness. (CS 7.173)

Shih-tsung did not believe that a ruler could bring his country happiness just by praying to Buddhist or Taoist deities. A ruler had to work hard and show true love for his people to win blessings for his country.

In Shih-tsung's opinion, what the people really needed was not Taoism or Buddhism, but rather a ruler who could provide his people with a contented and peaceful way of life. He remarked in 1187: "People all take happiness to be believing in Taoism or Buddhism, fasting, and reading scriptures. I have never caused the people [to suffer] injustice, and the world has become peaceful and joyful. [Am I] not superior to them [i.e., the two religions]?" (CS 8.199). The emperor obviously felt that his role as ruler of the empire was being threatened by the popularity of these two religions. He wanted his subjects not to believe in Buddhism and Taoism, but to be happy with the way of life he had provided for them. Yet discontent with his own life led him to seek advice from the Taoist Wang Ch'u-i. Shih-tsung summoned Wang to court to discuss Taoist methods of self-cultivation in 1187, the same year he told his people not to look to Taoism or Buddhism for happiness.

It appears that Emperor Shih-tsung had an ambiguous attitude toward religion. On the one hand, he was skeptical about the efficacy of religion and told his people that believing in the ruler was better than believing in religion. On the other hand, he never completely gave up hope for help from religion and from time to time would contact celebrated religious figures. His stance toward Buddhism and Taoism reflected the overall attitude of the Chin court. It did not trust the adherents of religions, but it settled for control rather than suppression. Imperial patronage was motivated more by the ruler's desire to raise revenues or secure services from the religious groups than by pious devotion.

Buddhism and Taoism and Chin Society

What attitudes toward Buddhism and Taoism were evident among the literati and the masses during the Chin? How did religious institutions affect the life and livelihood of Chin society?

Buddhism and Taoism are conspicuously present in Chin literary works. Li Ch'un-fu, the literatus who was most widely known as a lay Buddhist, became famous for bravely defending Buddhism against the criticisms of Sung Confucian scholars (KCC 9.105). And Chao Ping-wen, the best-known Confucian scholar to be fond of Buddhism and Taoism, enjoyed persuading other people to study these two religions. It is reported that Chao once personally taught someone how to perform the Buddhist salute. The incident apparently made him an object of ridicule among the literati. Perhaps because he did not want to be derided by other scholars, Chao removed all statements concerning the two religions from his collected works, the *Fu-shui chi* (Collected works from the Fu River), and published them separately (KCC 9.106; ISWC 17.6a). Chao Ping-wen is said to have published several studies on the Taoist classics. Unfortunately, only one of these studies is still extant.[17]

Among the Chin literati who believed in neither Buddhism nor Taoism, Liu Ch'i was probably the most outspoken. In commenting on Taoism, Liu Ch'i expressed doubts about the feasibility of attaining immortality through Taoist cultivation, curing illness with Taoist talismans and incantations, and turning misfortune into fortune by means of *chiao* sacrifices. In commenting on Buddhism, he expressed disbelief in fundamental Buddhist doctrines such as cause and effect (*yin-kuo*, i.e., *hetres* and *phala* in Sanskrit) and transmigration (*lun-hui*, i.e., *saṁsāra*). In comparing Confucianism with Buddhism and Taoism, Liu praised the former for guiding people with clearly defined sociopolitical rules and regulations and for never deluding people with "unknown matters," as Buddhism and Taoism did. Liu expressed pity for those "stupid and vulgar" people who failed to appreciate the real worth of their ordinary lives and followed Buddhism or Taoism simply because they were attracted to the strangeness and novelty of the religions. Liu Ch'i was especially upset that not only common folk but many scholar-officials as well believed in Buddhism and Taoism (*KCC* 12.141).

Like Liu Ch'i, Yüan Hao-wen was also disappointed to see so many Confucian scholars become followers of Buddhism. He expressed his admiration for their devotion, however, and his hope that Confucian scholars would promote Confucian teachings with the same kind of dedication and enthusiasm that the Buddhists exhibited toward Buddhism (*ISWC* 35.1b–2a). Yüan Hao-wen did not think very highly of the Ch'üan-chen sect of Taoism. Nonetheless, he once wrote:

> After this [i.e., Ch'iu Ch'u-chi's westward trek], two out of every ten people in the world were those who wore "yellow caps" [i.e., were Taoists].... Even those who were cruel, violent, and fierce and those who were most stupid and ignorant were all transformed by it [i.e., the Ch'üan-chen sect].... At a time when a father was unable to summon his son, when an elder brother was unable to overcome his younger brother, when the rites and righteousness could not be used to control the basic nature of the people, and when penalties were insufficient to punish their decadence, after the complete collapse [of the social order] and the irredeemable breakdown [of the political system], the so-called Ch'üan-chen school was able to save those people.... Alas! Is this the will of Heaven? (*ISWC* 35.22b–23a)

Yüan Hao-wen, as a Confucian scholar, would much rather have seen the Confucian system be the one to restore social order. Yet his own testimony demonstrates that it was the Taoist Ch'üan-chen sect that provided the people with shelter and relief during this period of great disorder. The numerous essays Yüan Hao-wen wrote on behalf of his many Taoist and Buddhists friends, moreover, form an important part of the source material for the study of Chin dynasty religion.

Some of the literati's lives were influenced by Taoism and Buddhism in more personal ways. For example, as a youth, the Chin dynasty poet Ma Chiu-ch'ou (1174–1232) is reported to have had serious health problems that he overcame by practicing Taoist breathing exercises (CCC 6.292). The scholar-official Wang Yü (fl. 1196–1201) suddenly deserted his wife one day to become a monk, but he later returned home to live with her as in the past (KCC 5.46; CCC 9.477). Although some Chin literati were dramatically influenced by Buddhism and Taoism, most Chin literati simply tried to maintain a friendly attitude toward them without abandoning Confucianism.

Following Liao practice, many Chin Buddhist devotees organized regional associations known as *i* (Buddhist societies) to support local Buddhist monasteries.[18] It is reported in a stele inscription written for T'ing-yü Monastery in I-chou (present-day I-hsien, Liaoning) that the monastery, which had housed 5,048 volumes of Buddhist sutras, burned down in 1146. A local resident by the name of Ma Yu organized one thousand people into a Buddhist society to purchase new sutras and to build a new monastery to house them (CWT 33.349). Another inscription, dated 1167, records that San-hsüeh Monastery in Hsing-chung prefecture (near present-day Ling-yüan, Liaoning) was supported by a Buddhist society of a thousand members. On the first day of the tenth month, all members, regardless of sex or age, were required to donate to the monastery two hundred cash and one peck of rice (CWT 34.366). From these two accounts we know that during the Chin dynasty the functions of the Buddhist societies included building monasteries, buying sutras, and providing monasteries with money and food. Although the two accounts cited above both give one thousand as the number of members in the societies, other sources reveal that the number varied from society to society. For example, Po-lin Ch'an Monastery in Wo-chou (present-day Chao-hsien, Hopei) was supported by a Buddhist society of three thousand members (CWT 43.467–68), and the Buddhist society associated with Hua-yen Monastery in the Western Capital had only eight hundred members (SYTP 20.5b). Sources also reveal that sometimes the name indicated the specific purpose of a society. The Buddhist society that built the Hua-yen-ching Pagoda (in present-day Hohhot) was called the Hua-yen Society (Li I-yu 1979, 365), and the Buddhist society that collected the *Bhagavat-sûtra* (*Po-ch'ieh ching*) at Hua-yen Monastery was known as the Po-ch'ieh Society (SYTP 20.4a). (While there were various Buddhist societies building monasteries or providing them with financial support, there are no records indicating the existence of Taoist societies comparable to the Buddhist *i*, although many Taoist monasteries were built with the help of their followers.)

In addition to the cash and gifts acquired through contributions from followers and the Chin court, many monasteries owned enough land to support themselves. The Buddhist Fu-yen Monastery in Tse-chou (present-day Chin-ch'eng, Shansi) is reported to have owned two thousand *mou* (approximately three hundred acres) of land, which provided the monks with enough revenue to survive (*SYTP* 23.22b).

Generally speaking, most Taoist and Buddhist monasteries were financially secure during the Chin dynasty, and some of them were quite wealthy. For example, the Taoist Ling-ch'üan Monastery in Lin-t'ung (in modern Shensi) owned, among other things, a wooded mountain and more than 150 *ch'ing* of land (close to 2,500 acres) (*CSTP* 155.9b–12b). The Buddhist Tz'u-hsiang Monastery in P'ing-yao (Shansi) is said to have had more than a thousand rooms and to have taken some fifteen years to complete (*SYTP* 22.13a). The Buddhist Yen-shou Monastery in Peking owned twenty-eight pawn shops (*SMCW* 1.16a). Sources reveal that in Chin times individual monks might also possess fortunes of their own:

> There were several dozen households of commoners who owed a certain rich monk some sixty to seventy thousand strings of cash, and they were unwilling to repay him. The monk related that he would report [the matter] to the authorities, and those who were in debt to him were greatly frightened. One after another, they bribed the interpreter [who worked for the local Jurchen official], requesting that the case be postponed. The interpreter said: "You people owe quite a bit of money. Even if the case is temporarily postponed for the present, it cannot be avoided forever. If you could thank me handsomely, I would see to it for you that he dies." They all assented gladly. After presenting the documents to the prefect, the monk, kneeling down, waited to hear the official's decision. The interpreter had secretly switched the monk's document with another piece of paper, and interpreted it [to the Jurchen official] thus: "It's been dry and without rain for a long time. [I], this monk, wish to burn this body that it might move Heaven to relieve the masses from the drought." Some twenty constables hurried the monk out, but the monk did not understand why they were arresting him. . . . After a little while, they went outside the city, to where the debtors had already made a pile of firewood. They pushed the monk onto the wood and lit the fire on all four sides. The monk cried and screamed, declaring that he was being wronged. Unable to escape, he finally burned to death. (*SMCW* 1.17b–18a)

Although no doubt an extraordinary case, the burning of this monk does illustrate the existence of conflict between wealthy monks and the masses.

One major factor in the relationship between the masses and the Buddhist monasteries during the Chin was the "twice-taxed" or "double-taxed" households (*erh-shui hu*). Double-taxed households were simply families of bond servants who paid taxes to their masters as well as to the state. According to the *Chin History*, the institution began under the Liao: "Many Liao people believed very strongly in Buddhism. [The Liao government] often gave law-abiding people to various monasteries. These people would divide their taxes, paying half to the government and half to the monasteries. They were therefore known as 'double-taxed households'" (*CS* 46.1033). Whereas during the Liao dynasty the term "double-taxed households" was used to refer to the slaves of both entrusted territories (*t'ou-hsia chün-chou*) and Buddhist monasteries, during the Chin dynasty the term was used exclusively to refer to the slaves of Buddhist monasteries. Members of double-taxed households who had been considered serfs during the Liao dynasty became slaves during the Chin (Chang Po-ch'üan 1983, 126).

The serfs given to Lung-kung Monastery in Chin-chou (Liaoning) too became slaves over a period of time. There were those among them who wanted to report the situation to the authorities, but they were murdered by the monks before they could do so. The scholar-official Li Yen (1123–75) memorialized: "According to Buddhist prescripts, monks are not to kill any living thing, let alone human beings. The Liao made these law-abiding citizens 'double-taxed households.' This was an extreme contravention of the Way. Now we have fortunately encountered a wise ruler, and I beg that all [members of double-taxed households] be freed to be loyal citizens" (*CS* 96.2127). The "wise ruler" was Shih-tsung, who accepted Li Yen's suggestion and consequently freed more than six hundred people. Another account also recorded in the *Chin History* claims that Shih-tsung was aware of the situation all along and issued an edict freeing the double-taxed households in 1162:

> After the fall of the Liao, Buddhist monks often hid the truth [that there were double-taxed households at their monasteries]. [Members of double-taxed households] were repressed and became slaves. Some of them, bringing forward solid evidence [of their mistreatment], appealed to the authorities, and the authorities sent up reports on each case [brought to their attention]. The emperor had always been aware of this matter. He therefore granted [the double-taxed households] amnesty. (*CS* 46.1033)

It is possible that the edict of 1162 was aimed at enriching the state treasury—it was also in 1162 that Shih-tsung issued the edict allowing sale of monk certificates and monastic name tablets. Freeing double-taxed households from bondage to the monasteries would have meant that the households no longer had to pay taxes to the monasteries and hence could contribute all due taxes to the state. The double-taxed households of Lü-shan Monastery, however, who provided only labor and paid no taxes to the monastery, were not among those favored by the amnesty (*CCC* 2.100): since they provided only forced labor to the monastery, their emancipation would not have increased the revenues of the state treasury. It was not until Li Yen had presented another memorial and engaged in debate with Shih-tsung that the emperor freed *all* double-taxed households, including those of Lü-shan.

Still, some double-taxed households were evidently not emancipated during Shih-tsung's reign, for shortly after Chang-tsung ascended the throne in 1190, a memorial was sent up requesting that double-taxed households be freed. To help the emperor deal with this problem, the assistant executive of the Secretariat, I-la Lü, suggested that if the state allowed all children of Khitan slaves the status of free citizens and prohibited the sale of slaves in the future, there would be no more slaves after the passage of another thirty years. Chang-tsung did not think I-la's method suitable and ordered further discussion of the matter. After more deliberation a solution was finally reached: all current double-taxed households who could provide evidence that they were not born slaves were to be freed, and those who possessed no such evidence were to continue paying half their taxes to the state and half to their monastic masters (*CS* 46.1035). Double-taxed households probably existed throughout the Chin dynasty.

Having presented the negative side of the monasteries as economic powers, we should also note their positive side. Because most monasteries were well-to-do, they were able to give relief to local populations at times of distress, to provide food and shelter to travelers, and to establish pharmacies that distributed medicine to those suffering from illness.[19] The philanthropic deeds of the Buddhists and Taoists certainly won them respect from the masses. Reflecting on the nature of the Buddhist societies and the evidence of economic conflict, we might surmise that the common people included both pious devotees and diehard disbelievers.

Concluding Remarks

While neither Buddhism nor Taoism enjoyed the level of imperial patronage under the Chin that it had during the T'ang and the Northern Sung, state patronage was still important. Although neither religion received sustained and genuine devotion from any of the Chin rulers, most of these rulers tried to give enough attention and patronage to both Buddhism and Taoism to keep their respective leaders satisfied. The Chin court never sided with any one particular religious group in order to purge another.

In this sense, it was neither partial nor necessarily warm toward either Taoism or Buddhism.

Both Taoism and Buddhism thrived under the Chin, but not without state control. Most Chin religious policies, whether they constituted friendly or unfriendly gestures toward Buddhism or Taoism, were designed to suit the interests of the state. Some measures, such as the sale of monk certificates, appear to have benefited both the government and the religious bodies: the state did raise funds to meet urgent needs, but in the long run it lost even more revenue due to the large number of tax-exempt priests created as a result of the sales. The sale of monk certificates also lowered the quality of the clergy by allowing undesirable elements to hide themselves among the pious. Several cases of open revolt led by monks caused the Jurchen Chin to tighten their control over the religious sects, even outlawing some of the more suspect. As P'an Kuei-ming (1983, 90) has written, "The power of the emperor in China was always higher than the power of the religious sects, and the Chin dynasty was no exception." The Chin generally used the same methods of control that other Chinese dynasties did.

Although both religions prospered throughout the Chin, Buddhism was probably more popular than Taoism in the early days of the dynasty. Chin Buddhism was basically a continuation of Liao and Northern Sung Buddhism; no new branches or sects were added during the Jurchen dynasty. Several new Taoist sects emerged during the Chin, however. One of these, the Ch'üan-chen sect, became the most popular religious sect in North China during the first half of the thirteenth century, overshadowing not only other Taoist sects but all Buddhist schools as well.

Many Chin dynasty Buddhists and Taoists advocated unification of the three religions. Hsing-hsiu and his disciples were the Buddhist representatives of this movement. Wang Che was the first religious figure in Chinese history to use the term "Three Doctrines," which appeared in the names of five religious congregations he established during the early years of his carreer. Unlike other advocates of the unification of the Three Doctrines who sometimes placed their own religion above the other two, Wang Che emphasized the equal importance of Taoism, Buddhism, and Confucianism.[20] His use of "Three Doctrines" in the names of his congregations is clear indication of his intention to treat all three religions impartially. Because of its emphasis on the cultivation of "inner elixir," Wang Che's school was considered a Taoist sect. In spite of that, Wang's Ch'üan-chen sect had a profound influence on the later development of the movement toward the unification of the Three Doctrines.[21]

The Jurchen Chin dynasty was at least as important to the development of Buddhism as the Southern Sung. All important later masters of Ts'ao-tung Ch'an Buddhism, for example, could trace their lines of transmission back to the Chin dynasty master Hsing-hsiu. To disregard Chin Buddhism would be to create a vacuum in the history of Chinese Buddhism. On the Taoist side, too, important developments took shape with the emergence of the new Taoist sects. The Ch'üan-chen sect, which dominated the religious scene for about a century after its founding in 1167, was especially important and became the representative of the alchemical tradition in Taoism. It is also one of the two major Taoist sects (the other being Cheng-i, representative of the magical and ritual tradition) still in existence today.

Taoists and Buddhists made voluminous collections of scriptures during the Chin dynasty. Under imperial sponsorship, the Taoists compiled the *Ta Chin hsüan-tu pao-tsang* (Precious scriptures of the mysterious capital of the Great Chin) in 6,455 volumes. This compilation, which was based on the Taoist canon compiled during the Northern Sung, was expanded by the Ch'üan-chen Taoists in 1244 to become the *Hsüan-tu pao-tsang* in 7,800 volumes. Unfortunately, a considerable portion of the *Hsüan-tu pao-tsang* was destroyed during the Yüan; the current Taoist canon, known as *Cheng-t'ung Tao-tsang* because it was first published during the Cheng-t'ung reign (1436–49) of the Ming dynasty, contains only 5,305 volumes (Liu Ts'un-yan 1975, 104, 114). As far as the compilation of the Taoist canon is concerned, the Taoists of the Chin, not those of the Southern Sung, carried on the tradition.

A Buddhist nun by the name of Ts'ui Fa-chen swore (and broke her arm to seal the oath) that she would raise the funds required to reprint the official edition of the Buddhist Tripitaka printed by the Northern Sung government. The project was started in 1139 and finally completed in 1173 (Li Fu-hua 1991, 3–4). The Chin Buddhist Tripitaka, commonly known as the *Chao-ch'eng Chin-tsang* (The Chin Tripitaka [discovered] at Chao-ch'eng [in Shansi]), in some 7,000 volumes, is a major achievement in the history of Buddhist private printing (Chung-kuo Fo-chiao hsieh-hui 1980, 100; Chiang Wei-hsin 1934; Chang Hsin-ying 1981, 35–36). It not only preserves the texts of the official Tripitaka of the Northern Sung, but also includes many additional important writings. This work is indeed important to the study of Buddhism in general and to the study of editions and textual criticism in particular (Chung-kuo Fo-chiao hsieh-hui 1980, 100). The Chin Buddhist Tripitaka was expanded during the Yüan and became known as the *Hung-fa tsang* (The Tripitaka of Hung-fa Monastery [in Peking]) (Su Pai 1964). The recent compilation of the *Chung-hua Ta-tsang-ching* (The great Tripitaka of China) was based on the *Chao-ch'eng Chin-tsang* (Chung-hua Ta-tsang-ching pien-chi chü 1984, 1). In light of the above, it is clear that the Chin Tripitaka carried on the tradition of the Buddhist Tripitaka in North China, and that it should be studied together with the Tripitakas printed under the Southern Sung.

The Chin dynasty was also a period during which many Buddhist sutras were engraved on stone tablets. According to an article by Wu Meng-lin (1981) on the *shih-ching* (sutras on stone tablets) found in the Fang-shan near Peking, the practice of engraving sutras on stone tablets started in the Sui dynasty and ended in the Ming, and was especially popular during the Sui-T'ang and Liao-Chin periods. Examining the rolls of donors who contributed to the carving of the sutras during the Chin, we find that they include members of the imperial family, high officials, and common people, as well as Buddhist priests. Some of the stone sutras carved during the Chin are not to be found anywhere else and are thus extremely valuable for the study of Buddhism.

Chin Buddhism and Chin Taoism are also indispensable to understanding specific aspects of Chin culture that, in turn, are essential to understanding the general development of Chinese culture between the Sung and Ming dynasties. For example, about two-thirds of all extant Chin *tz'u* poetry was written by members of the Ch'üan-chen sect. Two-thirds of all Chin *tz'u*, therefore, would be incomprehensible without a good understanding of Ch'üan-chen Taoism, and no serious study of Chin dynasty *tz'u* can be undertaken without considering the poetry the sect generated.[22] In the realm of art, some Chin Buddhist temples, pagodas, and pillars bearing Buddhist inscriptions still exist today and comprise valuable sources for the study of Chinese architecture, sculpture, and mural painting (Chung-kuo Fo-chiao hsieh-hui 1980, 100–101). The 1973 discovery of the Chin Buddhist murals of Yen-shang Temple in Fan-chih, Shansi, has provided raw material for the study of Chin dynasty painting and urban culture (P'an Chieh-tzu 1979; Karetzky 1980, 246). Archaelogical excavation of Chin tombs, including, during the last few decades, some Taoist tombs, has yielded many cultural relics related to Chin dynasty Taoism and Buddhism, relics that not only lend support to written sources for Buddhism and Taoism but also shed light on other aspects of Chinese culture.[23] For example, a still unearthed in 1975 in Ch'ing-lung, Hopei, proves that distillation technology existed in China at least as early as the Chin period. That particular still was employed in the Taoist practice of refining elixirs.[24] Portraits of the Twenty-four Paragons of Filial Piety carved in stone relief have been found in the tomb of P'an Te-ch'ung, a Ch'üan-chen Taoist who died in 1256. The motif can be found in tombs predating the Chin, but it is much more prevalent in tombs dating after 1161. This phenomenon is believed to be closely linked to the development of Ch'üan-chen Taoism, which advocated the virtue of filial piety (Hsü P'ing-fang 1960, 42–43; Ho-nan sheng po-wu-kuan and Chiao-tso shih po-wu-kuan 1979). The Twenty-four Paragons found in P'an's tomb not only verify the Ch'üan-chen sect's emphasis on filial piety, they can also help us to better understand the development of the paragons' story-cycle itself.[25]

In short, not only is a good understanding of Chin dynasty Buddhism and Taoism imperative for all students of Chinese religion, it is also necessary if we are to fully comprehend the development of other aspects, whether artistic or literary, of Chinese culture.

Notes

1. Both the line of Ch'u-yüan (Master Tz'u-ming of Shih-shuang Mountain, 987–1040), a teacher of Huang-lung and Yang-ch'i, and the line of Hui-chüeh, a fellow disciple of Ch'u-yüan's, continued into the Chin. Ch'u-yüan's line ended with Master I, who adhered to a policy of not transmitting his learning to unworthy disciples (*FSWC* 20.201–2; *ISWC* 37.14b–15a). According to Yüan Hao-wen (1190–1257), however, Hui-chüeh's line thrived because Chiao-heng (1150–1219), who carried on the line, was eager to expand the school and attracted many followers (*ISWC* 37.15a). Since Yüan Hao-wen was a friend of Chiao-heng's disciple Hung-hsiang, there should be no mistake in his identification of Chiao-heng as a follower of the Lin-chi branch of Ch'an Buddhism (*ISWC* 31.2a–2b). Other sources reveal that Chiao-heng also studied under the Ts'ao-tung Ch'an master Pao (1114–77) (*FTTT* 30.32a–32b; Wen Yü-ch'eng 1981, 137). The Yün-men branch of the Ch'an school, which was very popular in the early years of the Northern Sung, was still traceable during the early Chin (*CWT* 18.182).

2. From chapter 56 of the *Tao-te ching*; for an English translation, see Gia-fu Feng and Jane English 1972, 56.

3. From the *I ching*; for an English translation, see James Legge in van Over 1971, 107.

4. From chapter 44 of the *Tao-te ching*; for an English translation, see Wing-tsit Chan 1963b, 179.

5. For a study of the Ch'üan-chen sect in English, see Yao Tao-chung 1980.

6. The seven disciples of Wang Che are Ma Yü (Tan-yang, 1123–83), Sun Pu-erh (Ch'ing-ching-san-jen, 1119–82), T'an Ch'u-tuan (Ch'ang-chen, 1123–85), Hao Ta-t'ung (Kuang-ning, 1140–1212), Liu Ch'u-hsüan (Ch'ang-sheng, 1147–1203), Wang Ch'u-i (Yü-yang, 1142–1217), and Ch'iu Ch'u-chi (Ch'ang-ch'un, 1148–1227).

7. References are to the SKHP edition of *CSTP*.

8. T'ien-ch'ang Monastery was located at the site now occupied by Pai-yün Monastery. For a history of the latter, see Oyanagi 1928. In the Chin dynasty, all monastery names were given or approved by the state. T'ien-ch'ang Monastery was also known as Ta T'ien-ch'ang (the word *ta*, "great," was added to the title of some monasteries as an indication of special imperial favor) (*CWT* 36.383).

9. The word *chiao* means to offer wine without receiving a like offering in return. The sacrifice was originally practiced as part of the capping ceremony, marking a young man's passage into adulthood, and the wedding ceremony. Later, when Taoists performed sacrifices for local communities, they were known as *chiao* ceremonies. For an English description of the *chiao*, see Saso 1972.

10. According to Tsou Pao-k'u, Ch'ing-an Temple was a Buddhist nunnery at the time the former empress was in the Eastern Capital; however, it was transformed into a monastery at the end of Shih-tsung's reign (1189). Tsou (1984) also writes that there were at least two Buddhist temples built in the Eastern Capital during the Chin, Ch'ing-an Temple and Ch'ui-ch'ing Temple, and that both were built for Empress Chen-i. It was recorded in *FTTT* (30.32a) that Ch'ui-ch'ing Temple was built for an Empress Chen-i* (written with different characters) in 1170, but this is probably a scribal error. Thus, Shih-tsung built this second temple after his mother's death to commemorate her.

11. It is recorded in *FTTT* (30.32a) that on the first day of the tenth month of the eigth year of the Ta-ting era (1168), Master I of the Ch'an sect was summoned to the Eastern Capital to "establish" (*ch'uang*) Ch'ing-an Ch'an Temple and that five hundred monks were ordained. It is very unlikely that two Ch'ing-an Ch'an temples were built in the Eastern Captial during Shih-tsung's time. Since we know that the Ch'ing-an Ch'an Temple was in existence in 1155, the word "establish" here cannot mean that Master I built the temple. It is most likely that after the death of the former empress Chen-i in 1161, the temple underwent some changes and that Master I was chosen to head or to reorganize the temple. If this account is accurate, does it mean that Ch'ing-an Ch'an Temple changed from a nunnery to a monastery in 1168, rather than 1189 as reported in Tsou Pao-k'u's study? If Tsou's report (1984) is correct and if Ch'ing-an Ch'an Temple remained a nunnery until 1189, was it possible for Master I to be in charge of a nunnery and yet to ordain five hundred monks? To what temple did the monks belong? Further investigation is needed to clarify these points.

12. According to a study done by Imai (1975), the highest price paid for a monastic tablet was three hundred thousand cash; however, an inscription written for a stupa containing the ashes of the Ch'an master Pao records that he paid thirty million cash for a tablet for Ling-yen Temple (*CWT* 56.585). Given the normal price range at that time, the sum specified in this source is unrealistically high and is most likely a mistake.

13. For two examples of ordination by examination, see *HNIL* 42.217–19 and *SYTP* 20.50b. It appears that usually one first became a novice, studying under a master at a monastery, and then was later officially ordained when the opportunity arose (*HNIL* 42.217–19). It is not clear how

many novices were allowed at each monastery or what happened to those novices who were never officially ordained.

14. The Wu-hsing-p'i-lu sect here is probably another name for the P'i-lu sect, whose members have been identified by de Rachewiltz (1962a, 40 n. 13) as followers of the esoteric Diamond vehicle. In addition to the Ch'üan-chen and the P'i-lu, other sects banned include the K'ang-ch'an and the P'iao-ch'an, outlawed in 1188 (CS 8.201), and the T'ai-i and the Hun-yüan, banned in 1191. For a brief discussion of the K'ang-ch'an and the P'iao-ch'an, two heretical Buddhist sects, see de Rachewiltz 1962a, 40 n. 14. Practically nothing is known about the Hun-yüan sect. We do know that the ban of 1191 did not bring an end to the sect, because a certain Liu Hsien-hsien of the Yüan dynasty is known to have been a Hun-yüan Taoist (*LYWC* 11.14a). The Hun-yüan sect was later outlawed again in the Ming dynasty (de Rachewiltz 1962a, 42 n. 19).

15. The Korean scholar Lee Yung-bum has a different interpretation of Hai-ling's change in attitude toward Buddhism. According to Lee (1968, 31), after Hai-ling assumed the throne, he tried to sinicize everything; it was therefore only natural that he ban non-Chinese, heterodox Buddhism. If Hai-ling banned Buddhism because of its non-Chinese origin, as Lee argues, it is hard to explain why he also banned Taoism. It is more reasonable to argue that Hai-ling simply wanted to lower the prestige of organized religion, be it non-Chinese Buddhism or Chinese Taoism.

16. It is not clear whether this order of Hai-ling's was actually carried out. In his essay on the Sandalwood Buddha (*HLC* 9.11b), Ch'eng Chü-fu notes that the Buddha was housed at Ch'u-ch'ing Monastery for twenty years, from 1143 to 1163. If Ch'u-ch'ing was indeed leveled by order of the emperor, the Sandalwood Buddha must have been removed to another location. If this had been the case, Ch'eng certainly would have mentioned it in his essay. That no such mention was made suggests that Ch'u-ch'ing Monastery might have been only partially destroyed.

17. Chao is the ascribed author of the *Tao-te chen-ching chi-chieh* (*TT* 384–85).

18. For more on the history of *i*, see Kenneth K. S. Ch'en 1973, 281ff. For a study of *i* during the Liao dynasty, see Wang Chi-lin 1971. For a study of *i* during the Chin dynasty, see Katsura 1981.

19. For an example of feeding the hungry, see *CWT* 55.581. For two examples of distributing medicine, see *CWT* 55.579 and *ISWC* 35.4a–6a. For an example of providing food and shelter for travelers, see *CWT* 40.438. On the Ch'üan-chen sect and social relief, see Yao Tao-chung 1980, 185–89.

20. Chin Buddhism also advocated the unification of the Three Doctrines; however, it clearly placed Buddhism above Confucianism and

Taoism, as evidenced by the "San-chiao sheng-hsing pei" (Stele of the sacred image of the three religions), dated 1209, found at Shao-lin Monastery on Mt. Sung, Honan. On the stele is an image of the Buddha flanked by Lao-tzu on the left and Confucius on the right; the textual inscription says that Confucius' teacher was Lao-tzu and that Lao-tzu's teacher was the Buddha (Wen Yü-ch'eng and Kung Ta-chung 1975, 43). Image and inscription here both clearly rank Buddhism first in importance, Taoism second, and Confucianism third. Ellen Johnston Laing (1988–89, 118) has identified a Tz'u-chou pillow, dated 1178, with painted decoration illustrating a similar theme of unification: a Buddhist monk flanked by a Confucian scholar on the left and a Taoist priest on the right. Again, if position is any indication of importance, the Buddhist monk here is certainly accorded more than either the Taoist or the Confucian.

21. Lin Chao-en's writings, for example, were influenced by Ch'üan-chen teachings. It is known that Lin Chao-en was influenced by the Yüan dynasty Taoist Li Tao-ch'un (Berling 1980, 41), and Li Tao-ch'un is said to have belonged to the Ch'üan-chen sect (Ch'en Chiao-yu 1974, 326). The connection between the Ming dynasty advocates of the unification of the Three Doctrines and Wang Che's Ch'üan-chen sect has long been recognized. To some Ch'ing dynasty scholars, those Ming scholars who discussed the unification of the Three Doctrines were simply "remnants" of Wang Che's followers (SKTY 28.3080).

22. See Yao Tao-chung 1980, 196–202; and cf. Huang Chao-han 1988, 137. Some knowledge of Ch'üan-chen Taoism is also essential for understanding Yüan drama; see Yao Tao-chung 1980, 202–10.

23. Objects such as the Taoist cap and robe found in the tomb of the Chin Taoist Yen Te-yüan (1094–1189) offer an opportunity to visualize the life of Taoist priests during the Chin (Ta-t'ung-shih po-wu-kuan 1978, 1–7). The tomb of the Taoist Feng Tao-chen (1189–1265) has provided us with valuable objects and murals for the study of late Chin culture and art (Ta-t'ung-shih wen-wu ch'en-lieh-kuan and Shan-hsi Yün-kang wen-wu kuan-li-so 1962, 41). Another example of an archaeological find providing us with real evidence of the coexistence of Buddhism and Taoism during the Chin dynasty is the Chin tomb at Kan-ch'üan, Shensi, which contains both Buddhist and Taoist images (Chang Yen and Li An-fu 1989).

24. Ch'eng-te-shih pi-shu shan-chuang po-wu-kuan 1980, 471. For more on Ch'üan-chen's contribution to science, see Yao Tao-chung 1980, 215–18.

25. Hsü P'ing-fang (1960, 42) also writes that the Twenty-four Paragons of Filial Piety found in P'an's tomb formed the first complete set of such stories found in an archaeological context. Later archaeological finds, however, have yielded other complete story-cycles from tombs predating P'an's. Murals of the Twenty-four Paragons have been found in tombs

dating as early as 1158 (Shan-hsi-sheng k'ao-ku yen-chiu-so Chin tung-nan kung-tso chan 1985). A tomb dated 1195 contains murals depicting exactly the same twenty-four stories as found in the 1158 tomb—and in P'an Te-ch'ung's tomb (Wang Chin-hsien and Chu Hsiao-fang 1990). A set of Twenty-four Paragons in clay has also been reported discovered in a group of Chin tombs dated 1181 or earlier (the names of the twenty-four were not given in the report) (Shan-hsi-sheng k'ao-ku yen-chiu-so 1983, 55–56). The development of the Twenty-four Paragons cycle during the Chin dynasty deserves a separate study. As a traditional Chinese virtue, filial piety, while most often associated with Confucianism, was also valued and promoted by Taoism and Buddhism. Although it became part of the Taoist value system long before the Ch'üan-chen sect came into existence during the Chin, it was Wang Che who required his followers to study the *Book of Filial Piety*. Ellen Johnston Laing (1988–89, 84) feels that in addition to the efforts of the Ch'üan-chen Taoists, the popularity of filial piety as a motif in Chin tombs might partly be the result of Emperor Shih-tsung's promotion of the classic.

III

Literature
and
Art

7

FIVE PAINTINGS OF ANIMAL SUBJECTS OR NARRATIVE THEMES AND THEIR RELEVANCE TO CHIN CULTURE

Susan Bush

Earlier studies of Chin painting have focused primarily on literati art and landscape subjects or narratives in landscape settings (Bush 1986). This essay will discuss five scrolls depicting animal subjects or narrative themes that likely date from the mid-twelfth through the early thirteenth century: Chang Kuei's *Sacred Tortoise*, in the Peking Palace Museum; Chao Lin's *Six Horses* after T'ang T'ai-tsung's tomb reliefs, in the same museum; Chang Yü's *Wen-chi's Return to China*, in the Jilin Museum; Liu Yüan's *Dream of Ssu-ma Yu*, in the Cincinnati Art Museum; and Ma Yün-ch'ing's *Vimalakîrti Expounds Buddhist Sutras*, in the Peking Palace Museum. These scrolls have not previously been studied in connection with each other, nor has there been much attempt to link them with relevant cultural and institutional background. In the concluding section of this essay, the ties between artists and bureaucratic organizations will be assessed to provide grounds for addressing two questions: whether or not there was a Chin Academy of Painting, and what the status of "professional" painters was.[1]

The first scroll to be discussed, the *Sacred Tortoise* by Chang Kuei, is most unusual and not easily compared to any other contemporary work (Ku-kung po-wu-yüan 1985, pl. 45; *CKMS* 1:3.169, no. 62). In a short handscroll done in ink and colors on silk, a tortoise depicted in ink, with grass growing from his back (a sign of longevity), is placed horizontally on a sloping sandbank. From the tortoise's mouth a balloon-like cloud rises in cartoon fashion, containing the character *shou*, "longevity," written in seal script (fig. 1). The style of the painting is also quite unusual. The shell of the tortoise is distinctly patterned in a flat, decorative design, but his hind- and forefeet appear to be modeled or shaded. Both the sky and the water are tinted with blues that lighten at the point of juncture, giving the effect of a horizon. Swirling lines indicate the flow of water, and the cloud with the longevity character is lightly outlined and simulated by blank silk against the blue-tinted sky. Ocher color is used for the sand, which is textured by spattered dotting. To the lower right is a series of small, pointed rocks depicted with modulating outlines and painted with striated lines of ink in varying widths and tones. There are no classifiable *ts'un,* or brushwork patterns, in these rocks, and no sign throughout the work of Northern or Southern Sung Academy style. The painting is signed in the upper left: *sui chia Chang Kuei (hua),* "Painted by Chang Kuei of the Imperial Retinue." (The character read *hua,* "painted," is depicted in the form of a rather crude pictograph.) A Chin seal underneath the signature identifies Chang with "Ch'ing-ho," a literary synonym for a branch of the Chang family, presumably indicating the district (in modern Shantung province) that Chang Kuei's ancestors had made their ancestral seat. The other seals to the sides of the painting are Yüan and Ch'ing court seals.

The painting is identified as a Ming work in the eighteenth-century catalog of the Ch'ien-lung collection (*SCPC* 34.22; rpt. 2:1053A). There is, however, convincing evidence that Chang Kuei was a Chin painter. Collective biographies of artists indicate that Chang Kuei was active during the Cheng-lung era (1156–61) under the emperor Hai-ling (r. 1150–61) and that he was good at painting figures with correct forms and sharply defined garments. His technique was in the *chan-pi,* or "trembling brush," tradition, and his energetic outlining surpassed that of earlier masters (*THPC* 4.81; *YISCC* 14.661; Chu Chu-yü and Li Shih-sun 1958, 257). The titles of quite a few figure paintings are recorded under Chang's name in later collections: *Ch'en Lin [d. 217] Drafting a Dispatch, Assembled Worthies Collating the Classics, Autumn Moon on the Music Terrace [at Kaifeng], Description of Snow in the Liang Park [of Han], Officials Going into Retirement, Transmitting the Classics* (two paintings), *Making Music in Harmony* (two paintings), *Fourteen Images of Ancient Worthies* (*SKT* 2.148; rpt. 3:205B). The note appended to a poem by Yüan Hao-wen (1190–1257) entitled "On the Painting *Straddling the Ox*" confirms Chang Kuei's unusual signature (*YISCC* 14.661, no. 1311). "Written on the Painting of Geese and Reeds by Chang Kuei of the Chin," a poem by Yüan Hua (b. 1316), identifies Chang as a Chin artist who painted birds and flowers (*KHCS* 7.14b).[2]

The image and the inscribed character convey the wish for "longevity" simply and straightforwardly, almost redundantly. This work is quite unlike what is known of late Northern or Southern Sung Academy painting. Yet it can be assumed that the signature, *sui chia Chang Kuei,* indicates that the artist was currently part of "the Imperial Retinue," painting for an emperor; and the subject would have been appropriate for an important patron's birthday. It seems quite likely that this scroll could have been painted during the reign of Hai-ling, the ruler who shifted the Chin Central Capital to Peking (and thereby moved with him those in his retinue) and who evidently valued painting for its practical uses and possibly for its magical efficacy. Thus, he is said to have secretly commissioned painters to sketch the site of the Southern Sung capital at Hangchow, and on their return to have added to the painting a figure of himself on horseback atop Mt. Wu, overlooking West Lake, as an expression of his warlike intentions. This story, even if apocryphal, may indicate the priorities set at the mid-twelfth-century Chin court.[3]

Such paintings also raise the question of just how credulous or superstitious the Jurchen were in their approach to painting, or to the arts in general. Beliefs (and the practices that stem from them) that may seem "credulous" nowadays were thought of as eminently sensible in the twelfth century. A telling comparison can be made between the auspicious imagery valued in landscape arts by the Chin court and that prized by the Northern Sung. One story told to illustrate the simple views of the Jurchen, or at least their excessive belief in the power of geomancy (*feng-shui*) to protect the dynasty, involves the transportation of a mountain that embodied the "spirit of rule" (*wang-ch'i*) from the north, south to the palace gardens at Peking. Related symbolism can be identified in the documented removal of great water-eroded rocks from Hui-tsung's Ken-yüeh garden at Kaifeng for use at the site of the new Chin capital (Steinhardt 1983, 148). However credulous the Chin may have revealed themselves to be in their construction of rockeries, there was a Northern Sung precedent for their beliefs. In 1117, at the suggestion of a Taoist advisor, Hui-tsung constructed a mountain at the northeast corner of the Imperial City as a symbol of the male force (*yang*) that might favor the birth of male heirs. His lavish acquisitions for this garden are considered one of the causes for the fall of the dynasty (Yao Tao-chung 1980, 14–17); thus, even a Sung emperor, like Hui-tsung, could give credence to the power of geomancy to nurture the dynasty.

Official attitudes toward painting during the Northern Sung can also be inferred from the "Hua chi" (Notes on painting), the last section of the *Lin-ch'üan kao-chih* of Kuo Hsi (ca. 1010–ca. 1090). This record of Kuo Hsi's career at court provides insights into the relationship between artist and patron, and the special type of imagery it produced. Kuo's imperial screen *Whirling Snow in the North Wind* was evidently produced in 1074 to counter the effects of a great drought. Symbolism is easily read in certain landscape subjects done for specific purposes. For example, a screen done for the

Figure 1. Chang Kuei (fl. mid-12th cent.), *Sacred Tortoise*.

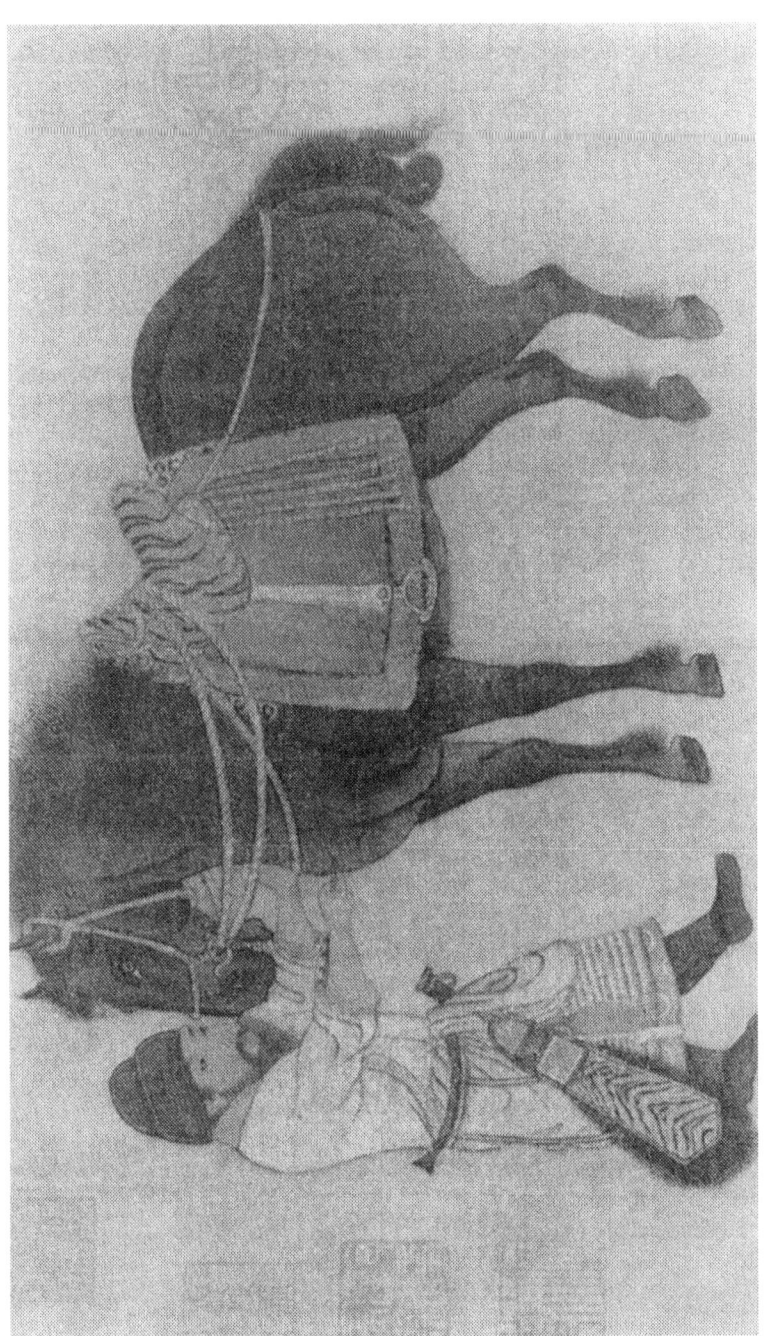

Figure 2. Chao Lin (fl. mid-12th cent.), *Six Horses*, detail.

eleventh hall of the Ching-ling Palace (the Imperial Shrine) showed a great boulder in eleven pieces with innumerable fragments, large and small, behind it: the rocks here appeared to refer to imperial descendants (Suzuki 1981; Po Sung-nien and Ch'en Shao-feng 1982). Kuo Hsi's son, Kuo Ssu (*chin-shih* of 1082, d. after 1123), who edited the *Lin-ch'üan kao-chih*, also describes a scroll that his father painted for the sixtieth (?) birthday of Wen Yen-po (1006–97), a long-tenured minister. It depicted an old man under a pine near a cliff, looking out at innumerable pines of different sizes linked in an uninterrupted view. This unusual composition was designed to express the wish for an unbroken line of descendants in high posts. It is noteworthy that the Kuo Hsi text's approach to subject matter has been thought to foreshadow the inclination of Chin scholars to read landscapes in social terms (Po Sung-nien and Ch'en Shao-feng 1982, 65). In contrast to Kuo Hsi's subtle landscapes, the *Sacred Tortoise* scroll seems to represent a fairly simple level of imagery, explicitly conveying in its literally descriptive style an appropriate and auspicious message for an imperial patron.

A straightforward illustration of early Chin cultural values is provided by a second painting, the *Six Horses* or *Six Steeds*, after the reliefs of T'ang T'ai-tsung's chargers originally in place at Chao-ling. A colophon by Chao Ping-wen (1159–1232), which bears the date 1220, authenticates the scroll and states that the artist was a certain Chao Lin of Loyang, a *tai-chao*, or court attendant, under Shih-tsung (r. 1161–89) (Koyama 1975, nos. 30–31; Ku-kung po-wu-yüan 1985, pls. 35–41; *CKMS* 1:3.170–75, no. 63, 5:4.109–11, no. 66; *SCHP* rpt. 1:336A–339B; Shen Fu 1980, 71). *Tai-chao* is not one of the official titles cited in the Chin dynastic history's treatise on officials and the bureaucracy; Chao Ping-wen presumably used the term as a casual reference to the post of court calligrapher or painter.[4] In standard biographies of artists, Chao Lin is recorded as having been active under Hsi-tsung (r. 1135–50) (Chu Chu-yü and Li Shih-sun 1958,332–33). Since no signature is given, he appears to have been responsible for both the painting of the horses and the accompanying inscriptions.

After the title inscription "Painting of T'ang T'ai-tsung's Six Horses," the scroll opens with a section of text loosely quoting the *Hsin T'ang-shu* biography of General Ch'iu Hsing-kung (early 7th cent.), famous for saving T'ai-tsung's life during the battle for Loyang (*TS* 90.3778–79). When the emperor's horse Whirlwind Victory (Sa-lu-tzu) was wounded, Ch'iu, the only member remaining of the emperor's party, managed to fight off the attacking enemy. Then, dismounting, he pulled the arrow from the horse's breast, gave the emperor his own horse to ride, and escorted him back to camp on foot. To commemorate this heroic exploit, the emperor had a stone image of Ch'iu extracting the arrow placed at Chao-ling. The textual inscription on the scroll ends with mention of the emperor's aim—"to exalt military service"—and the first image that follows in the painting is of Ch'iu Hsing-kung removing the arrow from Whirlwind Victory (fig. 2).

The original six steeds were the mounts ridden by T'ai-tsung in his early victories, and their images, carved in stone and celebrated in eulogies supposedly written by the emperor, were placed in front of the grave of Empress Wen-te (d. 636) on Mt. Chiu-tsung in Shensi. Between 644 and 649 this tomb complex was expanded and renamed Chao-ling. T'ai-tsung's grave was located two miles to the south of Wen-te's. In 1089, because it was inconvenient to visit these famous stone horses, a military governor of the district, Yu Shih-hsiung (1038–97), erected a stele of the "Six Steeds of Chao-ling," which included engraved line drawings of the horses along with inscriptions of the eulogies. From Yu's own inscription on the 1089 stele, we learn of a painting of T'ai-tsung's six horses attributed to Yen Li-pen (d. 673), presumably the original design for the sculptured reliefs, with eulogies said to have been composed by the Eighteen Scholars of T'ai-tsung's court (Ferguson 1931; 1935, 1–6; *CSTP* 139.10b–13a; Acker 1954–74, 2:210–12, 216).[5]

There are obviously some differences between the Chao Lin handscroll and its potential sources, the stone reliefs from Chao-ling and the engraved copies on the stele of 1089. The position and ordering of identifications and eulogies do not correspond exactly to what appears on the stele or what is presumed to have appeared on the sculptures. Moreover, the scroll is introduced by quotations from Ch'iu Hsing-kung's biography, no doubt to emphasize the value placed on military service and valor and thereby underline the virtues exhibited by the horses themselves. Most significantly, the horses are not strict imitations of T'ang originals, but free copies done in something like the current mode: their manes are not cut in the "three-blossom" fashion; their stirrups have added lower supports; their saddles are higher in front and in back. These features would seem to rule out strong influence from another possible source mentioned on Yu Shih-hsiung's stele of 1089: the painting done in the T'ang style attributed to Yen Li-pen, or a reproduction of it taken from a stone engraving. The variations in form and composition that occur on the scroll may or may not be Chin innovations; however, they are effective. For example, both Ch'iu Hsing-kung and Whirlwind Victory are shown on the scroll in seven-eighths rather than in strict profile view, evidently to compensate for the loss of three-dimensionality suffered in the transition from sculptured relief to painting (figs. 2, 3). The vigorous style of the Chao Lin painting has also been thought to be an attempt to transfer the monumentality of the stone reliefs into the small-scale format of the handscroll. Thus, vitality is

Figure 3. Ch'iu Hsing-kung and Whirlwind Victory.

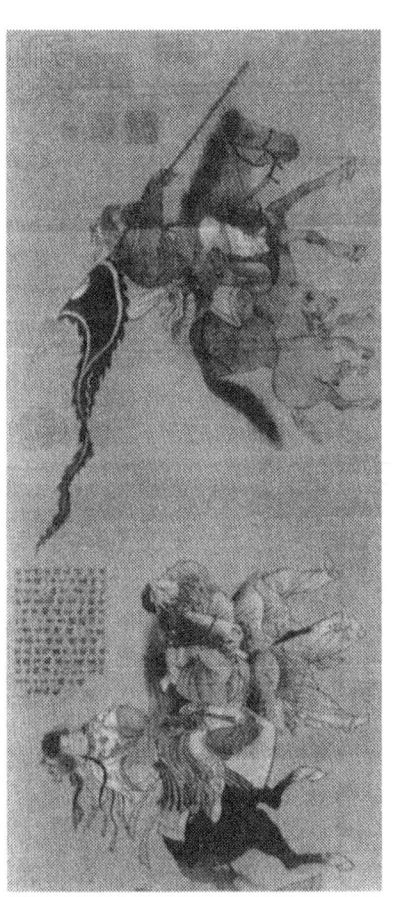

Figure 4. Chang Yü (?) (late 12th–early 13th cent.), *Wen-chi's Return to China.*

Figure 5. Chang Yü, *Wen-chi's Return to China*, detail.

Figure 6. Liu Yüan (fl. early 13th cent.), *Dream of Ssu-ma Yu*.

now emphasized pictorially by the hairs that rise from mane, tail, and body, or those that sprout from a beard and seem to quiver. The isolation of images against the plain ground and the following insertions of calligraphic texts would be considered archaistic features in a mid-twelfth-century work.

Chao Lin's scroll celebrates military valor and the establishment of dynastic rule through horsepower by references to T'ang precedents. Its meaning is underlined by quotations from Ch'iu Hsing-kung's biography, and its value is enhanced by the transcribed inscriptions and eulogies attributed to T'ang T'ai-tsung. The latter were appreciated in late Northern Sung by literati-connoisseurs such as Su Shih (1036–1101) and were to be commented on by Wang Yün (1227–1304) in a postscript to an anonymous painting of the *Six Steeds of Chao-ling* (*CSTP* 139.13a; *CCWC* 72.5b–6a). In light of Chin history, the Chao Lin scroll may remind us that the Jurchen exhibited an interest in the T'ang imperial tombs long before the court debates on the Chin as successors to the T'ang took place. When the Jurchen controlled the region of Sian, they carried on the Northern Sung restoration of the T'ang imperial graves. In 1134 a stele at Ch'ien-ling was engraved with an inscription in Jurchen and Chinese recording the restoration of T'ang Kao-tsung's temple buildings (Nishikawa 1966, no. 116). And sixty years later, a Chin inscription dated 1194 was carved on the reverse side of Yu Shih-hsiung's stele of 1089 (Ferguson 1935, 2). It seems likely that the Chao Lin scroll was appreciated at the Chin court primarily for its historical associations with T'ang T'ai-tsung, at least as far as we can judge from Wang Yün's comments.

Another Chin painting, probably done under Chang-tsung (r. 1190–1208), also features horses done in colors on silk and is definitely the work of a court painter. It is the handscroll *Wen-chi's Return to China*, which is signed: "Painted by Chang Yü of the Commission of Palace Services [*chih-ying ssu*]." In 1196 the Department of Painting (*t'u-hua shu*), which supervised painters and embroiderers in the palace, was reorganized and absorbed into the Commission of Palace Services (*CS* 56.1274). Thus, the signature suggests that this work was produced at the imperial palace sometime after 1196. The artist's name is nearly illegible, but it has been read as "Yü" by Kuo Mo-jo (1964; Su Hsing-chün 1964; *CKMS* 1:3.160–65, no. 59). Chang Yü's name is not recorded in the standard collective biographies of artists. The handscroll (fig. 4), formerly in the Ch'ing imperial collection, must be classified as an illustrative figure painting with genre elements. The signature and style, as well as the figure types, confirm its identification as a Chin work. Elements of costume can also be identified as specific to this period. It is true that the woman's fur hat with earmuffs appears in Liao tomb murals from the region of southern Manchuria, but the man's costume of fur-edged riding tunic worn over pantaloons, the relatively low saddles, and the lack of owners' brands on the horses diverge from Khitan fashion. It is also significant that Wen-chi's grieving husband is shown with a full beard, since the Jurchen were quite hirsute. They are also said to have worn their hair in two long strands or queues on their shoulders like the earlier Hsien-pei of the northeast. This mode contrasts with the intricately shaved hairdos, with braided locks usually falling in front of the ears, that were worn by the relatively hairless Khitan of the Liao dynasty (Johnson 1983, 130 n. 66). Thus, the well-known story of Ts'ai Yen, or Wen-chi, who was married to a Hsiung-nu ruler toward the end of Han and then recalled to China to carry on her family line, is evidently illustrated here in contemporary Jurchen costume.

That the scene described is Wen-chi's return to China would seem to be confirmed by the hunting falcon (a northeastern type), the hound, and the wrapped silver vase, all appropriate tribute gifts for barbarians to carry to a Chinese ruler. The colt by its mother's side that heads the procession may also be a reference to the children that Wen-chi has had to leave behind. Interestingly, Wen-chi's face is that of an older woman, with a prominent nose and double chins, and her booted foot, with muscle enough to exert pressure on the stirrup, has not been bound (fig. 5).[6] There is a striking contrast here between the demeanor of the barbarians, hunched over in their saddles with expressions of grief as they attempt to protect themselves against the bitter desert wind, and the two more stoical Chinese, Wen-chi, outwardly impervious to wind and grief, and the Chinese ambassador, who merely holds a fan up to his face. These details of Chang Yü's depiction of Wen-chi and her escorts impart an overtone of Chinese cultural superiority, in unspoken contravention, perhaps, of the 1191 decree prohibiting all reference to Jurchen as *fan*, "barbarians." It is also possible that the idealization of Wen-chi's bravery may reflect the general character of heroines portrayed in contemporary literature.

A question remains as to whether this composition originated with Chang Yü or was based on an earlier painting. In any case, the style of depiction, like the style of dress, hair, and the horses' trappings, seems acceptably Chin. The figures are again isolated against a plain ground, as in classical T'ang figure painting, and the wedge-shaped massing of the troops is reminiscent of a compositional device seen in the murals of Prince Chang-huai's tomb of 711 near Ch'ang-an (Fontein and Wu 1976, fig. 110). Another mannerism, which happens to reflect a Six Dynasties style, is the fluttering of scarves that adds to Wen-chi's presence. An earlier usage of this sort can be seen in the famous *Admonitions to the Court Ladies* attributed to Ku K'ai-chih (ca. 344–ca. 406), which was evidently in Chin Chang-tsung's collection (Toyama 1955, 26–27). It might be noted in this connection that Northern Wei Buddhist sculpture of the early sixth century, in the so-called Elongated Style with floating scarves, was revived in the region of northern Hopei under the Chin. Indeed, the touch of conscious archaism in the Wen-chi scroll and its conservative aspect are exactly what one might expect to find in a Chin composition of around 1200 that had developed from the figure style of the T'ang. The brushwork is still relatively straightforward, despite some decorative hooks. Hence, its modulations or variations in width help to describe the contours and textures of the images represented, in contrast to later brush techniques.

As for the content of the Wen-chi handscroll in the context of Chin culture, Linda Cooke Johnson (1974, 56–62, 66) has discussed it in connection with the Jurchen revival started by Shih-tsung and continued under Chang-tsung in an attempt to stem the increasing sinicization of the Jurchen people. No doubt the edicts banning Han Chinese dress account for the artist's scrupulous observation of costumes and trappings. The Wen-chi theme was, of course, popular throughout the history of Sung painting, and it allowed artists to depict exotic scenes and customs, like the simplified Liao encampments shown in twelfth-century album leaves in the Boston Museum. Southern Sung treatments of the subject have also been thought to have served as vehicles to express anti-Chin sentiments (Sirén 1956, 3: pls. 316–18; Wen Fong and Marilyn Fu 1973, 36–40). In these illustrations Wen-chi is usually standing or seated and is always grieving, as she is in the famous series of poems that is ascribed to her. By contrast, a heroic northern depiction of Wen-chi on horseback braving the elements with composure may have seemed particularly suitable in a painting made for palace ladies and their children at the Jurchen court. The courage displayed in the face of cold and grief was presumably not thought of as simply poignant, but as morally instructive; hence, the idealization of Wen-chi's figure may represent the painter's attempt to depict her as a paragon, a role model. As Johnson has noted, the story is classically Chinese in its connotations of filial piety, since Wen-chi leaves her non-Chinese husband and children to return to her homeland and remarry for the benefit of father and family. It should not be surprising that Chinese cultural values seem to be expressed in an archaistic figure painting employing Jurchen iconography. After all, with the translation of the Chinese classics into the Jurchen language, the Jurchen revival itself ultimately served to promote Confucian virtues (Johnson 1974; Tao Jing-shen 1976, 80–81).

Another narrative handscroll, the *Dream of Ssu-ma Yu*, was presumably produced in the milieu of the Chin court in the first part of the thirteenth century. This work in colors on silk also illustrates a literary theme and is signed by another unrecorded artist, a certain Liu Yüan of the Commission of Palace Services (*chih-ying ssu*). The inscription is above the painter's seal ("P'ing-shui Liu Yüan") and reads: "Composed by Liu Yüan of P'ing-shui, of the *chih-ying ssu*, disciple of San-t'ang Wang." The colophons attached to the scroll are of recent date. The painting was formerly in the collection of Chang Heng (1915–63), who inscribed the story of Ssu-ma Yu (late 11th cent.) in the main colophon. While in Loyang, Ssu-ma Yu, a great nephew of Ssu-ma Kuang (1019–86), once dreamt of the Southern Dynasties courtesan Su Hsiao-hsiao (late 5th cent.), who sang to him a *tz'u* to the tune of "The Golden Threads." In the early 1090s Ssu-ma Yu served in office at Hangchow, where he lived right next to Su Hsiao-hsiao's tomb. The romantic nature of the story was further enhanced when, within a year of his move to Hangchow, Ssu-ma Yu died in mysterious circumstances during an outing on a pleasure boat that caught fire. The scene depicted in the handscroll illustrates the apparition of Su Hsiao-hsiao as described in another *tz'u*, this written in response to hers, by Ch'in Kou (late 11th cent.), brother of Ch'in Kuan (1049–1100) and friend of Ssu-ma Yu (Sherman E. Lee and Wai-kam Ho 1968, no. 199; LTSS 20.224):

> The horn comb slanting above her hair—a cloud half rising.
> She gently marks time with the sandalwood clapper,
> And sings with all her heart the song of "The Golden Threads."
> Her dream wanders beyond the colored clouds and is lost forever.

The appearance of a female ghost to a budding scholar is a romantic theme that was well known in literature but extremely rare in art. In fact, there seems to be no comparable painting dating from the Sung period or earlier. On the one hand, the depiction of the singing girl is almost a genre subject, a dramatization of the performance of a romantic ballad. On the other hand, since she is an apparition from the past, the courtesan is distanced from the viewer. Her grief at the passing of time is also screened, as it were, by her covered mouth, and she is painted in three-quarters profile. And yet, hunched forward with a sleeve to her face, her figure is effectively theatrical and conveys a certain poignancy. Su Hsiao-hsiao is shown with the sandalwood clapper of the singing girl, another dramatic prop, and her ghostliness is emphasized by a swirling bank of fog and the curling, tentacle-like scarves that flutter in the wind, which also bends the candle flame. The artist has taken great pains with drapery folds and patterns, as well as with the construction of objects and their surface textures; but there is no display of bravura brushwork (fig. 6).

The Cincinnati *Dream of Ssu-ma Yu* exhibits stylistic traditions that originated in the Northern Sung. Su Hsiao-hsiao's relatively slender proportions and the mannneristic fluttering of her scarves (fig.7) reflect a

Sung Buddhist style still prevalent in twelfth-century murals of the Shansi region. These elements appear in the Buddhist tales painted in 1158 on the walls of Yen-shan Temple, on the northern slopes of the Wu-t'ai Mountains, under the direction of chief painter Wang K'uei, who may have received his training in the Northern Sung Academy of Painting. Curling scarves and patterned garments can be seen in the disheveled costumes of court ladies in the scene of Prince Siddhârtha's departure from the palace, and in the swirling drapery encircling Mâra's troops in the scene of the temptation. Architectural detail is carefully defined in these murals, and it is noteworthy that the steps and layered wooden siding depicted at the base of Siddhârtha's palace compare with those in the Cincinnati scroll (Karetzky 1980, 245–52, figs. 8, 13; P'an Chieh-tzu 1979, 4, 6, fig. 6, pl. 2). Moreover, a possible model for Liu Yüan's interpretation of the female figure with loose patterned garments can be seen in popular secular art in the woodcut illustration of four historical beauties that was found at Karakhoto in Central Asia (K. T. Wu 1950, 458, pl. 2).[7] Signed by printers, the Chi family of P'ing-yang, it is now accepted as a Chin print, and a prime example of the hedonistic imagery fostered by the popular culture of the middle Fen region. By the end of the Chin dynasty the P'ing-yang district had become a center for Buddhist art and secular theater as well as commercial and religious printing. Should the similarities in conservative style and romantic subject matter that appear in the print and the *Dream of Ssu-ma Yu* be interpreted as signs of regional influence on court art?

More information on this point is provided by the inscription on the painting. As in the Wen-chi handscroll, the term *chih-ying ssu* in Liu Yüan's signature implies that he was currently attached to the office, established in 1196, that provided paintings and silk embroideries for the Chin palace. The place-name in the signature, "P'ing-shui," corroborates a Chin date for the scroll, since the name was used only under the Jurchen. At that time P'ing-shui district was just south of the larger area of P'ing-yang and, like it, was a noted center of printing (CS 26.637). A source on Liu's teacher, San-t'ang Wang, sheds further light on the date of the scroll, as well as its regional affiliations and subject matter. A poem by Tuan Ch'eng-chi (1199–1279) entitled "A Colophon on San-t'ang Wang's Portrait of Myself" confirms the identity of San-t'ang Wang as a painting master in its comparison of the portraitist to Ku K'ai-chih (*HFSC* 7.45; *CCS* 58.20a–20b; rpt. 2:849B–850A). The poet Tuan Ch'eng-chi was a native of Chi-shan in Chiang-chou (Shansi), where P'ing-shui district too was located (*CS* 26.637). This supports the likelihood that the "P'ing-shui" in the Liu Yüan inscription refers to the district of the lower Fen region. Tuan Ch'eng-chi received a *chin-shih* degree at Kaifeng sometime during the Cheng-ta era (1224–32); thereafter he held the post of chief registrar of I-yang district near Loyang, which had been the Central Capital since 1217. After the fall of the Chin dynasty, he and his elder brother Tuan K'o-chi (1196–1254) went to the Lung-men Mountains, which are partly in Ho-chin district, Shansi. After his brother's death in 1254, Ch'eng-chi went to live with his family in the P'ing-yang area, where he refused to serve under the Mongols as superintendent of Confucian studies (CCS 58.1a–1b; rpt. 2:840A). Since Ch'eng-chi's poem does not appear in the *Erh-miao chi* (which includes the works of Tuan K'o-chi), it may have been composed after his move to the P'ing-yang area in 1254. The chronology is feasible: if San-t'ang Wang was an established artist in his thirties or forties in the 1220s, his disciple Liu Yüan must have been active during the late Chin, contemporary with, if younger than, Tuan Ch'eng-chi. This Liu Yüan of P'ing-shui attached to the *chih-ying ssu* should not be confused with the early Yüan sculptor of the same name, born in approximately 1248 in Pao-ti district south of Peking and eventually attached to the Yüan Imperial Archive (*mi-shu chien*) (Weidner 1982, 46–49, 212–13 n. 56).[8]

We may shed some light on the subject matter of the scroll and its relevance to late Chin culture by focusing on the name of the portraitist San-t'ang Wang. "San-t'ang" was the name given to the governor's estate in Kuo-chou (modern Ling-pao district, Honan), on the Yellow River midway between Ch'ang-an and Loyang. Ssu-ma Kuang was then residing in nearby Loyang, and Su Shih was of his circle. The subject of the Cincinnati *Dream of Ssu-ma Yu* has regional associations with Loyang, where Ssu-ma Kuang's great nephew had his dream, as well as links to Su Shih. Su himself had recommended Yu for a *chin-shih* equivalency examination, and it was the brother of Su's disciple Ch'in Kuan who wrote the *tz'u* that is illustrated in the painting. If we consider the importance of Ssu-ma Kuang and Su Shih for the sinicized Jurchen of the late Chin period, it may not surprise us that a painting of this type could have been produced by a court artist active toward the end of the dynasty (Tao Jing-shen 1976, 99–100). A literary romance with a student-hero would no doubt have had wide appeal at that time, when the scholar class was rapidly growing with the addition of new *chin-shih* degree graduates. Nevertheless, this subject is not likely to have been approved under an earlier emperor like Shih-tsung, who once censured Su Shih for his loose moral standards in consorting with singing girls (*CCS* 1.20b; rpt. 1:69B). Thus, the Liu Yüan handscroll may serve to suggest the decline of simple moral values at the late Jurchen court and the corresponding rise of the influence of the Northern Sung literati. The genre aspects of the narrative illustration and the specific references found in the inscription also underline the importance of the popular culture of the Ho and Fen regions toward the end of Chin.

Figure 7. Liu Yüan, *Dream of Ssu-ma Yu*, detail.

Figure 8. Attributed to Li Kung-lin (1049–ca. 1105), reattributed to Ma Yün-ch'ing (fl. 1229), *Vimalakīrti Expounds Buddhist Sutras*, detail.

As a final perspective on the subject matter, one might note that a few singing girls captured at the fall of both Northern Sung and Chin were able to lament their fates in *tz'u* set to memorized rhyme schemes (Sargent 1993, 230, 252). If Ssu-ma Yu's dream of Su Hsiao-hsiao portended an early death, the "soundless poem" sung in Liu Yüan's painting might well be a dirge for the Chin, as certain details suggest: the young scholar is dozing, caught off guard in a vulnerable pose while beside him, lying on a nearby table among his books, the blade of his elegant lacquer-hilted sword is cut off by the margins of the scroll.

The last painting to be discussed is a direct product of the late Northern Sung literati tradition in art, but it also exhibits some traces of regional influence. It is *Vimalakîrti and the Single Doctrine* (or *Vimalakîrti Expounds Buddhist Sutras*) in ink on paper, once attributed to the late Northern Sung painter Li Kung-lin (1049–ca. 1106) but now thought to be a copy executed by a Chin artist, Ma Yün-ch'ing, sometime around 1229. The reattribution was suggested because of an inscription on another painting of the same subject, this done by Wang Chen-p'eng (ca. 1280–1329) at the command of Yüan Jen-tsung (r. 1312–20) in 1308, as a copy of a composition by Ma Yün-ch'ing of the Chin that was to be followed by a second version, in color (*CPOT* 15.359, no. 696; *YISCC* 14.647–48). This inscription was recorded by the Ch'ing critic Wang Shih-chen (1634–1711), and the painting on which it occurs is now in the Metropolitan Museum of Art, signed as having been painted by Wang Chen-p'eng (Wen Fong and Hearn 1981–82, 28).[9] The handscroll in Peking, which is a classic example of Li Kung-lin's *pai-miao*, or "plain outline," method, has no signature, and its colophons date from the fifteenth through the seventeenth centuries. The earliest seals on it are of Yüan date and include one of Ch'iao K'uei-ch'eng's (fl. 1270–1313?), which, if genuine, would indicate that the painting was already extant in the thirteenth century. The style of the work, moreover, is consistent with a late Chin date.

The original that was copied first- or secondhand in the Peking and New York versions was presumably the Li Kung-lin handscroll painted in the *pai-miao* technique on silk and entitled *Vimalakîrti and the Single Doctrine* (*Wei-mo pu erh*). The location of this work is not currently known, but it is included in the catalog of Buddhist and Taoist paintings in the Ch'ien-lung imperial collection. There was no signature on it, but both the attribution to Li and the title appear in a poem by the Jurchen collector Wan-yen Shou (1172–1232). The author of the earliest colophon (dated to 1285), Shang T'ing (1209–88), notes that he first saw seen the scroll in Kaifeng, in 1229, in the collection of Ma Yün-ch'ing's father, a certain Liao-liao-chü-shih. Shang T'ing's own father had received a *chin-shih* degree in

1213, the same year Ma Yün-ch'ing's elder brother had. Hence, the painting had personal associations for Shang; he was apparently able to borrow it because of his friendship with the current owner. After the Mongol conquest he had no idea whether the scroll was still in existence, but in 1285 he learned of its whereabouts by way of Ch'iao K'uei-ch'eng and managed to see it again after fifty-six years. When he had first seen it in 1229, an inscription of the *Heart Sutra gâthâ* in the hand of Huang T'ing-chien (1045–1105) had appeared at the beginning of the scroll; unfortunately, this valuable piece of calligraphy had been lost by 1285 (*PTCL* 9.12, rpt. 1:109).

Ma Yün-ch'ing was evidently a figure painter and copyist with literati connections. The early Yüan writer Wang Yün owned a small portrait of Confucius with an inscription on it by K'ung Yüan-ts'o (1179?–1252?), fifty-first lineal descendant of Confucius and an official at the Chin court (*CS* 14.314). The painting bore a Chin reign era date in accordance with 1229 and was said to have been "brushed by Ma Yün-ch'ing, a student at the Imperial University" (*CCWC* 71.6b). Wang Yün records seeing in the Jade Hall of the Han-lin Academy Ma's copy of an Wu Tao-tzu (8th cent.) painting of Mt. T'ai and the Northern Dipper, with seven figures, some of whom were in armor. He further describes in some detail another painting with complex iconography, also done by Ma in the Wu tradition, depicting the five planets (corresponding to the Five Elements). Both Wan-yen Shou and Yüan Hao-wen wrote poems on another portrait by Ma, *Paper-clothed Recluse* (*YISCC* 14.647–48, no. 1254, citing *CCWC*; *CCS* 1.30b–31a, rpt. 1:33B–34A).

Apparently, there were a number of Ma brothers toward the end of the Chin dynasty who were competent portrait painters and who moved in literary circles. Ma Yün-han is said to have presented a portrait of Confucius to Wang O (1190–1273) on his retirement into mourning for a grandmother in 1230. Was this the same portrait later known to Wang Yün, or another version done by Ma Yün-ch'ing's brother? Yüan Hao-wen also knew the work of Ma Yün-han: he wrote poems on some landscapes by this artist and composed a eulogy for another of his paintings, *Reading the Classics*, that was evidently a portrait of Chu Hsi (1130–1200) (*ISWC* 38.520; *YISCC* 10.481, no. 661, 14.640–41, no. 1228–30, 14.648–49, no. 1257). Another brother, Ma T'ien-lai (1172–1232), also known as Ma Yün-chang (his *tzu* was originally Yüan-chang), was a scholar-official. He came from Chieh-hsiu in the region of Taiyuan, Shansi (*CS* 26.631), and spent nineteen years at the Imperial University. Around 1209 he was transferred to the first of a series of minor posts in the south. In 1213 he received a *chin-shih* degree in classical exegesis and thereafter became a compiler at the National Academy of History. Even after he became an official, however,

Figure 9. Ma Yün-ch'ing, *Vimalakīrti Expounds Buddhist Sutras*, detail.

Figure 10. Ma Yün-ch'ing, *Vimalakîrti Expounds Buddhist Sutras*, detail.

his usual dress was that of a commoner, and he still provided sculptural images and paintings on request. His practice of technical skills when in office was evidently unusual enough to require comment. Still, since he was a scholar-official, it is not surprising that the one painting of his described in later texts is a small scroll of bamboo and rocks with an unconventional air (THPC 4.80).

The Peking handscroll (fig. 8) now attributed to Ma Yün-ch'ing exemplifies a syncretic Confucian-Buddhism. The subject is the debate between the cultured Buddhist layman Vimalakîrti and the Bodhisattva of Wisdom, Mañjuśrî, as described in the *Ta-ch'eng ting-wang ching* (*Vimalakîrtinirdeśa sûtra*). The scene depicted is the moment when Vimalakîrti is proclaiming his doctrine of unity by a silence like a thunderclap, and Mañjuśrî, who is seated facing him, bends slightly forward with clasped hands to acknowledge the end of the debate (figs. 9, 10). In the middle distance are two subsidiary debaters: the Heavenly Maid, with upheld bowl of flowers and a blossom to toss, and the monk Śâriputra, shrinking from the rain of flowers, petals stuck to his robe. Since in the course of their debate, which concerned the position of women in Buddhism, the Heavenly Maid switched forms with the monk to prove that all, including gender, is an illusion, identification of which figure in the painting is which becomes difficult. Mañjuśrî and Vimalakîrti are depicted in stone engravings and murals from as early as the Six Dynasties period, when, according to the documentary record, a famous portrait of the latter was done by Ku K'ai-chih (Davidson 1954, 32–42; Sickman and Soper 1956, pl. 80; Soper 1959, 133; Bunker 1968, 33–43).

The Peking Palace Museum's handscroll is painted in the *pai-miao* technique, lending the figure of Vimalakîrti an affecting simplicity. If it is indeed a copy of Li Kung-lin's work, certain aspects of the ornamentation would seem to be in keeping with a twelfth- to thirteenth-century decorative style, and this would strengthen the likelihood of attribution to a Chin artist. Some of the scrollwork that serves as edging on the dais or throne, for example, is definitely twelfth century in type, and contrasting ink tones on the paper serve to emphasize different kinds of designs. Comparable vine scrolls occur on Tz'u-chou ware of late Northern Sung date, where strong contrasts in pattern are also favored (Mino 1980, 79, pl. 27). The decorative motifs that are depicted with loving detail in the Peking scroll have a generally flowery character. This is, of course, reminiscent of Chin Buddhist ornamentation of the Shansi region, which, like secular tomb carvings from the area, exhibits a delight in striking effects. An example of such ornamentation appears on an unusual stele of 1162 from the Lower Hua-yen Temple at Tatung, recording Chin restoration of the temple. In lieu of entwined dragons, the stele is topped by an engraved floral scroll, and it stands without a tortoise base on a rectangular plinth carved with peonies in ogival frames (Sekino and Takeshima 1934–35, 110–11). These examples of ornaments in different media are necessarily distinct from the subtle decorative detail of the Peking scroll, but they can serve as reminders of the middle Fen culture from which the Ma brothers emerged.

The Peking handscroll differs from the other Chin paintings discussed above in the religious import of its subject matter and the long artistic tradition that underlies it. Presumably, a high level of literary and calligraphic training would have been necessary in order to appreciate, study, and copy the revered original version by Li Kung-lin, graced with Huang T'ing-chien's calligraphy. Ma Yün-ch'ing is known to have been a student at the Imperial University and the brother of a scholar-official. Moreover, his family was wealthy enough at one time to own an important work of art—the Li Kung-lin scroll—and may also have been in contact with the Jurchen collector and painter Wan-yen Shou. In any case, Ma Yün-ch'ing and his brothers associated with well-known literary figures at the Chin Southern Capital toward the end of the dynasty. This was a time when Tao-hsüeh Confucian interests had come to the fore in scholarly circles but Ch'an Buddhism still exerted a strong influence. In copying Confucian, Buddhist, or Taoist subjects, Ma Yün-ch'ing was essentially following in the footsteps of Li Kung-lin, the most accomplished painter of Su Shih's group of friends and one whose later works always contained a moral message. Hence, Ma Yün-ch'ing's careful attempt to recreate Li's drapery or ornaments should be interpreted as concern with the transmission of an important painting, one appreciated for its subject matter as well as for its style. Vimalakîrti, the erudite Buddhist layman, could still be a model in Chin times, as he had been in Northern Sung, for the contemporary scholar with syncretic tendencies. When copying was done freehand on paper, slight variations in form and technique were inevitable: these would be Ma Yün-ch'ing's own additions to an enduring cultural tradition. His name was evidently known to later connoisseurs as a transmitter of Li Kunglin's style, not only for Wang Chen-p'eng, but also for Chao Meng-fu (1254–1322) (*CHSHF* 8.63). Thus, Ma Yün-ch'ing's figure painting represents a product of the artistic mainstream of the period and an example of the preservation and enrichment of Northern Sung literati culture at the end of Chin.

Far more is known about the "Academy" of the Northern and Southern Sung than about the organization of court painters under the Chin dynasty. The Han-lin Bureau of Painting (*t'u-hua yüan*) was set up under the Han-lin Academy in 984 as one of a series of palace workshops and formally organized with four ranks of painters (*tai-chao, i-hsüeh, chih-hou, hsüeh-sheng*) in 998. Its name was changed to the Office of Painting (*t'u-hua chü*) in 1095, when it was placed under the supervision of the Directorate of Inner Palace Services (*nei-shih sheng*). In addition, for a short period between 1104 and 1110, an Institute of Painting (*hua-hsüeh*) functioned along with other institutes of calligraphy, mathematics, and medicine as part of the reformed educational system set up under state auspices. Special examinations were held for artists in which literary interpretation of a set topic was as prized as painterly skill. Mi Fu (1052–1107) and Sung Tzu-fang (late 11th–early 12th cent.) were appointed as professors. This experiment in including the fine or technical arts in the state-sponsored curriculum was short-lived: in 1106 the institutes of painting and calligraphy were incorporated into the Imperial University, and in 1110 they became part of the bureaus of painting and calligraphy under palace supervision. Artists attached to these bureaus were granted certain privileges by the emperors, such as the right to wear purple silk robes, the golden belt, and the fish ornament, but they never achieved the status of scholar-officials (Ecke 1972, 50–58, 224–30; Cleveland Museum of Art 1980, xxv–xxx; Bush and Shih 1985, 134–38; Shimada 1981).

As for the situation under the Chin, it has been summarized by Wai-kam Ho:

> In the middle of the twelfth century, two official organs directly involved in the production and conservation of paintings are recorded in the dynastic history: *Shu-hua chü* (Bureau of Calligraphy and Painting), under the Directorate of the Imperial Archive; and *T'u-hua ch'u* [i.e., *shu*] (Department of Painting), under the Directorate of Construction and Manufacture. The former was a government bureau supervising state projects of painting and calligraphy. The latter seemed to be responsible for decorative paintings produced for the palace, and in 1196 it was reorganized and became part of the Commission of Palace Services. In addition, there were keepers of calligraphy and painting who were conservators of the imperial collection. (Cleveland Museum of Art 1980, xxix)

Because the Department of Painting was absorbed into the Commission of Palace Services, *chih-ying ssu*, in 1196, I have assumed that painting specialists were active at the Chin court after 1196 in those cases when the official designation *chih-ying ssu* is included in an artist's inscription—as on the handscrolls signed by Chang Yü and Liu Yüan. It would otherwise be difficult to date these two handscrolls, because they lack inscriptions or colophons by contemporaries and are not mentioned in the comments or catalogs of later connoisseurs.

The other three paintings discussed exhibit a higher degree of calligraphic skill or interest in calligraphy. The *Vimalakîrti and the Single Doctrine* is a late Chin work in the mainstream of the literati tradition and is attributed to Ma Yün-ch'ing, who signed another painting in 1229 while in the capacity of student at the Imperial University. This work has all the earmarks of a private study done for friends or scholarly patrons, rather than a painting composed for an emperor or his palace ladies. Of the two earlier works, the Chang Kuei *Sacred Tortoise* includes a seal-script character, and the Chao Lin *Six Horses* contains both a preface and accompanying identifications and eulogies for each horse. The subjects of these two scrolls seem highly appropriate for works made to be presented to an imperial patron, and their relatively unsophisticated styles would be in keeping with their attributions to the early Chin period. The *sui chia* of Chang Kuei's signature simply indicates that he was currently part of "the Imperial Retinue"; it is not the title of an office that would have been held by a court painter.[10] Chao Ping-wen's colophon of 1220, which authenticates the *Six Horses* scroll, specifically designates Chao Lin as a *tai-chao*, a title that during the Sung denoted a painter-in-attendance attached to the Bureau of Painting. Chao probably uses the term loosely here to refer to a court attendant with calligraphic or artistic skills. There is no evidence concerning the departments these last two artists might have been assigned to, or what positions, if any, they might have held at court.

According to Wai-kam Ho, the Chin "Academy" tried to attract the services of scholar-artists, several of whom were associated with the Imperial Archive or directly affiliated with its subordinate Bureau of Calligraphy and Painting. The men named are: Yang Pang-chi (d. 1181), Wang T'ing-yün (1156–1202), Wu Yüan-chih (late 12th–early 13th cent.), and Chang Kuei (said to be *chin-shih* of 1224) (Cleveland Museum of Art 1980, xxix–xxx). Yang Pang-chi (*chin-shih* of 1139) served under Shih-tsung as vice-director and later director of the Imperial Archive; however, in the course of his full bureaucratic career, he held a variety of other offices, including provincial posts and posts on the Board of Rites, the Board of War, and the Han-lin Academy (*CS* 90.2006–7). He was known for his painting, especially for his horses after Li Kung-lin and his landscapes after Li Ch'eng, which seem to have included figures.[11] Wang T'ing-yün is a prime example of the scholar-artist in Chin times, a poet, calligrapher, and painter who looked back to Northern Sung models. A *chin-shih* graduate of 1176, Wang classified the works in Chang-tsung's imperial collection and by 1192 had entered the Han-lin Academy (*CS* 126.2731; *ISWC* 16.227; Angela Lin Li 1980, 23–24). The identification of Wu Yüan-chih as director of the Bureau of Calligraphy and Painting has not been corroborated by specific references.[12] Like Ma Yün-ch'ing, Wu seems to have associated with eminent literary men of his time (*CCS* 24.4b, rpt.

1:394; *YISCC* 14.644, no. 1240–42; cf. Bush 1969, 107). Nor can Chang Kuei's connection with the Bureau of Calligraphy and Painting be substantiated: there are no seals on the *Sacred Tortoise* to support such a connection. Hence, there is no proof to date that either of the last two artists was ever affiliated with the Imperial Archive or its subordinate bureau. It is true that Li Shan (late 12th cent.), the most celebrated of all Chin landscape painters, and Wang Wan-ch'ing (late 12th–early 13th cent.), the adopted son of Wang T'ing-yün, were both attached to the Imperial Archive in the early thirteenth century, but neither of these men was placed specifically in the Bureau of Calligraphy and Painting. The evidence thus suggests that there were professional as well as literati painters working at the Chin court.

It is difficult to judge what the status of the professional painters might have been in the early Chin period, but by 1196 painters who specialized in narrative illustration were attached to the Commission of Palace Services under palace supervision. There was no Academy as such organized along the lines of the Northern or Southern Sung's, since there were no separate bureaus (or academies, *yüan*) of calligraphy or painting supervised by the palace. Moreover, there is no definite indication that titles and honors similar to those given Sung Academy painters were ever bestowed on Chin court painters—no indication, in other words, of an attempt to raise the status of the painting specialists working for the palace. On the other hand, two of these Chin court painters did sign their scrolls as members of the Commission of Palace Services, a practice we have no evidence of before this period. As for the scholar-painters under the Chin, doubtless the majority were amateur artists who painted for colleagues in time free from official or scholarly duties. Again, there were no separate institutes of calligraphy or painting in the state educational system comparable to those established for a brief time under Sung Hui-tsung; presumably, then, painting was not part of the official curriculum. Some aspiring scholars who also painted may have been students at the Imperial University, as were Ma T'ien-lai and Ma Yün-ch'ing. But since, as noted above, there were three Ma brothers who were artists (*THPC* 4.80), it seems likely that their own training had begun at home. It has been suggested that a number of scholar-artists were recruited and given positions in the Bureau of Calligraphy and Painting under the Imperial Archive. Apart from the rather ambiguous instance of Wang T'ing-yün's connoisseurship in the early Ming-ch'ang era (1190–96), there are no cases to prove this argument. Hence, it seems safer to make the general observation that scholar-artists served in a variety of posts in the Chin bureaucracy. Still, as one might expect, a large number of recorded calligraphers and painters held positions in the Han-lin Academy sometime after they had gained their *chin-shih* degrees.

In this connection, there is an inscription transcribed in Yüan times from a *pai-miao* handscroll, *Hunting in the Snow*, that is worth noting. It reads: "Painted by the *ying-feng* Huang Yeh before the emperor in the great Chin kingdom" (*THPC* 4.81; *SCHP* 55.1a–1b, rpt. 5:2739A). The term *ying-feng* is an abbreviation of the title *ying-feng Han-lin wen-tzu*, the initial position (subordinate seventh rank) held by scholars attached to the Han-lin Academy. Although men such as Wang T'ing-yün were evidently granted this post on the basis of their literary skills, several of them also had calligraphic and artistic talents (*CS* 55.1246, 126.2731, 125.2722–23 and 2726–27). It would seem that they displayed their skills before the emperor on occasion, as did the former Han-lin *tai-chao* of T'ang.

In terms of organizational structure, the situation at the Chin court does to some extent foreshadow what would occur in Yüan times. Then a scholar-official like Chao Meng-fu might serve in Peking in various posts on the Board of War and the Han-lin Academy and also be called on to do special paintings for the emperor or the emperor-to-be. Both literati and professional painters, such as Ho Ch'eng (ca. 1218–ca. 1309) and Wang Chen-p'eng, were attached to the Imperial Archive in early Yüan times, as was the famous sculptor Liu Yüan. There was also a Yüan Commission of Palace Services, both at the Summer Palace and at Ta-tu (Peking), which was in charge of palace decoration and furnishing ornamented objects like palanquins. No Yüan court painter is known to have been attached to it (Weidner 1982, 47, 73, 92, 112–13, 132–33).[13] In his book on historical sources for Yüan dynasty painters, Ch'en Kao-hua (1980, 2, 266) centers Yüan court painting in the Imperial Archive; he also notes that there was no Chin Academy of Painting. This would accord with the conclusions drawn from evidence presented above. There were painting specialists at the Chin court as well as scholar-officials in government posts who painted, but there was no organized "Academy" under palace supervision as in Sung times. Furthermore, there is no evidence that painting was highly valued at the early Chin court. From a historical perspective, painting seems to have come into its own only in the middle Chin period, during the reigns of Shih-tsung and Chang-tsung in particular. Even though members of the Jurchen imperial family collected Sung paintings of various types, in their art they tended to follow literati models, as did the most influential scholar-painters of the Chin. It is noteworthy that the models for early Yüan court artists of all types, regardless of origins, were the late Northern Sung styles preserved under the Chin: "those of the Li-Kuo School, Hui-tsung's Academy, and the literati painters Mi Fu, Wen T'ung [1018/9–79] and Li Kung-lin" (Weidner 1982, 191). By Yüan times, a painting specialist like Han Shao-yeh (late 13th cent.), attached to the Imperial Clothing Bureau (*yü-i chü*), did ink bamboos and monochrome landscapes in the Chin tradition (*THPC* 5.85). The very lack of a highly organized Chin Academy of Painting, in which painters produced works on imperial demand in specific artistic traditions, may have promoted the spread of literati subject matter among artists of all types. Did it also affect the issue of professionalism?

Kuo Hsi's notes on his career at court during the late eleventh century provide insights into the life of a professional artist working to meet the demands of an imperial patron. At this time, scholar-artists who took up the practice of painting elevated it from a technique to a fine art by linking it with poetry and calligraphy and regarding it as expressive of the artist's character. This amateur ideal is best expressed in Su Shih's writings on the ink bamboos done by his cousin, Wen T'ung. In turn, under Sung Hui-tsung an attempt was made to raise the status of court painters by treating them as the equals of court calligraphers and granting them some of the same privileges and honors as officials. Nonetheless, class distinctions were clearly drawn, and scholars were separated from non-scholars in the short-lived Institute of Painting (Ecke 1972, 82).

In the Chin dynasty, it has been suggested, there was no such keenly felt split between the scholar-artist and the court painter: "Perhaps due to the nomadic background of the Chin society and its traditional respect for crafts and craftsmen, the social demarcation between professionals and non-professionals, scholars and non-scholars was never clear-cut or rigid" (Cleveland Museum of Art 1980, xxix). Some of the material discussed above bears out this observation. It is true that Liu Yüan of the Commission of Palace Services now seems most likely to have been a secular figure specialist under the Chin, and not an early manifestation of the famous Yüan sculptor who produced a variety of religious images in several different techniques. But even if Liu Yüan's professionalism was limited to one art, the Chin dynasty Liu Yüan was evidently a court painter. Still, his mentor, San-t'ang Wang, was treated with great respect and affection by the poet and former Chin official Tuan Ch'eng-chi.

As far as professionalism is concerned, Ma T'ien-lai must remain the exemplary figure of a Chin artist working as both sculptor and painter. His importance also lies in the fact that he was a member of the scholar class who continued to produce modeled images when he held office (the first recorded instance of the practice of technical skills in office since the Six Dynasties period). Furthermore, his brother Ma Yün-ch'ing, a student at the Imperial University, painted copies of religious subjects by Wu Tao-tzu, yet his work was appreciated by well-known literary figures. There is no comparable continuity in the production of religious art by a scholar-official at the Southern Sung court; indeed, southern literati appear to have been highly sensitive about their status, even in connection with painting.

This reaction may have been stimulated by reinstitution of the Academy of Painting by Sung Kao-tsung (r. 1127–62). The scholar-official Chu Tun-ju (1081–1159), for example, denied authorship of his paintings when they were appreciated by Kao-tsung. He evidently feared that he would have to compete for advancement when painting before the emperor alongside the son of Mi Fu, Mi Yu-jen (ca. 1072–ca. 1151), whose posts at court were dependent on his artistic skills. Formerly an instructor in Sung Hui-tsung's Institute of Calligraphy, Mi Yu-jen authenticated the scrolls in the imperial collection while serving as auxiliary academician (*chih hsüeh-shih*) attached to the Hall for the Diffusion of Literature. When in this post, he is said to have painted only for the emperor and to have been berated by scholarly colleagues for not responding to their requests for landscapes (Chu Chu-yü and Li Shih-sun 1958, 51–52, 60). Then there is the case of Ma Ho-chih (d. ca. 1190), who illustrated the *Poetry* for, or with, Kao-tsung, probably between 1162 and 1187. Was he a scholar-official with a *chin-shih* degree, or should he simply be considered the foremost Academy painter who revived Wu Tao-tzu's style (*THPC* 4.63; Murray 1981, 93–102, 240–43)? Here modern scholarship has not yet disentangled the question of the status of an artist who painted expressly for a Southern Sung ruler. By Yüan times even notable scholar-officials painted for the emperor on demand, decorating the palace halls with murals.

It is dangerous to draw general conclusions on the basis of a minimal amount of evidence, and some of these issues will undoubtedly be clarified by further research. Still, it can be said that Ma T'ien-lai's attitude toward his art contrasts strongly with that of a few Southern Sung literati and many later scholar-critics. It is conceivable that he was motivated to produce images, whether Buddhist or Confucian, out of religious conviction. And it is also possible that his easygoing approach to the status of office was to some extent in keeping with the realities of the situation at the end of Chin. It was then that the largest number of *chin-shih* degrees was awarded, although there were not posts enough for all the successful candidates. Conceivably, in this period of flux the status of the literati was devalued along with their degrees, and scholars were necessarily less disparate from commoners. If so, this situation would in a sense foreshadow the diminished standing of the scholar class under Mongol rule, after the fall of the Chin.

Notes

1. Here professionalism will be considered in connection with secular figure or animal painters and copyists of religious subjects, not as a component of the Li-Kuo landscape tradition of the Yüan (see Barnhart 1977, 122–23).

2. I am grateful to Wai-kam Ho for this reference. He has suggested that Chang Kuei was a *chin-shih* degree graduate of 1224 attached to the Bureau of Calligraphy and Painting (*shu-hua chü*) of the Imperial Archive (see concluding section below). The seals on the *Sacred Tortoise* do not confirm this attribution, and Chang Kuei was an extremely popular name in the twelfth and thirteenth centuries (Ho 1980, 28–29; Cleveland Museum of Art 1980, xxix–xxx; Wang Teh-yi 1979–82, 2:1068–69).

3. Note that Hai-ling had expressed the same idea in the poem on the *West Lake Painting*, a poem that has also been attributed to a Han-lin scholar of the period (*CCS* 1.15a–19a; rpt. 1:26–28; Tao Jing-shen 1976, 43 and 141 n. 18).

4. As noted by Betty Ecke (1972, 51), "Han-lin Tai-chao and Han-lin Chih-hou were titles given to historians and experts learned in poetry, musicology and the arts."

5. References are to the SKSL edition of *CSTP*.

6. Significantly, the heroine has bound feet (i.e., of limited strength and usefulness) in a *pai-miao* copy of the Jilin handscroll now in the Osaka Municipal Museum; this copy, entitled *Consort Ming Crossing the Frontier*, refers to Wang Chao-chün, the Han concubine who was sent to be married to a Hsiung-nu ruler. Kuo Mo-jo has studied the signature and seals on the Osaka handscroll and considers it to be a late Ming or early Ch'ing work (Kuo 1964, 2.4–6; *CKMS* 1:3.159, no. 58).

7. Marsha Weidner, who argues that the Liu Yüan handscroll is likely to be a Chin work, has made the same comparison with this print (Weidner 1982, 212–13 n. 56).

8. Thus, the Liu Yüan painting should not be considered the work of this sculptor and placed in the early Yüan period (cf. Cheng Chen-to 1951–55, 8, no. 2; Sherman E. Lee and Wai-kam Ho 1968, no. 199).

9. I would like to express my thanks to Maxwell K. Hearn of the Metropolitan Museum of Art for the *CPOT* reference given above and for a set of reproductions of the Peking Palace Museum handscroll. The authenticity of the Metropolitan Museum's version has been questioned, partially on the basis of the signature in the inscription, which is actually identical to that in the *CPOT* text (cf. Weidner 1982, 139–40, 229–32). I am also indebted to Alfreda Murck of the same institution for providing detailed photographs of the Peking handscroll and for commenting on the quality of the copyist's hand.

10. In the late thirteenth century, *sui chia* was used as a verb-object phrase in biographies of Southern Sung painters, like Chao Po-chü (mid-12th cent.), who followed the Sung court to Hangchow; see *HCPI* A.3 and B.12, and cf. B.9–10.

11. In a conversation in December 1983, Wai-kam Ho noted that certain poetic descriptions of Yang's paintings indicated that figures played a

noticeable role in them. Ho has also pointed out that Jen Hsün (ca. 1110–ca. 1188), a scholar-official best known for his calligraphy and a model for Wang T'ing-yün in landscape painting, did one known architectural subject of the "ruled-line" type (Sherman E. Lee and Wai-kam Ho 1968, 92, 110 n. 104). For collections of contemporary poems on painting by Jen and Yang, see Ch'en Kao-hua 1984, 819–31.

12. It was Li Jih-hua (1565–1635) who stated that Wu Yüan-chih served in Chang-tsung's Painting Academy (*hua-yüan*) in the Ming-ch'ang era (*LYC* 2.31b). The person who actually served as director (*chih-ch'ang*) of the Bureau of Calligraphy and Painting in 1194 was the scholar-official Chang Chien (late 12th cent.) (*CSTP* 157.Chin 4.5a, 8a; *CS* 126.2734).

13. However, two court painters, one of them Liu Kuan-tao (late 13th–early 14th cent.), were attached to another palace office, the Imperial Clothing Bureau, under the Department of Imperial Manufacturing. Several scholar-officials painted murals for palace halls on imperial command or for temples on the order of the government (Weidner 1982, 70–72, 92).

8

JURCHEN LITERATURE UNDER THE CHIN

Jin Qicong

What is here designated "Jurchen literature" comprises both the oral literature of the Jurchen, in Jurchen, and the written literature the Jurchen, in Chinese. Since works in either category, we may assume, express ideas and emotions of Jurchen people, both must be considered within the scope of "Jurchen literature." Indeed, the major portion of Jurchen literature known to us is written by ethnic Jurchen using the Chinese language.

The most comprehensive treatment of Jurchen literature to date is found in Chao Chih-hui's (1989) study of Manchu literature, in which Jurchen, Su-hsiao, and Po-hai writers are considered together as proto-Manchus, a not unreasonable view. No monographic study of Jurchen literature during the Chin has yet appeared, and general histories of Liao, Chin, and Yüan literature tend to relegate the literature of Chin dynasty Jurchen writers to small sections or even to a few paragraphs. Despite this general neglect, progress has been made by Gisaburo Norikura Kiyose (1977) and Daniel Kane (1989), as well as by my own former students, in the field of historical linguistics, that is, the development of the Jurchen language, script, and phonology.

In the present essay, I will attempt to discuss systematically the birth and development, rules and special characteristics of Jurchen literature during the Chin, paying particular attention to the relationship between oral and written literatures and between literatures in the Jurchen and Chinese languages. I will conclude by postulating a rule of development for Jurchen literature that might also provide a model for Khitan literature of the Liao dynasty and Manchu literature of the Ch'ing.

Judging from extant records, the first songs to appear were shaman songs. The path by which ethnic Jurchen literature developed proceeds from these songs to folk ditties, "cursing songs" (*tsu-chou tz'u*), "songs of disentanglement" (*chieh-fen ko*), and "free lyric compositions" (*tzu-tu ko*). In more concrete terms, this evolution can be said to follow a saddle-shaped curve, rising gradually between the early and mid-twelfth century, falling sharply under the political and cultural influences of the 1150s, then rising again during the 1160s, before finally declining into eventual extinction during the thirteenth century.

The primary impediment to the formal development of Jurchen ethnic literature was the literature of the Jurchen's nearest neighbor, the Han Chinese. Even before the arrival of the Jurchen, the mature, formal, and eloquent structure of Chinese literature had infatuated the Po-hai, Khitan, and other ethnic groups. These peoples abandoned their own languages and literary forms and adopted the Chinese language to articulate their own passions and thoughts. Although some of their works are still preserved in the Han Chinese literary record, we have no way of reconstructing literary creations in their native Po-hai or Khitan forms.

The Jurchen were certainly no exception in this respect. By 1150 Han Chinese literary forms had already spread widely through the ranks of the Jurchen ruling house and nobility, relegating ethnic forms of literature to the narrow realm of the older generation and the lower classes. But just as ethnic Jurchen literature was edging toward extinction in the 1160s, it gained new life under Chin Shih-tsung's (r. 1161–89) revitalization of Jurchen culture. During this native revival, free lyric compositions, original in structure and form, began to spread. But even advocacy of literature in native Jurchen forms could not extirpate the Han Chinese literature that had already taken root among the Jurchen nobility. True Jurchen literature could only run a temporary parallel course with Han Chinese writing until, in the end, it was again engulfed by it. Even Shih-tsung's famous "native song" (*pen-ch'ü*) was translated into a four-character-line lyric that any poorly educated Chinese could understand.

Shaman Songs in the Jurchen Language (through the 11th Century)

In its most primitive stage, the literature of any people or society is generally oral, and the content of its earliest forms generally comprises songs of prayer and expressions of fear. The prayers can be further subdivided into songs for welcoming spirits and songs of praise; fear most often finds expression in curses and conciliatory compositions. Strictly speaking, prayer derives from fear. Primitive peoples fought a constant and losing battle against the elements of the natural world, the rain, wind, lightning, and thunder, as well as mountains and rivers, forces they imagined were controlled by specific spirits. Fearing these natural phenomena, and fearing even more their masters, they prayed for protection from the spirits' wrath.

Fear of nature may be observed in the oral verse "The Last Day of the World" ("Shih-chieh te mo-jih"), which was transmitted by generations of Tungus shamans in Manchuria.[1] These relatives of the Jurchen sang:

> Before long, it will begin to burn, the black earth,
> People's corpses will be strewn in corruption here, there, everywhere,
> Rivers and streams will stir into waves of blood,
> Mountains and hills revolve and whirl without end,
> Boulders from cliffs flying and falling, crashing, rumbling;
> In the intimated faltering of Heaven's void,
> The Great Sea will throw up rampant breakers,
> And the ocean's floor come forth, everywhere.

Under the psychological yoke of such a fear of nature, primitive people necessarily imagined the bodily forms of the spirits to be as terrible as the natural processes they controlled. A Tungus song extolling the might of Erlik, god of the underworld, provides a good example:

> Erlik, astride your black horse,
> You carry a bed of Black Sea wildcat skin;
> Your waist is too thick and strong,
> The lengthy belt will surely not be long enough.
>
> Your head, largest and without match,
> Will never be encircled by the hands of a man;
> Your eyebrows are as thick as fingers,
> Your beard, thick and black,
> Your face, blood-spotted and blurred.

Such spirits were usually invoked and offered sacrifices in exorcistic dance rituals, a practice that still survives in songs used by shamans during exorcistic rituals. At the beginning of their songs, I have heard Manchu shamans sing:

> *Abkai juse, fucihifusa, ejen sefu, coohai janggin, guwan i besise.*

> Son of Heaven above, Buddha and bodhisattvas, Lord and Teacher, Marshal of the Three Armies, sage Kuan Yü, Imperial Lord.

The spirits called on at the beginning of the verse are the deities being sacrificed to—deities who have already lost, however, the fearsomeness of Erlik.

Lamentably, no examples of works from this earliest stage of Jurchen literature have survived. The *Chin History* has preserved some cursing songs and songs of disentanglement, but the odes or hymns associated with sacrificial rites have been almost entirely lost. Only a single reference to them is found in the *Chin History* (28.693): "The [winter] Suburban Sacrifice of the Chin was rooted in their native customs; among them was a ritual for the worship of Heaven." Sacrifice to and worship of Heaven were rituals of considerable importance to the disciples of shamanism, and there is little doubt that part of the sacrificial ritual was accompanied by song. The passage in the *Chin History* further records: "[Shih-tsung] went on to tell his chief councilors: 'The ritual for the worship of Heaven is extremely important in my native kingdom. It is also fitting that you have now mentioned constructing an altar of sacrifice according to the ancient [Han] rule. My kingdom has expelled the rulers of the Liao and the Sung, and so holds the mandate to all under Heaven. How could the ritual of the [winter] Suburban Sacrifice not be performed?" (*CS* 28.694). Shih-tsung's statement shows that the Jurchen placed particular emphasis on sacrifices to Heaven. And the reference to the ritual for making obeisance to Heaven "in my native kingdom" points clearly to the Heaven worship of Jurchen shamanism.

In addition to the reverence and worship of certain deities and natural forces, Jurchen shamanistic practice also included rituals for cursing or revilement. Initially, malignant ghosts and evil spirits were reviled; later, men were. In the *Chin History* biography of Hsieh-li-hu, there is an extremely important passage that illustrates this:

> According to the customs of the [Jurchen] kingdom, if someone had been killed, a shaman was employed to curse and chant at the [deceased's] slayer. The shaman tied a blade to the end of a long pole and, accompanied by a crowd of people, went to the house [of the guilty man] to revile him: "I will take an ox of yours that has one horn pointing to Heaven and one horn pointing to earth, and a nameless horse that from before has a splotchy head, from behind a white tail, and from the sides wings to the left and right." The sound of this song was plaintive and shrill, like the sound of the [Chinese dirge] "Hao-li." After the shaman had drawn on the ground with the blade, [the guilty man's] livestock and valuables were seized, then the shaman withdrew. Once a person's house had been cursed like this, the finances of the household rapidly declined. (*CS* 65.1540)

If we juxtapose this passage and a case involving a Yakut shaman, the import of this passage becomes clearer. When a Yakut shaman wishes to carry on a dialogue with a spirit, he seeks out the individual (invariably ailing) whom the spirit has possessed, bows, and addresses the spirit: "What kind of livestock do you want? Speak, and I will give it to you. Leave the body of the sick one at once!" At that point the spirit typically speaks through the mouth of the shaman:

> Give me a white-backed cow
> And a colored horse,
> And then I will leave the sick one!

After the desired stock is brought into the courtyard, the shaman cries out in a loud voice: "Here it is, take it away! But now you must protect his life!"[2] This case is surely comparable to the cursing song of the shaman in Hsieh-li-hu's biography.

The cursing song of the biography can also be seen as a pretext for the shaman, under the guise of the evil spirit's demand, to take away the livestock and goods of the murderer—a real public punishment popularly exacted in early Jurchen tribes and hence called a "custom of their kingdom" in the *Chin History*. Such cursing songs might have had a prescribed structure and content. Even in Chinese translation, we can still see that the song had the typical head rhyme so characteristic of Jurchen literature. If the verses of the curse had been recorded in Jurchen, the opening words of two lines would have been in assonance: *emu* (one) and *gebu* (name). In short, during this early stage of Jurchen oral literature, shaman songs were the major form and eventually gave rise to special cursing songs.

The Rise and Decline of Free Lyric Composition in the Jurchen Language (11th–12th Centuries)

The shaman songs of early Jurchen culture were sung by the shaman alone to welcome descending spirits, to cure illness, or to curse and revile. Although the songs were passed orally from generation to generation, they remained essentially the same. This is corroborated by the case of the corresponding songs of the Manchu shamans, songs for the propitiation of Heaven, first written down no earlier than the Ch'ien-lung period (1736–96) (*MCCS* preface, 619–20). Original composition developed as Jurchen society evolved and human affairs became consequently more and more complex.

It was at this point that Jurchen folk songs began to be adapted, spontaneously, in response to particular situations; these adapted songs were called "free lyric compositions." A good example of the historical context for such a composition can be found in the *Chin History* biography of Madame T'ang-kua, Lustrous and Austere Resplendent Heir-giver to the Refulgent Progenitor, Wu-ku-nai (1021–74):

After the Refulgent Progenitor died, the Generational Progenitor [Ho-li-po, 1039–92] and his brother petitioned the Heir-giver before using troops, and she would admonish or praise them regarding their military engagements.... The Heir-giver went to I-t'un village with the Generational Progenitor and the Austere Ancestor [P'o-la-shu, 1042–94] in retinue. It turned out that both Huan-she and San-ta also came; at this time there was already a rift [between them and the two royal brothers]. After [Huan-she and San-ta] had become drunk with wine, their conversation became abusive and unreconcilable, and they advanced [on the royal brothers] with raised blades. The Heir-giver, rising and taking their hands, spoke to Huan-she and San-ta: "You are old friends of ours, going back to the days of my husband: How can you suddenly one morning forget the benevolence of my husband and contend with the likes of my children?" She thereupon composed a song herself, and the anger of Huan-she and San-ta was dispelled. (CS 63.1500)

The Generational Progenitor and the Austere Ancestor, Ho-li-po and P'o-la-shu, were both sons of Wu-ku-nai and T'ang-kua; Huan-she and his brother San-ta had previously been attached to Wu-ku-nai and lived in the Wan-yen clan village of I-t'un. But these latter two had begun to plot with Pa-hei, who opposed the sons of Wu-ku-nai. T'ang-kua went to I-t'un village specifically to win them over, and when they moved against Ho-li-po and P'o-la-shu, she personally used a song to dispel the conflict. Although the song with which she accomplished this feat is now lost, its contents must have been directed specifically to the circumstances of that instant.

Songs sung for the purpose of dispelling dissention are a type of folk literature that derive from shaman songs; however, the scope of their content was not confined to the older parameters and could in fact have a witty nature or a political reading. But how do we know that these songs were related to shaman songs? Because in her biography, we are told that T'ang-kua's father was a shaman. If she had not been born into a shaman family, she probably could not have composed her song as she did, spontaneously and in direct response to the situation. And how do we know that such songs could have political readings? Because T'ang-kua's song temporarily resolved the conflict between two different clans. Thus, the content of shaman songs evolved from the religious toward the political. It was from this kind of song that Shih-tsung's famous "native song," in which there were no religious overtones, eventually developed.

Children's songs are another form of oral literature. Centuries earlier, for example, when the Tibetan Fu Chien (339–85) was about to be made emperor of China, a children's ditty was bandied about in Ch'ang-an:

> Great fish in the Eastern Sea transform into dragons,
> The male a king, the female a princess.
> You ask, "Where are they?" East of the gates of Lo!
>
> (SLK 32.7b)

"Eastern Sea" is where Fu Chien was enfeoffed, and "east of the gates of Lo" where he had his residence. The song implicitly proposes that Fu Chien be made emperor.

A comparably politicized folk song was prevalent among the Jurchen tribes during the time of the conflict between Pa-hei, on the one side, and Ho-li-po and P'o-la-shu, on the other. The song advised:

> If you want to live,
> Attach yourself to Pa-hei;
> If you want to die,
> Attach yourself to Ho-li-po and P'o-la-shu.
>
> (CS 65.1542)

The politics is more explicit in this song than in the earlier one about Fu Chien. As noted, Jurchen folk songs and shaman songs, although composed in Jurchen, have been preserved only in Chinese. We know that in the original, however, they did not employ end rhyme, but head rhyme. In Jurchen the four lines of this folk song would have begun with words that were alliterated.

Although oral poetry in the Jurchen language began the transition from religious to political songs, its development was disrupted by Hsi-tsung's (r. 1135–50) and Hai-ling's (r. 1150–61) advocacy of Chinese literature. Jurchen literature consequently lost its currency among the Jurchen elite and was maintained only among Jurchen nativists and the lower levels of Jurchen society. Only after Hai-ling had been murdered and Emperor Shih-tsung had begun promoting Jurchen culture were shaman songs and folk songs resuscitated, eventually to evolve into the "native songs" of Shih-tsung and the Jurchen nobility.

The Introduction and Florescence of Chinese Literature (12th Century)

The Jurchen practice of writing in the Chinese language and in Chinese literary forms is related to the Chin court's wholesale adoption of Han institutions. Hsi-tsung's reign set this course: "[In 1137] the place where the emperor made his residence, which was called Hui-ning-fu, was established as the Upper Capital, and bureaucratic institutions were again altered. At a prior time the Sung envoy Yü-wen Hsü-chung [1080–1146] had been detained in the [Chin] state; at this time he received a position in the northern state [of Chin], and on its behalf he regularized and stabilized their institutions" (TCCC 9.136). Thus, the adoption of Han forms was done under the influence of Sung Chinese who had surrendered. (The Jurchen's military organization and titles continued to follow tribal custom, however, just as the Manchus' would during the Ch'ing centuries later.)

These members of the Sung intelligentsia who had surrendered not only influenced institutional reform in Chin China, but, more importantly, profoundly influenced Hsi-tsung:

> When Hsi-tsung was a child, his uncles, who were campaigning in the Central Plain, captured Han Fang of Yen and various other Confucian scholars to serve as his tutors. Later, he could compose poetry, "dip his brush in ink," sing songs of classical elegance, and wear the robes of a Confucian, take part in tea ceremonies, burn incense, and play both kinds of chess. Thus, he lost completely all semblance of old Jurchen ways. (TCCC 12.179)

Even though the sinicization of minorities in China usually begins with the ruling class, the rapidity of Hsi-tsung's sinicization is surprising since he grew up and continued to live in the Upper Capital within the boundaries of the Jurchen homeland.

This kind of blind sinicization could only result in the rejection of native culture and, concomitantly, dissention among the Jurchen themselves:

> After Hsi-tsung had ascended the throne, he was served by Confucian ministers, and flattery and sycophancy became the style. The Imperial Guard was dignified and austere; the actual palaces, however, were full of sensual delights, and the ministers and generals of merit from the old days were mostly distanced [from the court] and rejected. (TCCC 12.179)

Surely Jurchen literature could not be promoted in such an atmosphere, when even trusted advisors and generals who had helped to found the state were ignored.

Jurchen literature was apparently even denigrated and suppressed. This can be deduced from Hsi-tsung's attitude toward the Jurchen: "[Hsi-tsung] saw an old minister from the time of the founding of the state and said, 'Ignorant barbarian!' When the old minister saw him, he said, 'Just like a little Chinese boy' " (TCCC 12.179). Hsi-tsung's remark referred to the minister's lack of knowledge about Chinese culture. Yet the Han Chinese culture so loved by Hsi-tsung, as far as the old minister was concerned, did nothing more or less than vitiate the virile and unaffected ways of the Jurchen people. We, however, should look at Chin history and Chin literature from the standpoint of both the Han and the Jurchen ethnic groups. To continue the tradition of looking only at the regularization of institutional forms or adoption of Han customs is to maintain but a partial perspective. Our view should include Hsi-tsung's suppression and denigration of Jurchen literature and his abolition of Jurchen customs. In this regard, Hsi-tsung was not only the equal of Hai-ling, but in fact his forerunner.

Although he murdered Hsi-tsung to usurp his throne, Hai-ling was a loyal adherent to the cultural policies laid down by his predecessor. He effected policies that Hsi-tsung himself would never have dared to enact, however. Among them was the removal of the tombs of the first ten Chin rulers, including the tomb of the clan's founding ancestor, to Mt. Ta-fang. He also ordered all palaces and noble residences of the Upper Capital, including the Ch'u-ch'ing Temple, to be leveled and the ground they stood on plowed under. His aim, of course, was to destroy native Jurchen culture and eradicate even the very memory of the native Jurchen homeland.

This destroyer of Jurchen culture was well versed in traditional Chinese literary forms and styles. As a child, Hai-ling was called Po-lieh-han "because he looked like a Han Chinese boy"; moreover, he "was learned in the classics and histories because he never forgot what he had read" (*TCCC* 13.185, 187). Furthermore, "when young, he knew [Chinese] books well," and "his poetry excelled his contemporaries' " (*TCCC* 15.212). His literary ability is evident in the following two lines, which he wrote while a prince, on a friend's fan:

> If the handle of great authority rested in my hand,
> Then would a cleansing wind suffuse all under Heaven.
> (*KCC* 1.3; trans. Eng 1990, 227)

Such was the ambition of this man. One of his later poems, "Gazing at the Lower Yangtze on a Southern Expedition," is written in the same vein:

> Cart axles and writing are already standardized for myriad miles;
> Why should the southeast still be a detached, peripheral fiefdom?
> Our million-strong army will soon be encamped around West Lake,
> And I shall ride my horse to the highest peak of Wu.
> (*CCS* 1.15a)

Hai-ling could compose not only *shih* poetry, but also *tz'u* lyric meters. Here is an example of each:

On Mid-Autumn Festival, I Waited for the Moon in Vain
(Tune: "Immortals on Magpie Bridge")

Halted cups aren't raised,
Halted songs aren't sung,
Waiting for the Silver Toad to come out of the sea.
A patch of clouds comes from nowhere
And becomes an obstruction to the Great Unity under Heaven.

Tugging on my beard
And squinting my eyes,
I lament that my sword is not sharp enough.
One stroke should cut the purple cloud
And provide a better view of Ch'ang-o's form.

(CCS 1.16b–17a)

According to tradition, Ch'ang-o resided on the moon.

A Good Wish to General Han I on His Departure on a Southern Expedition
(Tune: "Nightingales Moving Happily")

Our banners are raised high,
Our horses are strong,
Neighing to the wind on the river islets.
Our tiger-killing generals,
Our eagle-shooting captains,
All look bright in their embroidered hats and robes.
They charge forward with bristling beards,
The sound of drums stirs the earth.
Laughing and talking,
All along the Yangtze,
Across our six armies fly.

On this expedition,
Your big golden seal will never fall,
For you will surely win honor.
As for the chain-cutting idea
And the whip-dropping plan,
There is no difference between antiquity and the present.
Utilize the Sleeping Dragon's strategic thinking,
And you will surely succeed.
Now in the southeast,
People are looking for rain after long draught,
And so are prepared to welcome you.

(CCS 1.17a–17b)

Allusions are made here to plans for unification of the empire that were advanced nine centuries earlier during the Three Kingdoms period; the strategy of the Sleeping Dragon, Chu-ko Liang (181–234), however, was to move north from a southern base.

In the early years of the Southern Sung, just when Hai-ling was composing these poems, the *tz'u* form was developing from shorter to longer tunes. Hai-ling's poems are not soft and sentimental, but vigorous and forceful. Thus, his style was rare among *tz'u* poets of that era, his poetics something neither Sung Hui-tsung (r. 1100–1125) nor Li Yü (937–78), as the effete rulers of fallen states, could ever have emulated.

Hai-ling more closely resembled Hsiao-wen-ti (r. 471–99) of the Northern Wei; and if he had succeeded in his southern expedition, he would have surpassed Hsiao-wen-ti. Hai-ling's ultimate failure can be ascribed to his excessive zeal for sinicization, which stirred extreme unrest among the Jurchen, and his lone insistence on mounting a southern expedition against the Sung, which ended in loss. As a result, his army was defeated abroad and unrest threatened his authority domestically, and in the end he was assassinated. The Southern Sung Chinese hated him for his aggression, and the Jurchen hated him for the changes he had imposed on their native culture. His biography in the official *Chin History* is consequently anything but unbiased (Ts'ui Wen-yin 1987 and 1990, 178–80). Yet his learning in the Chinese classics as well as his skill in traditional Chinese poetic forms are not to be slighted. His Chinese contemporaries, even in the Southern Sung, acknowledged this.

With Hsi-tsung's and Hai-ling's vigorous promotion of Chinese literature, Jurchen folk literature declined. Since it had never been recorded in Jurchen script, only transmitted orally, it was thus easily lost: not a single Jurchen song survives today from the entire twenty-some years of Hsi-tsung's and Hai-ling's reigns. We know virtually nothing of the Jurchen folk literature of this era; we can infer from its later flourishing during Shih-tsung's reign, however, that it must have continued to develop during those years, probably among the lower levels of Jurchen society, even while it was being suppressed from above.

The Revival of Jurchen Literature under the Reign of Shih-tsung (1161–89)

After its encounter with a literature as sophisticated as that of the Han Chinese, it was natural that the less developed Jurchen folk literature be absorbed. We can draw this conclusion from the comparable examples of the literature of the Po-hai (who shared a common ancestry with the Jurchen) and also that of the Khitan (who did not). This would also happen several centuries later to the folk literature of the Manchus, descendants of the Jurchen. We may safely say that even without the effort of Hsi-tsung and Hai-ling, Jurchen literature would have stood scant chance for survival. The political pressure they were able to bring into play, however, accelerated the demise of Jurchen folk literature by alternately ignoring its existence and distorting its natural course of development.

After his accession, Shih-tsung began to worry that total abandonment of Jurchen mores and culture might undermine the political stability of the dynasty. Determined to reverse the sinicizing trend of his two predecessors, Shih-tsung introduced two new policies. First, he encouraged all Jurchen princes and nobles to return to the Upper Capital—still the heartland of Jurchen culture, in spite of Hai-ling—there to be reimbued in the native Jurchen way of life. Although created only decades earlier by Wan-yen Hsi-yin (d. 1143) under the sponsorship of Emperor T'ai-tsu (r. 1115–23), the Jurchen script had fallen into disuse, and a number of princes were already unable to read or even to speak the Jurchen language. Shih-tsung's second measure was to make use of the Jurchen language, both oral and written, mandatory (CS 7.159).

Shih-tsung knew the importance of literature to his purpose. To keep native customs alive, he had Jurchen songs sung at all state banquets. His biography in the *Chin History* records: "[In 1173,] His Majesty came to the Sagely Reflection Hall. He ordered singers to sing Jurchen lyrical poetry. Looking at the crown prince and other princes, he said: 'I am always mindful of the deeds of the early years of the empire and do not dare to forget [them], not even for a minute. That is why I must listen to these songs from time to time, and why you, too, must know them' " (CS 7.159).

These were probably songs that had been passed down orally from the time of Su-tsung, that is, the late eleventh century. Although nothing of their specific content is known, we can conclude from Shih-tsung's words above that the songs must have recounted the deeds, ways, and mores of the Jurchen. They must have also have been more developed in nature than the songs for dispelling dissention, discussed above.

In 1186, Shih-tsung gave a grand banquet at the Supreme Martial Hall in the Upper Capital. All attending nobles, women, and ministers of state took turns dancing and making toasts, a Jurchen custom that was still preserved in Manchu family life into the early years of the Ch'ing dynasty. It was on such an occasion that an anecdote recorded in the *Chin History* took place:

> His Majesty said: "Since my arrival here several months ago, I have not heard anyone sing our native songs. Let me, then, sing one for you." He ordered the young aristocrats who sat in the lower part of the hall to come up and hear his song, which told of the hardships [encountered in] the founding of the empire and the difficulty of carrying on the cause. Coming to the verse "Sighing, I think long-

ingly of my forefathers. It is as if I can see them with my very eyes," his emotions overwhelmed him, his voice failed him, and at the end of the song, he wept.... Thereupon the imperial consorts sang native songs too, just as at a family banquet. Drunk, His Majesty sang again, and the banquet continued until the first drum. (CS 8.189)

The native song that Shih-tsung sang must have been a popular Jurchen song. It is recorded in translation in the *Chin History* (CS 39.892) in extremely refined Chinese of four-character lines, archaic in style and diction, and obviously indebted to the tradition of formal Chinese court odes. It has probably lost the simple style of the original Jurchen composition, now lost, which followed completely different rules of poetic organization, being written in a Tungusic language. The Ch'ien-lung emperor wrote a verse in imitation of this work, entitled "Yü-chih sheng-ching fu" (A rhapsody on the supreme capital by the imperial hand), which is preserved not only in an elegant Chinese rendition, but also in its Manchu original. If we derive anything from a comparison of the two versions of the text, it is that while the Chinese and Manchu compositions treat the same subject, they share little else in common. The Manchu song was composed in a polysyllabic language of the Altaic family, in this verse a simple, alliterative language that turns on assonance in the initial syllable of each word; the Chinese text, while generally considered a translation, is embedded in its own context of Chinese poetics, faithfully following the rules of end rhyme, tonal and grammatical antithesis and parallelism, and the apt use of allusion that are earmarks of the rhapsody form (*fu*). It is probably wiser to read them as two matching poems, one in Chinese and one in Manchu, meant to display the erudition of the emperor in both linguistic and literary traditions. Certainly, the translation of the native song in the *Chin History*, which adheres to the formal features of court and sacrificial odes, may be a display of Chinese literary virtuousity rather than an accurate translation of the sense and register of the original.[3] And the very fact that Shih-tsung let his native song be preserved in a Chinese translation that distorts the basic character of the original shows that his efforts at "re-Jurchenization" were limited in scope, making a true revival of Jurchen literature hardly possible.

Evidence for this judgment can be seen in the famous "Ta Chin te-sheng t'o-sung" stele erected by Emperor Shih-tsung to commemorate the conquest of Chin T'ai-tsu.[4] One of the most important among extant Chin monuments, the stele was erected in 1185, at the height of Shih-tsung's re-Jurchenization movement. Yet several of the stele's more salient characteristics belie the very nature of the movement. First, the Chinese text of the inscription is carved on the front, the more important *yang* side, and the Jurchen text on the back, the *yin* side. Second, the name of the author and calligraphers of the Chinese text and title inscription are all carved on the stone, whereas no name is attached to the Jurchen text, obviously a translation of the Chinese. Third, the Jurchen text is four lines shorter than the Chinese. Fourth, the Chinese text is embellished with many allusions to the Chinese classics, but none to any Jurchen cultural tradition. From this prominent example, it is apparent that during the reign of Shih-tsung, writing in the Jurchen language was largely limited to translations of Chinese texts.

Can we infer from this that during Shih-tsung's reign the Jurchen written language was not yet fully developed, not yet equal to the task of recording Jurchen literature? According to the official *Chin History*, in the first years of his reign, Shih-tsung's successor, the emperor Chang-tsung (r. 1190–1208), issued an imperial edict ending the use of the Khitan script; elsewhere the history records that in 1197 "an imperial edict was promulgated by which the royal princes were to begin using the Jurchen script" (CS 9.220 and 10.241). This was more than seventy years after the Jurchen script had been created and thirty years after Shih-tsung had begun his re-Jurchenization movement. Shih-tsung's efforts to introduce Jurchen script apparently bore no fruit until Chang-tsung's era.

Two pieces of evidence will serve to support this surmise regarding the delayed impact of Shih-tsung's movement. First, a text dating from Chang-tsung's reign (1206) demonstrates that Jurchen was already being used at that time for writing postscripts, colophons, and short inscriptions. The main body of the text on the "Ao-t'un Liang-pi chien-yin pei" (also known as the "T'ai-ho t'i-ming ts'an-shih"; Jin Qicong and Jin Guangping 1980, appendix 2) was composed and written in Chinese by a Jurchen named Ao-t'un Liang-pi, but it is followed by a postscript in Jurchen written by a friend of his, whose name in Chinese transcription reads something like "Pu Hsiu-hung." This postscript is a genuine Jurchen text, both composed and set down in Jurchen. Its author, however, seems to have been a Chinese writing in Jurchen—a phenomenon that is the result, no doubt, of the Jurchen civil service examinations that were introduced in 1165. (Actually, a stele erected in 1224 recording the names of successful exam candidates for that year includes a number of Han Chinese names.)

Second, an inscribed tablet discovered in the 1950s at P'eng-lai, Shantung, on which one of Ao-t'un Liang-pi's poems was preserved demonstrates that there were poets who wrote Chinese regulated verse (*ch'i-yen lü-shih*) in Jurchen. Although written in Jurchen, Ao-t'un's poem was a Chinese *lü-shih*, for it follows the strict rhythmic, rhyming, and stanzaic requirements of the Chinese genre closely. Even the extremely difficult antithesis requirement for the two middle couplets is clearly satisfied.

Writing Chinese poems in Jurchen was, of course, much more difficult than writing Jurchen alliterated poems. The only possible explanation for the motive behind this hybrid practice is that the influence of Chinese poetry on Jurchen aristocrats was already so deeply rooted, they not only had forgotten how to write traditional Jurchen poems but had also ceased to regard Jurchen poems as poetry. This was not simply the bizarre idea of a few Jurchen scholar-officials. A Jurchen *chin-shih* examination asked for a "Poem on the Loyalty with which Ministers Serve Their Emperor" (Jin Qicong and Jin Guangping 1980, appendix 1)—a topic eminently suited not for Jurchen alliterated folk poetry, but for regulated verse in the Chinese style. And if the government asked for Jurchen poems in the Chinese style, they would surely be written.

In his promotion of Jurchen folklore and Jurchen writing, Shih-tsung's aim was to enable educated Jurchen to write Jurchen literature in the Jurchen language. It was not until four or five decades later that the Jurchen written language was developed enough to replace the Khitan script. How could the emperor have ever imagined that the Jurchen script would be used to produce regulated verse that was neither Jurchen nor Chinese, but a strange combination of both?

The Development of Jurchen Literature in Chinese during the Re-Jurchenization Movement (Late 12th–Early 13th Centuries)

Emperor Shih-tsung's advocacy of Jurchen literature was a purely political action. But his program met with difficulties for two cultural reasons. First, the Jurchen script, which had been created under Emperor T'ai-tsu, was not put into practical use until Shih-tsung's own reign. Only then did Jurchen begin to be used for translations of the classics, instruction in schools, and the examination of *chin-shih* candidates. As a written language, Jurchen was not yet sufficiently developed for belles lettres, which continued to be recorded in Chinese. This was of course not what Emperor Shih-tsung had hoped. Second, at the end of the twelfth century, Chinese literature was not simply the literature of the Han Chinese people. For example, the *yüeh-fu* poetry of the T'ang era and the lyric meters of the Sung had absorbed much from the songs and music of neighboring tribal peoples. A literature with such power for assimilation is irresistibly attractive to the other literatures it comes in contact with, gaining a strength, richness, and vitality that it would surely not have as the exclusive literature of one ethnic group alone.

The people who embodied these two challenges were not Shih-tsung's political enemies, but his own son and grandson, the crown prince Hsüan-hsiao (1146–85) and the emperor Chang-tsung, over whose education he had taken personal care. His son, the crown prince Hsüan-hsiao, predeceased him. Of him Liu Ch'i (1203–50) writes: "Crown Prince Hsüan-hsiao was the son of Shih-tsung and the father of Chang-tsung; he was posthumously titled Hsien-tsung. He was fond of literature, composed poetry, and was good at painting human figures and other things; horses were his specialty. His paintings were greatly admired and are still treasured in many collections today" (KCC 1.3). The supplementary imperial biographies in the *Chin History* provide a revealing story about him:

> The emperor [i.e., Crown Prince Hsüan-hsiao] was sitting at a banquet in Ch'eng-Hua Hall. Imperial Tutor Shuang, Prince Shou, suggested: "Your Majesty is not yet well versed in the language of the dynasty. Why not replace the Han officials around you with Jurchen officials?" The emperor answered: "How can we dismiss officials who extol virtues and praise the good as well as serve us!" Shuang kowtowed and withdrew. (CS 19.412)

Note that the name of the banquet hall, Ch'eng-Hua, "Continuing Chinese Culture," suggests that the court regarded Chinese, not Jurchen, as the culture to be maintained, and that Emperor Shih-tsung's heir apparent, moreover, did not know Jurchen!

The crown prince's ignorance of his native language can be ascribed to his diligence in studying Chinese. According to the official *Chin History*, "He concentrated intensely on his studies and often held discussions with Confucian officials in Ch'eng-Hua Hall; after retiring to his bed, he would read until midnight without feeling fatigue" (CS 19.410). Thus, nothing but obsession with Chinese learning and scholarship accounted for Hsüan-hsiao's lack of knowledge of Jurchen. He was born in 1146, became crown prince in 1161, and died in 1185 at the age of forty. His lifestyle followed a course exactly opposite to the expectations of his father, and could be considered one of the greatest failures of Shih-tsung's policy of re-Jurchenization.

The crown prince's sons, the future emperors Chang-tsung and Hsüan-tsung, could have been no less sinicized since they were influenced more by their father than by their grandfather. According to the official *Chin History*, the crown prince set the schedule for his sons' lessons: "[In 1179,] emperors Hsüan-tsung and Chang-tsung began their education. Hsien-tsung told them: 'Every day you will first take instruction in written Chinese, which should continue until the *shen* hour [i.e., 3 to 5 p.m.], then you will take instruction in Jurchen small script and practice the spoken language of the dynasty' " (CS 98.2163). The time allocated to Jurchen was disproportionately limited and relegated to the end of a full day's study of Chinese. The result could be predicted.

The *Chin History* also records, however, that Emperor Chang-tsung could speak a little Jurchen:

> [In 1180] he was invested as prince of Chin-yüan commandery, and he began to study the language of the dynasty, Jurchen script, and the Chinese classics.... [In 1185] he was invested as Prince Yüan and put in charge of Ta-hsing-fu. When he came to court and thanked Emperor Shih-tsung in the language of the dynasty, Shih-tsung was both pleased and greatly moved. Addressing his ministers, Shih-tsung said, "I have ordered all the princes to learn the language of the dynasty; only Prince Yüan has studied it to any great extent, and I commend him highly for it." (CS 9.207–8)

Apparently the prince, who had outstripped his brothers in complying with their father's wishes, was actually able to say only a few courtesy words in Jurchen. No literary works in Jurchen by him survive, while a considerable amount of his Chinese poetry and prose has been preserved, the former in the *Kuei-ch'ien chih* (1.3):

Written in the Palace

The gold-and-enamel-colored clouds prop up the morning sun;
Where the houses are towering is the emperors' home.
When the curtains in the thirty-six palaces are all rolled up,
Flowers fly everywhere in the east wind.

Drinking at Night

What is so enjoyable about drinking at night?
It's the quietness—
Three cups of light wine,
One song from a cold lute.
Sitting long, the incense ash bends down;
Deep into night, lamps are about to bloom.
This is happiness upon happiness,
And no boundary for the realm of intoxication.

Two of his *tz'u* are also recorded in the *Kuei-ch'ien chih* (1.3):

On a Bone Fan
(Tune: "Butterflies Love Flowers")

In the flow of the Hsiang dragons with fine bones
Come upon one another as the waves in the river.

A tiny pin stranded with gold, like flowers entwined with grass;
A green silk ribbon tied into a sharing-heart knot.

Days are long in Gold Hall when there is a banquet;
[. . .] invites a cool breeze to penetrate.
Suddenly there comes an urgent request to go to court,
And one has to be nudged gingerly into perfumed sleeves.

Peeling Oranges
(Tune: "Soft Gold Cup")

Attractive are those young men of the Purple Mansion
When drinking heartily on shores of black silk.
Gentle as a river with nine bends;
Cold are their glass cups.

Gentle fingers, white as jade scallions,
Peel this pill of yellow gold.
The spring color, borrowed from T'ung-t'ing Lake,
Flies across peach-blossom faces.

There is nothing Jurchen about the poems cited above. The descriptions of houses, food, and utensils, the women, ideas, and emotions are all Chinese. Emperor Chang-tsung was actually following in the sinicizing tradition of Hai-ling rather than the re-Jurchenization of his own grandfather.

What those above were fond of was naturally adopted even more zealously by those below. Prince Mi-kuo, brother to Chang-tsung, was praised by Han Chinese literati of the last years of the Chin dynasty as a gifted poet. Two of his poems here (KCC 1.5) will suffice to illustrate his way of thinking:

*On the News that Chao Hsien-hsien
Is Reappointed to the Han-lin Academy*

Long in the light of the lotus candle, we have not heard
 your poems;
One morning you are picked above others by the emperor's
 grace.
The great master has been minister now in four reigns;
The Han-lin academician has enjoyed a good name for three
 dozen years.
People will say, a dragon has found its thunder and rain;
But I know that deer mean more to him than official attire.

> As for precious cliffs and empty valleys—dreams of the
>   western window—
> I believe they will still come to mind in autumn.

Chüeh-chü

> Say no more that the ford of Meng is more turbid than the Ching,
> For in times of peace it will turn clear.
> Then, north of the Yellow River, under the mulberry and *che* trees,
> We will speak only of the way of kingly governance, not of weapons
>   of war.

At Meng-chin, a county seat near the southern banks of the Yellow River, both life and the river were usually less turbulent than they were on the Ching River in the northwest. This poem, however, was composed at a time when the Mongols were driving relentlessly southward and threatening the very existence of the Chin, not just their northwestern frontier. Still, pinning his hopes on pacifist illusions of the moral governance of ancient Chinese kings, this poet-prince urged his companions on an excursion north of the Yellow River to talk of the *tao* instead of the military conflicts confronting them.

Mi-kuo's political opinions expressed the same pacifism on another occasion: " 'The power of our enemies has reached such limits that it cannot be resisted, and surrender is the only way is to save our clan,' he reasoned; 'It would be good if the Wan-yen clan were allowed to return to our native homeland, the Jurchen people not to become extinct. What more could be hoped for?' " (*KCC* 1.4). He did not know that this minimal hope was already impractical. What a contrast in attitude between Mi-kuo's poems and the traditional songs for dispelling dissention!

Such cultural refinement pervaded even the ranks of the Jurchen military leaders of the *meng-an* and the *mou-k'o*. Liu Ch'i notes that after the loss of the area north of the Yellow River to the Mongols, the hereditary leaders of the Jurchen military acquired a fondness for belles letters and the companionship of civilian scholar-officials, and he cites as examples six army officers who excelled at writing Chinese poetry (*KCC* 6.63).

Liu Ch'i wrote biographical notes for two of these officer-poets. The first reports:

> Shu-hu Sui—*tzu* Shih-hsüan, former personal name Hsüan and *tzu* Wen-po—was a Jurchen *meng-an* chief from Na-lin. Even though a [Jurchen] aristocrat, he worked as hard on poetry as a poor [Chinese] scholar. He was fond of the company of civilian scholar-officials. . . . He built a house in the countryside near the Shang River and

endured ragged clothes and crude food that he might concentrate on composing poetry. Thus, his compositions improved greatly. At the time I was in Huai-yang, and we often discussed classical scholarship. When the northern army entered Honan, he was entrusted with the command of the troops defending Po-chou. In the disorder at the end, he was killed—not yet forty at the time. A couplet from one of the poems he wrote as a youth describing the scenery of Honan went:

> The mountains are linked from Sung to Shao, an evening of mist and clouds;
> Plains connect Yao and Han, an autumn of grass and trees.
>
> (KCC 3.25)[5]

The second one, Wu-lin Ta-shuang, was also the hereditary chief of a *meng-an* who devoted himself to studying poetry. Like Shu-hu Sui, Wu-lin Ta-shuang also visited Liu Ch'i for lengthy discussions of poetry. Drinking with friends and making repartee in the company of noted literati, he lived the life of a Chinese poet as much as possible despite his poverty. When the city of Ch'en fell to the Mongols, he drowned himself; he was not yet thirty. One of his earlier couplets tells his literary personality:

> Parting in Heaven brings even more tears
> That fill the void and fly down as clear autumn rain.

Besides quoting his poems, Liu Ch'i praises him: "I always said that if he persisted, he would become the savant of his generation.... It is a great pity he was deprived of the opportunity to bring his promise to fruition" (KCC 3.26).

It is no surprise that a Chinese literatus such as Liu Ch'i liked those Jurchen aristocrats who delighted in drinking with men of letters and devoting themselves to poetry. Their obsession with Chinese poetry meant by necessity total abandonment of Jurchen literature. Consequently, Jurchen songs and poems could survive only for a while among common people before gradually fading away.

The Afterglow of Jurchen Literature in the Aftermath of the Chin

The literature of a people does not necessarily vanish abruptly with the loss of political dominance; it suffers, rather, gradual assimilation and eventual extinction. Official suppression or a vanquished people's fear of persecution at the hands of their new rulers may act as a cultural inhibitor and thus bring about the death of a basically oral literature—a phenomenon that is commonplace from the viewpoint of Chinese history.

The Mongols who crushed the Jurchen empire, however, seem to have cared relatively little about cultural matters. Jurchen literature consequently enjoyed an afterglow, now unfortunately visible only in a few words and names of Yüan drama, just as traces of Manchu survive in Peking opera. Some Yüan plays even have Jurchen heroes or heroines: Wang Jui-lan in Kuan Han-ch'ing's *Pavilion of Paying Respect to the Moon* (*Pai-yüeh-t'ing*), for example, or Wan-yen Yen-shou-ma in the southern drama *A Scion of a Noble House Opts for the Wrong Career* (*Huan-men tzu-ti ts'o-li-shen*), apparently based on an earlier drama, perhaps by Li Chih-fu, who also wrote *The Tiger's-Head Tablet for Power in Emergency* (*Pien-i hsing-shih hu-t'ou-p'ai*), featuring Wan-yen Shan-shou-ma, his wife Ch'a-ch'a, and his uncle Yin-te-ma. Their speech is larded with Jurchen words by necessity. Wang Jui-lan calls her father "A-ma" and her mother "A-che." More interesting is a song sung by Wan-yen Yen-shou-ma in which there are a number of Jurchen words and phrases. In printed versions of these plays such words and phrases are transliterated in Chinese characters, but not in the official transliterations promulgated by the Chin government. They must therefore have been transcribed directly from spoken Jurchen. (For a different view of the Jurchen nature of these plays, see West 1977a.)

The quantity of names, words, and even descriptions of Jurchen customs included in Yüan dramas cited above must represent a linguistic inheritance from the texts of Chin variety skits. Nonetheless, since Jurchen is found in Yüan compositions, we may say that bits of Jurchen literature survived the fall of Jurchen political power. We have to attribute this survival largely to the carelessness of Mongol literary censorship. Still, it is because it was recorded in Chinese characters that such Jurchen literature has been transmitted to the present day.

Conclusion

The oral phase of Jurchen literature started with shaman songs before the eleventh century, developed into original compositions by the mid-twelfth century and, finally, the more sophisticated original compositions of native songs by the end of the twelfth century. Afterwards, there was a prolonged decline relieved only by a slight afterglow in the recorded language of Yüan drama. Before the fall of the Chin dynasty, that is, during the mid- to late twelfth century, there was a radical decline in Jurchen language activity that was followed by a marked upsurge—the direct result of Emperor Hai-ling's and Emperor Shih-tsung's diametrically different policies. The Jurchen written language was not yet sufficiently developed when Shih-tsung tried to encourage composition of Jurchen literature in Jurchen. It was not until the years 1196–1212 that Jurchen civil service examinations provided the impetus, and Jurchen schools the means, for training a large number of men of letters in written Jurchen. What these Jurchen men of letters wrote, however, were not the shaman songs and native songs of the Jurchen oral tradition, culturally distinct in form and content from Chinese verse; what they wrote were not pure Jurchen compositions, but hybrids employing Chinese forms and Jurchen language, virtual translations from the Chinese. Both oral Jurchen literature recorded in Chinese and poetry composed by Jurchen in Chinese should be considered Jurchen literature because they express the emotions and experience of their Jurchen authors. Similarly, literature written in Chinese should by no means be considered the exclusive concern of Han Chinese, for it is shaped, in part, by the culture and literature of all the ethnic groups that form and have formed the Chinese nation. Jurchen literature should be of interest to the scholar not only because it prefigures Manchu literature in its development and evolution, but because it served as a cultural link between the earlier traditions of the Liao and Sung and later traditions of the Yüan.

Notes

1. This and the following song were collected by Nioradze (1925, chap. 12).

2. Collected in Nioradze 1925, chap. 2.

3. For the Chinese translation, see *THL*, Ch'ien-lung chap. 18; for the Manchu transcription, see the appendix in de Harlez 1884.

4. For a transcription of the stele's inscription, see Lo Fu-i 1937; for discussions of the inscription, see Jin Qicong and Jin Guangping 1980, chap. 3, sect. 26, and Wang Jen-fu 1987.

5. For a translation of another of Shu-hu's poems, see Eng 1990, 228.

9

SATIRE AND ALLEGORY IN ALL KEYS AND MODES

Wilt Idema

The *chu-kung-tiao*, or "all-keys-and-modes," is one of many varieties of prosimetric narrative in Chinese literature, a genre some scholars have referred to as "medley," "ballad," or "chantefable." It derives its peculiar name from its musical organization: the rhymed sections are written to song-sets, with two succeeding sets rarely belonging to the same musical mode. The life span of this particular prosimetric form does *not* neatly coincide with the beginning and end of the Chin dynasty. The *chu-kung-tiao* came into being at the end of the eleventh century and was still occasionally performed in the early decades of the fourteenth. Nor was the *chu-kung-tiao* practiced only in North China; we know that it was also popular in Hangchow.

Only a few *chu-kung-tiao* texts have been preserved. We have approximately one-third of the anonymous *Liu Chih-yüan chu-kung-tiao*, dating probably to the mid-twelfth century, which concerns the early career of Liu Chih-yüan, emperor (r. 947–48) of the Later Han during the Five Dynasties period. A second extant text is the *T'ien-pao i-shih chu-kung-tiao* (Anecdotes from the T'ien-pao era in all keys and modes), fifty song-sets of which are found dispersed throughout a number of *ch'ü* formularies and anthologies from as early as the sixteenth century. It is attributed to Wang Po-ch'eng, a dramatist active in the second half of the thirteenth century. We also have numerous references to the widespread popularity of a *chu-kung-tiao* concerning the romance between the student Shuang Chien and the courtesan Su Hsiao-ch'ing, along with what is probably a new prologue to the work written by a certain Yang Li-chai of the early Yüan dynasty (Crump 1983, 171–92). Only one *chu-kung-tiao* has survived in its entirety: the *Hsi-hsiang-chi chu-kung-tiao* (The story of the western wing in all keys and modes) by Tung Chieh-yüan, who is reported to have lived during the reign of the Chin emperor Chang-tsung (r. 1190–1208).

Though the genre does not coincide chronologically or geographically with the Chin, it has become closely associated with that dynasty and is considered by many to be its distinctive contribution to Chinese literature. For the Ming scholar Hu Ying-lin, the *Hsi-hsiang-chi chu-kung-tiao* even constitutes the whole of Chin literature: "Tung's work still circulates in the world nowadays. It is masterfully crafted, skilled, beautiful, the very acme of talent and feeling. Moreover, each syllable demonstrates 'basic color,' each word has an air of antiquity. It is indeed the progenitor of all musical plays, old and new. The total literary contribution of the Chin is exhausted in it" (*SSSF*, 560; trans. West 1977b, 50, *mod auct.*). Since the reevaluation of traditional vernacular literature in the wake of the Literary Revolution in the early decades of the twentieth century, the *Hsi-hsiang-chi chu-kung-tiao* has unanimously been considered one of the masterpieces of Chinese literature. Testimony to this are the numerous Western-language translations that have appeared over the last century or more.

In this essay I will consider the two major all-keys-and-modes extant, the *Hsi-hsiang-chi chu-kung-tiao* and the *Liu Chih-yüan chu-kung-tiao*. I prefer to deal with Tung's work first because it is our only complete text and is, in my opinion, more representative of the genre than the fragmentary *Liu Chih-yüan*; the peculiar characteristics of the latter will stand out in clearer relief when viewed against the apparent norms of the tradition exemplified in the *Hsi-hsiang-chi*. In neither case will I attempt a comprehensive analysis of the texts. I will try to limit myself to those aspects that have special relevance to social and cultural values that have been slighted or ignored in earlier studies. I will not treat the *T'ien-pao i-shih chu-kung-tiao*. The nature of its separated and disparate song-sets makes a comparable analysis extremely difficult. It would have to be discussed not only within the context of its genre but, because of its late date and authorship, within the context of dramatic literature (i. e., *tsa-chü*) as well. That is beyond the scope of this essay.

Before looking at these two *chu-kung-tiao*, however, I will briefly summarize my findings about the genre. The information on *chu-kung-tiao* in contemporary sources is scarce, and the number of preserved texts is exiguous. Nevertheless, available data provides a basis for certain tentative conclusions regarding the all-keys-and-modes as a genre. Although the *chu-kung-tiao* is a form of prosimetric storytelling, early sources prefer to treat it as a form of entertainment that combines music and song. A number of sources, moreover, point out the satiric nature of this specific type of song. Some of the authors known to us were regarded as satiric wits by their contemporaries. The audience of the *chu-kung-tiao* was probably to be found in relatively upper-class circles and was consequently rather small when compared to audiences of genres intellectually less demanding. This relatively restricted audience would also explain the small number of known performers. If this explanation holds, it is probably no coincidence that the number of known titles is so small. The all-keys-and-modes genre probably never experienced the pervasive popularity of storytelling or drama.

The earliest source concerning the *chu-kung-tiao* specifies the student as the main butt of its satire, a phenomenon borne out by the single complete example of the genre extant, Tung Chieh-yüan's version of the tale of Chang Kung and Ts'ui Ying-ying. If the *chu-kung-tiao* was primarily a northern genre, it had a counterpart in the southern *hsi-wen*, which also focused on the misdemeanor of students. This is not surprising: students, who emerged as a highly visible social group in the second half of the eleventh century, increased in number and importance under both the Chin and the Southern Sung dynasties.

There is an important difference, however, between the student-protagonists of the *chu-kung-tiao* and those of the *hsi-wen*. The authors of *chu-kung-tiao* are basically sympathetic toward the successful, upwardly mobile young men who are their protagonists, however much they may ridicule them during their days of obscurity and poverty. Chang Kung and Shuang Chien (and Liu Chih-yüan for that matter) are all eventually reunited with the objects of their love and they all set out on brilliant careers. But in early *hsi-wen* it is the ungrateful student that is the important theme. In their writings, the *shu-hui* of Hangchow demonstrate a basically negative attitude toward the successful and upwardly mobile student. We are tempted to interpret the plays concerning Ts'ai Po-chieh or Wang K'uei as expressions of jealousy aimed at former members of the *shu-hui* who had become officials through success in the examinations—expressions, that is, of a rudimentary antagonism against the establishment by an urban literati group excluded from the imperial bureaucracy. The emergence of such a group in the South, but not in the North, may be explained by the urbanization of some areas governed by the Southern Sung that was far more rapid and far more extensive than that experienced by any area under Chin rule. If the earliest *hsi-wen* reflect frustrated former friends' envy of the successful candidate, *chu-kung-tiao* reflect the firmly entrenched elite's smiling acceptance of the same. And if the earliest *hsi-wen* prefer to depict the student as a villain, the *chu-kung-tiao* prefer to portray him as a fool. The hero of the *chu-kung-tiao* may one day rise to metropolitan graduate or even emperor, but he is nevertheless a victim of circumstance, a slave to his passions, a piece of putty in the hands of a woman.

Social Satire and Sexual Allegory in the Hsi-hsiang-chi chu-kung-tiao

Tung Chieh-yüan's composition, it is generally known, is based on the "Ying-ying chuan," a classical tale by the T'ang dynasty literatus Yüan Chen. Yüan's tale, widely believed to be autobiographical in nature, recounts the romance of a certain Chang Kung, a student, and his cousin Ts'ui Ying-ying. Chang, en route to the capital and the state examinations, stops at P'u-chiu Monastery outside P'u-chou, where Ying-ying happens to be staying together with her mother and her younger brother. Chang is immediately taken with the girl, but she rejects his initial advances and berates him for his immodest proposals. She suddenly changes her mind, however, and visits him one night in his room. The visit blossoms into an affair, which Chang terminates formally after his departure from the monastery and arrival in the capital (despite a passionate letter from Ying-ying). Years later, both have married different partners. Chang visits Ying-ying but is refused a meeting.[1] Yüan Chen's friend Li Shen (d. 846) adapted the tale as a ballad, now lost except for the four fragments found in the *Hsi-hsiang-chi chu-kung-tiao* (*THH*, 10, 36, 69, 91).

The "Ying-ying chuan" enjoyed great popularity in the eleventh century. Both Ch'in Kuan (1049–1100) and his slightly younger contemporary Mao P'ang devoted segments of their *chuan-t'a* to descriptions of Ying-ying,[2] and Chao Ling-chih (1061–1134) adapted the "Ying-ying chuan" as a *ku-tzu-tz'u* (drum lyric). These literati all follow Yüan Chen's text closely; Chao Ling-chih's work alone is remarkable for its voiced disapproval of Chang's behavior. The "Ying-ying chuan" was also popular outside the milieu of the literati. In the introduction to his *ku-tzu-tz'u*, Chao Ling-chih states that "even female entertainers were all capable of narrating it in outline" (Liu Yung-chi 1957, 56)—wording that seems to imply that the tale told by these entertainers departed from Yüan Chen's text on points of detail. The tale's popularity continued during the Southern Sung dynasty: the "Ying-ying chuan" heads the list of *ch'uan-ch'i* in the "Hsiao-shuo k'ai-p'i" section of Lo Yeh's *Tsui-weng t'an-lu*.

It is very likely that Tung Chieh-yüan was influenced by popular versions of the "Ying-ying chuan" current during his lifetime, but it should be stressed that he returned to the original text in writing his adaptation. In contrast to Yüan and Ming playwrights who often were familiar only with abbreviated versions of T'ang *ch'uan-ch'i*, Tung frequently quotes from the original text verbatim and includes most of its poems, as well as Ying-ying's letter, in his own work. At the same time he draws on other sources to develop his theme. Tung Chieh-yüan knew the ballad by Li Shen; he quotes from it extensively four times. If these quotations were not doctored to fit the context, it would appear that Li Shen's ballad was more than simply a rhymed version of Yüan Chen's tale. While Yüan Chen alludes only briefly to the rebellion of the troops guarding the bridge across the Yellow River and to Chang Kung's averting the calamity threatening the monastery by appealing to an officer he has befriended, Tung quotes Li Shen's extended description of the rebels' plunder of P'u-chou (*THH*, 36)—the inspiration, perhaps, for Tung's own extended description of the troops' attack on the monastery, an attack that is not so much as mentioned in the "Ying-ying chuan." According to the text, the officer to whom Chang appeals for help is *not* Tu Ch'üeh, who "in about ten days ... restored order among the troops"; but another quotation from Li Shen's ballad suggests that Chang does request Tu Ch'üeh to come to the aid of the monastery and also mentions his sobriquet, Pai-ma-chiang-chün, "General on the White Horse" (*THH*, 69). The importance of Li Shen's narrative poem to the development of *Hsi-hsiang-chi* should not be underestimated.

In the development of his theme Tung Chieh-yüan also draws heavily from the story of Ssu-ma Hsiang-ju and Cho Wen-chün. Ever since Ssu-ma Ch'ien first recorded the impoverished poet's seduction of the young widow, the couple's elopement, and their subsequent life as wine-shop keepers, this romance has been one of China's most popular love stories, for all the moral criticism directed against Ssu-ma Hsiang-ju through the ages.[3] In our text Chang Kung is continually compared to Ssu-ma Hsiang-ju because of both his literary talent and his love for Ying-ying. The scene in which Chang tries to seduce Ying-ying with his zither playing (book 4) is directly inspired by Ssu-ma Hsiang-ju's seduction of Cho Wen-chün, though Chang plays alone in his room at night while Ssu-ma Hsiang-ju performed before Wen-chün's father and his guests in the light of day; even the song Chang Kung chants is closely modeled on that supposedly sung by Ssu-ma Hsiang-ju (*THH*, 83). The zither, of course, has always been the preferred musical instrument of the literatus, but in the "Ying-ying chuan" Chang does not play the zither. It is Ying-ying, when Chang is finally about to leave her, who performs at his request in one of the most moving scenes of the tale.

Tung Chieh-yüan adheres to the general line of development in the "Ying-ying chuan" up to the beginning of book 6, despite his many additions and changes in points of detail. But where Yüan Chen's tale has Chang depart for the capital on his own initiative and once there decide to break with Ying-ying, Tung Chieh-yüan's has him leave only after her mother has found out their affair and agreed to their marriage.

The plot of the last three books of the *Hsi-hsiang-chi chu-kung-tiao* may well be Tung Chieh-yüan's own invention, but it shows influence of other T'ang dynasty *ch'uan-ch'i* as well. The conclusion of book 6 is clearly inspired by the "Li-hun chi."[4] And the conclusion of book 7 is clearly inspired by the legend of the Le-ch'ang princess: Ying-ying comes face to face with her original fiancé, Cheng Heng, who has returned from the capital to claim her, and Chang Kung, who, after success in the capital, arrives only days behind Cheng Heng; the princess, a younger sister of the last emperor of the Ch'en dynasty, was captured by Yang Su (d. 606) but later returned by him to her husband. The anecdote is found in the *Pen-shih-shih* (The original incidents of poems) of Meng Ch'i, who lived in the second half of the ninth century.[5] In book 8 the monk Fa-ts'ung's offer to abduct Ying-ying and deliver her to Chang Kung recalls the young officer's offer to abduct Lady Liu and deliver her to Han I in Hsü Yao-tso's "Liu-shih chuan" (an abbreviated version is also included in the *Pen-shih-shih*), an incident already alluded to in book 7.[6]

Tung's work, however, is far more than a composite of its sources. All elements are inextricably fused into one new and coherent plot, which also contains episodes for which no source is readily identified. Tanaka Kenji (1954, 100–109) has pointed out that the main story line of the *Hsi-hsiang-chi chu-kung-tiao* consists of four waves of mounting expectation on the part of Chang Kung (and the audience), each wave dropping off abruptly in disappointment and unfulfilled desire. The first wave is halted in book 3, when Ying-ying's mother gives an unexpected interpretation to her promise to take her daughter's saviour into the family. The second wave is halted in book 4, when Chang Kung is sternly berated by Ying-ying. The third wave terminates in book 6, with her mother's discovery of their clandestine affair. The fourth is halted in book 7, when Chang discovers that Cheng Heng has preceded him by just a few days. Each wave repeats a comparable pattern of rising hope, initial disappointment, and renewed expectation.

If we also consider the requirements imposed by the prescribed points of suspense around the middle and end of each *chüan*, we cannot but admire the author's skill in plotting. On the one hand, he continually surprises the audience with sudden twists and turns in his story. On the other, he ensures that each new development in his narrative has been carefully prepared and, however unexpected at first sight, will appear in retrospect a logical outgrowth from the preceding action (Tanaka 1954, 109–12). In this respect Tung's *chu-kung-tiao* is quite different from Yüan Chen's tale, whose main attraction is the puzzling psychology of its heroine: "If *Ying-ying chuan* appeals to one's imagination, *Master Tung's Western Chamber Romance* surely gratifies one's sense of belief" (Li-li Ch'en 1976, xii). In view of the logical consistency of its intricate action, Tung Chieh-yüan's plot may be fully qualified as "well made."

Tung Chieh-yüan made his work a comedy by giving it a happy ending. The *Hsi-hsiang-chi chu-kung-tiao* is accordingly peopled with all the stock characters of comedy: the young lovers, the old parent, the disagreeable competitor who is favored by the parent, the resourceful servant who enables the lovers to maintain contact, and the friend who acts as a *deus ex machina* (Li-li Ch'en 1972, 135–37).

Like other comedies, the *Hsi-hsiang-chi chu-kung-tiao* contains many satiric elements, and most of them are directed primarily toward those characters who block the young lovers' hopes for the fulfillment of their love: Lady Ts'ui and Cheng Heng. Cheng Heng is a typical buffoon, fat and ugly and stupid yet full of self-conceit. He has secured official position through hereditary privilege and believes that his riches, aided perhaps by rumor, will buy him anything. He is in all ways portrayed as the negative example of the young man from a noble familiy who presumes on the power and wealth of his father, while lacking all ability himself.

Ying-ying's mother is a more complex character. As the widow of a minister, she is extremely status-conscious. Her every action is inspired by concern for the family honor. As a result, her love for her daughter takes the form of a desire to see Ying-ying suitably married to someone of her own class. Her opposition to Chang as a marriage candidate is motivated by both Ying-ying's previous engagement and Chang's low status as a student without an official post (and also, we assume, by his odd behavior). She reluctantly agrees to the marriage solely for fear of scandal, and she later is only too eager to believe the rumor that Chang has married someone else in the capital. Critics have noted that Lady Ts'ui is in many ways a personification of short-sighted conventional morality (Tanaka 1955, 96; Liu Wu-chi 1977, 26). Although she initially appears in all her strictness to be an awe-inspiring character, she is increasingly revealed to be a pathetic figure of fun who is helpless in difficult situations: in book 2, for example, when rebels have surrounded the monastery, and especially in book 6, when she discovers that her closely guarded daughter has long since lost her virginity.

In comedy, parents who cannot assert authority find their counterparts in servants who manipulate their superiors. In the *Hsi-hsiang-chi chu-kung-tiao*, the part of the wily servant is taken by Hung-niang, Ying-ying's servant-girl. Hung-niang's original task, the role in which she is introduced in book 1, is to see to it that her young mistress abides by Lady Ts'ui's instructions. As the story develops, she grows sympathetic toward the plight of the lovers, not only becoming their *postilion d'amour* but actually conspiring with Chang Kung in the seduction of Ying-ying. It is she who eventually persuades Lady Ts'ui to agree to the marriage. Moreover, Hung-niang's running commentary on the doings of her betters provides a sardonic accompaniment to action throughout the play (Tanaka 1955, 99–100).

While Fa-ts'ung is not Chang Kung's servant, their relationship is comparable in many ways to that of Hung-niang and Ying-ying. He prevents Chang from committing the terrible *faux pas* of rushing after Ying-ying; he acts as Chang's instrument, delivering to Tu Ch'üeh the letter asking for help; he supplies Chang with money from his own pocket for an engagement present; he offers to abduct Ying-ying and subsequently counsels the couple to take refuge with Tu Ch'üeh, by then governor of P'u-chou. At the same time, Fa-ts'ung is portrayed as a very unlikely monk. A former highwayman, he is not at all unhappy, despite his vows, to return temporarily to his old calling or to lead a band of provisionally armed monks and novices against the mutinous troops surrounding the monastery—and in so doing constructs one of the most boisterous, most farcical scenes in the work.

In many comedies the young lovers themselves are rather bland characters who leave the main stage, as well as the task of outwitting any figures of authority, to their servants. This is not the case in the *Hsi-hsiang-chi chu-kung-tiao*. For all the importance of the characters discussed above, Ying-ying and Chang Kung continue to act as the main protagonists.

Tung Chieh-yüan's work combines the characteristics of romantic comedy and tale of passion, but this does not necessarily make it the attack on feudal morality and paean to free love that many modern critics (e. g., Ling Ching-yen in his preface to *THH*; and Li-li Ch'en 1976, xv) would have it. The *Hsi-hsiang-chi chu-kung-tiao*, I believe, makes far more sense if read as a study in the follies of passion. If society's basic norms are transgressed by the lovers, those norms are not thereby questioned; the violation of such inviolable norms alone can manifest the force of the lovers' passion (Idema 1978b, 136–37). To modern readers, Marxist or not, traditional morality in matters of sex, love, and marriage may appear questionable, but there is no indication that Tung Chieh-yüan and his contemporaries shared such an opinion. They must have viewed the rites of marriage as the very cornerstone of social and cosmic order. Lovers who in their passion contravene these basic norms are not objects of admiration but prime targets of satire. Ying-ying and Chang Kung are the ideal embodiment of contemporary social values by right of family background, physical appearance, education, and accomplishments—until they become the victims of passion.

Ying-ying and Chang Kung fall in love at first sight; their passion increases when they chant poems across the garden wall at night. When troops attack the monastery, Ying-ying grasps the opportunity to ensure speedy realization of her desires, but her mother promptly reneges on the seeming promise of marriage. If Ying-ying does not immediately respond to Chang's proposal, however, the main hindrance is not her mother but her own sense of shame. The initial duplicity of her actions toward Hung-niang and Chang Kung may also be explained by this internal conflict between passion and shame. Only when Chang Kung appears to be on the brink of death with unrequited love does pity join with passion to conquer her shame and lead her to violate the taboo on premarital sexual relations. The gravity of her transgression is compounded by the fact that she is in mourning for her father. Having so disgraced herself, she is constantly occupied by the fear that her lover may reject her because her body is no longer pure. Tung Chieh-yüan's picture of Ying-ying is an ironic treatment of a refined young lady in the first throes of passion and all its subsequent stages (Tanaka 1955, 96–99; Liu Wu-chi 1977, 28–29).

Great lovers are either great heroes or great fools. The extent of their passion is measured and known by either the dangers they surmount or the indignities they subject themselves to willingly for the sake of their passion. In the first half of the *Hsi-hsiang-chi chu-kung-tiao*, Chang Kung is portrayed as a fool whose initial prudery makes him all the more suitable a victim of passion. As soon as he sees Ying-ying, he loses all self-control. He neglects his studies and attends only to schemes for approaching Ying-ying and winning her. He makes a fool of himself when he first tries to follow Ying-ying into her apartment and makes an even greater fool of himself when he attends the masses being said for her late father. Thinking that his plan to repel the mutinous troops has obtained him Ying-ying as a wife, he finds that he has been made into her brother. At the suggestion of Hung-niang, he tries to seduce Ying-ying with his zither playing but finds that in the dark he has embraced the servant-girl instead of her mistress. And when he responds to Ying-ying's invitation to rendezvous in her room, he is dumbfounded by her stern lecture. All his plans to win Ying-ying backfire or fail, and by the beginning of book 5 he is reduced to a physical wreck.

Tung Chieh-yüan rounds out his picture of Chang Kung as fool by underlining his self-conceit in the second half of book 2, his vanity and impatience in book 3, his lasciviousness in the first half of book 4 and his physical clumsiness in the second half, when he climbs into Ying-ying's garden and, "Jumping from the eastern side, / Falls on the western side, flat on his face" (*THH*, 90). To bring Chang Kung's foolishness into even greater relief, Tung Chieh-yüan provides him with a foil in the character of his friend Tu Ch'üeh, who is portrayed as both a perfect civil official and an infallible military commander. Yet if the *Hsi-hsiang-chi chu-kung-tiao* has any single central character, it is Chang Kung. Tung Chieh-yüan has obviously decided to continue K'ung San-chuan's tradition of "poking fun at students" (Li-li Ch'en 1972, 137; Tanaka 1955, 98).

The first four books of the *Hsi-hsiang-chi chu-kung-tiao* show man as a victim of the passion inspired in him by woman, the power of *yin* over *yang*. The second part of the work shows its mirror image, the reassertion of *yang* over *yin*. Chang Kung's fate reaches its nadir when he climbs into Ying-ying's garden, but his fortune improves once Ying-ying visits him in his room on her own initiative. As soon as Lady Ts'ui's consent to their marriage offers the prospect of the regularization of their relations, Chang Kung shows himself capable of controlling his passion in order to resume his rightful place in society by departing for the capital and the examinations. Chang's newfound mastery over his desires is brought out most dramatically upon his return from his successful trip to the capital when he refuses to "squabble over a woman" with Cheng Heng (THH, 148). Chang Kung is still in love with Ying-ying but is now so in command of his passion that he will not make a fool of himself again. Nor is there any need for him to do so, because Ying-ying elopes with him that very night to the haven of Governor Tu's yamen.

Actually, the author of the *Hsi-hsiang-chi chu-kung-tiao* may be much closer in sentiment here to Yüan Chen's "Ying-ying chuan" than to Wang Shih-fu's play. In the *tsa-chü*, Chang Kung's departure for the capital is a condition imposed upon him by Lady Ts'ui: he is allowed to return and claim Ying-ying only if he obtains official position. Success in the examinations turns the fool into a hero who has earned his right to a bride, but his activities are still inspired by the same passion. In the "Ying-ying chuan," Chang explains his decision to leave Ying-ying by describing her as a *yu-wu*, an extraordinary being that will destroy a man with the unbridled passion it inspires in him. In the *Hsi-hsiang-chi chu-kung-tiao*, Chang Kung's departure for the capital marks his resumption of social responsibility, his successful bridling of passion. If Chang Kung can indeed control his desires, Tung Chieh-yüan might have argued, there is no further need to deny the lovers a happy married life in which "the husband leads and the wife follows." Once Chang Kung regains his sanity, the main force of the satiric drive is directed instead against his rival Cheng Heng, the arrogant son of a high official.

In connection with the preceding paragraph, it may be instructive to compare the *Hsi-hsiang-chi chu-kung-tiao* to the legend of the White Snake as it appears, for example, in Feng Meng-lung's *Ching-shih t'ung-yen* (Universal words to warn the world).[7] This *hua-pen* opens with an evocation of West Lake and its frequent floods. The main story recounts a young man's encounter with a young lady in mourning during a terrible shower of rain on the occasion of the Ch'ing-ming festival. She excites a great passion in him and casts a spell from which he cannot flee, even though she repeatedly brings him to disaster. The young woman is eventually revealed to be the transfiguration of a white snake and is exorcised by a Buddhist monk, who buries her beneath Lei-feng Pagoda. The young man thereupon shaves his head and becomes a monk. Throughout most of the *hua-pen* the lady in white is depicted as a sympathetic character. Still, she is clearly the personification of the lethal passion a woman may arouse in a man: she is a subterranean creature associated with death and mourning, the grave (the Ch'ing-ming festival), and the supremacy of *yin* over *yang* (the floods and rain).

If the legend of the White Snake illustrates the Buddhist solution to the danger of woman (man's overcoming lust by cutting all social ties and renouncing the world), the *Hsi-hsiang-chi chu-kung-tiao* may be seen as offering a more "Confucian" solution: marriage—if man can sufficiently control his passion. In book 1 Ying-ying operates within the same kind of associative contexts as the heroine of the White Snake legend in several ways. Following the prologue, the book opens with a description of the Yellow River where it is most impressive; we are told repeatedly that Ying-ying is in mourning and so wears white; the action is set at a monastery that serves as her father's temporary resting place and the site of his obsequies. Whether she wills it or not, Ying-ying is surrounded by the aura of death, and the passion she inspires is potentially lethal. Modern beliefs in the salutary effects of romantic love should not prevent a correct appreciation of the traditional fear of sexual passion as a disruptive power. Ying-ying's devastating charms not only affect Chang Kung, but upset the congregation of monks and the local community as well. Prey to Ying-ying's powers of attraction, the rebels in book 2 may also be viewed as an extension of her power to destroy. Here it might be pointed out that in the opening line of his ballad, Li Shen compares lovers who cannot meet to the swallow and the shrike who each fly in opposite directions (*THH*, 10). The call of the shrike was traditionally believed a portent of rebellion.

The theme of the *Hsi-hsiang-chi chu-kung-tiao* is further underlined in its correlation of action and location. All readers of Chinese poetry are acquainted with the customary correspondences between action and season. This may also be observed in Tung Chieh-yüan's work: the lovers meet in spring, carry on their affair through summer, and part in autumn; the following spring is one of unfulfilled love-longing, while the final reunion takes place in autumn. The correlation of action and location is equally important. Chang Kung does not come under the spell of Ying-ying in P'u-chou, where he has come seeking teachers, but outside the city and its ordered society, at the monastery. Once installed there, his situation deteriorates every time he leaves his study; conversely, his fortunes seem to improve whenever people come to visit him. When he attends masses for the late minister Ts'ui, rebels besiege the monastery and threaten to abduct Ying-ying; when he visits Lady Ts'ui, she reneges on the apparent promise of marriage; when he steals into Ying-ying's garden, he is sternly rebuked by her. But when he plays the zither in his own room, he almost succeeds in seducing Ying-ying; she eventually fulfills his desires by coming to his room; and it is there too that Hung-niang informs him that Lady Ts'ui has agreed to the marriage. Chang Kung's fortunes improve dramatically when he arrives in the capital; they suffer a temporary setback when he returns to the monastery; and his marriage becomes definite only when the couple flees to the administrative seat in P'u-chou. The monastery and the women's quarters are consistently depicted as the negative antipode of the scholar's study and the official yamen. If the Buddhist monastery commonly served as hostel (and so a quite plausible location for the action of the play), by T'ang times it already had a reputation as a place of debauchery. It is certainly no coincidence that Tung Chieh-yüan remembers to note, reliably or not, that the P'u-chou monastery had been founded by the notorious Wu Tse-t'ien, the only woman in Chinese history who occupied the dragon throne and who almost succeeded in exterminating the imperial clan.

The *Hsi-hsiang-chi chu-kung-tiao* is more than a simple love comedy. As a tale of great passion, it is a comprehensive satire of a society set awry by desire: a society in which soldiers rebel, monks fight, parents lack authority, servants usurp the powers of their superiors, daughters surrender their chastity, and students neglect their studies. Yet the situation is not viewed as hopeless. After all, desire belongs to human nature and may be regulated. Throughout the work the presence of Tu Ch'üeh, the personification of Confucian norms, holds out the promise of a return to normalcy, which is eventually achieved.

The theme of Tung Chieh-yüan's work is uncomfortably close to that of Wang Po-ch'eng's *T'ien-pao i-shih chu-kung-tiao*, a work that, in the words of one of its prologues, is an "indictment" against Yang Kuei-fei and the passion she inspired in Hsüan-tsung, a passion that "overturned an empire." Ying-ying in mourning is probably a reflection of the same menacing archetypal image cast by the white body of Yang Kuei-fei as she emerged from the hot springs of the Hua-ch'ing Palace. Both women excite passions that compel men to violate the ultimate taboo of incest: Hsüan-tsung marries his own daughter-in-law; Chang Kung and Ts'ui Ying-ying become brother and sister before they become lovers.

The *Hsi-hsiang-chi chu-kung-tiao* is an intensely erotic text. It contains numerous scenes of love-longing, usually in the shape of extensive monologues by Chang Kung or Ying-ying, which are very much in the tradition of the erotic lyrics of the Northern Sung (Li-li Ch'en 1972, 144–45; and 1976, xxv–xxvii). The text also contains descriptions of actual lovemaking that exhibit a frankness quite remarkable for traditional Chinese literature of that time (Li-li Ch'en 1972, 139–40). All this is only to be expected in view of the subject matter of Tung Chieh-yüan's work. We also encounter explicit sexual allusions, however, at places where at first thought we would hardly expect them. These passages are usually explained away as regrettable but unavoidable lapses into bad taste on the part of the author who, as a commercial artist, had to attract the attention of his audience at any cost. But such explicit sexual allusions are not found in, for example, the *Liu Chih-yüan chu-kung-tiao*'s many scenes of love-longing or its descriptions of lovemaking; they are not necessarily characteristic, then, of the genre. Of course, we might also explain this occasional bawdiness as part and parcel of Tung Chieh-yüan's irreverence toward his subject matter, one of the distinguishing traits of satire. Yet something more may be involved.

Fa-ts'ung, who has finally succeeded in breaking through the rebels' ranks and is covered with blood, is explicitly compared (in book 2) to a penis after defloration:

> In an hour he had broken through the encircling troops;
> The monk's heroic bravery was truly great.
> To the top of his head he was red all over.
>
> Perhaps I shouldn't say this, but he was exactly like the you-know-what
> When for the first time it emerges from the vagina.
>
> (*THH*, 46)

Despite the apology that introduces the simile, it appears that this is not an incidentally facetious comparison. Rereading the preceding battle scene, we cannot escape the impression that the comparison between monk and erect male member inspires many details in the portrait of Fa-ts'ung: his weapon is an iron cudgel; his horse is "an elephant without tusks" (*THH*, 38); and his opponents aim for his nose. (The identification of monk and penis is also quite common in later vernacular literature.)

If Fa-ts'ung is consistently compared to the penis, his enemy must just as consistently be interpreted as the vagina, and their battle as an allegorical description of sexual congress. Indeed, many details point in this direction. For a fuller understanding of these, we should first recall the basic tenets of sexual theory and practice in traditional China.

According to traditional Chinese physiology, a man is endowed with a limited amount of vital energy, one of the physical manifestations of which is his semen. A man's primary concern should be the preservation of this vital energy and, possibly, its reinforcement, if he is to ensure his health and longevity. The Taoists went so far as to claim that cultivation of one's vital energy would eventually lead to physical immortality. One way to strengthen this vital energy was through the "art of the bedchamber." Emission of semen was carefully restricted to those occasions when a man copulated with his principal wife in order to obtain male offspring to continue the family line. A man's seed had its counterpart in a woman's vaginal secretions, but she was not fertile unless she experienced orgasm.

Any useless spilling of seed was considered detrimental; but a man could strengthen his vital energy through sexual intercourse with other women, it was believed, if he could suppress the emission of semen and send his activated vital energy back to the brain by way of the Yellow River of his spine marrow. He could even reinforce his vital energy by imbibing the vaginal fluids of his sexually aroused partner.

Sexual intercourse was still fraught with danger, however, for a woman might easily incite a man to frequent emissions in order to reinforce her own vital powers. Female beauty was consistently compared to a killing blade, and a woman was said to carry "a sword between her thighs." One frequently quoted line in Yüan drama reads: "The gate that gave us birth is the door to our death." The Chinese imagination never tired of vixen or female ghosts who assumed human guise that they might rob vital powers from those men foolish enough to be seduced by them.

The art of the bedchamber as a general rule for sexual moderation in marriage was widely known. As a recipe to increase one's potency by frequent copulation with concubines and courtesans, it was secret lore that dated back to beyond Han times (and reaches into the twentieth century). In writing it was usually couched in the language of allegory, borrowing the terminology of alchemy or military science (van Gulik 1961).

Fa-ts'ung's main opponent is the rebel chief Sun Fei-hu. Like Fa-ts'ung, he is a character invented by Tung Chieh-yüan, and his name is ominous. The surname Sun is homophonous to the word *sun*, "monkey," an animal renowned for its lechery. The *fei-hu*, or "flying tiger," is a mythical beast that sucks out the brains of its victims. We are reminded of another mythical animal, the *nao*, or "monkey bitch," which was believed to suck out the brains of the tigers that carried her on their backs. The term was consequently used to designate courtesans who sap young male admirers of all their vital energy (*THCY*, 54). The depiction of Sun Fei-hu may also have been inspired by the features of the God with White Eyebrows (Pai-mei-shen), the protective deity of bordellos, whose appearance is said to be almost identical to that of Kuan Yü. Sun Fei-hu's horse is compared to Red Hare (*THH*, 36), the charger Lü Pu bequeathed to Kuan Yü, and both Sun's turban and his beard are red. Sun Fei-hu is seconded by two rebel officers. Together, they carry three cutting weapons: sword, battle-axe, and spear. If Fa-ts'ung represents the penis, this threesome may well represent the vagina, "the door to our death." Their battle is the act of sexual intercourse, and their aim is the eternal impotence of their opponent:

Your hands should be cut off, your brains knocked out,
Your ears chopped off, and, with legs tied together,
You ought to be hung upside down from the gate until death!

(*THH*, 41)

I would like to suggest here that, not the battle scene in book 2 alone, but the whole of Tung Chieh-yüan's work may be read as an allegorical treatment of the Chinese *ars amatoria*, specifically, the art of the bedchamber as practiced in bordellos. Those inclined to reject this interpretation should note the remarkable claim made by the persona of the author in the second stanza of the very first song of the *Hsi-hsiang-chi chu-kung-tiao*:

Behind the bed-curtains of the best bordellos
My savoir-faire is very much famed.
I have the smartest blades all yield to me!
Never once have I made a mess of things—
Sophistication is my style of life!

(*THH*, 1)

In no other prologue is a comparable claim ever encountered.

In the allegorical scheme I will here propose, student Chang stands for the male party, while various other characters—Fa-pen, Fa-ts'ung, Tu Ch'üeh—represent specific aspects of his person at different times. (It is unnecessary to point out that the character for the surname Chang also means "to extend" or "to expand.") While Chang represents the male sex as a whole, he is often more specifically intended to represent male sexual desire. And the monk Fa-ts'ung, as we have seen, may stand for the male member or more generally for the physical aspects of lust. When, unwilling to lend Chang money from the monastery's funds, he hands over his own limited savings, we may understand the gold, *chin*, to stand for semen, *ching* (Roy 1981).

If the able Fa-pen represents common sense, Tu Ch'üeh represents self-control. The character for the surname Tu, meaning "to suppress" or "to block," is glossed in early dictionaries as *sai*, a technical term for the suppression of a man's ejaculation. Moreover, he is mounted on a white horse—clearly identified as dominated will in the allegorical scheme of the sixteenth-century novel *Hsi-yu chi* (Journey to the west). For our discussion, it is most significant that when Tung Chieh-yüan opposes Tu Ch'üeh to Sun Fei-hu in book 3, he does not exploit the opportunity for yet another exciting battle scene, but has Sun Fei-hu submit immediately to Tu without a struggle: male self-control can annihilate any danger that woman presents. Just as Tu Ch'üeh's wise government ensures the prosperity of the body politic, self-control can ensure physical health.

A man who spends foolishly, however, invites his own doom, and such a man is represented by Cheng Heng. The character for the surname Cheng is the same character used for the name of the ancient state notorious for its "lascivious songs"; it is also the same character used to designate a minor role-type in Chin dynasty farce, which, though not yet fully understood, may have been the role of "lecher" (Hu Chi 1957, 145). Cheng Heng's first argument supporting his claim on Ying-ying concerns the amount of money he has already spent on her:

> As a bridal gift,
> I brought masses of top-grade gold and silver,
> A hundred thousand cash-strings' worth of brand-new jewelry,
> Scores of gowns,
> And embroidered capes and long skirts.
>
> (THH, 165)

In contrast to many plays and stories in which the villain is eventually forgiven and is included in the happy ending, especially if he is a relative, Cheng Heng dies. The manner of his death too is significant: he throws himself down from the steps to the hall of Tu Ch'üeh's yamen and splits open his skull.

Ying-ying, naturally, represents the female sex. As a girl's name, Ying-ying, "Oriole," was never very popular, perhaps because the bird, a fine singer and a sign of spring, was also a common metaphor for courtesans. While representing women as a whole, Ying-ying also specifically represents a woman's sense of shame, which must be overcome before she can become sexually aroused.

Other aspects of Ying-ying's person, like Chang's, may be represented by other characters. Lady Ts'ui may represent the calculating mind of conventional morality and Hung-niang, "Reddy," female sexual desire. The household of Ying-ying, Lady Ts'ui, and Hung-niang closely resembles the trio of courtesan, madam, and servant-girl so often portrayed on the Yüan stage. At times descriptions of Ying-ying ("Her slim waist— a dancer's—/ Could be held in one hand"[THH, 13]) indeed suggest a high-class courtesan rather than the daughter of an upper-class family, while the mother is actually cursed as an "old and experienced madam" (THH, 69, 159). Ying-ying's brother Huan-lang remains outside of this circle, still the shadowy character of the "Ying-ying chuan."

Even though a woman may eventually benefit her partner, provided his ability to control his desires, her very presence constitutes a menace to him. This aspect of her person, we have noted, is represented by the mutinous troops and their leader, Sun Fei-hu. Sun's apparent masculinity does not oppose this identification: as a rebel he represents *yin*. Nor does his attempt to abduct Ying-ying run counter to what he would represent: a man must exert self-control or he will be destroyed by the passion a woman inspires, he will be unable to derive any benefit from sexual intercourse. In Ying-ying and Sun Fei-hu we see the two antagonistic aspects of woman, the source of life and the destructive force. As the latter prevails, the former retreats.

This allegorical interpretation may be further developed if we read book 1 as a fourfold confrontation of *se*, or *rupa*, and *k'ung*, or *sûnyata*. In each confrontation the charms of phenomenal reality in its most seductive aspect, woman, triumph over the eternal truth of emptiness. *Se* is represented by Ying-ying, Hung-niang, or both; and the Buddhist law is successively represented by the splendors of P'u-chiu Monastery, the full moon (a common metaphor for the universal Buddha-nature), the pious discourse of the abbot, and the entire *sangha*'s veneration of Buddha according to the *dharma*. In each case Chang's thoughts, at first impressed by these symbols of emptiness, are overwhelmed by *se* the moment he observes Ying-ying or Hung-niang.

More specifically, book 1 relates the inception of sexual contact. Ying-ying's mourning recalls the white robes of Kuan-yin so frequently encountered in Buddhist iconography. But we must remember too that a woman's genitalia were often likened to a monastery, in which there was "a living Kuan-yin who plays with a monk," and that intercourse might be referred to as a visit to this sanctum (Wolfe 1980, 25). Book 2 continues this allegorical description of sexual intercourse, utilizing the well-tried metaphor of battle (Lévy 1969). In this case the union is a defloration. The entry of Tu Ch'üeh in book 3 signals the exercise of self-control, but masculine restraint is of limited benefit without the stimulation of the feminine sex. Chang might have expected to be treated to a gargantuan meal by Lady Ts'ui, but he finds he is unable to eat.

The extended description of zither playing in the seduction of Ying-ying may be read as a camouflaged description of the foreplay necessary to excite a woman: the labia minora were called "zither strings" (*ch'in-hsüan*). The sexual nature of Chang's playing is strongly suggested in his injunction to his fingers with its unmistakable reference to masturbation:

My ten fingers,
I have never betrayed you.
Now I'll see what tricks you can do!

I've slept alone all of my life,
So you've not been idle a single day.
Tonight's zither playing
Is something altogether different;
If you can play a heart-rending melody,
I'll have Ying-ying learn to love.

Fingers!
When I have such luck,
You too will be sure to find relief!

(*THH*, 83)

The foreplay is successful in part: Chang embraces Hung-niang and Ying-ying is tempted. Chang is emboldened to send her the following poem:

My longing for you grows only more intense,
So I idly entrust it to my zither playing.
Such a joy, and in spring, moreover—
The flower-heart is bound to be moved.
Do not oppose your secret passion!
Why should you cling to an idle reputation?
Do not hate the light of the moon for its brightness;
Rather cherish the dense flower shadows.

(*THH*, 88)

The "flower-heart" might be explained as "[your] heart like a flower"; it also refers to the clitoris. Such a word would be completely out of place in the conventional circumlocutions of Chinese love poetry.

The man must not place all his trust in his manipulations, however; he must wait for true signs that the woman has overcome shame, which will ultimately culminate in orgasm. If he penetrates her "secret garden" too hastily, he will miss his objective, encountering instead only bitter disappointment. So long as she fails to come, all his effort is spent in vain and his virility will continue to diminish. The description of Chang's illness at the beginning of book 5 is suggestive:

How could my heart's sickness develop to this extreme?
These last few days I hardly breathe, wish only to sleep,
My tongue is shrunk, my lips are parched,
I haven't a single drop to spit.

(*THH*, 101)

But according to the doctor's diagnosis, "though he looks shriveled, he is actually not ill at all" (*THH*, 103). It is only when for love she puts aside her sense of shame and gives herself over to him completely that he may gain his objective. Once she has yielded, her desire will persuade her common sense of the wisdom of her action, primarily of benefit to the man. (Ying-ying even explicitly compares herself to a medicine: "When taken for a long time, / It replenishes the cinnabar field, restores failing *yang*" [*THH*, 106].) Now he really has "picked the flower." Chang does not win highest honors in the examinations but third place, becoming not a *chuang-yüan*, "principal graduate" (usual in this type of story), but a *t'an-hua*, "he who picks the flower."

The last two books of the *Hsi-hsiang-chi chu-kung-tiao* exemplify the belief often stated in old sex texts that even though self-interest might draw a woman to a man who foolishly spends himself without restraint, in the long run she will find herself more satisfied by one who regulates his spending carefully. If intercourse could be thought of as a visit to a monastery, a man's absorption of a woman's vital energy might be represented by Ying-ying's flight to the yamen. When Ying-ying elopes with Chang, she drives Cheng Heng to spend himself finally in a violent and extravagant death. Our *ars amatoria* ends with a stark warning against lechery, one which might appear rather out of place in a romantic comedy:

> The general, offering a golden cup brimming with wine,
> Said, "Do not refuse today to drink without restraint!"
> How happy our couple was!
> The crash had killed that oaf Cheng Heng:
> His jaws were locked,
> His breath blocked in his throat,
> His skull was split,
> His blood soiled the steps.
> Outside the rear gate
> The corpse was laid out.
> On a sign were written a few lines that read:
> "All his life this man was a lecher—
> This time it cost him his life."
>
> [*Coda*]
> One may see rakes who force themselves to love;
> There have been blades since time immemorial.
> But who ever found, like this man in his youth, among flowers, his death?

(*THH*, 167)

In summary, if I put forward an allegorical reading of the *Hsi-hsiang-chi chu-kung-tiao* with considerable diffidence, it is because such a reading seems to make sense at some places far more than at others and also because I know of no premodern commentator who even hints at the possibility of such a reading. Still, I believe that the text contains enough clues to warrant an attempt to reconstruct the allegorical underpinnings of the work. Even if my own attempt is not fully convincing, it may still speak for the validity of the approach. The allegorical reading proposed here explains certain aspects of the text that have been problematic for earlier scholars: for example, the space devoted to the battle of Sun Fei-hu and Fa-ts'ung; the seemingly out-of-place sexual allusions; the character of Cheng Heng and the manner of his death.

As a text that is both a moving love story and an allegorical treatment of the *ars amatoria*, Tung Chieh-yüan's composition has a nearly contemporary counterpart in Western literature in the *Roman de la rose*. Of course, the nature of the art of love taught in each work is quite distinct. A perhaps more fundamental difference is the relation between the two levels of meaning in these texts. Though the allegorical meaning will never fully explain all the details of the surface narrative, which unavoidably develops its own dynamics, it may still be said that the purpose of the surface narrative in the *Roman de la rose* is to represent the allegorical meaning. The meaning of the allegory is primary, and the surface narrative is secondary. In the *Hsi-hsiang-chi chu-kung-tiao* that relation is reversed: the surface narrative remains primary; it is what is taken over and developed by later adaptations. The allegorical meaning, which may be simultaneously perceived, only serves to increase our appreciation of the work's satiric drive.

The society that allowed the irreverent art of Tung Chieh-yüan to flourish must have been free of the intolerance usually associated with Neo-Confucianism. It is perhaps no coincidence that in dynastic China Tung's work was reprinted only during the last century of the Ming dynasty, another rare period of relatively liberal attitudes.

Low Burlesque and Genre Parody in the Liu Chih-yüan chu-kung-tiao

In general discussions of the *chu-kung-tiao* most space is devoted to Tung Chieh-yüan's composition as the prime example of the genre, and no one can deny the *Hsi-hsiang-chi chu-kung-tiao* its literary preeminence. But the anonymous *Liu Chih-yüan chu-kung-tiao* is an interesting text in its own right. For one thing, the preserved fragments represent the earliest printing of a work of vernacular fiction known to date. All the vernacular texts from Tun-huang are in manuscript, and the earliest preserved printings of vernacular narrative and drama we have date only from the end of the thirteenth and the beginning of the fourteenth centuries. In the *Liu Chih-yüan chu-kung-tiao* fragments all care has been taken to bring out the musical structure of the text as clearly as possible (Idema 1978a, 63). While the text is thus suitable for performance by either professional or amateur, the very fact of the printing strongly suggests that texts like this also served a considerable reading public. Moreover, the selection of the *Liu Chih-yüan chu-kung-tiao* for printing suggests that it enjoyed, for whatever reason, at least a certain reputation in its time.

In many ways the *Liu Chih-yüan chu-kung-tiao* is a less complex work than the *Hsi-hsiang-chi chu-kung-tiao*. Its relatively simple musical structure is one reason for assuming that it predates Tung Chieh-yüan's work. The prose sections of the *Liu Chih-yüan chu-kung-tiao* are much simpler, too. At the same time both compositions share, in Li-li Ch'en's phrase, a great many "thematic ingredients": scenes of love-longing and descriptions of lovemaking, scenes of the heroine's doubts over whether or not to offer herself to her lover, drawn-out parting scenes, scenes of the villain's confident appeal to a judge who turns out to be on the other side, and so on (Li-li Ch'en 1972, 139–41; Idema 1972, 269–70; 1978b, 132; and 1978a, 76–77). Of course this may be explained by the extreme homogeneity of the tradition of the genre. I personally find the correspondences so numerous and so specific that I would not *a priori* exclude the possibility that the anonymous author of the *Liu Chih-yüan chu-kung-tiao* may have been acquainted with an earlier adaptation of the "Ying-ying chuan" reworked by Tung Chieh-yüan into the *Hsi-hsiang-chi chu-kung-tiao*, just as Shang Tao reworked an earlier version of the romance of Shuang Chien and Su Hsiao-ch'ing.

The *Liu Chih-yüan chu-kung-tiao* is not only simpler in composition than Tung's text, it is also quite different in mood. This contrast has been described and explained variously. Cheng Chen-to argues that the artlessness (*pen-se*) of the *Liu Chih-yüan chu-kung-tiao* reflects the pristine energy that informed the genre in the early years of its development, whereas the *Hsi-hsiang-chi chu-kung-tiao* exemplifies the refined decadence of later years (Cheng 1957, 931). This has been more negatively rephrased by Li-li Ch'en, who holds that the author of the *Liu Chih-yüan chu-kung-tiao* did not yet know how to fully exploit the possibilities of the genre and simply superimposed his story on the form, while Tung Chieh-yüan was "ready to exploit all the possibilities presented by the verse-forms to write highly decorated verses which could please both a discerning reader and a sophisticated audience" (Ch'en 1970, 521). Others have tried to explain the contrast of artlessness and literary sophistication by reference to the (assumed) intended audience of both works: while Tung Chieh-yüan must have written his work for performance in the best houses of pleasure before audiences of literary aficionados and other connoisseurs, the *Liu Chih-yüan chu-kung-tiao* would have been written for streetside and marketplace performances before "a simple audience" (Li-li Chen 1970, 520; Doleželová-Velingerová and Crump 1971, 6). Still others have postulated that these two works reflect different world views: while Tung Chieh-yüan's reflects the aspirations of the literati, the *Liu Chih-yüan chu-kung-tiao* reflects the culture of the peasantry (T'ai Ching-nung 1981, 102–8). The contrast between the two works has also been explained by their reference to different source materials: Tung Chieh-yüan borrowed his theme from romantic fiction, while the *Liu Chih-yüan chu-kung-tiao* is unique in depicting a historical hero as represented in popular legend (Doleželová-Velingerová and Crump 1971, 12). All of these explanations agree that the source of the contrast between the two works lies in the social milieus from which they originated. It remains to be seen to what extent this view can be substantiated by a more detailed analysis of the text.

At the outset we should stress that any analysis of the *Liu Chih-yüan chu-kung-tiao* is severely hampered by the fragmentary nature of the text: only one-third of the original has been preserved. Fortunately, the authors of all-keys-and-modes had their characters frequently recapitulate preceding action, so the last two books contain many hints concerning what must have happened in the missing pages. Moreover, we have several complete later versions of the legend of Liu Chih-yüan and Li San-niang, which may help in reconstructing an outline of events.

The *Liu Chih-yüan chu-kung-tiao* takes its theme from a series of popular story-cycles inspired by the Five Dynasties period, a chaotic century spanning the final decades of the T'ang and the first years of the Sung. By the end of the Northern Sung, "history of the Five Dynasties" was a recognized specialization of the professional storytellers of Kaifeng (*TCM*, 30). The earliest preserved account of these story-cycles is the fourteenth-century *Wu-tai-shih p'ing-hua* (Simple narrative of the history of the Five Dynasties).

Liu Chih-yüan (d. 948) was the founder and first emperor of the penultimate of the Five Dynasties, the Later Han dynasty. The legend of his marriage to Li San-niang, his departure for the army, and their eventual reunion, has little basis in historical fact but for many centuries was immensely popular (Aoki 1932, 224–26). It was developed into a *chu-kung-tiao*, retold in the *Han-shih p'ing-hua* (Simple narrative of the history of the Han) in the *Wu-tai-shih p'ing-hua*, and adapted for the stage as both a *tsa-chü* (by Liu T'ang-ch'ing, now lost, but see Fu Hsi-hua 1957, 146–47) and a southern play entitled *Pai-t'u chi* (Story of the white hare).

Pai-t'u chi is one of a famous quartet of early *ch'uan-ch'i* and is now known through three versions. According to the prologue of the fifteenth-century edition only recently discovered, the play was written by the Yung-chia Shu-hui, a literary association in Wenchow. Since these three editions already show quite considerable differences among themselves, they cannot serve as authorities for details of action in the lost books of the *Liu Chih-yüan chu-kung-tiao*. We should also be aware of the different characteristics of the genres: the prescribed points of suspense in the all-keys-and-modes and its unexpected twists and turns might have brought about the inclusion of numerous new elements in the *Liu Chih-yüan chu-kung-tiao* that were not retained in later versions of the legend. Not nearly enough narrative detail is supplied by these later versions, at first sight at least, to fill in all of the eight books missing. On the other hand, it appears that the *Liu Chih-yüan chu-kung-tiao* never included some of the incidents most conspicuous in later versions: there is no reference to Li San-niang's biting through the umbilical cord of her newborn boy, nor is there any mention of a hare, white or otherwise.[8] Nonetheless, a comparison between corresponding sections in the *Liu Chih-yüan chu-kung-tiao* and the later versions of the legend may help us to classify the nature of the treatment of the material in the all-keys-and-modes (Crump 1970).

Li-li Ch'en has rightly noted that the heroes of *pien-wen* belong to the high mimetic or even romantic mode in Northrop Frye's classification of fiction, while the heroes of the *Liu Chih-yüan chu-kung-tiao* and the *Hsi-hsiang-chi chu-kung-tiao* belong to the low mimetic and ironic modes. She states that both works involve the development of a "domestic situation, the type of situation to be found in what Frye calls the New Comedy of Plautus and Terence" (Ch'en 1972, 135). Tung Chieh-yüan's work, as we have seen, may indeed be fruitfully analyzed as such a comedy, but the application of this term to the *Liu Chih-yüan chu-kung-tiao* is far more problematic. It does not end with a marriage, for instance, but opens with one, and the final reunion of husband and wife is brought about through the mediation of their son. The *Liu Chih-yüan chu-kung-tiao* may have a happy ending, but that does not automatically make it a comedy. Its main theme is the spectacular rise of its title hero from humble beginnings to the highest position in the empire. Both the *Hsi-hsiang-chi chu-kung-tiao* and the *Liu Chih-yüan chu-kung-tiao* open with descriptions of young men who set out in the world by leaving home to seek their fortunes. Chang Kung is a minister's son who travels in order to study; after his success in the capital and assignment to an official post, he only comes to occupy a social position that we feel has been his due all along. Liu Chih-yüan may claim an illustrious line of descent, but by the beginning of the story he has already been driven from his home, despised by his stepbrothers as little better than a bastard, and forced to wander, a penniless farmhand.

The low origins of emperors and heroes—or, at any rate, the drastic decline in family fortune shortly before their births or during their youth—is commonplace in traditional Chinese fiction. The first chapter of the *San-kuo chih yen-i* (Romance of the Three Kingdoms) has Liu Pei plaiting sandals and straw mats for a living, while Chang Fei plies the trade of butcher. As a rule, however, this meanness is only touched upon to bring out more clearly the hero's subsequent spectacular rise. The emphasis is on his feats of arms, which enable him to conquer all his enemies and realize his destiny. In contrast, the *Liu Chih-yüan chu-kung-tiao* never actually comes to Liu's ascent to the throne, and the text as we have it scarcely deals with his military career. Book 1, with its description of Liu's defeating Li Hung-i in a tavern brawl, raises the expectation that we will hear a catalog of heroic deeds comparable to the saga of the early adventures of Chao K'uang-yin, founder of the Sung dynasty, but this does not happen. In the first book Liu Chih-yüan begins as an unwanted stepbrother and finishes an unwanted brother-in-law. In book 2 he is forced to leave the pregnant young wife he loves, but immediately afterward he is forced under threat of court martial to commit bigamy by marrying his commander's daughter. Book 3 opens with the description of their sumptuous wedding feast; it may well have ended with Li Hung-i bringing Li San-niang's baby to Liu Chih-yüan, referred to by him in book 11:

That year, when a cold snow was falling,
That Hung-i was just too mean!
Wrapped in paper and carried in a sack—
Thus he brought [your baby] to Ping-chou.
And damn it!
In front of the barracks he raised a commotion,
All over the main street.

(Uchida 1974, 281–84)

In book 11 we again encounter Liu Chih-yüan, now governor-general of Ping-chou. He disguises himself as a camp follower in order to test Li San-niang's loyalty, only to be humiliated by her brothers. In the final book, Liu, although intent on revenge, is happily reunited not only with his first wife but with all his enemies as well. The *Liu Chih-yüan chu-kung-tiao* is a narrative of the misadventures and tribulations of a future emperor during his days of obscurity. Because of the nature and treatment of these adventures, it is best appreciated as an example of low burlesque, the portrayal of a noble person in ludicrous situations.

Throughout the text, the *Liu Chih-yüan chu-kung-tiao* contrasts Liu's future greatness with his present poverty. Liu himself is not without ambitions when he leaves home without a single cash: "If things remain always as they are now,/ When will I ever make known my might?" (Uchida 1974, 244). He is even more explicit when he contemplates leaving Li San-niang because of his treatment at her brothers' hands:

At present we live during the Five Dynasties
And experience the wreck of T'ang.

> The common people have lost their way,
> The multitudes are anxious and afraid.
> Braves parade themselves, heroes flourish;
> The man who gets ahead is of firm resolve.
> In Taiyuan prefecture they mark the faces of new soldiers;
> I would like to go there but still have my doubts—
> Not that I cannot reach a decision,
> Do not blame me for pacing up and down,
> It's just that I cannot bear to leave my Li San-niang.
>
> (Uchida 1974, 267)

He appears completely unaware of the throne that lies in store for him, and in practice his ambitions are modest enough. When hired by Squire Li as a farmhand and visited by San-niang in his room at night, he is afraid of losing his newly won security:

> This night the Hidden Dragon was really greatly alarmed.
> Hastily, in front of his earthen bed,
> He politely bowed and asked,
> "Madam, in the middle of the night—
> Why did you come here?
> Quickly leave my room—
> Really, that is best.
> If the squire should learn of this,
> I would surely land in trouble!"
>
> (Uchida 1974, 255–56)

We can hardly blame the common run of people for not instantly recognizing the future emperor in such a man, though there are a few privileged persons who are allowed to observe Liu's true dragon nature when it manifests itself unbeknownst to him. Such people—Squire Li, Li San-niang, Commander Yüeh—immediately want to affiliate themselves with Liu in order to share in his future glory. They force their favors on an unwilling Liu Chih-yüan, favors that turn out to be disasters in disguise. Squire Li insists on hiring Liu as a farmhand despite the objection of his sons, and his daughter San-niang insists on marrying him though well aware of the opposition of her brothers; yet he is driven from the farm and his wife with the death of his parents-in-law. Commander Yüeh, ignoring Liu's protests that he is already married, insists on marrying his daughter to him; yet the ceremony is barely concluded before Liu's country kin begin to turn up.

In these first books Liu Chih-yüan is never in control of his circumstances. Even his rare displays of martial prowess serve only to compound his tribulations. His barroom victory over his future brother-in-law Li Hung-i converts Hung-i and his brother Hung-hsin, as well as their wives, into implacable foes set on his destruction. When he displays his might in book 2 by drawing an exceptionally stiff bow, it earns him a soldier's pay but also an extra and unwanted wife. Even in books 11 and 12, as governor-general of Ping-chou, Liu is no more in control of circumstances than before. Visiting Li San-niang as a poor camp follower, he is robbed of his official seal and ignominiously chased off, taken for a beggar by her brothers. When they fight with staves, the brothers and their wives again defeat Liu, this time backed by his companions, the formidable fighters Shih Hung-chao and Kuo Wei. In book 12, when Liu orders his troops to fetch Li San-niang, he is informed that she has just been kidnapped by bandits, who easily fight off his two trusted generals. The bandits fortunately turn out to be his stepbrothers.

As if underlining the extent to which Liu's fate is determined by circumstances outside himself, the author repeatedly depicts Liu Chih-yüan asleep at crucial moments in the first books of the story. In book 1 he is asleep when found by Squire Li and when approached by Li San-niang. In book 2 he is away drinking when Li Hung-i and Li Hung-hsin attempt to ambush him in the peach garden they have ordered him to guard at night. Liu is again sound asleep when they set fire to the cowshed where they have him watching over a buffalo with calf; he is saved by a sudden downpour of rain but, as if in mockery of the divine intervention that saves him, falls asleep immediately afterward when another downpour startles the buffalo and Liu's mule, causing them to break loose and run off. And he is "taking a good rest" when Commander Yüeh instructs a sergeant to act as matchmaker for his daughter and Liu (Uchida 1974, 276). In many ways Liu Chih-yüan is portrayed as a most unlikely candidate for emperor: even his own troops mistake him for a common bandit in book 12. Such a man's ascension to the throne can indeed be attributed only to fate.

The characterization of Liu Chih-yüan as a dragon trapped in a mud puddle, at the mercy of circumstance, contrasts sharply with his portrayal in the *Han-shih p'ing-hua* (*HSPH*, 159–76). The *Han-shih p'ing-hua* dwells on the poverty that forces Liu's mother to remarry, but her new husband (no mention of Liu's stepbrothers) is depicted as a very considerate man who takes great pains to provide his stepson with a good education. Liu is an extremely unruly youth, however, who is tattooed all over and addicted to drinking, whoring, and gambling. He is not turned out, but simply decides not to return home when he has gambled away the sizable amount of money entrusted to him by his stepfather for paying taxes. After his marriage to Li San-niang and the death of his parents-in-law, Li Hung-hsin and Li Hung-i do indeed want to be rid of him. But Liu Chih-yüan does not sneak away in the middle of the night; at Li San-niang's suggestion he departs with considerable trading capital. The *Han-shih p'ing-hua* passes over Liu's second marriage; his subsequent military career is imputed solely to his bravery. The humiliations he suffers when disguised as a camp follower are played down, unlike the extensive description devoted to his magnificent return to fetch San-niang on the following day.

This contrast in characterization must be explained largely by the difference in genre. It is clearly observable, for example, that as popularized history the *Han-shih p'ing-hua* avoids elements in the legend that are in conspicuous conflict with the data of traditional historiography, such as Liu's second marriage, whereas the all-keys-and-modes is free to invent. The *Han-shih p'ing-hua* tries to cast Liu Chih-yüan as a founding emperor in the heroic mold, while the *chu-kung-tiao* ridicules its own protagonist.

Liu Chih-yüan also appears in an early *hua-pen* roughly comparable in date to, or perhaps even slightly earlier than, the *Wu-tai-shih p'ing-hua*: that is, the "Shih Hung-chao lung-hu chün-ch'en hui" (Shih Hung-chao: The meeting of dragon and tiger, prince and baron), included in chapter 15 of Feng Meng-lung's *Ku-chin hsiao-shuo* (Stories from past and present). The greater part of the *hua-pen* is taken up with an account of the adventures and misadventures of Shih Hung-chao and Kuo Wei during their days of obscurity. Because of its portrayal of Shih Hung-chao as a blustering fool, this *hua-pen* has been treated as an example of low burlesque in vernacular fiction (Průšek 1955).

Liu Chih-yüan appears only in the final section of the *hua-pen*. To please his wife, the chancellor Sang Wei-han has Liu, highest military officer of the realm, kowtow to the tips of his boots protruding below a curtain and then forgets about him. When the enraged Liu Chih-yüan offends the chancellor in court the following day, he is degraded to governor-general of Ping-chou, a demotion that eventually enables him to establish his own Han dynasty. This humiliating incident recalls Liu's misadventures in the *chu-kung-tiao*, and, like his forced flight and his bigamous marriage, his degradation to Ping-chou proves a blessing in disguise. There are other correspondences between the "Shih Hung-chao lung-hu chün-ch'en hui" and the *Liu Chih-yüan chu-kung-tiao*; but although it is quite conceivable that the *hua-pen*'s account of Sang Wei-han's treatment of Liu may derive from the latter work, it cannot be proven (Idema 1984a).

If the *Han-shih p'ing-hua* subordinates the legend of Liu Chih-yüan and Li San-niang to an account of Liu's career, the reverse occurs in the *Pai-t'u chi*. Here the emphasis is on their separation and final reunion. Liu's adventures before meeting Squire Li are not dealt with; he is simply introduced as a local good-for-nothing given to gambling. After marrying the squire's daughter, he enjoys the good life until the death of his parents-in-law. Then his wife's brothers, hoping to be rid of him, apportion him a bewitched melon field. Liu finds a handbook on military strategy and a miraculous suit of armor in the field and decides to leave for Ping-chou. Once there, he impresses Commander Yüeh, who marries his daughter to Liu. She rears San-niang's child, brought to her while Liu is on campaign, as if it were her own. Years later, after Liu's return, his son encounters a woman while pursuing a white hare. She recounts the sad story of her life to him, which he repeats to his father back home. Realizing that the boy must have met his mother, Li San-niang, Liu first visits her incognito. Their final reunion takes place the next day.

The two extant late-Ming editions of this play, the *Liu Chih-yüan pai-t'u chi* published by the Fu-ch'un-t'ang of Nanking and the *Pai-t'u chi* included in the *Liu-shih-chung ch'ü*, both adhere to the same basic story line, yet they exhibit numerous and extensive differences of narrative detail. Where the *Liu-shih-chung ch'ü* version stresses the miraculous elements of the story, the *Liu Chih-yüan pai-t'u chi* presents a strongly rationalizing version of the action. In the former, for example, it is Commander Yüeh's daughter who observes a red glow over Liu Chih-yüan while he lies sleeping one winter's night and thereupon covers him with her father's finest red mantle. But in the *Liu Chih-yüan pai-t'u chi*, Commander Yüeh himself arranges the couple's marriage only after Liu has scored a victory as commander of the vanguard. Both versions coincide in treating their material as melodrama, which precludes an ironic handling of heroes. And in their melodrama the focus is less on the military career of Liu Chih-yüan than on the suffering of his first wife. Li San-niang's misery during pregnancy, delivery, and long years of loyal waiting is presented in fine detail; she becomes an exemplar of the patiently suffering wife.

The characterization of Li San-niang in the *Liu Chih-yüan chu-kung-tiao* is quite different; she is portrayed as anything but an obedient daughter and wife. In all other preserved versions of the legend it is Squire Li who, having observed a sign of his future greatness, decides to marry her to Liu; in the *Liu-shih-chung ch'ü* version of the *Pai-t'u chi*, Li San-niang also observes such a sign. In the *Liu Chih-yüan pai-t'u chi*, her father plots matters in such a way that she will fall in love with Liu; yet in the all-keys-and-modes, it is Li San-niang who takes the initiative (Idema 1972, 271–72). Burning incense to the moon at midnight, she spies a small snake, which she follows to the room of the farmhand and, observing the red glow about him, is overwhelmed with joy:

Once a soothsayer told my fate:
I was meant to make it far.
I could become the empress,
Be the mother of the nation,

>   Marry a famous prince.
>   This night bears out that master's words:
>   At the end of T'ang, dragon and snake are not yet distinguished,
>   Among the common people emperors hide.
>   While still on the farm, I'll attach myself to this lucky man.
>
>   [*Coda*]
>   If I fail in this marriage,
>   When will I enter Chao-yang Palace?
>   Without pupils in one's eyes, one will ever be poor.
>   (Uchida 1974, 255)

She forces the alarmed Liu Chih-yüan to pledge his troth, "but other than this, nothing happens" (Uchida 1974, 256). At the earliest opportunity and with feigned innocence, she tells her parents of the vision:

>   Early in the morning, at break of day, she visited her parents
>   And told them again the circumstances:
>   "Last night as I burned my incense,
>   In the farmhands' room I frequently looked.
>   I saw a snake, its golden gleam shining bright;
>   It moved about, wriggling and slithering.
>
>   Suddenly it fled up a blue linen shirt!
>   I recognized that newly arrived fellow.
>   Into his nose it wildly bored,
>   Yet he never even tossed or turned!
>   Such a strange affair—
>   Father, what do you guess it could mean?"
>   (Uchida 1974, 255)

Her scheme works perfectly; her father orders her to marry Liu: "San-niang, do not disobey your father. / We will take that young man into the family as a son-in-law" (Uchida 1974, 257).

Li San-niang shows the same mettle in book 11, when Liu Chih-yüan visits her incognito. The action at this point seems a mirror image of the legend of Ch'iu Hu and his virtuous wife. When, after a long absence, Ch'iu Hu returns to his native village as a high official, he makes improper proposals to a woman picking mulberry leaves, not realizing that she is his own wife. He even offers her the gold his prince has given him for the support of his family if she will grant him her favors. But his wife refuses the gold and later rejects Ch'iu Hu as a husband. When Liu Chih-yüan returns as a beggar, he discloses his true position to Li San-niang and shows her his gold seal of office. She snatches the seal from him and refuses to return it. After she has forced him to make love to her, she explains that she will keep the seal to ensure that he will come again to fetch her. In other versions there is no mention of a gold seal or else, as in the *Liu-shih-chung ch'ü* version, it is Liu Chih-yüan who voluntarily leaves the seal with her as a pledge of his promise to return. When Li San-niang eventually arrives and the daughter of Commander Yüeh offers to cede to her the position of principal wife, San-niang first displays indifference; but when the offer appears sincere, she asks for a heavenly sign, and a miracle duly takes place. We cannot escape the impression that her initial reluctance is feigned and that she requests a miracle for the purpose of consolidating her new position of prominence, for only in this way can she be sure of having realized her ambitions.

The anonymous author of the *Liu Chih-yüan chu-kung-tiao* stresses the bond of love between Liu and Li San-niang, especially in the parting scene in book 2, but it is less love than self-interest that inspires Li San-niang's behavior. Knowing full well how she herself seized the opportunity for advancement offered in the person of Liu, she is aware that others may do the same, and therefore she does not resign herself to accept what the future may bring but decides to take action for herself. As a squire's daughter who pairs herself with an impecunious farmhand, she is the rustic counterpart to the refined young girls and beautiful courtesans who attach themselves to poor but talented students whose future importance they foresee. In her determined pursuit of self-interest Li San-niang is no different from her brothers; what distinguishes her from them is her farsightedness.

Correspondences in the characterization of Cheng Heng and the Li brothers have been noted elsewhere (Li-li Ch'en 1972, 137). But while Cheng Heng appears only in the last two books of the *Hsi-hsiang-chi chu-kung-tiao*, Li Hung-i is introduced at the beginning of book 1 and, along with his brother (and the shrews who are their wives), makes appearances in every one of the preserved books of the *Liu Chih-yüan chu-kung-tiao*.

An innkeeper thus describes Li Hung-i's character as a local bully to Liu Chih-yüan:

Before Ch'i-weng saw him, he had twisted his brow into a frown:
"My guest, I'll tell you all the details.
Speaking of this man's doings—
Whatever it is, he wants to do it on the cheap.
Snatching a seat, he drinks himself into a stupor;
An uninvited guest, he gobbles down your cakes.

He knows no high or low, he acts against all reason;
If people cross him, he's as cruel as a ghoul.
He'll torture you to death and never let up a bit!

[*Coda*]
He is more evil than the local plague.
No one in the village calls him Li Hung-i—
The whole region simply refers to him as the living pest!"

(Uchida 1974, 280)

Li Hung-i immediately demonstrates the aptness of this characterization by abusing the innkeeper—whereupon Liu gives him a well-deserved beating, sending him into a stuttering rage. His evil character is evident and compounded by his personal ugliness and his preposterous clothing. In book 2, for example, when he bursts in upon Li San-niang and Liu Chih-yüan, who are taking leave of each other,

Suddenly they heard a loud shout
That scared our couple to death.
He had dressed up quite curiously:
The face he showed, all grimy and grisly,
A shiny black turban, a cord round his waist,
Leather boots (to rabbits once the cause of sorrow),
His stomacher was a yard of crimson flowers,
His linen shirt was woven of coarse hemp.

In his hand he carried a thorny club,
Which had once defeated five villages' instructors.
His ears looked like dried mulberry leaves;
His nose stuck up, his eyes were hollow.
His thighs were thick, his buttocks high: a hefty buffalo!
His coarse lips were meant to drink local brew.
He cursed: "Motherfucking rotten pauper!
Our sister, that child—you seduced her!"

[*Coda*]
He opened wide his mulberry-eating, candy-chewing mouth
And gave a shout just like an ox's bellow;
Not Liu Chih-yüan alone but even a *ch'i-lin* would flee at the sight of that!

(Uchida 1974, 273)

Throughout the text Li Hung-i and Li Hung-hsin place themselves in opposition to Liu Chih-yüan, and the sole attempt to mollify them appeals exclusively to their greed:

> A flagpole placed before the gate will exempt you from statutory labor,
> Your leather boots he will have changed for shoes.
> And at the capital,
> Your linen shirts will become purple silk gowns.
> (Uchida 1974, 258)

But their greed and meanness are teamed with stupidity; their schemes to harm Liu Chih-yüan only miscarry and fall back upon themselves. Their attempt to waylay Liu Chih-yüan in the peach garden results in Li Hung-i's thrashing his own brother, Hung-hsin (it was in a peach garden too that Liu Pei, Kuan Yü, and Chang Fei swore their brotherhood; here it has become the site of fratricide). Their attempt to burn Liu to death also fails, and the incident that eventually compels Liu to flee is brought about by his own inattention. The brothers' fortune reaches its lowest point when, in book 12, they lodge a complaint with the governor-general against their brother-in-law Liu Chih-yüan, only to discover that the governor-general is Liu himself.

Local bullies are depicted in the *Liu Chih-yüan chu-kung-tiao* as the dominant, but by no means the only, aspect of the general unpleasantness of rural life. Buildings in the village are crude: the walls of the inn in book 1 are plastered with cow dung, its pots and bowls set on an earthen bench. The first detail of Squire Li's farm that is mentioned is the cowshed. Liu Chih-yüan sleeps on an earthen bench in the farmhands' quarters, and his nuptial chamber is described as a "thatched hut," a "poor dwelling," a "reed cottage" (Uchida 1974, 259). Our impression of this simplicity is deepened with the second book's detailed description of the luxuriousness of the wedding chamber in Ping-chou on the night of Liu's second marriage. In contrast, the *Han-shih p'ing-hua* (*HSPH*, 163) describes the farm in palatial terms:

> One saw nothing but
> Plastered walls and red doors,
> Painted pavilions and jade-like buildings.
> In the morning a light haze capped the courtyards,
> At night a thin mist covered the ponds.

When the gatekeeper of Liu Chih-yüan's new father-in-law, Commander Yüeh, announces the arrival of two uninvited guests in book 2, we learn that not only Li Hung-i and Li Hung-hsien but all country people dress curiously:

> He said: "Two fellows are there, strong and sturdy,
> They are dressed up in the country way:
> Their padded jackets are with coarse thread made
> And dyed a deep brown color;
> Their stomachers are crimson flowers
> Embroidered with candy figures;
> Leggings of white linen with ox-hide socks,
> Shining black turbans bulging out.
> Their speech is crude, their behavior rustic and rude.
> In Sha-t'o they live, at Li Family Farm.
> In their hands they carry thorny clubs.
> Looking for Chih-yüan, they call him 'our Liu.' "
> (Uchida 1974, 280)

And while the wedding of Liu Chih-yüan and the daughter of Commander Yüeh is a grand affair, the celebration of his wedding to Li San-niang degenerates into a drunken riot:

> Those rustics,
> Filling their bowls with wine,
> Drank themselves into a stupor, red of face.
> They boxed and kicked
> And shrieked and shouted—
> A melee of guests and friends!
> The music was never once played in tune:
> Exactly like what happens in a picture of Yao's people.
> (Uchida 1974, 259)

The reference to a "picture of Yao's people" (*Yao-min t'u*), with its idyllic representations of happy and contented peasants, is of course ironic.

The village is viewed as a seat of ignorance. When Liu Chih-yüan vainly tries to persuade Li San-niang to return him his official seal, he reasons:

> If I have the seal, I am governor-general,
> But what will become of me if I lose it?
> On it there are eight characters,
> Explaining my multitude of duties.
> Because you've been trapped all your life in a village,
> You have no idea of the facts of state and law.

There are so many extraordinary things—
I cannot bear to explain them to you.

(Uchida 1974, 285)

And in book 12 Li San-niang herself cites her country ignorance as a reason for declining the position of principal wife:

From the time I was a child, I have lived in a village.
I would not know how to put on the phoenix robe;
Given the golden headdress, how could I wear it?

(Uchida 1974, 300)

Later, appealing for a diving miracle, she again refers to her rural background: "I was born and raised in a country village; /Certainly, it seems I do not understand etiquette" (Uchida 1974, 301). Throughout the text the word *ts'un*—"village," "rustic"—is consistently used as a term of opprobrium. The anonymous author of the *Liu Chih-yüan chu-kung-tiao* was evidently convinced of the "idiocy of rural life."

This unpleasant picture of rural life characterized by dirt, greed, meanness, stupidity, and utter absence of sophistication was, I believe, a new phenomenon in Chinese literature. It is the very opposite of the bucolic idealization of country life that found its first prominent advocate in T'ao Yüan-ming (365–427) and was so eagerly cultivated by literati-poets of the Southern Sung dynasty in their days of retirement. The author of the *Liu Chih-yüan chu-kung-tiao* was well aware of this contrast; we know this from his ironic reference to the "picture of Yao's people."

But this disagreeable picture is different too from earlier negative descriptions of the countryside. In T'ang times and earlier, any official appointment outside the capitals was viewed as a "demotion to the provinces"; no distinction was made between the local seat of government and the surrounding countryside. In the *Liu Chih-yüan chu-kung-tiao*, it is the rural village as opposed to the provincial town that is the object of revulsion. Many T'ang texts, such as the works of Po Chü-i (772–846) or Liu Tsung-yüan (773–819), depict the misery of the rural population, but these texts never make rural people the objects of ridicule. Furthermore, the cited sources of rural misery are sought outside the countryside: misguided domestic policies, the emperor's personal extravagance, long foreign wars, high taxes, the harshness of corvée labor, onerous military service, a rapacious local government, cruel clerks and usurious merchants. In the *Liu Chih-yüan chu-kung-tiao*, however, this misery has no such traceable source—even though the action takes place in chaotic times. Misery is simply presented as an inevitable characteristic of rural life.

The cause of this new contempt for rural life must lie in the rapid urbanization that China, including the North China plain, experienced in the eleventh and twelfth centuries. As the city population developed its own increasingly distinctive lifestyle, the country rustic became a figure of fun. The *Tu-ch'eng chi-sheng* (TCM, 97) explains the origins of short skits parodying country bumpkins:

> The *tsa-pan* is occasionally called *tsa-pan**; it is also called *niu-yüan-tzu*; it is also called *pa-ho*, "acting out country folks." It is a dispersal piece in a comedy. During the time that the court was at the capital [i. e., up to 1126], villagers seldom got to enter the city, so people composed these pieces. For the most part they costumed themselves as villagers from the regions of Shantung or Hopeh to provide a few laughs.

The stage representation of villagers as yokels not only proved its viability in the heavily urbanized dominions of the Southern Sung dynasty, but also survived in North China under the Chin dynasty and was carried over into Yüan drama. Tanaka Kenji, basing himself on titles of Chin dynasty farces cataloged in the *Yüan-pen ming-mu* and those passages of Yüan *tsa-chü* that he takes to be residuals of Chin farces, argues that the Chin stage knew both the bucolic idealization of the country life and its opposite, the ignorant farmer as a figure of ridicule (Tanaka 1968, 177–78; West 1977b, 26–28). The latter was common on the urban stage and among literati, as Tu Jen-chieh's *Chuang-chia pu-shih kou-lan* testifies. It may be pointed out here that the protagonist, a villager who enters a theater for the first time in his life, is not simply any peasant, but appears to be a village headman.[9] The urbanites' disdain for the idiocy of rural life must have been coupled with pride in their own far more varied and interesting existence. Such pride is also detectable in Meng Yüan-lao's description of the hustle and bustle of early twelfth-century Kaifeng in his *Tung-ching meng Hua lu*, as well as in Chang Tse-tuan's meticulous depiction of the same in his handscroll painting *Ch'ing-ming shang-ho t'u* (A visit to the river on the Ch'ing-ming festival). Even though the legend of Liu Chih-yüan and Li San-niang might have been a widely circulating folktale, it is impossible to view the *Liu Chih-yüan chu-kung-tiao* as a true reflection of peasant culture. On the contrary, its contemptuous description of rural life, with heavy emphasis on the villagers' grotesque appearance, reflects the pride and prejudices of a decidedly urban audience, which may well have been broader than the narrow circle of literati but certainly included them.

At this point it may be pertinent to reconsider the "simplicity" of the *Liu Chih-yüan chu-kung-tiao*. Its anonymous author does not display the extensive erudition of Tung Chieh-yüan, but he does appear to have enjoyed at least a sound general education, and his work may well contain more literary echoes than is usually assumed.

The *Liu Chih-yüan chu-kung-tiao* contains two explicit references to other texts. Following the second song-set of book 1, the author purports to quote a certain *Wu-tai shih* (History of the Five Dynasties) (Uchida 1974, 243). If the passage is a quotation, it is not one from either of the two canonical histories by that title; but then such works were printed only in very small editions and consequently were rare. The "quotation" may derive from an abbreviated version of one of the histories or some other work popular at the time but now lost. Similarly, the *Shih-ch'i tai* (Seventeen dynasties) mentioned in the first song probably refers to some popular compendium.

There are other allusions, less explicit. In book 2, when Liu Chih-yüan is hesitant to leave Li San-niang, he refers to the preface to the *Book of Filial Piety*, a common primer (Uchida 1974, 264). And the description of the inn in book 1 reads:

If, in the span of a hundred years' time,
One could always be drunk—
It would amount to thirty-six thousand times!

(Uchida 1974, 245)

The lines allude to a couplet by Li T'ai-po (701–62), the drunken immortal whose portrait adorns the inn's cow dung–plastered walls:

Three hundred days and six times ten,
Day after day I'm plastered, drunk.[10]

Liu Chih-yüan's lengthy monologue in book 2 bemoaning his untenable position at the farm seems to parody Po Chü-i's well-known *hsin yüeh-fu*, "Ching-ti yin yin-p'ing" (Drawing a silver flask from the well). The final lines of Po Chü-i's poem, sung by a girl who eloped with her lover but is eventually sent away by his parents, read:

This is my message for other foolish girls:
Be careful not to entrust yourself lightly to a man.[11]

The last lines of the first stanza of Liu Chih-yüan's complaint, in which he fondly remembers his deceased parents-in-law, read:

I admonish all other young swells:
May you never in any existence
Become a "married-in" son-in-law.

(Uchida 1974, 268)

Later in the same book (p. 273) the author assumes familiarity with the tale of strife between the swallow and the sparrow, known to us through two *fu* from Tun-huang, witty satires on the corruption of the law courts.[12] Actually, the other three texts share a satiric intent, too.

In this connection, we may also consider the relation of the *Liu Chih-yüan chu-kung-tiao* to painting. Describing the dismay of Li Hung-i and his brother upon the discovery of the identity of the governor-general, the anonymous author refers to Chang Seng-yu and Wu Tao-tzu, both proverbially famous for their vivid pictorial representations of the horrors of hell (Uchida 1974, 293). We have already encountered the ironic reference to the "picture of Yao's people." The only preserved contemporary example of this theme is Li Kung-lin's (ca. 1049–ca. 1106) *Chi-jang t'u* (Picture of [Yao's people] singing and dancing), which has been described as something of an exception in his oeuvre, "the motif being intensively realistic, and the treatment rather humorous" (Sirén 1956, 2:44). The same no doubt can be said of the *Huo-lang t'u* (A peddler) by the Southern Sung painter Li Sung (ca. 1190–ca. 1230), the finest treatment of a motif that was then quite popular and that is evoked in book 11 in the final stanza of the song in which Li San-niang orders Liu Chih-yüan to come and fetch her:

> You motherfucking, matchless liar!
> [For years you] had me,
> All alone, keep an empty room.
> If you're late, you need hope for nothing!
> Don't say it's twenty-five ounces;
> Even if it were a jade seal and gold box,
> If I were to hear the rum-tum-tum of the snakeskin drum,
> Making its rounds of village and hamlet
> And croaking out its scorched sound,
> I'd swap your golden seal for candy!
>
> (Uchida 1974, 286)

In such passages, the *Liu Chih-yüan chu-kung-tiao* shows an affinity, not with specific literati paintings, but with the realistic genre painting associated with the Sung Imperial Academy of Painting and its humorous observations of scenes from daily life.

In contrast to the *Hsi-hsiang-chi chu-kung-tiao*, which in its present form may have been meant to be read as much as sung (its prose sections are basically written in classical literary language), the *Liu Chih-yüan chu-kung-tiao* must have been written primarily for performance, since both verse and prose are written in the contemporary vernacular. Once we overcome the difficulties presented by this peculiar twelfth-century idiom, the anonymous author of our text shows himself an expert practitioner of light verse. Each individual stanza is written as a self-contained unit that simultaneously functions within the song-set as a whole. The author almost completely eschews the use of parallelism, the favorite device of high literature so amply employed by Tung Chieh-yüan; thus, rhyme assumes a more than usual importance in his verse. Especially in the last lines of stanzas, rhyme is often used to great effect in underlining key words or phrases (Idema 1972, 265–66). Quite often proper names provide the rhyme words in such final lines. In the translations of selected passages above, I have tried as far as possible, often at the expense of correct English usage, to maintain the original word order to illustrate this phenomenon.

Two more examples may perhaps be given here. When Li Hung-i is defeated by Liu Chih-yüan and flees,

> He stuttered and stuttered time and again:
> "I haven't yet done with you, scum!"
>
> (Uchida 1974, 249)

And in the final song-set of book 1, Li Hung-i and his brother are egged on by their wives to get rid of Liu Chih-yüan:

> Moreover, they had no defense against their wives at their sides,
> Who relentlessly trumpeted in their ears:
> "Have him sliced!"
>
> (Uchida 1974, 260)

The author of our text also evinces his control of the material in the similes he uses, either in the parallel couplets that often follow a song-set or in the body of the songs themselves. These similes and images may be taken from rural life and so emphasize the rusticity of the action. The fight between Li Hung-i and Liu Chih-yüan, for instance, is thus described:

> That rustic hit out with his fists;
> Chih-yüan remained unhurried.
> By stepping aside he evaded the blow;
> To catch a water buffalo he had his own way.
> With all his strength he clenched his fist,
> Just like the threads of a silkworm's cocoon.
>
> (Uchida 1974, 248)

The wedding of Liu and Li San-niang is concluded when "cattle and sheep have returned to the fold" (Uchida 1974, 259). And in book 11, Li Hung-i's fury upon seeing Liu is thus described:

Again he saw the strolling player who stole his golden pots;
Once more he met the quack who sold fake medicine.

(Uchida 1974, 287)

On the other hand, the protagonists are consistently compared to the greatest figures from Chinese history and mythology, even though their actual circumstances do not in the least warrant such comparison. One can only assume that the author was fully aware of this incongruity but exploited its possibilities to the full in line with the intended nature of his work as low-burlesque satire. Upon Li San-niang's entrance we are told:

Even though she was a country girl,
Her devastating appearance was without par.
Lo-p'u, Hsi-shih, and also Ta-chi
Could not yet compare with this beauty.

(Uchida 1974, 257)

These three women were proverbial for their fatal attractions: the goddess of the River Lo, an apparition of whom overwhelmed the poet Ts'ao Chih (192–232); Hsi-shih, whose charms destroyed the kingdom of Wu; and Ta-chi, who was responsible for the downfall of the Yin empire. The comparison between these beauties and Li San-niang, whose amorous advances threaten only the newly acquired social security of the farmhand Liu Chih-yüan, is intentionally overstated; the studied sequence of the enumeration precludes naiveté. When Liu's brothers-in-law try to burn him to death, even Huang Ch'ao, whose armies devastated all of China, becomes a "veritable Buddha" by comparison (Uchida 1974, 265).

Another clear-cut example occurs in book 11, when Liu Chih-yüan throws the food offered him into Li Hung-i's face:

Hung-hsin boiled with fury;
Hung-i burst with wrath;
The two sisters-in-law were enraged.
Together they surrounded Liu Chih-yüan
And cursed him: "You pauper, how dare you?
With good food, with good fare,
We have filled your mule's belly!
Think: we harbor no bad intentions,
But you have to be so touchy!
Whether you eat it or not,
Is all up to you.

But all of a sudden you fly into a rage—
You haven't changed your old pauper's nature!"
So the four had finished speaking;
Together they advanced.
Chih-yüan knew no fear,
He manifested his might.
San-niang by his side
Said a silent prayer,
Earnestly imploring divine Heaven to lend a little help.
From head to foot she trembled:
Grief damaged her dazzling appearance,
Furrows broke her "lace eyebrows."

[Coda]
Liu Chih-yüan, how brave he was!
His carrying pole he used so well,
That alone he defended himself on all four sides.

(Uchida 1974, 288)

This ordinary squabble is then compared to the most momentous battle of the early Five Dynasties period, the defeat of the redoubtable general of the Liang dynasty, Wang Yen-chang, by the combined good luck of five future emperors.

A favorite technique of the author of the *Liu Chih-yüan chu-kung-tiao* is repetition of identical phrases in different circumstances. In the inn (in book 1),

Clay pots and china jars were arranged on an earthen bench;
The taste surpassed a Kao-yang.

(Uchida 1974, 245)

And when Li San-niang observes Liu Chih-yüan for the first time, she sees:

On an earthen bench there was lying a young man:
His impressive seven feet were beautiful,
His awe-inspiring jade body was godlike.
With closed eyes he was sound asleep,
Not a single thing did he ever hear.

(Uchida 1974, 254)

The repetition of the key word "earthen bench" suggests that the young farmhand presents a sight as delectable to the young maiden as jugs of wine to the thirsty Liu Chih-yüan. In book 3 the same term "dumbfounded" (*ch'ing ssu ch'ih*) is used to describe the bashfulness of Commander Yüeh's daughter on her wedding night and the consternation of Liu Chih-yüan when questioned by village relatives about his bigamous marriage (Uchida 1974, 279, 281). And Liu Chih-yüan's question at the outset of his peregrinations—"When will I ever manifest my might?"—is echoed in book 11 in the description of his fight with his brothers-in-law and their wives: "Chih-yüan knew no fear,/He manifested his might."

The *Liu Chih-yüan chu-kung-tiao* reveals itself an expertly executed low-burlesque satire on the divine institution of the emperor that may elevate most unlikely candidates to the throne; the imbecility of the rural life is a subsidiary theme. The main tale is aptly introduced by the prologue, in which the author poses as a disillusioned literatus convinced by his study of the *Seventeen Dynasties* that history is an uninterrupted succession of wars that confound the natural hierarchy of society. It is this somber tone that tempts us to date the text to the chaotic years following the Jurchen conquest of Kaifeng in 1126.

In conclusion, if the *Liu Chih-yüan chu-kung-tiao* is indeed a low-burlesque satire, it is probably also a parody of the genre to which it formally belongs. Here, of course, we can only speculate, having no earlier example of the genre. The only complete example we have most likely dates from a later period, while early references to the genre and its characteristics are few. Yet in view of the consistency between the earliest descriptions of the genre and the *Hsi-hsiang-chi chu-kung-tiao*, it appears that Tung Chieh-yüan's composition represents the main line of development of the genre in both style and subject.

In the preceding pages we have noted numerous examples of the author's tendency to overturn existing symbols and stories—the peach garden, Po Chü-i's *hsin yüeh-fu*, the tale of Ch'iu Hu—as well as his tendency to parody himself through the repetition of identical phrases in disparate circumstances. In the same way, his work as a whole parodies the conventional subject matter and techniques of the all-keys-and-modes as exemplified by the *Hsi-hsiang-chi chu-kung-tiao*. The protagonists are not a brilliant student and a refined young lady, but a poor farmhand and a village girl; the setting is not a sumptuous monastery, but the countryside; the story does not end with a marriage, but opens with one.

Many of the thematic ingredients display similar contrasts: in Tung Chieh-yüan's work Chang Kung steals into Ying-ying's garden to be sent away, but here it is Li San-niang who surprises Liu Chih-yüan in his room, and when Liu does jump across the wall to see San-niang it is not to make love but to take leave; in Tung Chieh-yüan's work Fa-ts'ung lifts one of the bandit chiefs bodily from his saddle, but here it is Shih Hung-chao who is so humiliatingly defeated by one of the bandits.

We see the same phenomenon where suspense-building techniques are concerned. When Chang Kung wants to rush after Ying-ying upon first spying her, he is grabbed from behind by Fa-ts'ung; when Liu Chih-yüan, fearful of his brothers-in-law, sneaks into his own room, he is grabbed from behind by his wife. The first book of the *Hsi-hsiang-chi chu-kung-tiao* ends with the sudden entrance of a novice who shouts, "Disaster!" In the *Liu Chih-yüan chu-kung-tiao* the action is so often interrupted by the sudden arrival of a messenger that it becomes a running gag. In book 1 the arrival of Li San-niang's brothers is announced just when Liu Chih-yüan is about to accept the proposal of marriage. In book 3 the gatekeeper announces the arrival of villagers looking for Liu just when he is being entertained by Commander Yüeh after the wedding. In book 12 this technique is used no less than four times: when Liu Chih-yüan is about to dispatch troops to fetch Li San-niang, he is informed that she has been kidnapped by bandits; when Kuo Yen-wei is struggling to hold his own against those bandits, he is informed of the arrival of yet another column of bandits; when Liu Chih-yüan and Li San-niang finally celebrate their reunion, they are informed that her brothers and their wives are starving; and when Liu Chih-yüan brings himself to pardon these villains, someone announces the arrival of a stalwart young man.

Personally, I can appreciate book 12 only as a spoof on the *t'uan-yüan* convention. Not only is Liu Chih-yüan united with Li San-niang and reconciled with his brothers-in-law and their wives, but the very bandits who kidnapped San-niang turn out to be the stepbrothers who once chased Liu away from home. Having heard that he is governor-general, they have come to join him, led by their mother, while the stalwart who appears out of the blue at the finale is Liu's younger brother. The relatively early date may well be an argument in favor of reading the *Liu Chih-yüan chu-kung-tiao* as a parody of the all-keys-and-modes; genres tend to attract parodies not in their heydays but when they either are outworn or have just emerged.

Much of the "simplicity" of the *Liu Chih-yüan chu-kung-tiao* is a carefully cultivated artlessness or even non-art. Once the nature of the text as low burlesque and parody is clear, we understand the author's confident conclusion of his work in the final coda:

I had hoped that this new composition
Would please you well, discerning gentlemen—
With a head and tail and a conclusion: the *Liu Chih-yüan*!

(Uchida 1974, 305)

Notes

1. For a modern edition of the "Ying-ying chuan," see Wang Pi-chiang 1955, 135–40; and for a translation, see Hightower 1973.

2. *Chuan-t'a* was a type of dancing song (described in West 1977b, 66). Preserved texts are reproduced in Liu Yung-chi 1957, 70–117. Those by Ch'in and Mao are on pp. 89–106. Ch'in's is translated by Josephs (1976), who mistakes it for a *ch'an-ta*.

3. SC 117. 2999–3074; trans. Watson 1961, 2:297–342, and Hervouet 1972. Evaluations in later ages studied by Hervouet (1964) and Idema (1984b).

4. For the Chinese text, see Wang Pi-chiang 1955, 49–51; and for a translation, see Elizabeth Wang 1961, 295–301.

5. For the Chinese text, see Wang Meng-ou 1974; and for a translation, Levy 1969.

6. For the Chinese text of "Liu-shih chuan," see Wang Pi-chiang 1955, 52–55; and for a translation, Elizabeth Wang 1961, 1–13.

7. This is an example of a demon story and dates from the Yüan or, more likely, the early Ming (Hanan 1973, 188–97, 241). Recent translations can be found in H. C. Chang 1973, 205–61; and Y. W. Ma and Joseph S. M. Lau 1978, 355–78. Of the voluminous secondary literature on the White Snake, see especially Lévy 1971.

8. For a comparison of the various versions of the legend of Liu Chih-yüan and Li San-niang vis-à-vis a reconstruction of the narrative of the *chu-kung-tiao*, see Cheng Chen-to 1957, 921–30; Aoki 1932, 217–30; and Doleželová-Velingerová and Crump 1971, 115–22. Kim 1981 stresses the many features of Liu's legend that link the early version to southern Shansi and shows that these features were lost when the story became popular in the South.

9. For the Chinese text of this song-set, see Sui Shu-sen 1964, 31–32; and for a translation, Idema and West 1982, 187–89, and Crump 1983, 107–24.

10. From his "Tseng nei"; see *Ch'üan T'ang shih* 184.1884.

11. From his "Ching-ti yin yin-p'ing"; see *Ch'üan T'ang shih* 427.4707–8.

12. For the text of these two *fu*, see Wang Chung-min 1957, 249–66; and for a translation of one, Waley 1960, 11–12.

10

CHILLY SEAS AND EAST-FLOWING RIVERS: YÜAN HAO-WEN'S POEMS OF DEATH AND DISORDER, 1233-35[1]

Stephen H. West

In 1211 the first Mongol armies invaded the area within the Great Wall and in a decisive battle defeated a Jurchen army of an estimated four hundred thousand men. In 1213 they forced the transfer of the imperial capital from Yenching to Pien-liang, and in 1215-16 they carried out sustained and effective attacks in Shansi and Shensi, leaving behind them a wake of destruction and death. In 1230, after the brief respite of the late 1220s when their attention shifted westward, the Mongols, under the leadership of Ogödei, decided to engage in a decisive battle with the Chin. After being thwarted in their attempts to take the T'ung-kuan region, they split their forces and, making use of an alliance with the Sung, attacked the Chin from the southwest, crossing the Wei River at Pao-chi, gradually working their way south along the Han, and finally driving northward into Honan toward the capital at Pien-liang (Sun K'o-k'uan 1968, 1-84; Yao Ts'ung-wu 1970, 226-28; KCC 11.121-30).

In April 1231, under the leadership of Subotai, the northern soldiers surrounded the capital at Pien and, finding the fortifications too solid to fall easily, began a year-long siege. Despite excellent physical defenses, by the end of that year the situation inside Pien had grown desperate. Food was dwindling—one account says that the dead were stripped of flesh, children were eaten, and all leather goods were boiled for food (KCC 11.121-30)—and Ai-tsung, the last emperor of the Chin, fled the capital in January 1233 to Kuei-te, in the province of Sung, where he ended his own life a year later rather than surrender to the combined Mongol-Sung force (CS 18.393-403).

On March 3, Ts'ui Li, one of four generals in charge of defending the city, slaughtered the leading civil ministers and surrendered the capital to

Subotai. On May 30, Ts'ui sent all members of the royal family to the Green City (Ch'ing-ch'eng) south of Pien-liang, the site of the temporary palace that housed the emperor during his annual Southern Suburban Sacrifice.[2] The male members of the Wan-yen clan were executed, and the women were dispatched northward the day after. Altogether, thirty-seven carts were needed to transport the empress, the dowager, the consorts, and the five hundred kinswomen of the imperial family. All court artisans, craftsmen, and men of letters were also sent northward under Mongol patronage, to be scattered over North China in forced resettlement. Yüan Hao-wen, a leading literary figure of the day, was among them. He was sent to the Green City for processing as a political prisoner on June 8, 1233. Four days later he began his deportation to Liao-ch'eng in Shantung under the protection of Chang Jou, a former Chin general in Mongol service, and Yeh-lü Ch'u-ts'ai, whose determination had saved the inhabitants of the capital from slaughter (de Rachewiltz 1962b).

Yüan Hao-wen's poems are a single voice in this period of violence and chaos, just as his life is a single story in that same collective tragedy. His poems from this period have been justly praised as unparalleled in their expression of despair. They are seen by traditional and modern critics alike as some of the finest examples of historical poems ever written and are extolled for the way in which they carefully trace and lament the decline and subsequent extinction of the Chin (*OPSH* 8.115–24). I would like to look closely at several of these poems, along with selections of historical writings from the period 1233–35, and examine their relationship to Yüan Hao-wen's life—not to test historical accuracy or reconstruct the facts of his life, but to see how he worked his imagination and self-awareness into a vision of a dying culture.

I will treat here the more significant of his poems written between May 1233 and December 1234, from the time that Ts'ui Li surrendered the capital to the end of the year in which the last Chin emperor met his self-imposed death. They are:

"P'ai-t'i: Hsüeh-hsiang-t'ing tsa-yung shih-wu-shou"
"In the Farcical Style: Random Chants at the Kiosk of Snowy Perfume, Fifteen Verses" (*YISCC* 12.559–63)

"Kuei-ssu ssu-yüeh erh-shih-chiu-jih ch'u ching"
"June 8, 1233: Going out of the Capital" (*YISCC* 8.387–88)

"Kuei-ssu wu-yüeh san-jih pei-tu san-shou"
"June 12, 1233: Fording Northward, Three Verses" (*YISCC* 12.568)

"Huai-yu"
"Right of the Huai" (*YISCC* 8.391)

"Ch'iu-yeh"
"Autumn Night" (YISCC 8.395–96)

"Hsü hsiao-niang-ko shih-shou"
"Continuing the Song of the Maidens, Ten Verses" (YISCC 6.307–8)

"Sung Chung-hsi chien chien Ta-fang"
"Sent to Chung-hsi with a Communication to Ta-fang" (YISCC 10.501)

"Meng-kuei"
"Dreaming of Return" (YISCC 8.390)

"Chia-wu ch'u-yeh"
"Exorcism Night, *Chia-wu* Year" (YISCC 8.396)

The focus of my investigation will be the three poems that open the cycle "Random Chants at the Kiosk of Snowy Perfume," since they introduce the major themes and images that Yüan elaborates on in other poems and mark a departure in his treatment of symbol and political allegory.

The cycle of fifteen poems on the Kiosk of Snowy Perfume was written sometime between May 30 and June 8, 1233, that is, in the week or so between the imperial family's and Yüan Hao-wen's departure from the capital. During this period, Yüan was free to roam through the imperial parks and gardens, free to visit, as he did, the former emperor's inner chambers. A contemporary account by Yang Huan (Wang Teh-yi 1979–82, 3:1517–18; Chan Hok-lam 1976), *A Record of the Old Palaces of Pien (Pien ku-kung chi)*, places the Kiosk of Snowy Perfume in the area where the emperor and the women of the court, including the empress and consorts, had their bedchambers: "The Hall of Pure Harmony is the main sleeping chamber. West of the Hall of Pure Harmony is the Kiosk of Snowy Perfume. North of Snowy Perfume is the location of the empress's and consorts' [bedchambers]" (PKKC 2:340; NTCK 18.222–23).

That Yüan would entitle these "In the Farcical Style" is a matter of irony. The *p'ai-t'i* form was used primarily for comic or satirical verse and, as the name denotes,[3] was associated with court jesters who entertained the emperor and his court, presumably within the inner chambers. Since the name "Snowy Perfume" couples attributes common to court lovelies, the irony is doubled: where court jesters once entertained the beauties of the emperor, here in the back chambers, Yüan now laments their dispersion into the cold northlands of Mongolia.

The sorry fate of court beauties is itself a frequent theme in Chinese literature, but these poems go beyond that—they function as a nexus of political event and personal fortune. The fall of the capital was not only the first major action to signal the sure fate of the Chin, it was also a time when Yüan Hao-wen's own life hung in the balance.[4] In historical retrospect it was, and is, easy to see the gradual decline of the Chin dynasty, the relentless and certain advance of Mongol supremacy. But the Chin maintained the hope, even in the besieged capital, that they could turn the Mongols back and restore unity to the Central Plain. The reverie was broken, however, with Ai-tsung's flight and Ts'ui Li's capitulation, which severed all but the slimmest threads of hope for political revival.

Yüan Hao-wen's own life had been a microcosm of the Chin retrenchment: he had been continually chased about central China since 1214, and many times he had returned from those flights to find once-settled areas laid waste by Mongol raids. He had lost his brother and his friends in the 1212–18 invasions, and he was familiar with death as an ever-present phenomenon, but never, before this time, as a process. Another person's death—even if that person is close—maintains certain aspects that can be objectively described or publicly dealt with: the loss is wept over, assimilated, rationalized in literature. So it was in Yüan Hao-wen's earlier poetry, carefully crafted lamentations of grief that remained, nevertheless, objective. It was rather the process of dying—the slow and relentless starvation of the capital, the play of chance in whether one lived or died—that challenged his impulse to rationalize and brought him face-to-face with the reality of his own extinction.

It is from this nexus that the cycle of fifteen poems emerges. Yüan begins the cycle with three poems that establish the coordinates of his structure of reference and introduce the master tropes that will govern his poetry over the next two years: the cold seas of political chaos and the flowing rivers of cultural dissolution.

In the Farcical Style:
Random Chants at the Kiosk of Snowy Perfume
(Number One of Fifteen)

Cold seas violently flow—myriad states become fish;
Spirit's pattern is vast, vague—in the end, like what?
The Six Classics may be mastered under a bookish student,
But broad blades and long lances have no trust in him.

The first poem of the cycle describes the chaos that accompanied the decline of the Chin. *Ts'ang-hai heng-liu*, "cold seas violently flow," is a phrase that is repeated several times in Yüan Hao-wen's poetry, invariably referring to great disorder (Wixted 1982, 304 n. 19; Suzuki 1965, 200–202). Its classical source is the preface to the *Ku-liang chuan*, where Fan Ning uses these words to summarize the ills that afflicted China during the time of the state of Chou's decline: "All under Heaven was unsettled, the Way of the king had ended. Confucius gazed at the violent flow of the cold seas and sighed deeply, saying, 'Since King Wen has died, does culture not rest in me?' This means that since the Way of King Wen was lost, the one who would revive it was [Confucius] himself" (*KLC* preface, 1a).

The phrase has another referent, however: the *Chin shu* biography of a certain Wang Ni:

> When Loyang fell, [Wang Ni] avoided the disorder in Chiang-hsia [in modern Hupei]. At that time Wang Ch'eng was the inciting notary of Ching-chou, and he treated [Wang Ni] with deep favor. Ni had early on lost his wife and had only one son. He had no house to dwell in and lived simply in a pasture in an open cart. He had a single ox; each time he traveled, he had his son drive it. At night [he and his son] would sleep together in the cart. He often sighed, saying, "The *cold seas violently flow,* place after place is insecure." Suddenly [his patron] Ch'eng died, and the region of Ching was smitten by hunger and famine. Ni had no way to get food, and so he killed his ox and broke up the cart, roasted the meat and ate it. Once it was gone, father and son died. (*CSH* 49.1382, emphasis added)

This is also the anecdote that Su Tung-p'o, the major literary influence in Yüan's life, refers to in his poem "Reading Chin History" ("Tu Chin shih"):

> *The cold seas violently flow,* blood makes a ford;
> Spear and sword come out contesting, struggling to claim truth.
> Could the Central Plain be without the powerful and eminent?
> Heaven dispatched flocks of the brave to slay men of Chin.
>   (*SWCK* 49.15a, emphasis added)[5]

The opening words of the poem, then, have well-attested antecedents both in antiquity—that is, in the Warring States period—and in the era of the Six Dynasties. The latter, a period of disunion and violent warfare, provides an obvious analogy to Yüan's life: Six Dynasties Chin was a northern dynasty that had been established under alien rule and was ultimately pressured by another alien dynasty. He thus feels a great affinity with Six Dynasties figures who were themselves buffeted by political change and harried by danger in their native lands. In the last two poems of the cycle, for instance, he makes conscious allusion to both Pao Chao and Yü Hsin:

Random Chants at the Kiosk of Snowy Perfume
(Number Fourteen of Fifteen)

Ten thousand portals, a thousand gates, all have names
And clearly pass before my eyes—I memorize as I walk;
The writer of rhapsodies may now have a brush to portray the
    "Overgrown City,"
But it will never give shape to this strip of broken heart.

"Overgrown City" is an allusion to Pao Chao's famous "Ruined City" ("Wu ch'eng fu"), a description of Kuang-ling, near modern Yangchow. The inhabitants of Kuang-ling (except for the young girls, who were given to army officers, and the young boys, who were spared) were put to the sword in 457 after supporting an insurrection against the Liu-Sung court. Yüan sees a parallel between Pao Chao's composition on Kuang-ling and his own on Pien-liang—sketched, but incomplete because it fails to include his own broken heart.

Random Chants at the Kiosk of Snowy Perfume
(Number Fifteen of Fifteen)

Evening clouds, loft and kiosk, sentiments of past and present;
Earth ages, Heaven grows rank, vexation has yet to settle.
Hoary-headed bound ministers—how many are left?
Sorrow, in their center, slays Yü Lan-ch'eng.

This is a reference to Yü Hsin's life and his well-known "Rhapsody Lamenting South of the River" ("Ai Chiang-nan fu"). Sent as an envoy to the North, Yü Hsin was detained there, after his own dynasty had fallen, because of his literary talents. He attained high posts under the Western Wei and later the Northern Chou, but he continued to lament the demise of his own state of Liang and the hardships of life in the North. Thus, Yü Hsin presented Yüan Hao-wen with the perfect analogue for his own impending situation under the Mongols.

The poem, then, may also be read as personal reflection—a statement of the peril confronting Yüan's own life—and as historical analogy—a description of the peril awaiting anyone caught in the epicycle of dynastic decline.

The second line of the first poem of the cycle expands on the doublet of political disorder and personal safety. "Spirit's pattern" (*shen li*) refers to the subtle working of the Way of Heaven, vague and vast because, unclearly stated in a world of chaos, it is beyond the ken of human beings. Politically, the point is that, just as in the time of the Six Dynasties, the issue of legitimacy is now unclear. The Chin armies that were centered around the exiled emperor were still capable of mounting temporary resistance to the armed forces of the Mongols and the Southern Sung; the line may thus be understood to ask, What is Heaven's intent in regard to its mandate to rule? That is, the poem may allude to the slim possibility of a Chin restoration, but it also wonders to whom the mandate to rule will pass next.

Questioning Heaven—the provenance of the mandate to rule—is a major device in Yüan Hao-wen's poetry. In a poem entitled "June 8, 1233: Going out of the Capital," for instance, he poses a similar question:

The rise and decline [of dynasties]—who can understand the intent of the Heavenly Noble,
In leaving behind the Green City to survey past and present?

And in another poem written after the fall, "Sent to Chung-hsi with a Communication to Ta-fang," he writes:

Ever aging, the Heavenly Noble is truly bursting in chaos;
Since the disorder, human affairs have turned limitless in vexation.

Poems such as those cited here question the fate of the Chin—not only in the contemporary world, but in the context of history as well. Chin literati were aware of the complicated problem of political legitimacy in an age that lacked unified rule. If they failed to retain the mandate, the obvious corollary was to question why. Heaven was not only obscure in its bestowal of the mandate, but silent and inscrutable in its reasons for removing it.

The Chin had deliberated for nearly ten years over the question of from whom they had received the mandate (Chan Hok-lam 1984), and their decision to claim descent from the Northern Sung was probably an effort to assume the authority of the past (which they might also have done by claiming descent from the Liao), as well as an attempt to clarify their status in relation to the Southern Sung, who could claim not only political legitimacy but blood descent from the Northern Sung. Never extinguished by the Chin, the Southern Sung could continue to presume on Heaven's protection; and now on the point of extinguishing the Chin, the Southern Sung seemed to belie the Chin assertion that they themselves were the true inheritors of the mandate. Now the empire was up for grabs between barbarian invaders, the southern successors to the Northern Sung, and the Jurchen Chin. In such great periods of chaos, as Yüan Hao-wen says in the first poem of the "Snowy Perfume" sequence, all states are thrown into confusion (*wan kuo yü*).

As a reflexive statement, "spirit's pattern" of the same poem refers to the uncertainty and insecurity of Yüan's own future, a point emphasized in the final couplet of the poem where he complains of his helplessness as a student of the classics, unused and useless in a period of violence and warfare.

There is a deeper level to this poem, however, that deals with something akin to the death of culture. *Ts'ang-hai heng-liu* may allude to political disorder, but because of the Confucian ideal of politics as an extension of practiced morality and social order, it carries with it the idea of cultural dissolution, return to a precivilized state. To the Confucian, culture, civilization, and the political state are one, their distinguishing features the institutional forms created by heightened moral order. The phrase *hengliu*, of course, is reminiscent of the famous passages in *Mencius* on the beginnings of civilization:

> At the time of Yao, all under Heaven had not yet been settled. Floodwaters *violently flowed*, inundating all under Heaven. Herbaceous and woody plants flourished and thickened, beasts and birds multiplied, the five grains did not ripen. Birds and beasts pressured people; tracks of beasts and trails of birds crisscrossed in the Central Kingdom. Yao alone worried about it. (3A/4, emphasis added)

> All under Heaven was born over a long time: one period of order, one period of chaos. At the time of Yao, waters flowed backwards and inundated the Central Kingdom. Snakes and dragons resided there. People had no place to find stability. In lowlands they made nests; in highlands they made caves. (3B/9)

Mencius postulates here the recurrent cycles of order and disorder that are a part of life itself. Yao, Shun, and Yü were responsible for bringing human life out of darkness—they expelled the beasts that plagued people, they drained the waters that prevented settlement, they brought agriculture into being as the highest activity of civilized human beings. They also brought something else: the written word. Indeed, the documents ascribed to the sage-kings are themselves the origin of the classical tradition.

We sometimes overlook the fact that in Confucian eyes culture and history begin simultaneously. The sage-kings who brought civilization to the Central Kingdom also brought into being a cultural tradition that was eventually epitomized in the Six Classics. These writings represented history as an unfolding of moral truth in action, and culture as the apprehension of that moral truth and its embodiment in institutional form. Government and society were created by the extension of individual morality into a common sphere of collective will and purpose, but they also embodied *wen*—the expression of humanity as cultural pattern.

"Spirit's pattern" in the second line of Yüan's first "Snowy Perfume" poem, then, refers not only to the concept of political mandate or personal future, but also to the hazy notion of alternating cycles of order and chaos—which are represented in the larger scheme by the existence or disappearance of culture and civilization. Consequently, the last three characters of the first line carry certain overtones of the *Tso chuan's* decision concerning the importance of Yü, the mythic dredger: "Comely indeed, the meritorious effort of Yü; his lustrous virtue went far indeed. If it had not been for Yü, would we probably not be fishes?" (CCCC 20.8a).

Fan Ning's remark about Confucius viewing the shifting waves of the ocean of chaos is important, because it describes the point at which Confucius dedicated himself to the written word, to compiling the *Spring and Autumn Annals* and copying the *Poetry* from the archives of the court musicians. It is this sensibility, then, that allows the final couplet to be read thus: the Six Classics, which have dominated the civilized world, providing pattern and principle for cultural life, will be punished, unused and untrusted, in the new age of chaos.

These three points of reference—the age of the sage-kings, the Six Dynasties, and Yüan Hao-wen's own situation—as well as a fourth, which Yüan introduces in the second poem of the "Snowy Perfume" sequence, provide the touchstones of his poetry on the theme of dissolution for the next two years:

> *Random Chants at the Kiosk of Snowy Perfume*
> (Number Two of Fifteen)
>
> Loyang's walls and pylons transformed to ash and smoke,
> Evening Kuo and morning Yü are just before the eyes.
> Speak for me to that pair of swallows in the apricot garden,
> "Where will you build your nest in the coming year?"

This poem makes absolute the points of contact between the Six Dynasties, the end of the Sung, and the demise of the Chin. Commentators either are silent on the use of Loyang in line one (Hao Shu-hou 1959, 59) or suggest that it is a general metaphor for a capital city and, by analogy, for Pien-liang (Oguri 1963, 82–83). Loyang was, of course, an ancient capital and cultural center of the Central Plain. Its use is, on one level, meant to conjure up the ancient seat of the grand kings and dynasties of antiquity. There can be little doubt, however, that in the general scheme of historical translocation, this image of the ruined capital is also meant to refer back to the beginning of the Six Dynasties, to the fall of the Eastern Chin and the sack of Loyang, which left the city in rubble until it was rebuilt by the T'o-pa Wei some 150 years later. But there is also a possibility of direct reference to the Sung as well. Chao K'uang-yin, founder of the Sung, was a native of Loyang. According to imperial rescripts preserved in the *Hsü Tzu-chih t'ung-chien ch'ang-pien* and the *Sung hui-yao chi-kao*, when Chao established his capital at Pien, he dispatched artisans to make a map of Loyang and to expand the former imperial city of the Northern Chou according to that plan: "Chien-lung, third year, fifth month [June–July 983]: In this month began the great ordering of the palaces and pylons, done in imitation of the model of the Western Capital [i.e., Loyang]" (*HTCCP* 2:68).[6]

Such information, repeated in several *pi-chi* sources, would have been known to Yüan Hao-wen, and the doubled referent serves his purpose beautifully. By collapsing time into a single image with multiple reference points in history, he can stress the recurrent nature of chaos in Chinese history. The fall of Loyang, which ushered in four hundred years of ever-worsening disorder in Six Dynasties China, presents a case parallel to the fall of Pien-liang, occupied by the Jurchen Chin after the demise of Northern Sung, much as the Six Dynasties state of Chin had occupied Loyang after Three Kingdoms Wei. By extension, an epoch of political confusion and cultural imperilment lay ahead of Yüan Hao-wen's own time, just as the fall of Chin had preceded the dark ages of the Six Dynasties period.

The second line of the poem above is a reference to an episode recorded in the *Spring and Autumn Annals* and its ancillary texts. Because of the phrasing of the line, commentators trace the allusion to the passage in the *Kung-yang chuan* where the minister Hsün Hsi advises Duke Hsien of the state of Chin: "If you, my lord, use my, this minister's, schemes, then, indeed, today you will be able to seize Kuo and tomorrow you will be able to seize Yü with ease" (*KYC* 10.63b). This is clear criticism of the Southern Sung court's shortsighted policy of allying with the Mongols against the Chin. Chin was to Sung as Kuo was to Yü—outer protection—and the extinction of one would assure the extinction of the other. Yüan repeats this theme in a poem written after settling in Liao-ch'eng, in modern Shantung, under the patronage of the interim myriarchs who controlled North China between 1234 and the final conquest of 1276. The poem is part of a series he began en route from the capital in June 1233, but it was probably finished sometime after the suicide of the last Chin emperor.

Continuing the Song of the Maidens
(Number Ten of Ten)

For a thousand *li* the Yellow River had yoked the soldiers' thrust,
Kuo and Yü were clearly cloven in our eyes.
Say for me to those many generals West of the Huai,
"No use bragging about Ts'ai-chou merit."

The last line of this poem refers to the success of the Southern Sung generals who finally took Ts'ai-chou after Ai-tsung's death, killing the young kinsman whom Ai-tsung had appointed his heir. There is also certainly implicit here a reference to the Chin emperor's request to the Sung for help in withstanding the Mongol invasion:

> The emperor counseled [his envoys], saying, "The Sung have been deeply ungrateful to me. Since ascending the throne, I have severely admonished the border generals not to violate the southern border [with Sung]. Whenever there has been a border official who has requested on his own to levy a campaign, I have always severely reprimanded him. . . . Now they take advantage of my exhaustion and weariness, occupying my Shou-chou, enticing my Teng-chou, attacking my T'ang-chou. How shallow are their schemes! Great Yüan has extinguished forty states and by this reached the kingdom of Hsi-hsia; after the loss of the Hsia, they reached me. When I am lost, inevitably they will reach Sung. 'When the lips are gone, the teeth are cold.' This is a natural principle. If they unite with me, then that which is done for me will also be done for them. You, my ministers, should enlighten them on this." But when they got to the Sung [court], the Sung would not assent [to the alliance]. (CS 18.400)

The very site that is associated with these first fifteen poems, the Green City itself, serves to reinforce the lesson for Southern Sung. Forgetting the historical exemplars of the *Spring and Autumn Annals*, the Northern Sung had allied with the Chin to conquer the Liao—and had then been exterminated by the Chin. It was at the Green City that the Chin generals accepted the surrender of Hui-tsung and Ch'in-tsung, the last two monarchs of Northern Sung; it was there that they gathered the women of the former ruling house of Chao; and it was from there that the remnants of the imperial clan set out for Manchuria. The irony was not lost on Yüan Hao-wen, as we noted in the poem above:

> The rise and decline [of dynasties]—who can understand the intent
>   of the Heavenly Noble,
> In leaving behind the Green City to survey past and present?

But it is better expressed by his contemporary Liu Ch'i:

> Five *li* south of the Ta-liang city walls is [a place] called the Green City. It is the exact site where Nianhan received the surrender of the two Sung emperors at the beginning of the Chin. At that time the

empress and consorts and imperial kinswomen were all sent there. Consequently, they were all taken prisoner and sent northward. Later, when the last emperor went eastward at the end of the T'ien-hsing reign period, Ts'ui Li surrendered the city to the northern soldiers, who also set up their permanent fort at the Green City. And the empress, consorts, and other members of the inner clan all were sent there. Most of them were butchered. Is this not to be marveled at? (KCC 7.68–69)[7]

So, as Yüan says, the lesson is before the eyes—not only in ancient history in the fate of Yü, but in recent memory in the very demise of the Northern Sung. But I suspect another reference may be found on the level of cultural continuity. In Tso Ch'iu-ming's commentary on this passage, a minister of Yü, Kung-chih-ch'i, remonstrates with the duke of Yü:

"Kuo is the outer side of Yü; if Kuo is lost, Yü will inevitably follow it. Chin cannot be allowed to open up [its covetous heart], and violence cannot be allowed to become a habitual practice. Once would be called excessive; could a second occurrence be allowed? That which the aphorism professes—'Cheekbone and jawbone lean on each other: when the lips are gone, the teeth are cold'—certainly it is Kuo and Yü of which this speaks." (CCCC 5.9b–10a)

The duke responds that Chin will not exterminate Yü because, he says, "They are of my ancestral clan." Kung-chih-ch'i counters this argument by elaborately demonstrating that not only do Kuo and Yü and Chin all derive from King Wen's extended clan, but that the duke of Chin himself has exterminated collateral branches of his own grandfather and great-grandfather's clan in order to secure his position. The duke did not heed his advice, and as predicted, Yü did not survive until the twelfth-month sacrifice.

I think this is a subtle reference to the fact that as inheritors and perpetuators of the civilization of the Central Plain, the Southern Sung and the Chin shared a common cultural ancestry. Through its campaign against the Chin, the Southern Sung was not only participating in its own destruction, but was hastening the end of its own cultural legacy.

The message of the closing couplet of the second of the "Snowy Perfume" poems,

> Speak for me to that pair of swallows in the apricot garden,
> "Where will you build your nest in the coming year?"

is ostensibly directed at the palace women who were sent to the Green City and then northward, but it may be an oblique reference to the Sung as well: their shortsightedness indeed put their own existence in danger; they would have no place to nest the next year.

In the third poem of the "Snowy Perfume" series Yüan introduces the other master trope of his poetry of this period, the east-flowing river. This is a favorite image in Chinese poetry, a metaphor for the passage of time, for emotions in spate, for that which is irretrievably lost. The image carries with it as well its earlier uses in Yüan's private repertoire of imagery. In a cycle of five poems written after the imperial decision to go on eastward campaign, Yüan uses the river as a symbol for the onslaught of the Mongol invasion and the changes it would work in central China:

January 1233: On Events after the Emperor's
Departure on Eastern Campaign
(Number Two of Five)

Cruel and harsh, dragon and snake daily battle in contest;
Shield and spear simply desire to end life and spirit.
Water issues from high plains, mountains and rivers change;
Wind blows from battlefields, shrubs and trees are putrid.[8]
(YISCC 8.384)

In his poems written after the capital had fallen, however, the river refers rather to the result of those changes and disruptions in the physical universe—the irretrievable loss of the Chin and the impending death of culture and civilization as Yüan Hao-wen knew it:

Random Chants at the Kiosk of Snowy Perfume
(Number Three of Fifteen)

Falling sun, green mountains—the whole a strip of sorrow—
The Great River funnels eastward, will not flow back;
If we could make the Kiosk of Happy Spring exist longer,
Time after time we would ascend its highest level to gaze at Sung-chou.

The falling sun, the flowing river, the relentless movement toward night, toward the ocean, signal the end of the Chin and the progress of life toward death.

The Kiosk of Happy Spring was in fact a real site in the capital. It had survived both the Chin and the Mongol conquests:

> The T'ung-le-yüan of the Southern Capital was the old Palace of Dragon Virtue [Lung-te-kung] built by Hui-tsung. The lofts and belvederes and the flowers and stones in [this garden] were quite extraordinary. In spring, in the third month of every year, flowers bloomed. When it came to the fifth or sixth month, lotus blossoms opened. Officials allowed commoners [in] to see the sights. Although it was never restored or added to, still its prospects and seasonal phenomena were like those of old times [during the Sung].
>
> At the end of the Cheng-ta reign period the northern soldiers entered Honan, and the capital made plans for defense. The officials razed it completely. The heavy lumber from its lofts and kiosks was transformed into battle towers [on the city wall] and the T'ai-hu rocks were all bored through [and split] to serve as catapult stones. Even now it is nothing more than a deserted district, with broken-down foundations and overgrown weeds. All that remains is the one kiosk, Happy Spring. Now, this kiosk was constructed entirely of horse chestnut and was completely unsurfaced, with no plaster above or below. Even if one wanted to destroy it, it would not be possible. Will the world ever see such superb craftsmanship again? (KCC 7.69)

Because of its solidity, the kiosk represents hope: so long as it stands, so will the Chin. In measured anticipation of the revival of the Golden Dynasty, Yüan Hao-wen would climb that tower and gaze toward Sung-chou, where imperial forces were attempting to rally citizens to halt the Mongol flood.

In the poem, however, Happy Spring carries the irony of the seasons. The capital fell, not in the autumn of the year, but in the spring. The verdant mountains outside the city, the blossoming trees of the imperial palace, the seasonal delights in the prospect that the kiosk offered reflect a time that is out of joint with emotion. Spring is a time of birth, not death. But just as the earth itself has transformed under this dark force from the north, so has time lost its proper correlative.

Spatial and temporal dislocation become historical translocation as well. In the vague image of the Six Dynasties, Kaifeng and central China become the area of Kiangnan, the land of the southern courts of the Six Dynasties. The waters of the Yellow River become the greatest of all waters, the Yangtze, or Kiang. Yüan Hao-wen becomes an Yü Hsin, wandering far into the north, dispossessed from his southern home, a land visible to him now only in imagination.

Continuing the Song of the Maidens
(Number Four of Ten)

From high places on green mountains [I] gaze afar at southern realms;
Slowly, slowly Kiang waters circle as they flow around city walls.
I want my whole body to follow those waters away,
Without a turning of the head, straight to the bottom of the sea.

Dreaming of Return

Careworn and haggard in southern cap, a single Ch'u prisoner;[9]
A homing heart, the Yangtze, the Han daily flow eastward.
Green mountains recurrent and vivid—a dream of home and state;
Yellow leaves soughing and sighing—an autumn of wind and rain.
In poverty I have poetry, but skill becomes a curse;
Since disorder I have had no tears that can bolster sorrow.
In the remaining years, if brothers are alive to meet,
Content with our lot of coarse pickled food, all affairs will end.

It is no surprise that Yüan Hao-wen's poems from this period become more linear in their imagery, expressing in the metaphor of the river not only the passage of time and the past, but also the diaspora of humanity from the center of the civilized world of China into a desert of sand and brambles.

June 12, 1233: Fording Northward
(Number One of Three)

By the side of the road, prostrate, lie prisoners filling the gang;
Passing, departing felt-covered carts flow like water.
Crimson powder laments as it follows Uighur horses—
"For whom, a step, a turn of the head?"

(Number Two of Three)

From camp to camp wooden Buddhas are cheaper than firewood,
Racks of bells for court music fill the marketplace.
"How much did the caitiffs plunder?" Sir, do not ask,
"Great ships transport the entirety of Pien capital here."

(Number Three of Three)

Whitening bones hither and thither, like scattered hemp;
How many years of mulberry and catalpa have turned to dragon's sand?[10]
Simply know that north of the River living souls are finished;
Broken buildings and scattered smoke now number the homes.

Continuing the Song of the Maidens
(Number One of Ten)

Youths of Wu line the roads, singing songs as they march;
Ten by ten, five by five, they harmonize the songs' sounds.
They sing tunes of young girls meeting each other,
Knowing not the feelings of departing their homes or leaving their kingdom.

(Number Six of Ten)

Goose accompanies goose as they come across the Yellow River,
People sing, people weep, sounds of geese are mournful.
When geese come to autumn's advent, they can depart to the south;
But southern people fording north, when will they return?

(Number Eight of Ten)

In times of peace, married and wed, never leaving home,
Fresh and bright young men, small and tiny girls,
Nourished and raised for the last three hundred years,
Only to be led to the desert and traded for oxen or sheep.

(Number Nine of Ten)

Hungry crows sit and guard human bodies in the grass;
Blue cloth still kept in old-style scarves.
Sixth-month southern winds from myriad miles away,
If mindful of white bones, would have turned them to dust.

The preceding poems complete the myth of recurrent chaos. The sage-kings brought civilization to China by clearing the flood, driving serpents and reptiles from the Central Kingdom to make it habitable for men. But now the carefully cultivated lands of China—and with them, the civilization that had been framed by the models of culture and the collective body of wills that mirrored a moral universe—were to be left behind, and the brambles of the wilderness would press in once again.

Continuing the Song of the Maidens
(Number Seven of Ten)

Bambooed creeks and plum-treed embankments, silent and
  without dust,
The second month in Kiangnan, a spring of mist and rain.
Brokenhearted this day on the Ho-p'ing Road,
Over a thousand *li* of thorny clumps, not a single person appears.

As a process, literature often serves as a means of systematically organizing and assigning meaning to a single event or set of events that are confronting the writer. Yüan Hao-wen does this by creating a historical context and tapping one of the ritual myths of Chinese culture, the alternation of the world between the binary poles of chaos and order. By making concurrent references to the age of the sage-kings, the Six Dynasties, and the end of the Northern Sung, Yüan Hao-wen telescopes history across time and reasserts the role of political disorder in the epicycle of dynastic decline. But by introducing the imagery of dissolution and exodus, he suggests a return to a precivilized state as well.

The myth of chaos is itself cyclical. The *ts'ang-hai*, or "chilly seas," of Yüan Hao-wen's first "Snowy Perfume" poem certainly alludes to the well-known trope from the *Lieh-hsien chuan*, a metaphor for recurrent periods of long-enduring transformations (*LHC* 3.25b). This is probably an echo (albeit in a different key) of the Mencian idea, cited above, of periods of chaos and disorder followed and preceded by periods of moral and cultural rebirth: the great era of political stability initiated by King Wu, King Wen, and the Duke of Chou, for example, an era modeled on the sage-kings' administrations, was followed by an era of disorder that led Confucius to write the *Spring and Autumn Annals*. One of the points of the *Mencius* passage, which is repeated in the preface to the *Ku-liang chuan*, is that during such periods of chaos the responsibility to nourish, perpetuate, and maintain cultural traditions devolves upon the individual.

On the one hand, this stressed importance of the role of the individual has nourished the concept of the Confucian eremite, the recluse who works at moral refinement until called upon to serve the social weal. On the other hand, it has also led to active and aggressive attempts to preserve historical sources. As noted above, the sage-kings ushered in writing—and with it, literature, especially the literature of history, the repository of the civilization's cultural and moral values. And it was these classics that Confucius was moved to edit, thereby providing a body of materials that would lead to a canonical, unambiguous understanding of the virtues of correct behavior.

Yüan Hao-wen, in recognition of the fact that imagination entails responsibility, was moved to preserve the resources of his own age. The chaos he imagined built a symbolic world of dissolution even while it established a context for his actions as a historian. As early as May 1233—approximately the same time he wrote the "Random Chants at the Kiosk of Snowy Perfume"—Yüan sent Yeh-lü Ch'u-ts'ai a letter in which he pleaded for the safety and sought the employment of fifty-four eminent members of the Chin literati. In curious contrast to his poetry of exodus, which evinces a certain resignation to the dispersal of Chinese civilization, he wrote:

> Although these [fifty-four] men are various and uneven in their enterprise of learning as well as in their actions and conduct, on the whole they are in every case the budding [talents] of Heaven's citizens who will prove of use to the world. In the past hundred years the instruction and education [of the literati], their study and practice, have been of the highest sort, yet those who have been able to come to a successful completion are not many—since the start of "loss and disorder" [i.e., 1211], [the count] has stopped at only thirty or forty men. Now, to bring them to birth is hard, to bring them to completion even harder. Indeed, that they should not be slain by weapons, not be slain by cold and hunger, but that the creator of all things should help them along and give them to a dynasty that will unite anew [all under Heaven]—is it not, most likely, that it was intended? Or was it unintended?
>
> I sincerely hope that through your efforts they can be brought to escape the shame of doing others' bidding, can halt their employment in fleeing and running, can be gathered and nourished and dispersed [throughout North China, there] to dwell. Their provisioning in the halls of study need not be exhaustive or complete. Congee is sufficient to make the mouth sticky, cotton floss is enough to cover the body—this is no great expenditure. This being so, to bestow [such favors] on the various households [of these men] firmly makes them already [one's own] flesh and bone. On another day, when you seek men to control affairs in a hundred ways, then you will be able to take them left and right at your picking. Ceremonial vest and cap, ritual and music, the hawser and rope [i.e., great principles] of government, literary splendor—all exist completely in this.... If we postulate that they will not be used by the world, then these various men will be able to establish their words and integrity—they cannot be left to vanish unseen, to remain silent and rot together with the grasses and trees.[11]

Yüan's own attentions were turned to the preservation and compilation of historical sources and other writings that he considered part of the cultural repository. The zealousness of his activities is described in a funerary inscription written by his disciple Hao Ching:

> When Pien-liang was lost, the elders [of the Chin] were all finished and the master himself became the ancestrally venerated craftsman of the whole age. As the elder uncle of writing, he trod alone for thirty years. Those who would create inscriptions for men of meritorious achievement and virtue hastened to his door. There were a hundred or more of those [funerary inscriptions] that had precedents, that had proper format, that had purport, and that had interest.
>
> He wrote *A Study of Tu [Fu's] Poetry* [*Tu-shih hsüeh*], *The Classical Elegance of [Su] Tung-p'o's Poetry* [*Tung-p'o shih ya*], *The Embroidered Loom* [*Chin-chi*], *Self-Admonitions in Prose and Poetry* [*Shih-wen tzu-ching*], and other collected writings to point out [the proper direction to follow] and to bestow [teachings] on those who would learn. When Our Way was in ruin, when literary gleanings were dim and obscure, the master alone was capable of shaking and encouraging [writing and the Way], raising its splendor to the heavens, [thus] enabling students to have something they might return to and look up to, to recognize the uprightness of prose and poetry, to pass along its life's pulse undiminished and unbroken. His meritorious achievements in this world were great indeed.
>
> Whenever it was a matter of assuming the responsibility of writing—taking into account the fact that when the clan of the Golden Springs possessed the world, canons and statutes, their rules and regulations nearly achieved the status of those of Han and T'ang; and that when a state is lost, its history arises—he took it upon himself. And just at that time, since the veritable records of the state history were at the bureau offices of the noble Chang [Jou], myriarch of the Shun-t'ien circuit, he spoke of it to Chang and had him make it known by memorial that he desired to write a narrative history. The memorial was accepted, and he had just begun to clear a room [to work in] when he was stopped by someone.
>
> The master then said, "It is not possible to have the comeliness of a whole age vanish and go unheard." And so, he compiled the *Collection of the Central Plain* [*Chung-chou chi*] in a hundred or more *chüan*, and he also wrote *A Record of the Words and Deeds of the Rulers and Ministers of the Golden Springs* [*Chin-yüan chün-ch'en yen-hsing lu*].
>
> Back and forth across the four quadrants he plucked and culled whatever had been omitted or neglected. Whenever he found some-

thing, he would always make a personal record in meticulous characters on inch-wide paper. Even when deeply drunk, he never forgot [the task he had set himself].

At this point he randomly recorded the affairs of the modern age in [writings totaling] over a million characters, had the [pages] tightly bound, and stored them away. They filled a room of several pillars, which he called the Kiosk of History from the Fringelands [Yeh-shih-t'ing]. He died before attacking the documents. (LCC 35.1a–6b)

According to Yüan Hao-wen's preface to his *Record of the Southern Capped* (*Nan-kuan lu*), he had indeed asked that a copy of the veritable records be sent on eastern campaign with the last emperor:

When the capital was surrounded, I was cabinet overseer for the Eastern Bureau. Learning that a naval force was about to campaign to the east, I spoke to the various ministers, requesting that one copy of the state history be written out in tiny characters and packed on a single horse that would follow the imperial entourage [wherever it went].

Even though the ministers concurred, [the plan] was never put into effect. During Ts'ui's revolt all veritable records of the successive reigns were seized by the marshal of Man-ch'eng [i.e., Chang Jou]. Many indeed were the affairs of the illustrious rulers and stalwart ministers that were worthy of being passed on to later generations. In no more than twenty or thirty years, men of the world would no longer know of them. There was nothing to be done about those things I knew nothing of—but could I bear to cast aside those I knew of without recording them? I have therefore attached to this the random affairs of the former court, consolidated them, made them one, and named them *Record of the Southern Capped*. (CCJC 37.6a)

These texts and several others, including Yüan's own poems, his preface to the *Collection of the Central Plain* (CCC, preface), and many of his funerary inscriptions, attest to Yüan Hao-wen's zealousness in preserving historical documents and materials, and thereby the best of the classical tradition. There may have been other factors involved: an attempt to clear his name of complicity in the Ts'ui Li affair, for instance. That is, his historiographical work may have been intended as conspicuous testimony that his actions during Ts'ui's coup (when he helped compose an inscription for a commemorative stele honoring Ts'ui Li) stemmed only from a concern with the archival materials that would allow the survival of the dynasty in the cultural tradition and collective memory, if not in actual fact (Hsü K'un 1974, 73–76).

But there can be little doubt that in Yüan Hao-wen's eyes his major purpose was the preservation of Chinese culture in general and, once the threat of total extinction was over, the preservation of the Confucian Way in particular. On the last day of the year in which Ai-tsung died (1234), on the eve of lunar New Year, Yüan wrote a poem, "Exorcism Night, *Chia-wu* Year," the last two couplets of which read:

Spiritual merit and sagely virtue—three thousand tablets;
Ta-ting and Ming-ch'ang [reigns]—five decades.
The sexagenary cycle has revolved twice, today it has come to an end;
Vainly I take my aging tears and sprinkle them in the Heavens of Wu.

His lament—tears shed for Ai-tsung's grave in the South, for the short-lived dynasty that came to its end after a bare 120 years—is also praise for the divine merit of the founders of the dynasty, for the history of sagely (i.e., Confucian) virtue that filled three thousand wooden tablets, for the fifty years of the golden age of the Chin dynasty, the reigns of Shih-tsung and Chang-tsung, often likened in historical sources to the reigns of Yao and Shun as eras of virtue and harmony (Yao Ts'ung-wu 1959; *CCWC* 32.11a). In 1247, Yüan Hao-wen argued together with Chang Te-hui at the court of Khubilai in Karakorum against the proposition that "the Liao was destroyed because of Buddhism and the Chin was lost because of Confucianism" (Sontag 1978, 37).[12] And while he himself never served in the government of the Mongols, his letter to Yeh-lü Ch'u-ts'ai and his trip to Karakorum clearly demonstrate his interest in persuading his conquerors to adopt the Confucian Way.

Although Yüan Hao-wen was stopped from working on the veritable records of the Chin, he pursued his studies on his own; his unofficial history of the fall of the Chin, *A Random Chronicle of the Year 1232–33* (*Jen-ch'en tsa-pien*), formed the basis for much of the standard *Chin History* and accounts for the traditional stature of the history as the best of those compiled under the Mongol reign (Chan Hok-lam 1970 and 1981). His ardor never diminished; as his protégé's account makes clear, he ended his life in pursuit of historical sources. Yüan took upon himself the status of "official of wild grain" (*pai-kuan*)— a historian who draws his materials from the "alleys and lanes" where common folk tell tales and recount events. As he wrote himself in his "personal postface" to the *Collection of the Central Plain*,

> In normal times, what need would there have been for an "official of wild grain"?
> Since the disorder, the brush of history has been burned and tattered.
> Bequeathed manuscripts from a hundred years—Heaven has let them exist—
> Clutching them in my arms, I wipe away the tears and look toward empty mountains.
>
> (*YISCC* 13.611)

There can be little doubt that Yüan Hao-wen's sense of mission as a historian was partly a product of his poetry. Only an imagination that could create such a world of chaos and disorder could create as well the concomitant responsibility of archivist and scribe. He was a failure in many respects: he failed the *chin-shih* examinations three times; he was accused at least twice of factionalism; he held minor and undistinguished posts until elevated by Ts'ui Li. His poetry, as much as it envisioned the death of a culture, also offered Yüan Hao-wen the opportunity to redeem a life he saw primarily as a failure, and it created a place for him as successor to a lineage of protectors of culture that stretched back to Confucius.

We can view poetry in many ways. It may be a universal expression of emotion or aspiration, a piece for personal contemplation, a fossilized abstraction of one person's imagination and experience. But it is always a human document intimately related to and subsumed under the experiences of life. In the case of Yüan Hao-wen's poems of lamentation, poetry was an extension of his imagination and self-awareness into a created world of cultural dissolution.

That this world to some extent existed is verified in history—the Mongols were the most brutal conquerors known until the advent of this century. But in Yüan Hao-wen's verse that world was also partly imagined, partly created. His concurrent references to other historical and prehistorical periods of chaos substantiated the principle of repeating cycles of order and disorder and recalled a felt need to preserve culture in the nadir of civilized life. In this sense, then, as a personal document his poetry was not so much a description of the death of the Chin as it was a creation of context for self-expression through cultural preservation. His desire to protect culture in its written form found its roots in the legend of Confucius and was very much a corollary to the ideal Confucian model of self-cultivation as the source of all order and harmony. But in his very zealousness we are also led to conclude that other, self-interested factors might have figured in—his repeated failures in the examinations, his retreat from official life under censure for factionalism, his impotence in governmental circles, and his desire to clear his name of complicity in the Ts'ui Li affair. And while his contributions to history and poetry now shine as brilliant cultural and literary artifacts, they also provided him a means to sustain his own life during a period of darkness. They offered a method by which to transcend the world of chaos and failure in a synthesis of ritual and private symbols that led at once to the preservation of Chin culture and the position of redeemer, a position that lent his own life esteem and worth.

Notes

1. This essay is a revised version of an article first published in the *Journal of the American Oriental Society* (West 1986). In my revisions I have availed myself of the helpful finding list for Yüan Hao-wen's poetry compiled by J. T. Wixted (1981), whose other works on Yüan Hao-wen (esp. 1982) are the fullest in English to date.

2. Called "Green" because it originally consisted of a compound of mock-halls constructed of green curtains and hangings in which the emperor warmed himself during the twelfth-month sacrifices. See *TCM* 10.3b and *SSYT* 5.2a.

3. In earlier texts, the word *p'ai* was used interchangeably with and often glossed as *ch'ang*, "singer," which is obviously etymologically related to *ch'ang*, "to sing" (the later *ch'ang** is a gender-specific derivative); see Wang Li 1982, 362. These court singers specialized in music with lyrics that were either pointed satire or farce. The genre was known by several names: *p'ai-ko* (a term found under the category "Musical Lyrics for Dance Tunes" [*wu-ch'ü ko-tz'u*] in the Sung compendium of *yüeh-fu* lyrics, *Yüeh-fu shih-chi*), *p'ai-hsieh-t'i*, and *p'ai-yu-t'i*. Kuo Mao-ch'ien (1978, 3:219–20) characterizes the music and its performance as comic and cites sources from the earliest texts to the *Sui shu* that describe *p'ai-ko* as music sung by dancers who were led by dwarves, court entertainers noted for their sharp tongues. This does not vary much from the description in the *T'ai-ho cheng-yin p'u*, Chu Ch'üan's musical formulary from the fifteenth century, in which Chu defines *p'ai-ko* as "hyperbolic metaphor, wanton and excoriating" (*THCY* 3:13). T'ao Tsung-i's recension of Yang Huan's account includes a set of nineteen "palace poems," which Shih Kuo-ch'i, the Ch'ing critic of Yüan Hao-wen's verse, points out are clearly written by a consort of the Chin emperor (see *YISCC* 12.561). I think there is enough similarity between Yüan's cycle of fifteen poems and the palace cycle of nineteen to warrant further investigation.

4. In a postscript to a poem Yüan remarks: "In the coup d'état during the first month of the *kuei-ssu* year there were those in the recalcitrant faction

who wanted to harm me. I relied on Li Chung-hua to rescue me and set me free." See Hsü K'un 1974, 58, 69.

5. Cf. Wixted 1982, 174. The "Chin" in this poem is, of course, the Six Dynasties state of that name.

6. See also 3:369 (dated K'ai-pao 9/4) and 367 (dated K'ai-pao 9/3); and *SHY ts'e* 187, *fang-yü* 1.2a.

7. See also Hao Ching's "Ch'ing-ch'eng hsing" (*LCC* 11.7b–8b).

8. See also West 1974.

9. The "prisoner" is the subject of a passage in the *Tso chuan*, Ch'eng-kung 9 (*TC* 12.27b–28a). The marquis of Chin first identified the prisoner as a native of Ch'u by the cap he wore. The prisoner described himself as a court entertainer by virtue of birth. An advisor to the marquis, however, after hearing an account of his lord's interrogation of the man, recognized the prisoner as a man of humanity, loyalty, conscentiousness, and quick-witttedness—a superior man—and he counseled the marquis to free him immediately and return him to Ch'u. The point here is that Yüan not only is a prisoner of the Mongols, but also has the moral worth to be employed as an advisor or official.

10. Mulberries and catalpa were planted by people for the benefit of their children and grandchildren.

11. Relying on the variorum recension of the text in Yao Ts'ung-wu 1970.

12. See also Yao Ts'ung-wu 1962.

Glossary

A-che	阿者
A-ku-nai	阿古廼
A-ku-ta	阿骨打
A-ma	阿馬
A-shu	阿疏
"Ai Chiang-nan fu"	哀江南賦
Ai-tsung	哀宗
An Lu-shan	安祿山
"Ao-t'un Liang-pi chien-yin pei"	奧屯良弼餞飲碑
Ch'a-ch'a	茶茶
chan-pi	戰筆
Chan-t'an-Fo	栴檀佛
Ch'an (Zen)	禪
Ch'an-men K'ung-hsüeh	禪門孔學
ch'an-ta	纏達
Chang Chi	張籍
Chang Chien	張建
Chang Chiu-ch'eng	張九成
Chang-ch'iu	章邱
Chang Chü	張琚
Chang Chüeh	張殼
Chang Chung-yen	張中彥
Chang Fei	張飛
Chang Hao	張浩
Chang Heng	張珩
Chang Hsiao-ch'un	張孝純
Chang Hsin-chen	張信真
Chang Hsing-chien	張行簡
Chang-huai	章懷
Chang Hui	張暉
Chang I-yün	張怡雲
Chang Jou	張柔
Chang Ku-ying (Chung-chieh)	張轂英 (仲杰)
Chang Kuei	張珪
Chang Kung	張恭

Chang Lei	張耒
Chang Pang-hsien	張邦憲
Chang Pang-yen	張邦彥
Chang Seng-yu	張僧繇
Chang Shang-ying	張商英
Chang Shih	張栻
Chang Ta-chieh	張大節
Chang Tao-ling	張道陵
Chang-te	彰德
Chang Te-hui	張德輝
Chang Tsai	張載
Chang Tse-tuan	張澤端
Chang-tsung	章宗
Chang Wan-kung	張萬公
Chang Yü (d. ca. 218)	張裕
Chang Yü (late 12th–early 13th cent.)	張瑀
ch'ang ("singer")	倡
ch'ang* ("singing girl")	娼
ch'ang ("to sing")	唱
Ch'ang-o	嫦娥
Ch'ang-tzu	長子
ch'ang-wu	常無
ch'ang-yu	常有
Chao	趙
chao-an	招安
Chao-ch'eng Chin-tsang	趙城金藏
Chao Feng	趙渢
Chao Fu	趙孛
Chao-hsien	趙縣
Chao I	趙翼
Chao K'uang-yin	趙匡胤
Chao Lin	趙霖
Chao-ling	昭陵
Chao Ling-chih	趙令畤
Chao Meng-fu	趙孟頫
Chao Ping-wen (Hsien-hsien)	趙秉文 (閑閑)
Chao Po-chü	趙伯駒
Chao Ssu-wen	趙思文
Chao-yang	昭陽
chao-ying	照應
Ch'ao Chiung	晁迥
Ch'ao Pu-chih	晁補之

che	柘
Che-chiang t'ung-chih	浙江通志
Chen-i	貞懿
Chen-i*	貞儀
Chen-kuan cheng-yao	貞觀政要
chen-k'ung	真空
Chen Ta-tao	真大道
Chen-ting	真定
Chen-tsung	真宗
Chen-yu	貞祐
Ch'en	陳
Ch'en I-jen	陳以仁
Ch'en Liang	陳亮
Ch'en Lin	陳琳
Ch'en Shan	陳善
Ch'en Shih-cheng	陳師正
cheng	正
Cheng Heng	鄭恆
Cheng-ho	政和
Cheng Hsüan	鄭玄
Cheng-i	正一
Cheng-lung	正隆
Cheng-ta	正大
Cheng-t'ung Tao-tsang	正統道藏
ch'eng	誠
Ch'eng-Chu	程朱
Ch'eng Hao	程顥
ch'eng-hsiang	丞相
Ch'eng-Hua	承華
Ch'eng I	程頤
Chi (family)	姬
Chi (place-name)	薊
Chi-hsien	汲縣
Chi-jang t'u	擊壤圖
chi-lu chieh	寄祿階
Chi-shan	稷山
Chi-tse	雞澤
Chi-yang	濟陽
ch'i	氣
Ch'i	齊
ch'i-chih chih hsing	氣質之性
Ch'i-hsia	棲霞

ch'i-lin	麒麟
Ch'i-tan (Khitan)	契丹
Ch'i-weng	七翁
ch'i-yen lü-shi	七言律詩
Ch'i-yin	棲隱
Chia	郟
Chia I (200–168 B.C.)	賈誼
Chia I (d. 1222)	賈益
Chia K'uei	賈葵
Chia Tao	賈島
"Chia-wu ch'u-yeh"	甲午除夜
Chiang-chou	絳州
Chiang-hsia	江下
Chiang Kuo-ch'i	姜國器
Chiang Yen	江淹
chiao (sacrifice)	醮
chiao ("teaching")	教
Chiao-heng	教亨
chiao-shou	教授
ch'iao-chün	峭峻
Ch'iao K'uei-ch'eng	喬簣成
chieh-chen	節鎮
chieh-fen ko	解紛歌
Chieh-hsiu	介休
chieh-tu shih	詳度使
chien	建
chien-hu	監戶
Chien-lung	建隆
chien-tang kuan	監當官
ch'ien-hu	千戶
Ch'ien-ling	乾陵
Ch'ien-lung	乾隆
chih-ch'ang	直長
chih-chih ko-wu	致知格物
Chih-chiu	智究
chih-hou	祇候
chih hsüeh-shih	直學士
chih-ying ssu	祇應司
chin	金
Chin-ch'eng	晉城
Chin-chi	錦機
Chin-chou	錦州

Chin-ling	金陵
chin-shih	進士
chin-shih chü	近侍局
"Chin-shih t'i-ming chi"	進士題名記
Chin wu tsung yeh	晉吾宗也
Chin-yüan	金源
Chin-yüan chün-ch'en yen-hsing lu	金源君臣言行錄
ch'in-hsüan	琴絃
Ch'in Kou	秦覯
Ch'in Kuan	秦觀
Ch'in Kuei	秦檜
Ch'in-tsung	欽宗
ching ("semen")	精
ching ("seriousness")	敬
Ching	涇
Ching-chao	京兆
Ching-chou	荊州
ching-i	經義
Ching-ju	淨如
Ching-ling	景靈
Ching-shih t'ung-yen	警世通言
"Ching-ti yin yin-p'ing"	井底引銀缾
Ching-yen	精嚴
ch'ing	頃
Ch'ing-an	清安
Ch'ing-ch'eng	青城
"Ch'ing-ch'eng hsing"	青城行
Ch'ing-ching ching	清淨經
Ch'ing-ho	清河
Ch'ing-li	慶曆
Ch'ing-lung	青龍
Ch'ing-ming	清明
Ch'ing-ming shang-ho t'u	清明上河圖
ch'ing ssu ch'ih	情似癡
Chiu-tsung	九嵕
Ch'iu Ch'u-chi (Ch'ang-ch'un)	丘處機(長春)
Ch'iu Chün	邱濬
Ch'iu Hsing-kung	丘行恭
Ch'iu Hu	秋胡
"Ch'iu-yeh"	秋夜
Cho Wen-chün	卓文君
Chou Ang (Te-ch'ing)	周昂(德卿)

Glossary

Chou Ssu-ming	周嗣明
Chou Tun-i	周敦頤
Chou Yü	周瑜
Chu Hsi	朱熹
Chu-ko Liang	諸葛亮
Chu-ko Tan	諸葛誕
chu-kung-tiao	諸宮調
Chu Tun-ju	朱敦儒
chü-tzu	舉子
chü-tzu pei	舉子輩
Ch'u Ch'eng-liang	褚承亮
Ch'u-ch'ing	儲慶
Ch'u-yüan	楚圓
ch'ü	曲
Ch'ü-fu	曲阜
ch'ü-hua	曲話
chuan-t'a	轉踏
chüan	卷
ch'uan-ch'i	傳奇
ch'üan	權
Ch'üan-chen	全真
Ch'üan-chen ch'i-tzu	全真七子
ch'üan-nung shih ssu	勸農使司
Ch'üan Tsu-wang	全祖望
Chuang-chia pu-shih kou-lan	莊家不識构闌
Chuang Chou	莊周
Chuang-tzu	莊子
chuang-yüan	狀元
ch'uang-	㓷、創
ch'uang-chien	創建
chüeh-chü	絕句
Ch'ui-ch'ing	垂情
chün	軍
chung	中
Chung-ching	中京
Chung-hua Ta-tsang-ching	中華大藏經
Chung-yung	中庸
Ch'ung-fu	崇福
"Ch'ung-hsiu Mien-pi-an chi"	重修面壁庵記
ch'ung-tan	沖淡
Ch'ung-yang li-chiao shih-wu lun	重陽立教十五論
Duke of Chou	周公

Erh-miao chi	二妙集
erh-shui hu	二稅戶
Fa-lü	法律
Fa-pao	法寶
Fa-pen	法本
Fa-ts'ung	法聰
Fa-t'ung	法通
Fa-yen	法言
fan	番
Fan-chih	繁峙
Fan Chung-yen	范仲淹
Fang-shan	房山
fang-yü chou	防禦州
Fei-hsiang	肥鄉
Fei-shui	淝水
fei-tung	飛動
Fen	汾
Feng Ch'en	馮辰
feng-liu	風流
Feng Meng-lung	馮夢龍
Feng Pi	馮璧
feng-shui	風水
Feng Tao-chen	馮道真
feng-ya	風雅
Fo-chien Hui-ch'in	佛鑒慧勤
Fo-hsüeh wei t'i, Ju-hsüeh wei yung	佛學為體，儒學為用
Fo-kuo K'o-ch'in	佛果克勤
Fo-yen Ch'ing-yüan	佛眼清遠
fu ("prefecture")	府
fu ("rhyme-prose")	賦
Fu Ch'i	傅起
Fu Chien	符堅
Fu-ch'un-t'ang	富春堂
fu-lu	符籙
Fu-shan	福山
fu-shih	府試
Fu-yen	福嚴
Fu-yü	福裕
Hai-chou	海州
Hai-hui	海慧
Hai-ling	海陵
Han (pass)	函

Glossary

Han (river)	漢
Han Ch'i-hsien	韓企先
Han Fang	韓昉
Han Hsi-fu	韓希甫
Han I	韓翊
Han-lin	翰林
Han-p'u	函普
Han Shao-yeh	韓紹曄
Han T'o-chou	韓佗冑
Han Yü (Ch'ang-li)	韓愈(昌黎)
hao	豪
Hao Ching	郝經
"Hao-li"	蒿里
Hao Ta-t'ung (Kuang-ning)	郝大通(廣寧)
Heng-hai	橫海
ho	和
Ho Ch'eng	何澄
Ho-chin	河津
Ho-chung-fu	河中府
Ho-li-po	劾里鉢
Hou Chih	侯摯
Hou Yüan-hsien	侯元仙
Hsi-hsia	西夏
Hsi-hsiang-chi chu-kung-tiao	西廂記諸宮調
Hsi-shih	西施
Hsi-tsung	熙宗
hsi-wen	戲文
Hsi-yu chi	西遊記
Hsiang-ling	襄陵
Hsiang-shan	香山
Hsiang-yang	襄陽
Hsiang Yü	項羽
Hsiao Chih-ch'ung	蕭志沖
Hsiao-ching	孝經
Hsiao Fu-tao	蕭輔道
Hsiao Pao-chen	蕭抱珍
Hsiao-shen	蕭愼
"Hsiao-shuo k'ai-p'i"	小說開闢
Hsiao-wen-ti	孝文帝
Hsieh-li-hu	謝里忽
Hsieh Liang-tso	謝良佐
Hsieh Ling-yün	謝靈運

Hsien	獻
hsien-chüeh	顯訣
Hsien-pei	鮮卑
Hsien-ti	獻帝
Hsien-tsung (1146–85)	顯宗
Hsien-tsung (r. 1251–59)	憲宗
Hsien-yang	咸陽
hsin	心
Hsin	忻
hsin-chien	新建
hsin-hsüeh	心學
Hsin-lun	新論
hsin-shu	心術
hsin yüeh-fu	新樂府
hsing	性
Hsing-chung	興中
hsing-erh-hsia	形而下
hsing-erh-shang	形而上
Hsing-hsiu (Wan-sung-lao-jen)	行秀 (萬松老人)
hsing-li hsüeh	性理學
hsing-ming	性命
hsing-t'ai	行台
hsing tao	行道
Hsiu-chen	修真
hsiu tao	修道
hsiu-ts'ai	秀才
Hsiung-nu	匈奴
Hsü Heng	許衡
"Hsü hsiao-niang-ko shih-shou"	續小娘歌十首
Hsü Tao-chen	許道真
Hsü Wei	徐璧
Hsü Yao-tso	許堯佐
Hsü Yu-jen	許有壬
Hsüan-chen	玄真
Hsüan-ho	宣和
Hsüan-hsiao	宣孝
hsüan-hui yüan	宣徽院
Hsüan-tsung (r. 712–56)	玄宗
Hsüan-tsung (r. 1213–24)	宣宗
hsüeh	學
hsüeh-sheng	學生
hsüeh-t'ien	學田

Glossary 313

Hsün Hsi	荀息
Hsün-tzu	荀子
Hsün Yü	荀彧
Hu Li	胡礪
hu-lu	忽魯
Hu Tzu	胡仔
Hu Ying-lin	胡應麟
Hu Yüan	胡瑗
"Hua chi"	畫記
Hua-ch'ing	華清
hua-hsüeh	畫學
hua-pen	話本
Hua-yen	華嚴
Hua-yen ching	華嚴經
hua-yüan	畫院
Huai	淮
Huai-yang	淮陽
"Huai-yu"	淮右
Huan-lang	歡郎
Huan-men tzu-ti ts'o-li-shen	宦門子弟錯立身
Huan-she	桓赦
Huan T'an	桓譚
Huang Ch'ao	黃巢
Huang-chi shu	皇極書
Huang-fu Shih	皇甫湜
Huang-lung	黃龍
Huang T'ing-chien	黃庭堅
Huang Yeh	黃謁
Hui-chi	惠寂
Hui-chüeh	慧覺
Hui-ning-fu	會寧府
Hui-tsung	徽宗
Hun-yüan	混元
Hung Ch'eng-ch'ou	洪承疇
Hung-fa tsang	弘法藏
Hung Hao	洪皓
Hung-hsiang	弘相
Hung Mai	洪邁
Hung-niang	紅娘
hung-tz'u k'o	宏詞科
Huo-chou	霍州
Huo-lang t'u	貨郎圖

i ("art")	藝
i (Buddhist societies)	邑
i ("intent")	意
i ("uprightness," "integrity")	義
I	顗
I ching	易經
I-chou	宜州
I-hsien	義縣
i-hsüeh	藝學
I-la Lü	移刺履
i-li hsüeh	義理學
I-t'un	邑屯
I-yang	宜陽
I Yin	伊尹
Jen-ch'en tsa-pien	壬辰雜編
jen-ch'ing	人情
Jen Hsün	任詢
jen-i	仁義
Jen-tsung	仁宗
jen-yü	人欲
jou-tao	柔道
Ju	儒
ju ch'i wei jen	如其為人
Juan Chi	阮籍
Jung-chai sui-pi	容齋隨筆
"Kai-chien t'i-ming pei"	改建題名碑
K'ai-pao	開寶
kami	神
Kan-ch'üan	甘泉
K'ang-ch'an	糠禪
kao	高
Kao Ch'ung	高沖
Kao K'o-chiu	高可久
Kao Lin	高霖
Kao-p'ing	高平
Kao Shih-t'an	高士談
Kao-tsu	高祖
Kao-tsung	高宗
Kao-yang	高陽
Ken-yüeh	艮嶽
ko-wu	格物
k'o te erh chih	可得而知

Glossary

Koryo	高麗
Ku-chin hsiao-shuo	古今小說
ku-hsüeh	古學
ku-jen	古人
Ku K'ai-chih	顧愷之
ku-tzu-tz'u	鼓子詞
ku-wen	古文
Kuan-chung	關中
Kuan Chung	管仲
Kuan Han-ch'ing	關漢卿
kuan-hu	官戶
Kuan-yin	觀音
Kuan Yü	關羽
Kuang-en	廣恩
Kuang-ling	廣陵
Kuang-wu	光武
"Kuei-ssu ssu-yüeh er-shih-chiu-jih ch'u ching"	癸巳四月二十九日出京
"Kuei-ssu wu-yüeh san-jih pei-tu san-shou"	癸巳五月三日北渡三首
Kuei-te	歸德
K'uei-wen-ko	奎文閣
kung-chi chien	宮籍堅
Kung-chih-ch'i	宮之奇
kung-wei chü	宮闈局
Kung-yang	公羊
k'ung	空
K'ung Yüan-ts'o	孔元措
Kuo	虢
Kuo-chou	虢州
Kuo Hsi	郭熙
kuo-hsiang	國相
kuo-shih	國師
Kuo Ssu	郭思
kuo-tzu chien	國子堅
kuo-tzu hsüeh	國子學
kuo-tzu t'ai-hsüeh	國子太學
Kuo Wei	郭威
Kuo Yen-wei	郭彥威
Lao Tan	老聃
Lao-tzu	老子
Lao-tzu	老子
Le-ch'ang	樂昌
Lei-feng	雷風

Lei Yüan (Hsi-yen)	雷淵 (希顔)
li ("clerks")	吏
li (linear measure)	里
li ("principle," "structure")	理
li ("profit," "utility")	利
li ("rites," "ceremonies")	禮
Li Ch'ang-yüan	李長源
Li Ch'eng	李成
Li Chih-fu	李直夫
Li Ch'in-shu	李欽叔
Li Ching (T'ien-ying)	李經 (天英)
Li Ch'iung	酈瓊
Li Chün-min	李俊民
Li Ch'un-fu (Chih-ch'un, P'ing-shan)	李純甫(之純、屏山)
Li Chung-lüeh	李仲略
Li Han	李翰
Li Ho	李賀
Li Hsi-an	李熙安
Li Hsi-ch'eng	酈希城
Li Hsien-ch'eng	李獻誠
Li Hsien-fu	李獻甫
"Li-hun chi"	離魂記
Li Hung-hsin	李洪信
Li Hung-i	李洪義
Li Jih-hua	李日華
Li Kung-lin	李公麟
Li Po (T'ai-po)	李白(太白)
Li San-niang	李三娘
"Li sao"	離騷
Li Shan	李山
Li Shen	李紳
Li Sung	李松
Li Tao-ch'un	李道純
Li Yen	李晏
Li Yü	李煜
li-yüeh	禮樂
liang hsin liang neng	良心良能
Liang Su	梁肅
Liao-ch'eng	聊城
Liao-chou	遼州
Liao-liao-chü-shih	了了居士
Liao-yang	遼陽

Glossary

Lieh-tzu	列子
lien	廉
Lin-an	臨安
Lin Chao-en	林兆恩
Lin-chi	臨濟
Lin-ch'üan kao-chih	林泉高致
Lin-i	臨沂
Lin-t'ung	臨潼
ling	令
Ling-ch'üan	靈泉
Ling-pao	靈寶
Ling-yen	靈巖
Ling-yüan	淩源
Liu An-shih	劉安世
Liu Cheng	劉整
Liu Chi	劉汲
Liu Ch'i	劉祁
Liu Chih	劉摯
Liu Chih-yüan	劉智遠
Liu Chih-yüan chu-kung-tiao	劉智遠諸宮調
Liu Chih-yüan pai-t'u chi	劉智遠白兔記
Liu Ch'u-hsüan (Ch'ang-sheng)	劉處玄(長生)
Liu Hsiang	劉向
Liu Hsien-hsien	劉閧閧
Liu K'ai	柳開
Liu Kuan-tao	劉貫道
Liu Kuang-ch'ien	劉光謙
Liu Kung-ch'üan	柳公權
Liu Pei	劉備
"Liu-shih chuan"	柳氏傳
Liu-shih-chung ch'ü	六十種曲
liu-shou	留守
Liu T'ang-ch'ing	劉唐卿
Liu Te-jen	劉德仁
Liu Tsung-yüan	柳宗元
Liu Ts'ung-i	劉從益
Liu Yü	劉豫
Liu Yü-hsi	劉禹錫
Liu Yüan	劉元
Lo-p'u	洛浦
Lo Yeh	羅燁
lu	路

Lu-lung	盧龍
Lü	呂
lü-fu	律賦
Lü Pu	呂布
Lü-shan	閭山
Lü Tsu-ch'ien	呂祖謙
Lü-tsung	律宗
Lü Wen-huan	呂文煥
Lü Wen-te	呂文德
lüeh	略
lun-hui	輪迴
Lun-yü	論語
Lung-kung	龍宮
Lung-men	龍門
Lung-te-kung	龍德宮
Ma Chih-chi	麻知幾
Ma Chiu-ch'ou	麻九疇
Ma Ho-chih	馬和之
Ma T'ien-lai (Yün-chang, Yüan-chang)	馬天來(雲章、元章)
Ma Yu	馬祐
Ma Yü (Tan-yang)	馬鈺(丹陽)
Ma Yün-ch'ing	馬雲卿
Ma Yün-han	馬雲漢
Man-ch'eng	滿城
Mao Hsi-ts'ung	毛希琮
Mao Hui	毛麾
Mao P'ang	毛滂
Mao-shan	茅山
Meng	孟
meng-an	猛安
Meng Ch'i	孟啓
Meng Chiao	孟郊
Meng-chin	孟津
Meng Huo	孟獲
"Meng-kuei"	夢歸
mi-feng	彌縫
Mi Fu	米芾
Mi-kuo	密國
mi-shu chien	祕書監
Mi Yu-jen	米友仁
Miao	苗
miao-hsüeh	廟學

miao-t'i	妙體
miao-yu	妙有
Ming-ch'ang	明昌
ming-chiao	名教
ming-li chih wen	名理之文
mou	畝
mou-k'o	謀克
Mu Hsiu	穆修
Na-lin	納鄰
"Nan-hsing ch'ien-chi hsü"	南行前集序
Nan-kuan lu	南冠錄
nan-mien	南面
nao	猱
nei-shih chü	內侍局
nei-shih sheng	內侍省
nei-tan	內丹
niu-yüan-tzu	紐元子
nu-pei hu	奴婢戶
Nü-chen (Jurchen)	女真
Nü-chen kuo-tzu-hsüeh	女真國子學
Ou-yang Hsiu	歐陽修
Ou-yang Hsün	歐陽詢
Pa-hei	跋黑
pa-ho	拔和
pai-hu (po-hu)	百戶
pai-kuan	稗官
Pai-ma-chiang-chün	白馬將軍
Pai-mei-shen	白眉神
pai-miao	白描
Pai-t'u chi	白兔記
Pai-yüeh-t'ing	白月亭
Pai-yün (Po-yün)	白雲
p'ai	俳
p'ai-hsieh-t'i	俳諧體
p'ai-ko	俳歌
"P'ai-t'i: Hsüeh-hsiang-t'ing tsa-yung shih-wu-shou"	俳體雪香亭雜詠十五首
p'ai-yu-t'i	俳優體
Pan-jo hsin-ching	般若心經
Pan Ku	班固
P'an Te-ch'ung	潘德沖
P'ang Han	龐漢

P'ang Yün	龐雲
Pao	寶
Pao Chao	鮑照
Pao-chi	寶雞
pao-ching an-min	保境安民
Pao-te	保德
Pao-ti	寶坻
P'ei Hsiu	裴休
pen-ch'ü	本曲
pen-se	本色
Pen-shih-shih	本事詩
P'eng-lai	蓬萊
pi-chi	筆記
P'i-lu	毗盧
P'iao-ch'an	瓢襌
pien	變
Pien-ching	汴京
Pien-i hsing-shih hu-t'ou-p'ai	便宜行事虎頭牌
Pien-liang	汴梁
pien-wen	變文
Ping-chou	並州
p'ing-chang cheng-shih	平章政事
P'ing-chou	平州
P'ing-shui	平水
P'ing-yang	平陽
P'ing-yao	平遙
po-chi-lieh	勃極烈
Po-ch'ieh ching	薄伽經
po-chin	勃董
Po-chou (Anhwei)	亳州
Po-chou (Shantung)	博州
Po Chü-i	白居易
Po-hai	渤海
Po-lieh-han	孛烈漢
Po-lin	柏林
P'o-la-shu	頗剌淑
Pu Hsiu-hung	卜修洪
Pu-yi	溥儀
P'u-chao	普照
P'u-chiu	普救
P'u-chou	蒲州
Sa-lu-tzu	颯露紫

sai	塞
san-chiao	三教
san-chiao ho-i	三教合一
san-chiao kuei-i	三教歸一
"San-chiao sheng-hsing pei"	三教聖形碑
san-chiao t'ung-yüan	三教同源
San-hsüeh	三學
san-kuan	散官
San-kuo chih yen-i	三國志演義
san-she	三舍
San-ta	散達
San-t'ang Wang	三堂王
sang-luan shih	喪亂詩
Sang Wei-han	桑維韓
se	色
seng-cheng	僧正
seng-lu	僧錄
Sha-t'o	沙陀
Shang	商
Shang-ching	上京
shang-shu sheng	尚書省
Shang-tang	上黨
Shang Tao	商道
Shang T'ing	商挺
Shao	少
Shao-lin	少林
Shao Yung	邵雍
shen	紳
Shen-chou	紳州
shen li	神理
Sheng-an	聖安
sheng Nü-chen pu-tsu chieh-tu shih	生女真部族詳度使
shih ("commissioner")	使
shih ("literatus")	士
Shih chi	史記
shih-ch'i	士氣
Shih-ch'i tai	十七代
Shih-chia-chuang	石家庄
Shih Chieh	石介
"Shih-chieh te mo-jih"	世界的末日
shih-ching	石經
Shih Cho	史倬

shih chung	時中
shih-feng	士風
shih-hsiang	使相
Shih Hsüeh-yu	史學優
Shih Hung-chao	史弘肇
"Shih Hung-chao lung-hu chün-ch'en hui"	史弘肇龍虎君臣會
Shih I-sheng	施宜生
Shih Kuo-ch'i	施國祁
Shih-lu	石魯
Shih-shuang	石霜
Shih-tsu	世祖
Shih-tsung	世宗
Shih-wen tzu-ching	詩文自警
shou	壽
Shou	壽
Shou-chou	壽州
Shu-Han	蜀漢
Shu-hu Kao-ch'i	尤虎高琪
Shu-hu Sui (Hsüan, Shih-hsüan, Wen-po)	尤虎遂 (玹、士玄、溫伯)
shu-hua chü	書畫局
shu-hui	書會
shu-mi yüan	樞密院
shu-yüan	書院
Shuang	爽
Shuang Chien	雙漸
Shun	舜
Shun-t'ien	順天
ssu	寺
Ssu-ma Ch'ien	司馬遷
Ssu-ma Hsiang-ju	司馬相如
Ssu-ma Kuang	司馬光
Ssu-ma Yu	司馬楢
ssu-nung ssu	司農司
ssu wen, ssu tao	斯文斯道
Su-hsiao	肅蕭
Su Hsiao-ch'ing	蘇小卿
Su Hsiao-hsiao	蘇小小
Su Shih (Tung-p'o)	蘇軾 (東坡)
Su-t'o-shih-li	蘇陀室利
sui chia Chang Kuei (hua)	隨駕張珪 (畫)
Sui shu	隋書
Sui-te	綏德

Glossary

sun	猻
Sun Fei-hu	孫飛虎
Sun Fu	孫復
Sun Ming-tao	孫明道
Sun Pu-erh (Ch'ing-ching-san-jen)	孫不二(清靜散人)
Sung (mountain)	嵩
Sung (province)	宋
Sung Chiu-chia	宋九嘉
Sung-chou	宋州
"Sung Chung-hsi chien chien Ta-fang"	送仲希兼簡大方
Sung Tzu-fang	宋子方
ta	大
Ta-an	大安
Ta-chi	妲己
Ta Chin hsüan-tu pao-tsang	大金玄都寶藏
"Ta Chin te-sheng t'o-sung"	大金得勝陀頌
Ta Ch'ing-an	大清安
Ta Ch'u-ch'ing	大儲慶
Ta-fang	大房
Ta-hsing	大興
Ta-hsing-fu	大興府
ta-li ssu	大理寺
Ta-liang	大梁
Ta-tao	大道
ta-t'i	大體
Ta T'ien-ch'ang	大天長
Ta-ting	大定
Ta-tu	大都
Ta Yung-an	大永安
tai-chao	待詔
T'ai	泰
t'ai-ch'ang ssu	太常寺
T'ai-chia	太甲
T'ai-ch'ing	太清
t'ai-fu chien	太府監
T'ai-ho	泰和
"T'ai-ho t'i-ming ts'an-shih"	泰和題名殘石
t'ai-hsüeh	太學
T'ai-hu	太湖
T'ai-i	太一
T'ai-tsu	太祖
T'ai-tsung	太宗

tan	石
tan-ting	丹鼎
T'an Ch'u-tuan (T'an Yü, Ch'ang-chen)	譚處端(譚玉、長真)
t'an-hua	探花
Tang Huai-ying (Shih-chieh)	党懷英(世傑)
T'ang	湯
T'ang-chou	唐州
T'ang-ku (Tangut)	唐古
T'ang-kua	唐括
tao	道
tao-cheng	道正
Tao-hsüeh	道學
Tao-hsüeh fa-yüan	道學發源
Tao-hsün	道詢
tao-lu	道錄
tao-te	道德
Tao-te chen-ching chi-chieh	道德真經集解
Tao-te ching	道德經
tao-t'ung	道統
T'ao Yüan-ming	陶淵明
te-hsing	德行
T'e-lin	忒鄰
Teng-chou	鄧州
Teng Yen	鄧儼
t'i-chü	提舉
t'i-chü hsüeh-shih kuan	提舉學事官
T'i-hsüan ta-shih	體玄大師
t'i-tien	提點
T'iao-hsi yü-yin ts'ung-hua	苕溪漁隱叢話
T'ieh-le	鐵勒
tien-ch'ien tu tien-chien ssu	殿前都點檢司
T'ien-ch'ang	天長
T'ien Ch'üeh	田穀
T'ien-hsing	天興
T'ien-hui	天會
t'ien-li	天理
T'ien-pao i-shih chu-kung-tiao	天寶遺事諸宮調
T'ien-sheng	天聖
T'ien-shih	天師
t'ien-tao	天道
Ting-hsien	定縣
ting-li	定理

Glossary 325

T'ing-yü	廳峪
T'o-pa	拓跋
t'ou-hsia chün-chou	投(頭)下軍州
tsa-chü	雜劇
tsa-pan	雜扮
tsa-pan*	雜旺(雜班)
Ts'ai-chou	蔡州
Ts'ai Kuei	蔡珪
Ts'ai Po-chieh	蔡伯喈
Ts'ai Sung-nien	蔡松年
Ts'ai Yen (Wen-chi)	蔡琰(文姬)
ts'an-chih cheng-shih	參知政事
ts'ang-hai heng-liu	滄海橫流
ts'ang-hai heng-liu ch'u-ch'u pu-an	滄海橫流處處不安
Ts'ao Chih	曹植
Ts'ao Ts'ao	曹操
Ts'ao-tung	曹洞
Tse-chou	澤州
ts'e-lun	策論
Tseng Kung	曾鞏
"Tseng nei"	贈內
Tso Ch'iu-ming	左邱明
Tso Yung	左容
tsu-chou tz'u	詛咒詞
Tsu-lang	祖朗
Ts'ui Fa-chen	崔法珍
Ts'ui Li	崔立
Ts'ui Ying-ying	崔鶯鶯
ts'un (brushwork patterns)	皴
ts'un ("village," "rustic")	村
tsung-kuan	總管
tsung-kuan fu	總管府
tsung-shih chiang-chün ssu	宗室將軍司
Tu-ch'eng chi-sheng	都城紀勝
"Tu Chin shih"	讀晉史
Tu Ch'üeh	杜確
Tu Fu	杜甫
Tu Jen-chieh	杜仁傑
tu-kang	都綱
tu po-chi-lieh	都勃極烈
tu-pu chang	都部長
Tu-shih hsüeh	杜詩學

tu yüan-shuai fu	都元帥府
t'u-hua chü	圖畫局
t'u-hua shu	圖畫署
t'u-hua yüan	圖畫院
Tuan Ch'eng-chi	段成己
Tuan K'o-chi	段克己
t'uan-yüan	團圓
Tung-ch'ang-fu	東昌府
Tung Chieh-yüan	董解元
Tung Cho	董卓
Tung Chung-shu	董仲舒
Tung-p'ing	東平
Tung-p'o shih ya	東坡詩雅
Tung-t'ing	洞庭
T'ung-chou	通州
t'ung-hsing	同姓
T'ung-hui Yüan-ming	通慧圓明
T'ung-kuan	童關
T'ung-le-yüan	同樂園
Tzu-chang	子張
tzu ch'eng i chia	自成一家
Tzu-kung	子貢
tzu-tu ko	自度歌
tz'u	詞
Tz'u-chou	磁州
tz'u-fu	詞賦
Tz'u-hsiang	慈相
tz'u-jen	詞人
Tz'u-ming	慈明
tz'u-shih	刺史
wai-tan	外丹
Wan-ch'üan	萬全
wan kuo yü	萬國魚
Wan-yen	完顏
Wan-yen Hsi-yin	完顏希尹
Wan-yen Hu-nü	完顏胡女
Wan-yen Shan-shou-ma	完顏山壽馬
Wan-yen Shou	完顏璹
Wan-yen Tsung-hsien	完顏宗憲
Wan-yen Tsung-pi	完顏宗弼
Wan-yen Wu-lu	完顏烏祿
Wan-yen Yen-shou-ma	完顏延壽馬

Glossary

Wang An-shih	王安石
Wang Chao-chün	王昭君
Wang Che (Ch'ung-yang)	王嚞 (重陽)
Wang Chen-p'eng	王振鵬
Wang Ch'eng	王澄
wang-ch'i	王氣
Wang Ch'u-i (Yü-yang)	王處一 (玉陽)
Wang Ch'üan	王權
Wang Chün	王濬
Wang Hsi-chih	王羲之
Wang Jo-hsü (Ts'ung-chih)	王若虛 (從之)
Wang Jui-lan	王瑞蘭
Wang K'uei	王逵
Wang Ni	王呢
Wang O	王鶚
Wang P'an	王磐
Wang Po-ch'eng	王伯成
Wang Shih-chen	王士禎
Wang Shih-fu	王實甫
Wang T'ing-yün (Tzu-tuan)	王庭筠 (子端)
Wang Tse	王澤
Wang Tseng	王曾
Wang T'ung	王通
Wang Wan-ch'ing	王萬慶
Wang Wei	王維
Wang Yen-chang	王彥章
Wang Yü (fl. 1196–1201)	王彧
Wang Yü (1204–36)	王鬱
Wang Yün	王惲
Wei (river)	渭
Wei (state)	魏
Wei Ch'eng-te	魏成德
Wei-hui	衛輝
Wei-mo pu ehr	維摩不二
wei-na	維那
wei tao	為道
wei wen	為文
Wei Ying-wu	韋應物
wen	文
wen-chang	文章
Wen-chi	文姬
Wen Chung-tzu	文中子

wen-hsüeh	文學
wen-jen	文人
wen-shih	文士
Wen-te	文德
Wen T'ung	文同
wen-ya	文雅
Wen Yen-po	文彥博
Wo-chou	沃州
Wu (king)	武
Wu (state)	吳
"Wu ch'eng fu"	蕪城賦
Wu Chi	吳激
Wu-ch'i-mai	吳乞買
Wu-chu	悟銖
wu-ch'ü ko-tz'u	舞曲歌辭
Wu Hsi	吳曦
wu-hsing	五行
Wu-hsing-p'i-lu	五行毗盧
Wu-ku-nai	烏古廼
Wu-lin-ta	烏林答
Wu-lin Ta-shuang	烏林答爽
wu pei	吾輩
Wu San-kuei	吳三桂
Wu-tai shih	五代史
Wu-tai-shih p'ing-hua	五代史評話
Wu-t'ai	五台
Wu Tao-tzu	吳道子
Wu-ti	武帝
Wu Tse-t'ien	武則天
wu-wu	戊午
Wu-ya-shu	烏雅束
Wu Yüan-chih	武元直
yang	陽
Yang-ch'i	楊岐
Yang Hsiung (Tzu-yün)	揚雄(子雲)
Yang Huan	楊奐
Yang Kuei-fei	楊貴妃
Yang Li-chai	楊立齋
Yang Pang-chi	楊邦基
Yang P'u (Yang P'o)	楊朴
Yang-shan	仰山
Yang Shih	楊時

Yang Su	楊素
Yang-tzu	揚子
Yang Yün-i (Chih-mei)	楊雲翼(之美)
Yao (mountains)	崤
Yao (sage-king)	堯
Yao-min t'u	堯民圖
Yeh	葉
Yeh-lü Ch'u-ts'ai	耶律楚材
Yeh-lü Tzu-jang	耶律資讓
Yeh Shih	葉適
Yeh-shih-t'ing	野史亭
Yen	燕
Yen Chen-ch'ing	顏真卿
Yen Hui	顏回
Yen Li-pen	閻立本
Yen-shan (=Yen-shang)	岩山 (岩上)
Yen-shang (=Yen-shan)	岩上 (岩山)
Yen-shou	延壽
Yen Te-yüan	閻德源
yin (female principle)	陰
yin (protection system)	蔭
yin-kuo	因果
Yin-te-ma	銀德馬
ying-feng	應奉
ying-feng Han-lin wen-tzu	應奉翰林文字
Ying-ko	盈歌
Ying-yang	穎陽
"Ying-ying chuan"	鶯鶯傳
Yu Shih-hsiung	游師雄
yu-wu	尤物
yu-yu pu-p'ing chih ch'i	幽憂不平之氣
Yü (sage-king)	禹
Yü (state)	虞
Yü-chang	豫章
"Yü-chih sheng-ching fu"	御製盛京賦
Yü-chou	裕州
Yü Hsin	庾信
yü-i chü	御衣局
Yü Lan-ch'eng	庾蘭城
Yü Shih-nan	虞世南
yü-shih t'ai	御史台
Yü-wen Hsü-chung	宇文虛中

yüan	院
Yüan	原
Yüan Chen	元稹
Yüan-feng	元豐
Yüan Hao-wen	元好問
Yüan Hua	袁華
yüan-jung	圓融
Yüan-kai	圓蓋
yüan-pen	院本
Yüan-pen ming-mu	院本名目
Yüan-tao	原道
Yüan-yu	元祐
yüeh	樂
yüeh-fu	樂府
Yüeh-fu shih-chi	樂府詩集
Yüeh I	樂毅
Yün-chou	鄆州
Yün-men	雲門
Yung-chia Shu-hui	永嘉書會
"Yung shuo"	庸說

BIBLIOGRAPHY OF WORKS CITED

Primary Sources

CCC
Chung-chou chi 中州集. Comp. Yüan Hao-wen 元好問. Peking: Chung-hua shu-chü, 1959.

CCCC
Ch'un-ch'iu ching-chuan chi-chieh 春秋經傳集解. Comp. Tu Yü 杜預. Shanghai: Shang-hai ku-chi ch'u-pan-she, 1978.

CCJC
Shih-lien-an hui-k'o Chiu Chin-jen chi 石蓮盦彙刻九金人集. Comp. Wu Chung-hsi 吳重憙. Facsimile rpt. of 1909 ed. Taipei: Ch'eng-wen ch'u-pan-she, 1967.

CCS
Ch'üan Chin shih 全金詩. Comp. Kuo Yüan-yü 郭元釪. Facsimile rpt. of 1711 ed. Taipei: Hung-hao p'ei, 1968.

CCWC
Ch'iu-chien hsien-sheng ta-ch'üan wen-chi 秋澗先生大全文集. By Wang Yün 王惲. SPTK ed.

CCYT
Ch'üan Chin Yüan tz'u 全金元詞. Comp. T'ang Kuei-chang 唐圭璋. Peking: Chung-hua shu-chü, 1979.

CFTC
Chi-fu t'ung-chih 畿輔通志. Comp. Huang P'eng-nien 黃彭年 et al. Facsimile rpt. of 1910 ed. Taipei: Hua-wen shu-chü, 1968.

CHCC
Chih-cheng chi 至正集. By Hsü Yu-jen 許有壬. SKCP ed.

CHSHF
Ch'ing-ho shu-hua fang 清河書畫舫. By Chang Ch'ou 張丑. Chih-pei ts'ao-t'ang ed. of 1763.

Ch'üan T'ang shih 全唐詩
Comp. P'eng Ting-ch'iu 彭定求 et al., ed. Wang Ch'üan 王全 et al. Peking: Chung-hua shu-chü, 1960.

Chuang-ching chi 莊靖集
By Li Chün-min 李俊民. In CCJC.

CJMTC
Chu Ju ming-tao chi 諸儒鳴道集. Comp. student(s) of Chang Chiu-ch'eng 張九成. 1236 ed. of text comp. ca. 1159–68. Shanghai Library. Microfilm of above ed., Harvard-Yenching Library. (There is also a Ming manuscript copy in Peking Library's rare book collection.)

CJWC
Chan-jan chü-shih wen-chi 湛然居士文集. By Yeh-lü Ch'u-ts'ai 耶律楚材. Peking: Chung-hua shu-chü, 1986.

CKC
Ching-ting Chien-k'ang chih 景定建康志. Comp. Chou Ying-ho 周應和 et al. Rpt. of 1801 ed. Taipei: Commercial Press, 1983.

CKL
Ch'o-keng lu 輟耕錄. By T'ao Tsung-i 陶宗儀. TSCC ed.

CKMS
Chung-kuo mei-shu ch'üan-chi 中國美術全集. Ed. Chung-kuo mei-shu ch'üan-chi pien-chi wei-yüan-hui 中國美術全集編輯委員會. Vol. 1. Peking: Jen-min ch'u-pan-she, 1984.

CLC
Ch'en Liang chi 陳亮集. By Ch'en Liang 陳亮. Rev. and enl. ed. Peking: Chung-hua shu-chü, 1987.

CPOT
Chi'h-pei ou-t'an 池北偶談. By Wang Shih-chen 王士禎. Peking: Chung-hua shu-chü, 1982.

CS
Chin shih 金史. By T'o-t'o 脫脫 et al. Peking: Chung-hua shu-chü, 1975.

CSCS
Chin-shih chi-shih 金詩紀事. Comp. Ch'en Yen 陳衍. Shanghai: Commercial Press, 1936.

CSH
Chin shu 晉書. By Fang Hsüan-ling 房玄齡 et al. Peking: Chung-hua shu-chü, 1974.

CSL
Chin-ssu lu 近思錄. Ed. Chu Hsi 朱熹 and Lü Tsu-ch'ien 呂祖謙. SPPY ed.

CSPC
Pa-ch'iung-shih chin-shih pu-cheng 八瓊室金石補正. Comp. Lu Tseng-hsiang 陸增祥. SKHP ed.

CSPM
Chin-shih chi-shih pen-mo 金史紀事本末. Ed. and comp. Li Yu-t'ang 李有棠. Peking: Chung-hua shu-chü, 1980.

CST
Ch'üan Sung tz'u 全宋詞. Comp. T'ang Kuei-chang 唐圭璋. Peking: Chung-hua shu-chü, 1965.

CSTP
Chin-shih ts'ui-pien 金石萃編. Comp. Wang Ch'ang 王昶. SKSL ed. SKHP ed.

CTC
Chin-lien cheng-tsung chi 金蓮正宗紀. By Ch'in Chih-an 秦志安. TT ed.

CTFC
Cheng-ting fu-chih 正定府志. By Cheng Ta-chin 鄭大進 et al. Facsimile rpt. of 1756 ed. Taipei: Hsüeh-sheng shu-chü, 1968.

CTL
Chi Teng lu 繼燈錄. By Yüan-hsien 元賢. ZZ ed.

CTS
Chiu T'ang-shu 舊唐書. By Liu Hsü 劉昫 et al. Shanghai: Chung-hua shu-chü, 1975.

CTW
Ch'üan T'ang wen 全唐文. Comp. Tung Kao 董誥 et al. Facsimile rpt. of 1819 ed. Peking: Chung-hua shu-chü, 1978.

CTYL
Chu-tzu yü-lei 朱子語類. Comp. Chu Hsi 朱熹. Facsimile rpt. of 1473 ed. Taipei: Cheng-chung shu-chü, 1970.

CWKWC
Hui-an hsien-sheng Chu Wen-kung wen-chi 晦庵先生朱文公文集. By Chu Hsi 朱熹. SPPY ed.

CWT
Chin-wen tsui 金文最. Comp. Chang Chin-wu 張金吾. Facsimile rpt. of 1895 ed. Taipei: Ch'eng-wen ch'u-pan she, 1967.

CWTS
Chin-wen tsui 金文最. Comp. Chang Chin-wu 張金吾. Peking: Chung-hua shu-chü, 1990.

CWY
Chin-wen ya 金文雅. Ed. and comp. Chuang Chung-fang 莊仲方. Facsimile rpt. of 1891 ed. Taipei: Ch'eng-wen ch'u-pan she, 1967.

CYSC
Ch'üan Yüan san-ch'ü 全元散曲. Comp. Sui Shu-sen 隋樹森. Peking: Chung-hua shu-chü, 1964.

ECC
Erh-Ch'eng chi 二程集. By Ch'eng Hao 程顥 and Ch'eng I 程頤. Peking:

Chung-hua shu-chü, 1981.

Fan-sheng lu 繁勝錄
By Hsi-hu-lao-jen 西湖老人. In *Tung-ching meng Hua lu wai ssu-chung* 東京夢華錄外四種, pp. 111–28. Shanghai: Ku-tien wen-hsüeh ch'u-pan-she, 1956.

FSWC
Hsien-hsien lao-jen Fu-shui wen-chi 閑閑老人滏水文集. By Chao Ping-wen 趙秉文. SPTK ed.

FTTT
Fo-tsu li-tai t'ung-tsai 佛祖歷代通載. By Nien-ch'ang 念常. Taipei: Hsien-wen-feng ch'u-pan kung-ssu, 1975.

HCPI
Hua-chi pu-i 畫繼補遺. By Chuang Su 莊肅. Peking: Jen-min mei-shu ch'u-pan-she, 1963.

HFSC
Ho-fen chu-lao shih-chi 河汾諸老詩集. Ed. Fang Ch'i 房祺. Peking: Chung-hua shu-chü, 1958.

HHS
Hou-Han shu 後漢書. By Fan Yeh 范曄. Peking: Chung-hua shu-chü, 1973.

HLC
Ch'eng Hsüeh-lou wen-chi 程雪樓文集. By Ch'eng Chü-fu 程鉅夫. Facsimile rpt. of 1395 ed. Taipei: Kuo-li chung-yang t'u-shu-kuan, 1970.

HNC
Hu-nan chi 滹南集. By Wang Jo-hsü 王若虛. In *CCJC*.

HNIL
Hu-nan i-lao chi 滹南遺老集. By Wang Jo-hsü 王若虛. SPTK ed.

HNTC
Ho-nan t'ung-chih 河南通志. Ed. Sun Hao 孫灝 et al. Facsimile rpt. of 1882 ed. Taipei: Hua-wen shu-chü, 1969.

HNYL
Chien-yen i-lai hsi-nien yao-lu 建炎以來繫年要錄. By Li Hsin-ch'uan 李心傳. KHCP ed. Peking: Chung-hua shu-chü, 1988.

HSPH
Han-shih p'ing-hua 漢史平話. In *Hsin-pien Wu-tai-shih p'ing-hua* 新編五代史平話. Peking: Chung-hua shu-chü, 1959.

Hsüan-ch'ü lu 軒渠錄
By Lü Pen-chung 呂本中. In *Shuo-fu* 說郛, ed. T'ao Tsung-i 陶宗儀. Wan-wei-shan-t'ang ed. of 1647.

HTCCP
Hsü Tzu-chih t'ung-chien ch'ang-pien 續資治通鑑長編. Comp. Li T'ao 李燾. Peking: Chung-hua shu-chü, 1979.

HTCTC
Hsü Tzu-chih t'ung-chien 續資治通鑑. Comp. Pi Yüan 畢沅 et al. Peking: Chung-hua shu-chü, 1957.

HTK
Hsü T'ung-k'ao 續通考. Comp. Chi Yün 紀昀 et al. Facsimile rpt. of Wu-ying-tien ed. Taipei: Hsin-hsing shu-chü, 1963.

HYC
Ch'ang-ch'un chen-jen hsi-yu chi 長春真人西遊記. By Li Chih-ch'ang 李志常. SPPY ed.

HYHC
Chin-lien cheng-tsung hsien-yüan hsiang-chuan 金蓮正宗仙源像傳. By Liu T'ien-su 劉天素 and Hsieh Hsi-ch'an 謝西蟾. TT ed.

ISWC
I-shan hsien-sheng wen-chi 遺山先生文集. By Yüan Hao-wen 元好問. SPPY ed.

KCC
Kuei-ch'ien chih 歸潛志. By Liu Ch'i 劉祁. Peking: Chung-hua shu-chü, 1983.

KHCP
Kuo-hsüeh chi-pen ts'ung-shu 國學基本叢書. Ed. Wang Yün-wu 王雲五. Shanghai: Commercial Press, 1929. Rpt. Taipei: Commercial Press, 1968.

KHCS
Keng-hsüeh-chai shih-chi 耕學齊詩集. By Yüan Hua 袁華. SKCP ed.

KKPC
Kung-kuan pei-chih 宮觀碑誌. TT ed.

KLC
Chien-pen fu-yin Ch'un-ch'iu Ku-liang chuan chu-shu 監本附音春秋穀梁傳注疏. Comp. and annot. Fan Ning 范寧, subannot. Yang Shih-hsün 楊士勛. In *Shih-san-ching chu-shu* 十三經注疏. Taipei: I-wen yin-shu-kuan, 1983.

KS
K'ung-shih tsu-t'ing kuang-chi 孔氏祖庭廣記. By K'ung Yüan-ts'o 孔元措. Facsimile rpt. of Yüan ed. Taipei: Kuang-wen shu-chü, 1970.

KSHY
Kan-shui hsien-yüan lu 甘水仙源錄. By Li Tao-ch'ien 李道謙. TTCY ed.

KYC
Chien-pen fu-yin Ch'un-ch'iu Kung-yang chuan chu-shu 監本附音春秋公羊傳注疏. Comp. and annot. Ho Hsiu 何休, subannot. Hsü Yen 徐彥. In *Shih-san-ching chu-shu* 十三經注疏. Taipei: I-wen yin-shu-kuan, 1983.

LCC
Ling-ch'uan chi 陵川集. By Hao Ching 郝經. SKCP ed.

LH
Lun-heng 論衡. By Wang Ch'ung 王充. Shanghai: Jen-min ch'u-pan-she, 1974.

LHC
Lieh-hsien chuan 列仙傳. By Liu Hsiang 劉向. In *Lieh-hsien ch'üan chuan* 列仙全傳. Facsimile rpt. of Ch'ing ed. Taipei: Kuang-wen shu-tien, 1974.

LSSI
Lo-shih shih-i 羅氏識遺. By Lo Pi 羅璧. Hsüeh-hai lei-pien ed.

LTSS
Li-tai shih-shih ch'ang-pien 歷代詩史長編. Ed. Yang Chia-lo 楊家駱. Taipei: Ting-wen shu-chü, 1971.

LYC
Liu-yen-chai pi-chi 六硯齋筆記. By Li Jih-hua 李日華. SKCP ed.

LYWC
Lin-yüan wen-chi 麟原文集. By Wang Li 王禮. SKCP ed.

MCCS
Ch'in-ting Man-chou chi-shen chi-t'ien tien-li 欽定滿洲祭神祭天典禮. SKCP ed.

MSHH
Men-shih hsin-hua 捫虱新話. By Ch'en Shan 陳善. Shanghai: Commercial Press, 1920.

MSTW
Ma Shih-tien wen-chi 馬石田文集. By Ma Shih-tien 馬石田. SKCP ed.

MTCS
Ming-tao chi-shuo 鳴道集說. Li Ch'un-fu 李純甫. Facsimile rpt. of Ming ed. In *Chung-kuo tzu-hsüeh ming-chu chi-ch'eng* 中國子學名著集成. Taipei: Shih-chieh shu-chü, n.d. Also, microfilm copies deposited in Peking Library and the Library of Congress of an undated (Ming) manuscript once in the rare book collection of the former Peiping Library.

NTCK
Nan-ts'un Ch'o-keng lu 南村輟耕錄. By T'ao Tsung-i 陶宗儀. Peking: Chung-hua shu-chü, 1959.

OPSH
Ou-pei shih-hua 甌北詩話. By Chao I 趙翼. Peking: Chung-hua shu-chü,

1981.

OYWC
Ou-yang Wen-chung-kung wen-chi 歐陽文忠公文集. By Ou-yang Hsiu 歐陽修. SPTK ed.

OYWT
Ou-yang wen-ts'ui 歐陽文粹. By Ou-yang Hsiu 歐陽修. Comp. Ch'en Liang 陳亮. SKCP ed.

Pai-t'u chi 白兔記
In *Ming Ch'eng-hua shuo-ch'ang tz'u-hua yeh-k'an shih-liu-chung fu Pai-t'u chi ch'uan-ch'i i-chung* 明成化說唱詞話叢刊十六種附白兔記傳奇一種. Facsimile rpt. of 15th-cent. ed. Shanghai: Shang-hai-shih wen-wu pao-kuan wei-yüan-hui, 1973.

PCC
P'an-ch'i chi 磻溪集. By Ch'iu Ch'u-chi 邱處機. TT ed.

PCS
Pa-ch'iung-shih chin-shih pu-cheng 八瓊室金石補正. Comp. Lu Tseng-hsiang 陸增祥. SKSL ed.

PHKS
Pu-hsü Kao-seng chuan 補續高僧傳. By Ming-ho 明河. ZZ ed.

PKKC
Pien ku-kung-chi 汴故宮記. By Yang Huan 楊奐. In *Yüan wen-lei* 元文類, ed. Su T'ien-chüeh 蘇天爵. Shanghai: Shang-wu yin-shu-kuan, 1936.

PTCL
Pi-tien chu-lin 秘殿珠林. By Chang Chao 張照 et al. Facsimile rpt. of 1744 manuscript. Taipei: Palace Museum, 1971.

SC
Shih chi 史記. By Ssu-ma Ch'ien 司馬遷. Peking: Chung-hua shu-chü, 1962.

SCHP
Shih-ch'ü pao-chi hsü-pien 石渠寶笈續編. By Wang Chieh 王杰 et al. Facsimile rpt. of 1793 manuscript. Taipei: Palace Museum, 1971.

SCPC
Shih-ch'ü pao-chi 石渠寶笈. By Chang Chao 張照 et al. Facsimile rpt. of 1745 manuscript. Taipei: Palace Museum, 1971.

SCPM
San-ch'ao pei-meng hui-pien 三朝北盟會編. Comp. Hsü Meng-hsin 徐夢莘. Facsimile rpt. of 1879 ed. Taipei: Wen-hai ch'u-pan-she, 1962.

SHSWC
Sung hsüeh-shih wen-chi 宋學士文集. By Sung Lien 宋濂. KHCP ed.

SHTC
Shan-hsi t'ung-chih 山西通志. Comp. Wang Hsüan 王軒 et al. Facsimile rpt. of 1892 ed. Taipei: Hua-wen shu-chü, 1969.

SHY
Sung hui-yao chi-kao 宋會要輯稿. Comp. Hsü Sung 徐松. Facsimile rpt. of mansucript copy. Taipei: Shih-chieh shu-chü, 1964.

SJIS
Sung-jen i-shih hui-pien 宋人軼事彙編. Comp. Ting Ch'uan-ching 丁傳靖. Shanghai: Commercial Press, 1935. Rpt. Peking: Chung-hua shu-chü, 1981.

SKC
San-kuo chih 三國志. By Ch'en Shou 陳壽. Peking: Chung-hua shu-chü, 1982.

SKCP
Ssu-k'u ch'üan-shu chen-pen 四庫全書珍本. Facsimile rpt. of manuscript copy. Taipei: Commercial Press, 1971–77. Shanghai: Shang-hai ku-chi ch'u-pan-she, 1987.

SKCS
Ssu-k'u ch'üan-shu 四庫全書. Comp. Chi Yün 紀昀 et al. SKCP ed.

SKHP
Shih-k'o shih-liao hsin-pien 石刻史料新編. Taipei: Hsin-wen-feng ch'u-pan kung-ssu, 1977.

SKSL
Shih-k'o shih-liao ts'ung-shu 石刻史料叢書. Ed. Yen Keng-wang 嚴耕望. Taipei: I-wen yin-shu-kuan, 1967.

SKT
Shih-ku-t'ang shu-hua hui-k'ao 式古堂書畫彙考. By Pien Yung-yü 卞永譽. Facsimile rpt. of 1682 ed. Taipei: Chung-hua shu-chü, 1958.

SKTM
Ssu-k'u ch'üan-shu tsung-mu 四庫全書總目. Comp. Chi Yün 紀昀 et al. Peking: Chung-hua shu-chü, 1981.

SKTY
Ssu-k'u ch'üan-shu tsung-mu t'i-yao 四庫全書總目提要. Comp. Chi Yün 紀昀 et al. In *Ho-yin Ssu-k'u ch'üan-shu tsung-mu t'i-yao chi Ssu-k'u wei-shou shu-mu Chin-hui shu-mu* 合印四庫全書總目提要及四庫未收書目禁燬書目, ed. Wang Yün-wu 王雲五. Taipei: Commercial Press, 1971.

SLK
Shih-liu-kuo ch'un-ch'iu chi-pu 十六國春秋輯補. By T'ang Ch'iu 湯球. TSCC ed.

SMCW
Sung-mo chi-wen 松漠紀聞. By Hung Hao 洪皓. SKCP ed.

SPPY
Ssu-pu pei-yao 四部備要. Comp. Lu Fei-k'uei 陸費逵 et al. Shanghai: Chung-hua shu-chü, 1934–36.

SPTK
Ssu-pu ts'ung-k'an 四部叢刊. Comp. Chang Yüan-chi 張元濟. Shanghai: Commercial Press, 1929.

SS
Sung shih 宋史. By T'o-t'o 脫脫 et al. Peking and Shanghai: Chung-hua shu-chü, 1977.

SSHP
Sung-shih hsin-pien 宋史新編. By K'o Wei-ch'i 柯維騏. Facsimile rpt. of 1557 ed. Taipei: Shih-chieh shu-chü, 1974.

SSPM
Sung-shih chi-shih pen-mo 宋史記事本末. By Ch'en Pang-chan 陳邦瞻. Peking: Chung-hua shu-chü, 1977.

SSSF
Shao-shih shan-fang pi-ts'ung 少室山房筆叢. By Hu Ying-lin 胡應麟. Peking: Chung-hua shu-chü, 1958.

SSYT
Sheng-shui yen-t'an lu 澠水燕談錄. By Wang P'i-chih 王闢之. In *Pi-chi hsiao-shuo ta-kuan* 筆記小說大觀. Yangchow: Chiang-su Kuang-ling ku-chi ch'u-pan-she, 1983.

STPC
Su Tung-p'o chi 蘇東坡集. By Su Shih 蘇軾. Taipei: Commercial Press, 1967.

STTC
Shan-tung t'ung-chih 山東通志. By Sun Pao-t'ien 孫葆田 et al. Facsimile rpt. of 1915 ed. Taipei: Hua-wen shu-chü, 1969.

SWCK
Su Wen-chung-kung shih ho-chu 蘇文忠公詩合注. By Su Shih 蘇軾. Ed. Feng Ying-liu 馮應榴. 1793 ed.

SWCY
Shih-wu chi-yüan 事物紀原. By Kao Ch'eng 高承. Taipei: Commercial Press, 1971.

SYC
Shui-yün chi 水雲集. By T'an Ch'u-tuan 譚處端. Chin ed. in rare book collection of Peking Library.

SYHA
Sung Yüan hsüeh-an 宋元學案. By Huang Tsung-hsi 黃宗羲 and Ch'üan Tsu-wang 全祖望. Rpt. of Li-tai hsüeh-an 歷代學案 ed. Taipei: Shih-chieh shu-chü, 1966.

SYPI
Sung Yüan hsüeh-an pu-i 宋元學案補遺. Rpt. of Li-tai hsüeh-an 歷代學案 ed. Taipei: Shih-chieh shu-chü, 1962.

SYSK
Shan-yu shih-k'o ts'ung-pien 山右石刻叢編. Comp. Hu P'ing-chih 胡聘之. SKSL ed.

SYTP
Shan-yu shih-k'o ts'ung-pien 山右石刻叢編. Comp. Hu P'ing-chih 胡聘之. SKHP ed.

TC
Fu shih-yin Ch'un-ch'iu Tso chuan chu-shu 附釋音春秋左傳注疏. Comp. and annot. Tu Yü 杜預, subannot. K'ung Ying-ta 孔穎達. In *Shih-san-ching chu-shu* 十三經注疏. Taipei: I-wen yin-shu-kuan, 1983.

TCCC
Ta Chin-kuo chih chiao-cheng 大金國志校證. By Yü-wen Mao-chao 宇文懋昭. Ed. Ts'ui Wen-yin 崔文印. Peking: Chung-hua shu-chü, 1986.

TCKC
Ta Chin-kuo chih 大金國志. By Yü-wen Mao-chao 宇文懋昭. KHCP ed.

TCKM
Tzu-chih t'ung-chien kang-mu 資治通鑒綱目. Comp. Chu Hsi 朱熹. Chu-wen-t'ang ed. Soochow, 1804.

TCM
Tung-ching meng Hua lu 東京夢華錄. By Meng Yüan-lao 孟元老. In *Tung-ching meng hua lu wai ssu-chung* 東京夢華錄外四種, pp. 1–87. Shanghai: Ku-tien wen-hsüeh ch'u-pan-she, 1956.

THCY
T'ai-ho cheng-yin p'u 太和正音譜. Comp. Chu Ch'üan 朱權. In *Chung-kuo ku-tien hsi-ch'ü lun-chu chi-ch'eng* 中國古典戲曲論著集成, vol. 3, pp. 3–231. Peking: Chung-kuo hsi-chü ch'u-pan-she, 1959.

THH
Tung Chieh-yüan Hsi-hsiang chi 董解元西廂記. By Laureate Tung 董解元. Ed. Ling Ching-yen 凌景埏. Peking: Jen-min wen-hsüeh ch'u-pan-she, 1962.

THL
Tung Hua lu 東華錄. By Wang Hsien-ch'ien 王先謙. Shanghai: Ts'un-ku-chai, 1911.

THPC
T'u-hui pao-chien 圖繪寶鑒. By Hsia Wen-yen 夏文彥. Rpt. of I-shu ts'ung-pien ed. Taipei: Shih-chieh shu-chü, 1962.

TK
Wen-hsien t'ung-k'ao 文獻通考. Comp. Ma Tuan-lin 馬端臨. Facsimile rpt. of Wu-ying-tien ed. Taipei: Hsin-hsing shu-chü, 1963.

TMC
Ta Ming I-t'ung-chih 大明一統志. By Li Hsien 李賢 et al. Taipei: T'ung-i ch'u-pan yin-shua kung-ssu, 1965.

TS
Hsin T'ang-shu 新唐書. By Ou-yang Hsiu 歐陽修 and Sung Ch'i 宋祁. Peking and Shanghai: Chung-hua shu-chü, 1975.

TSCC
Ts'ung-shu chi-ch'eng chien-pien 叢書集成簡編. Ed. Wang Yün-wu 王雲五. Taipei: Commercial Press, 1966.

TT
Tao-tsang 道藏. Rpt. of Commercial Press ed. Taipei: I-wen yin-shu kuan, 1962.

TTCY
Tao-tsang chi-yao 道藏輯要. By P'eng Wen-ch'in 彭文勤. Taipei: Hsin-wen-feng ch'u-pan kung-ssu, 1977.

TTPN
Tsung-t'ung pien-nien 宗統編年. By Chi Yin 紀蔭. ZZ ed.

TWTL
Tsui-weng t'an-lu 醉翁談錄. By Lo Yeh 羅燁. Shanghai: Ku-tien wen-hsüeh ch'u-pan-she, 1957.

WCL
Wei Ch'i lu 偽齊錄. Comp. Yang Yao-pi 楊堯弼. Ou-hsiang ling-shih ed.

YHYF
Yung-hsi yüeh-fu 雍熙樂府. Comp. Kuo Hsün 郭勛. SPTK ed.

YISCC
Yüan I-shan shih-chi chien-chu 元遺山詩集箋註. By Yüan Hao-wen 元好問. Annot. Shih Kuo-ch'i 施國祁. Peking: Jen-min wen-hsüeh ch'u-pan she, 1958.

YISS
Yüan I-shan shih chu 元遺山詩注. By Yüan Hao-wen 元好問. Taipei: T'ai-wan Chung-hua shu-chü, 1970.

YKC
Yün-kuang chi 雲光集. By Wang Ch'u-i 王處一. TT ed.

YS
Yüan shih 元史. By Sung Lien 宋濂 et al. Peking: Chung-hua shu-chü, 1976.

ZZ
Dai Nihon zoku Zôkyô 大日本續藏經. Kyoto: Zôkyô shoten, 1905–12.

Secondary Sources

Acker William R. B.
1954–74   *Some T'ang and Pre-T'ang Texts on Chinese Painting*. 2 vols. Leiden: E. J. Brill.

Aoki Masaru 青木正兒
1932   "Ryû Chi-en shokyûcho kô" 劉知遠諸宮調考. *Shinagaku* 支那學 6:195–230.

Aubin, Françoise
1987   "The Rebirth of Chinese Rule in Times of Trouble: North China in the Early Thirteenth Century." In *Foundations and Limits of State Power in China*, ed. S. R. Schram, pp. 113–46. London: School of Oriental and African Studies.

Barnhart, Richard
1977   "Yao Yen-ch'ing, T'ing-mei, of Wu-hsing." *Artibus Asiae* 39:105–23.

Berling, Judith A.
1980   *The Syncretic Religion of Lin Chao-en*. New York: Columbia University Press.

Bol, Peter K.
1982   "Culture and the Way in Eleventh Century China." Ph.D. diss., Princeton University.
1983   "Why Was There a Literati Culture in Chin?" Paper presented at the Conference on Cultural Values in North China during the Twelfth and Thirteenth Centuries, Oracle, Arizona, December 1983.
1987   "Seeking Common Ground: Han Literati under Jurchen Rule." *Harvard Journal of Asiatic Studies* 47:461–538.
1992   *"This Culture of Ours": Intellectual Transition in T'ang and Sung China*. Stanford: Stanford University Press.

Buell, Paul D.
1985–86   "The Sung Resistance Movement, 1276–1279: An Episode in Chinese Regional History." *Annals of the Chinese Historical Society of the Pacific Northwest*, no. 3, pp. 138–86.

Bunker, Emma
1968 "Early Chinese Representations of Vimalakîrti." *Artibus Asiae* 30:28–52.

Bush, Susan
1965 " 'Clearing after Snow in the Min Mountains' and Chin Landscape Painting." *Oriental Art*, n.s. 11:163–72.
1969 "Literati Culture under the Chin (1122–1234)." *Oriental Art*, n.s. 15:103–12.
1986 "Chin Literati Painting and Landscape Traditions." *National Palace Museum Bulletin* 21, no. 4/5:1–24.

Bush, Susan H., and Victor H. Mair
1977–78 "Some Buddhist Portraits and Images of the Lü and Ch'an Sects in Twelfth- and Thirteenth-Century China." *Archives of Asian Art* 31:32–51.

Bush, Susan, and Hsio-yen Shih, comps. and eds.
1985 *Early Chinese Texts on Painting*. Cambridge: Harvard-Yenching Institute and Harvard University Press.

Chaffee, John W.
1985 *The Thorny Gates of Learning in Sung China: A Social History of Examinations*. Cambridge: Cambridge University Press.

Chan Hang-lun 詹杭倫
1993 *Chin-tai wen-hsüeh shih* 金代文學史. Taipei: Kuan-ya wen-hua shih-yeh yu-hsien kung-ssu.

Chan Hok-lam (Ch'en Hsüeh-lin 陳學霖)
1970 *The Historiography of the Chin Dynasty (1115–1234): Three Studies*. Münchener ostasiatische Studien, no. 4. Wiesbaden: Franz Steiner Verlag.
1976 "Yang Huan." *Papers on Far Eastern History* 14:37–59.
1981 "Chinese Official Historiography at the Yüan Court: The Composition of the Liao, Sung, and Chin Histories." In *China under Mongol Rule*, ed. John D. Langlois, Jr., pp. 56–106. Princeton: Princeton University Press.
1984 *Legitimation in Imperial China: Discussions under the Jurchen-Chin Dynasty (1115–1234)*. Seattle: University of Washington Press.
1987 "Chin kuo-hao chih ch'i-yüan chi ch'i shih-i" 金國號之起源及其釋義. In *Liao Chin shih lun-chi*, ed. Ch'en Shu and Sung Te-chin, vol. 3, pp. 279–309.

1991 " 'Ta Chin' (Great Golden): The Origin and Changing Interpretation of the Jurchen State Name." *T'oung Pao* 77:253–99.
1992 "The Organization and Utilization of Labor Service under the Jurchen Chin Dynasty." *Harvard Journal of Asiatic Studies* 52:613–64.

Chan Hok-lam and Wm. Theodore de Bary, eds.
1982 *Yüan Thought: Chinese Thought and Religion under the Mongols.* New York: Columbia University Press.

Chan, Wing-tsit
1963a *A Source Book in Chinese Philosophy.* Princeton: Princeton University Press.
1963b Trans. and ed. *The Way of Lao Tzu (Tao-te ching).* Indianapolis: Bobbs-Merrill.
1967 Trans. *Reflections on Things at Hand; The Neo-Confucian Anthology, Compiled by Chu Hsi and Lü Tsu-ch'ien.* New York: Columbia University Press.
1982 "Chu Hsi and Yüan Neo-Confucianism." In *Yüan Thought,* ed. Chan Hok-lam and Wm. Theodore de Bary, pp. 197–231.
1986 *Chu Hsi and Neo-Confucianism.* Honolulu: University of Hawaii Press.

Chang, H. C.
1973 *Chinese Literature, Popular Fiction and Drama.* Edinburgh: Edinburgh University Press.

Chang Hsin-ying 張信英
1981 "Kuan-yü Fo-chiao Ta-tsang-ching te i-hsieh tzu-liao" 關於佛教大藏經的一些資料. *Shih-chieh tsung-chiao tzu-liao* 世界宗教資料, 1981, no. 4:34–40.

Chang Lu 張祿, ed.
1955 *Tz'u-lin chai-yen* 詞林摘艷. Peking: Wen-hsüeh ku-chi k'an-hsing-she.

Chang Po-ch'üan 張博泉
1981 *Chin-tai ching-chi shih lüeh* 金代經濟史略. Mukden: Liao-ning jen-min ch'u-pan she.
1983 "Liao Chin 'Erh-shui-hu' yen-chiu" 遼金二稅戶研究. *Li-shih yen-chiu* 歷史研究,1983, no. 2:120–29.
1984 *Chin shih chien-pien* 金史簡編. Mukden: Liao-ning jen-min ch'u-pan-she.
1985 "Chao Ping-wen chi ch'i ssu-hsiang" 趙秉文及其思想. *Hsüeh-hsi yü t'an-so* 學習與探索, 1985, no. 3:135–40.

Chang Po-ch'üan 張博泉 and Ch'eng Ni-na 程妮娜
1987   "Wan-yen A-ku-ta lüeh-lun" 完顏阿骨打略論. In *Liao Chin shih lun-chi*, ed. Ch'en Shu and Sung Te-chin, vol. 1, pp. 335–56.

Chang Po ch'üan 張博泉 et al.
1986   *Chin shih lun-kao* 金史論稿. Vol. 1. Tung-pei shih ts'ung-shu 東北史叢書. Ch'ang-ch'un: Chi-lin wen-shih ch'u-pan-she.

Chang Yen 張燕 and Li An-fu 李安富
1989   "Shan-hsi Kan-ch'üan Chin-tai i-k'u ch'ing-li chien-pao" 陝西甘泉金代瘞窟清理簡報. *Wen-wu* 文物, 1989, no. 5:75–80.

Chao Chih-hui 趙志輝 et al.
1989   *Man-tsu wen-hsüeh shih* 滿族文學史. Vol. 1. Mukden: Shen-yang ch'u-pan-she.

Chao Ming-ch'i 趙鳴岐
1987   "Liao-tai sheng Nü-chen te she-hui pien-ko chi Chin te chien-kuo" 遼代生女真的社會變革及金的建國. In *Liao Chin shih lun-chi*, ed. Ch'en Shu and Sung Te-chin, vol. 3, pp. 95–121.

Chao T'ing-p'eng 趙廷鵬 et al.
1987   "Fu tao ts'ang-sang chü pien kung: Lun Yüan I-shan te sang-luan shih" 賦到滄桑句便工：論元遺山的喪亂詩. In *Yüan Hao-wen yen-chiu wen-chi* 元好問研究文集, ed. Shan-hsi-sheng ku-tien wen-hsüeh hsüeh-hui 山西省古典文學學會 and Yüan Hao-wen yen-chiu hui 元好問研究會, pp. 76–94. Taiyuan: Shan-hsi jen-min ch'u-pan-she.

Chao Tung-hui 趙冬暉
1987   "Lun Chin Hsi-tsung shih-ch'i kuo-chia cheng-t'i te chuan-pien" 論金熙宗時期國家政體的轉變. In *Liao Chin shih lun-chi*, ed. Ch'en Shu and Sung Te-chin, vol. 2, pp. 226–44.
1989   "Chin-tai k'o-chü chih-tu yen-chiu" 金代科舉制度研究. In *Liao Chin shih lun-chi*, ed. Ch'en Shu and Sung Te-chin, vol. 4, pp. 212–35.

Chao Yung-ch'un 趙永春
1989   "Sung Chin chiao-p'in chih-tu shu-lun" 宋金交聘制度述論. In *Liao Chin shih lun-chi*, ed. Ch'en Shu and Sung Te-chin, vol. 4, pp. 248–60.
1991   "Chin Hsi-tsung te kuan-chih kai-ko chi ch'i li-shih ti-wei" 金熙宗的官制改革及其歷史地位. *Pei-fang min-tsu wen-hua* 北方民族文化 2:78–81.

Ch'en Chiao-yu 陳教友
1974 "Ch'ang-ch'un Tao-chiao yüan-liu" 長春道教源流. In *Tao-chiao yen-chiu tzu-liao* 道教研究資料, comp. Yen I-p'ing 嚴一萍, vol. 2, part 4. Taipei: I-wen yin-shu-kuan.

Ch'en Chih-ch'ao 陳智超
1986 "Chen Ta-tao chiao hsin shih-liao—Chien p'ing Yüan Kuo-fan 'Yüan-tai Chen Ta-tao chiao k'ao'" 真大道教新史料—兼評袁國藩《元代真大道道教考》. *Shih-chieh tsung-chiao yen-chiu* 世界宗教研究, 1986, no. 4:16–24.

Ch'en Kao-hua 陳高華
1976 "Li-hsüeh tsai Yüan-tai te ch'uan-po ho Yüan-mo Hung-chin-chün tui li-hsüeh te ch'ung-chi" 理學在元代的傳播和元末紅巾軍對理學的衝擊. *Wen shih che* 文史哲, 1976, no. 2:77–83.
1980 Ed. *Yüan-tai hua-chia shih-liao* 元代畫家史料. Shanghai: Jen-min mei-shu ch'u-pan-she.
1984 Ed. *Sung Liao Chin hua-chia shih-liao* 宋遼金畫家史料. Peking: Wen-wu ch'u-pan-she.

Ch'en, Kenneth K. S.
1956 "The Sale of Monk Certificates During the Sung Dynasty: A Factor in the Decline of Buddhism in China." *Harvard Theological Review* 49:307–27.
1964 *Buddhism in China: A Historical Survey*. Princeton: Princeton University Press.
1973 *The Chinese Transformation of Buddhism*. Princeton: Princeton University Press.

Ch'en Lai 陳來
1986 "Lüeh-lun *Chu Ju ming tao chi*" 略論《諸儒鳴道集》. *Pei-ching ta-hsüeh hsüeh-pao che-hsüeh she-hui k'o-hsüeh pan* 北京大學學報哲學社會科學版, 1986, no. 1:30–38.

Ch'en, Li-li
1970 "The Relationship between Oral Presentation and the Literary Devices Used in *Liu Chih-yüan* and *Hsi-hsiang-chi chu-kung-tiao*." *Literature East and West* 14:519–27.
1972 "Outer and Inner Forms of *Chu-kung-tiao*, with Reference to *Pien-wen*, *Tz'u* and Vernacular Fiction." *Harvard Journal of Asiatic Studies* 32:124–49.
1973 "Some Background Information on the Development of *Chu-kung-tiao*." *Harvard Journal of Asiatic Studies* 33:224–37.
1976 Trans. and ed. *Master Tung's Western Chamber Romance (Tung Hsi-hsiang-chi chu-kung-tiao): A Chinese Chantefable*. Cambridge:

Cambridge University Press.

Ch'en Ping 陳兵
1984 "Lüeh-lun Ch'üan-chen tao te san-chiao ho-i shuo" 略論全真道的三教合一說. *Shih-chieh tsung-chiao yen-chiu* 世界宗教研究, 1984, no. 1: 7–21.

Ch'en Shu 陳述
1986 *Ch'i-tan cheng-chih shih-kao* 契丹政治史稿. Peking: Jen-min ch'u-pan-she.

Ch'en Shu 陳述 and Sung Te-chin 宋德金, eds.
1987–92 *Liao Chin shih lun-chi* 遼金史論集. 5 vols. Vol. 1, Shanghai: Shang-hai ku-chi ch'u-pan-she, 1987. Vols. 2–5, Peking: Shu-mu wen-hsien ch'u-pan-she, 1989, 1992.

Ch'en Yüan 陳垣
1962 *Nan-Sung ch'u Ho-pei hsin Tao-chiao k'ao* 南宋初河北新道教考. Peking: Chung-hua shu-chü.

Cheng Chen-to 鄭振鐸
1951–55 Ed. *Wei-ta te i-shu ch'uan-t'ung t'u-lu* 偉大的藝術傳統圖錄. Shanghai: Shang-hai ch'u-pan kung-ssu.
1957 "*Sung Chin Yüan chu-kung-tiao k'ao*" 宋金元諸宮調考. In his *Chung-kuo wen-hsüeh yen-chiu* 中國文學研究, vol. 3, pp. 843–970. Peking: Tso-chia ch'u-pan-she.

Ch'eng-te-shih Pi-shu shan-chuang po-wu-kuan 承德市避署山庄博物館
1980 "Chin-tai cheng-liu-ch'i k'ao-lüeh" 金代蒸餾器考略. *K'ao-ku* 考古, 1980, no. 5: 466–71, 405.

Chiang I-pin 蔣義斌
1992 "Ch'üan-chen chiao-tsu Wang Ch'ung-yang ssu-hsiang ch'u-t'an" 全真教祖王重陽思想初探. In *Sung shih yen-chiu chi* 宋史研究集, vol. 22, pp. 305–27. Taipei: P'an-an yin-shua-so.

Chiang Sung-yen 蔣松岩
1989 "Chin-tai yü-shih-t'ai ch'u-t'an" 金代御史臺初探. In *Liao Chin shih lun-chi*, ed. Ch'en Shu and Sung Te-chin, vol. 4, pp. 196–211.

Chiang Wei-hsin 蔣唯心
1934 "Chin-tsang tiao-yin shih-mo k'ao" 金藏雕印始末考. *Kuo-feng* 國風 5, no. 12: 1–34.

Ch'ien Chung-shu 錢鍾書
1984 *T'an-i lu* 談藝錄. Peking: Chung-hua shu-chü.

Ch'iu Han-sheng 邱漢生 et al., eds.
1984 *Sung Ming li-hsüeh shih* 宋明理學史. Vol. 1. Peking: Jen-min ch'u-pan-she.

Chou Hui-ch'üan 周惠泉 and Mi Chih-kuo 米治國, eds.
1986 *Liao Chin wen-hsüeh tso-p'in hsüan* 遼金文學作品選. Ch'ang-ch'un: Shih-tai wen-i ch'u-pan-she.

Chu Chu-yü 朱鑄禹 and Li Shih-sun 李石孫, eds.
1958 *T'ang Sung hua-chia jen-ming tz'u-tien* 唐宋畫家人名辭典. Peking: Chung-kuo ku-tien i-shu ch'u-pan-she.

Chu Chung-yü 朱仲玉
1984 "Chin shih shih-hsi" 金史試析. *Wen-shih chih-shih* 文史知識, 1984, no. 4:21–25.

Chu Liang-chih 朱良志
1987 "Shih-lun Yüan Hao-wen te 'i ch'eng wei pen' shuo" 試論元好問的"誠為本"說. In *Yüan Hao-wen yen-chiu wen-chi* 元好問研究文集, ed. Shan-hsi-sheng ku-tien wen-hsüeh hsüeh-hui 山西省古典文學學會 and Yüan Hao-wen yen-chiu hui 元好問研究會, pp. 192–202. Taiyuan: Shan-hsi jen-min ch'u-pan-she.

Chung-hua Ta-tsang-ching pien-chi chü 中華大藏經編輯局
1984 "Chung-hua Ta-tsang-ching Han-wen pu-fen kai-lun" 中華大藏經漢文部分概論. *Shih-chieh tsung-chiao yen-chiu* 世界宗教研究, 1984, no. 4:1–14.

Chung-kuo Fo-chiao hsieh-hui 中國佛教協會
1980 *Chung-kuo Fo-chiao* 中國佛教. Peking: Chih-shih ch'u-pan-she.

Chung-kuo hsi-ch'ü ch'ü-i tz'u-tien 中國戲曲曲藝詞典
1981 Shanghai: Shang-hai tz'u-shu ch'u-pan-she.

Cleveland Museum of Art
1980 *Eight Dynasties of Chinese Painting: The Collections of The Nelson Gallery–Atkins Museum, Kansas City, and The Cleveland Museum of Art*. Cleveland: The Cleveland Museum of Art.

Crump, J. I.
1970 "Liu Chiu-yüan in Chinese 'Epic,' Ballad, and Drama." *Literature East and West* 14:154–71.
1983 *Songs from Xanadu: Studies in Mongol Dynasty Song-Poetry (San-ch'ü)*. Michigan Monographs in Chinese Studies, no. 47.

Ann Arbor: Center for Chinese Studies, University of Michigan.

Davidson, J. Leroy
1954   *The Lotus Sutra in Chinese Art: A Study in Buddhist Art to the Year 1000.* New Haven: Yale University Press.

De Bary, Wm. Theodore
1953   "A Reappraisal of Neo-Confucianism." In *Studies in Chinese Thought*, ed. Arthur F. Wright, pp. 81–111. Chicago: University of Chicago Press.
1982   "Introduction." In *Yüan Thought*, ed. Chan Hok-lam and Wm. Theodore de Bary, pp. 1–25.

De Harlez, Charles
1884   *Manuel de la langue mandchoue.* Paris: Maisonneuve frères & Ch. Leclerc.

De Rachewiltz, Igor
1962a "The *Hsi-yu lu* 西遊錄 by Yeh-lü Ch'u-ts'ai 耶律楚材." *Monumenta Serica* 21:1–128.
1962b "Yeh-lü Ch'u-ts'ai (1189–1243): Buddhist Idealist and Confucian Statesman." In *Confucian Personalities*, ed. Arthur F. Wright and Denis Twitchett, pp. 189–216. Stanford: Stanford University Press.

Dolby, William
1976   *A History of Chinese Drama.* London: Paul Elek

Doleželová-Velingerová, Milena, and J. I. Crump, trans.
1971   *Ballad of the Hidden Dragon (Liu Chih-yüan chu-kung-tiao).* Oxford: The Clarendon Press.

Ecke, Tseng Yu-ho
1972   "Emperor Hui Tsung, the Artist: 1082–1136." Ph.D. diss., New York University.

Endô Jitsuo 遠滕實夫
1934   *Chôkonka kenkyû* 長恨歌研究. Tokyo: Kensetsusha.

Eng, Joe
1990   "Laughter in a Dismal Setting: Humorous Anecdotes in the *Kuei-ch'ien chih*." *Harvard Journal of Asiatic Studies* 50:223–38.

Fan Shou-k'un 范壽琨
1991   "Lun Chin-tai te K'ung-miao chien-chih chi ch'i tso-yung" 論金代的孔廟建置及其作用. Paper presented at the Interna-

tional Symposium on Liao-Chin and Khitan-Jurchen Histories, Tatung.

Feng, Gia-fu, and Jane English, trans.
1972   *Tao-te-ching*. New York: Vintage Books.

Feng Yüan-chün 馮沅君
1956   *Ku-chü shuo-hui* 古劇說彙. Peking: Tso-chia ch'u-pan-she.

Ferguson, John C.
1931   "The Six Horses at the Tomb of the Emperor T'ai Tsung of the T'ang Dynasty." *Eastern Art* 3:61–71.
1935   "The Six Horses of T'ang T'ai Tsung." *Journal of the North China Branch of the Royal Asiatic Society*, ser. 2, 67:1–8.

Foccardi, Gabriele, trans. and ed.
1981   *Tales of an Old Drunkard*, by Lo Yeh 羅燁. Wiesbaden: Otto Harrassowitz.

Fong, Wen, and Maxwell K. Hearn
1981–82 "Silent Poetry: Chinese Paintings in the Douglas Dillon Galleries." *Metropolitan Museum of Art Bulletin* 39, no. 3:4–80.

Fong, Wen, with Marilyn Fu
1973   *Sung and Yüan Paintings*. New York: The Metropolitan Museum of Art.

Fontein, Jan, and Wu Tung
1976   *Han and T'ang Murals: Discovered in Tombs in the People's Republic of China and Copied by Contemporary Chinese Painters*. Boston: Museum of Fine Arts.

Forke, Alfred, trans.
1962   *Lun-heng: Miscellaneous Essays of Wang Ch'ung*. 2d ed. 2 vols. Rpt. New York: Paragon Books.

Franke, Herbert
1975   "Chinese Texts on the Jurchen: A Translation of the Jurchen Monograph in the *San-ch'ao pei-meng hui-pien*." *Zentralasiatische Studien* 9:119–86.
1976   Ed. *Sung Biographies*. 3 vols. Münchener ostasiatische Studien, no. 16. Wiesbaden: Franz Steiner Verlag.
1978a   "Chinese Texts on the Jurchen II: A Translation of Chapter One of the Chin-shih." *Zentralasiatische Studien* 12:413–52.
1978b   *From Tribal Chieftain to Universal Emperor and God: The Legitimation of the Yüan Dynasty*. Munich: Verlag der Bayerischen Akademie der Wissenschaften.

1981 "Jurchen Customary Law and the Chinese Law of the Chin Dynasty." In *State and Law in East Asia*, ed. Dieter Eikemeier and Herbert Franke, pp. 215–33. Wiesbaden: Otto Harrassowitz.

1982 "Wang Yün (1227–1304): A Transmitter of Chinese Values." In *Yüan Thought*, ed. Chan Hok-lam and Wm. Theodore de Bary, pp. 153–96.

1983 "History of the Chin." In *The Cambridge History of China*. Forthcoming.

1987 "The Role of the State as a Structural Element in Polyethnic Societies." In *Foundations and Limits of State Power in China*, ed. S. R. Schram, pp. 87–112. London: School of Oriental and African Studies.

1989 "The Legal System of the Chin Dynasty." In *Ryû Shiken hakushi shôju kinen Sôshi kenkyû ronshû* 劉子健博士頌壽紀念宋史研究論集, ed. Kinugawa Tsuyoshi 衣川強, pp. 387–409. Kyoto: Dôbôsha.

1990 "The Forest Peoples of Manchuria: Khitans and Jurchens." In *The Cambridge History of Early Inner Asia*, ed. Denis Sinor, pp. 400–423. Cambridge: Cambridge University Press.

Fu Hsi-hua 傅惜華
1957 *Yüan-tai tsa-chü ch'üan-mu* 元代雜劇全目. Peking: Tso-chia ch'u-pan-she.

Fu, Shen
1980 "Chinese Calligraphy." In *Traditional and Contemporary Painting in China*, ed. Committee on Scholarly Communication with the People's Republic of China, pp. 68–86. Washington, D.C.: National Academy of Sciences.

Han Ping-fang 韓秉方 and Ma Hsi-sha 馬西沙
1984 "Lin Chao-en san-chiao ho-i ssu-hsiang yü san-i chiao" 林兆恩三教合一思想與三一教. *Shih-chieh tsung-chiao yen-chiu* 世界宗教研究, 1984, no. 3:64–83.

Han Yao-tsung 韓耀宗
1985 "A-ku-ta chien-kuo ch'ien Nü-chen te she-hui hsing-chih" 阿骨打建國前女真的社會性質. In *Sung Liao Chin shih lun-ts'ung* 宋遼金史論叢, vol.1, ed. Ts'ui Wen-yin 崔文印, pp. 226–36. Peking: Chung-hua shu-chü.

Hanan, Patrick
1973 *The Chinese Short Story; Studies in Dating, Authorship, and Composition*. Cambridge: Harvard University Press.

Hao Shu-hou 郝樹侯
1959   *Yüan Hao-wen shih-hsüan* 元好問詩選. Peking: Jen-min wen-hsüeh ch'u-pan-she.

Hargett, James M.
1989   *On the Road in Twelfth Century China: The Travel Diaries of Fan Chengda (1126–1193).* Münchener ostasiatische Studien, no. 52. Stuttgart: Franz Steiner Verlag Wiesbaden.

Hervouet, Yves
1964   *Un poète de cour sous les Han: Sseu-ma Siang-jou.* Paris: Presses universitaires de France.
1972   Trans. *Le chapitre 117 du Che-ki: Biographie de Sseu-ma Siang-jou.* Paris: Presses universitaires de France.

Hightower, James R.
1973   "Yüan Chen and 'The Story of Ying-ying.'" *Harvard Journal of Asiatic Studies* 33:90–123.

Ho-nan-sheng po-wu-kuan 河南省博物館 and Chiao-tso-shih po-wu-kuan 焦作市博物館
1979   "Ho-nan Chiao-tso Chin-mu fa-chüeh chien-pao" 河南焦作金墓發掘簡報. *Wen-wu* 文物, 1979, no. 8:73–126.

Ho, Wai-kam
1980   "Religious Paintings." In *Traditional and Contemporary Painting in China*, ed. Committee on Scholarly Communication with the People's Republic of China, pp. 22–34. Washington, D.C.: National Academy of Sciences.

Höke, Holger, trans.
1980   *Die Puppe (Mo-ho-lo)—Ein Singspiel der Yüan-Zeit*, by Meng Han-ch'ing 孟漢卿. Veröffentlichungen des Ostasien-Instituts der Ruhr-Universität Bochum, no. 26. Wiesbaden: Otto Harrassowitz.

Hsiao Kung-ch'in 蕭功秦
1985   "Yüan-tai li-hsüeh san-lun tui Meng-ku kuei-tsu t'ung-chih shih-tai te she-hui cheng-chih tso-yung te k'ao-ch'a" 元代理學散論對蒙古貴族統治時代的社會政治作用的考察. *Chung-kuo che-hsüeh* 中國哲學 13:21–35.

Hsü K'un 續琨
1974   *Yüan I-shan yen-chiu* 元遺山研究. Taipei: Chung-hua shu-chü.

Hsü P'ing-fang 徐苹芳
1960   "Kuan-yü Sung Te-fang ho P'an Te-ch'ung mu te chi-ko wen-

t'i" 關於宋德方和潘德沖墓的幾個問題. *K'ao-ku* 考古, 1960, no. 8:42–45.

Hu Chi 胡忌
1957   *Sung Chin tsa-chü k'ao* 宋金雜劇考. Shanghai: Ku-tien wen-hsüeh ch'u pan she.

Huang Chao-han 黃兆漢
1988   "Ch'üan-chen ch'i-tzu tz'u p'ing-shu" 全真七子詞評述. *Hsiang-kang Chung-wen ta-hsüeh Chung-kuo wen-hua yen-chiu-so hsüeh-pao* 香港中文大學中國文化研究所學報 19:135–62.

Huang Ming-fen 黃鳴奮
1985   "Su Shih te 'shih-ch'i' lun" 蘇軾的"士氣"論. *Hsia-men ta-hsüeh hsüeh-pao (Che-hsüeh she-hui k'o-hsüeh pan)* 廈門大學學報(哲學社會科學版), 1985, no. 4:101–8.

Huang Shih-chien 黃時鑒
1981   "Yüan Hao-wen yü Meng-ku-kuo kuan-hsi k'ao-pien" 元好問與蒙古國關係考辯. *Li-shih yen-chiu* 歷史研究, 1981, no. 1:127–40.

Hucker, Charles O.
1985   *A Dictionary of Official Titles in Imperial China.* Stanford: Stanford University Press.

Idema, Wilt
1972   Review of *Ballad of the Hidden Dragon (Liu Chih-yüan chu-kung-tiao)*, trans. Milena Doleželová-Velingerová and J. I. Crump. *T'oung Pao* 58:260–77.
1978a   "Performance and Construction of the *Chu-kung-tiao.*" *Journal of Oriental Studies* 16:63–78.
1978b   Review of *Master Tung's Western Chamber Romance (Tung Hsi-hsiang-chi chu-kung-tiao): A Chinese Chantefable*, trans. and ed. Li-li Ch'en. *T'oung Pao* 64:132–44.
1980   "Shih Chün-pao's and Chu Yu-tun's *Ch'ü chiang chih*: The Variety of Mode within Form." *T'oung Pao* 66:217–65.
1984a   "The Meeting of Dragon and Tiger, Prince and Baron: Contrastive Structure and Complex Theme." *Nachrichten der Gesellschaft für Natur- und Völkerkunde Ostasiens* (Hamburg) 136:65–74.
1984b   "The Story of Ssu-ma Hsiang-ju and Cho Wen-chün in Vernacular Literature of the Yüan and Early Ming Dynasties." *T'oung Pao* 70:60–109.
1984c   Trans. and ed. *Het verhaal van de westerkamers in alle toonaarden*, by Tung Chieh-yüan 董解元. Amsterdam: Meulenhoff.

Idema, Wilt, and Stephen H. West
1982   *Chinese Theater 1100–1450: A Source Book*. Münchener ostasiatische Studien, no. 27. Wiesbaden: Franz Steiner Verlag.

Imai Hidenori 今井秀周
1975   "Kinchô ni okeru jikan meigaku no hatsubai" 金朝における寺觀名額の發賣. *Tôhô shûkyô* 東方宗教 45:48–70.

Jan Yün-hua
1976   "Li P'ing-shan." In *Sung Biographies*, ed. Herbert Franke, vol. 2, pp. 577–82.
1979   "Li P'ing-shan and His Refutation of Neo-Confucian Criticism of Buddhism." In *Developments in Buddhist Thought: Canadian Contributions to Buddhist Studies*, ed. Roy C. Amore, pp. 162–93. Waterloo, Ontario: Wilfrid Laurier University Press.
1982   "Chinese Buddhism in Ta-tu: The New Situation and New Problems." In *Yüan Thought*, ed. Chan Hok-lam and Wm. Theodore de Bary, pp. 375–417.

Jao Tsung-i 饒宗頤
1968   "San-chiao lun yü Sung Chin hsüeh-shu" 三教論與宋金學術. *Tung hsi wen-hua* 東西文化, no. 11:24–32.

Jen Chi-yü 任繼愈
1980   "T'ang Sung i-hou te san-chiao ho-i ssu-ch'ao" 唐宋以後的三教合一思潮. *Shih-chieh tsung-chiao yen-chiu* 世界宗教研究, 1980, no. 1:1–6.

Jen Erh-pei 任二北, comp. and annot.
1981   *Yu-yü chi* 優語集. Shanghai: Shang-hai wen-i ch'u-pan-she.

Jin Qicong 金啓孮
1984   *Nü-chen-wen tz'u-tien* 女真文辭典. Peking: Wen-wu ch'u-pan-she.

Jin Qicong 金啓孮 and Jin Guangping 金光平
1980   *Nü-chen yü-yen wen-tzu yen-chiu* 女真語言文字研究. Peking: Wen-wu ch'u-pan-she.

Johnson, Linda Cooke
1974   "The Art of the Jurchen Revival, a Court Movement in Chin Dynasty China." Master's thesis, San Jose State University.
1983   "The Wedding Ceremony for an Imperial Liao Princess: Wall Paintings from a Liao Dynasty Tomb in Jilin." *Artibus Asiae*

44:107–36.

Josephs, Hillary K.
1976 "The Chanda, a Sung Dynasty Entertainment." *T'oung Pao* 62:179–98.

Kane, Daniel
1989 *The Sino-Jurchen Vocabulary of the Bureau of Interpreters*. Indiana University Uralic and Altaic Series, vol. 153. Bloomington: Indiana University, Research Institute for Inner Asian Studies.

Kao Shu-lin 高樹林
1986 "Chin-ch'ao hu-k'ou wen-t'i ch'u-t'an" 金朝戶口問題初探. *Chung-kuo shih yen-chiu* 中國史研究, 1986, no. 2:31–39.

Karetzky, Patricia Eichenbaum
1980 "The Recently Discovered Chin Dynasty Murals Illustrating the Life of the Buddha at Yen-shang-ssu, Shansi." *Artibus Asiae* 42:245–60.

Katsura Kajunshi 桂華淳祥
1981 "Kindai yûkai no ikkôsatsu" 金代邑會の一考察. *Indogaku Bukkyôgaku kenkyû* 印度學佛教學研究 29:737–40.

Kim Moon Kyung 金文京
1981 "Ryû Chi-en no monogatari" 劉智遠の物語. *Tôhôgaku* 東方學 62:66–82.

Kiyose, Gisaburo Norikura
1977 *A Study of the Jurchen Language and Script: Reconstruction and Decipherment*. Kyoto: Hôritsubunka-sha.

Koyama Fujio 小山富士夫 et al.
1975 *Kokyû hakubutsuin* 故宮博物院. 2 vols. Tokyo: Kodansha.

Kracke, E. A.
1953 *Civil Service in Early Sung China, 960–1067, with Particular Emphasis on the Development of Controlled Sponsorship to Foster Administrative Responsibility*. Harvard-Yenching Institute Monograph Series, no. 13. Cambridge: Harvard University Press.

Ku-kung po-wu-yüan 故宮博物院
1980 *Sung Li Kung-lin Wei-mo yen-chiao t'u-chüan* 宋李公麟維摩演教圖卷. Tientsin: T'ien-chin jen-min mei-shu ch'u-pan-she.
1985 *Ku-kung po-wu-yüan ts'ang ming-hua hsüan* 故宮博物院藏名

畫選. Peking: Wen-wu ch'u-pan she.

Kubota Ryôon 久保田遠
1931   *Shina Ju Dô Butsu sankyô shi ron* 支那儒道佛三教史論. Tokyo: Tôhô shoten.

Kuo Mao-ch'ien 郭茂倩
1979   *Yüeh-fu shih-chi* 樂府詩集. 4 vols. Peking: Chung-hua shu-chü.

Kuo Ming-chang 郭明璋
1978   "Chin-yüan yü pei-Ya chu pu-tsu kuan-hsi chih yen-chiu" 金源與北亞諸部族關係之研究. Master's thesis, Kuo-li Cheng-chih ta-hsüeh, Mu-cha.

Kuo Mo-jo 郭沫若
1964   "T'an Chin-jen Chang Yü te Wen-chi kuei Han t'u" 談金人張瑀的文姬歸漢圖. *Wen-wu* 文物, 1964, no. 7:1–6.

Kuo Shao-yü 郭紹虞
1961   *Chung-kuo wen-hsüeh p'i-p'ing shih* 中國文學批評史. Peking: Chung-hua shu-chü.

Laing, Ellen Johnston
1973   "Li Sung and Some Aspects of Southern Sung Figure Painting." *Artibus Asiae* 37:5–38.
1988–89 "Chin 'Tartar' Dynasty (1115–1234) Material Culture." *Artibus Asiae* 49:73–126.

Langlois, John D., Jr., and Sun K'o-k'uan 孫克寬
1983   "Three Teachings Syncretism and the Thought of Ming T'ai-tsu." *Harvard Journal of Asiatic Studies* 43:97–139.

Lee, Sherman E., and Wai-kam Ho
1968   *Chinese Art under the Mongols: The Yüan Dynasty (1279–1368)*. Cleveland: The Cleveland Museum of Art.

Lee, Thomas H. C.
1977   "Life in the Schools of Sung China." *Journal of Asian Studies* 37:45–60.
1985   *Government Education and Examinations in Sung China*. Hong Kong: Chinese University of Hong Kong Press.

Lee Yong-bum 李龍範
1968   "Liao Chin Fo-chiao chih erh-ch'ung t'i-chih yü Han-tsu wen-hua" 遼金佛教之二重體制與漢族文化. *Ssu yü yen* 思與言 6, no. 2:27–32.

Lei Hai-tsung 雷海宗
1934–35   *Chung-kuo t'ung-shih hsüan-tu* 中國通史選讀. Peking: Ch'ing-hua ta-hsüeh.

Lévy, André
1969   "Un text burlesque du xvie siècle dans le style de la chantefable." *Bulletin de l'Ecole Française d'Extrême-Orient* 56:119–24.
1971   "Le *Serpent Blanc* en Chine et au Japon: Excursion à travers les variations d'un thème." In his *Etudes sur le conte et le roman chinois*, pp. 97–113. Paris: Publications de l'Ecole Française d'Extrême-Orient.

Levy, Howard S.
1969   "The Original Incidents of Poems." *Sinologica* 10:1–54.

Li, Angela Lin (Li Tsung-ch'in 李宗憻)
1980   "Tu Chin Li Shan Feng-hsüeh shan-sung t'u cha-chi" 讀金李山風雪杉松圖札記. *Ku-kung chi-k'an* 故宮季刊 14, no. 4:19–40.

Li Fu-hua 李富華
1991   "Chao-ch'eng Chin-tsang yen-chiu" 趙城金藏研究. *Shih-chieh tsung-chiao yen-chiu* 世界宗教研究, 1991, no. 4:1–18.

Li Han 李涵
1989   "Chin ch'u Han ti shu-mi-yüan shih-hsi" 金初漢地樞密院試析. In *Liao Chin shih lun-chi*, ed. Ch'en Shu and Sung Te-chin, vol. 4, pp. 180–95.

Li Hsi-hou 李錫厚
1985   "Shih-lun Liao-tai Wang T'ien Han-shih chia-tsu te li-shih ti-wei" 試論遼代王田韓氏家族的歷史地位. In *Sung Liao Chin shih lun-ts'ung* 宋遼金史論叢, vol. 1, ed. Ts'ui Wen-yin 崔文印, pp. 251–66. Peking: Chung-hua shu-chü.

Li I-yu 李逸友
1979   "Hu-ho-hao-t'e-shih wan-pu Hua-yen-ching t'a te Chin-tai pei-ming" 呼和浩特市萬部華嚴經塔的金代碑銘. *K'ao-ku* 考古, 1979, no. 4:365–74.

Li Shu-t'ien 李樹田
n.d.   *Hai-hsi Nü-chen shih-liao* 海西女真史料. Ch'ang-ch'un: Chi-lin wen-shih ch'u-pan-she.
1989   *Chin pei hui shih* 金碑匯釋. Ch'ang-ch'un: Chi-lin wen-shih ch'u-pan-she.

Li T'ang 李唐
1978   *Chin T'ai-tsu* 金太祖. Taipei: Ho Lo t'u-shu ch'u-pan-she.

Lin, Shuen-fu
1978   *The Transformation of the Chinese Lyrical Tradition: Chiang K'uei and Southern Sung Tz'u Poetry*. Princeton: Princeton University Press.

Liu Ch'ing 劉慶
1987   "Chin-tai shu-shen chih-tu ch'u-t'an" 金代贖身制度初探. In *Liao Chin shih lun-chi*, ed. Ch'en Shu and Sung Te-chin, vol. 3, pp. 228–42.
1989   "Liao Chin chün-shih kai-ko shu-lun" 遼金軍事改革述論. In *Liao Chin shih lun-chi*, ed. Ch'en Shu and Sung Te-chin, vol. 4, pp. 16–25.

Liu, James T. C. (Liu Tzu-chien 劉子建)
1964   "The Neo-Traditional Period (ca. 800–1900) in Chinese History: A Note in Memory of the Late Professor Lei Hai-tsung." *Journal of Asian Studies* 24:105–7.
1970   "Nan-Sung chün-chu ho yen-huan" 南宋君主和言宦. *Ch'ing Hua hsüeh-pao* 清華學報, n.s. 8:340–49.
1972   "Yüeh Fei (1103–41) and China's Heritage of Loyalty." *Journal of Asian Studies* 31:291–97.
1973   "How Did a Neo-Confucian School Become the State Orthodoxy?" *Philosophy East and West* 23:483–505.
1974   "China: History of Southern Sung." In *The New Encyclopedia Britannica*, 15th ed., vol. 4, pp. 335–37.
1977   "The Jurchen and Southern Sung Background of the Mongol Rule: A Reassessment in Intellectual History." *Canada-Mongolia Review* 3, no. 2:83–90.
1984   "Ch'in Kuei te ch'in-yu" 秦檜的親友. *Shih-huo* 食貨 14, no. 7/8:34–47.
1985   "Polo and Cultural Change: From T'ang to Sung China." *Harvard Journal of Asiatic Studies* 45:203–24.
1988   *China Turning Inward: Intellectual-Political Changes in the Early Twelfth Century*. Harvard East Asian Monographs, no. 132. Cambridge: Council on East Asian Studies, Harvard University.

Liu Shih-p'ei 劉師培
1937   "Liu Shih-p'ei nan-pei wen-hsüeh pu-t'ung lun" 劉師培南北文學不同論. Annot. Hsü Wen-yü 許文雨. In *Wen-lun chiang-shu* 文論講疏, ed. Hsü Wen-yü, pp. 387–434. Shanghai:

Commercial Press.

Liu Su-yung 劉肅勇
1987   *Chin Shih-tsung chuan* 金世宗傳. Sian: San Ch'in ch'u-pan-she.

Liu Tse 劉澤
1987   "Yüan Hao-wen tsai kuei-ssu chih pien chung te ssu-hsiang chuan-che" 元好問在癸巳之變中的思想轉折. In *Yüan Hao-wen yen-chiu wen-chi* 元好問研究文集, ed. Shan-hsi-sheng ku-tien wen-hsüeh hsüeh-hui 山西省古典文學學會 and Yüan Hao-wen yen-chiu hui 元好問研究會, pp. 274–88. Taiyuan: Shan-hsi jen-min ch'u-pan-she.

Liu Ts'un-yan
1975   "The Compilation and Historical Value of the Tao-tsang." In *Essays on the Sources for Chinese History*, ed. Donald D. Leslie, Colin Mackerras, and Wang Gungwu, pp. 104–19. Rpt. Columbia: University of South Carolina Press.

Liu Wu-chi 柳無忌
1968   *An Introduction to Chinese Literature*. Bloomington: Indiana University Press.
1977   "Yü Wang *Hsi-hsiang* ho-ch'eng shuang-pi te Tung Chieh-yüan *Hsi-hsiang-chi*" 與王西廂合稱雙璧的董解元西廂記. *Yu-shih hsüeh-chih* 幼獅學誌 14, no. 3/4:1–61.

Liu Yung-chi 劉永濟, comp.
1957   *Sung-tai ko-wu chü-ch'ü lu-yao* 宋代歌舞劇曲錄要. Shanghai: Ku-tien wen-hsüeh ch'u-pan-she.

Lo Chi-tsu 羅繼祖
1987   "Wan-yen Liang hsiao i" 完顏亮小議. In *Liao Chin shih lun-chi*, ed. Ch'en Shu and Sung Te-chin, vol. 2, pp. 256–61.

Lo Ch'iu-ch'ing 羅球慶
1957   "Pei-Sung ping-chih yen-chiu" 北宋兵制研究. *Hsin Ya hsüeh-pao* 新亞學報 3, no. 1:169–270.

Lo Fu-i 羅福頤
1937   *Man-chou chin-shih chih* 滿洲金石志. Mukden: Man-Jih wen-hua hsieh-hui. Rpt. Taipei: T'ai-lien kuo-feng ch'u-pan-she, 1974.

Lü Ssu-mien 呂思勉
1982   *Lü Ssu-mien tu-shu tsa-chi* 呂思勉讀書雜記. Shanghai: Shang-hai ku-chi ch'u-pan-she.

Ma, Y. W., and Joseph S. M. Lau, eds.
1978   *Traditional Chinese Stories, Themes and Variations*. New York: Columbia University Press.

Makino Shûji
1983   "Transformation of the *Shih-jen* in the Late Chin and Early Yüan." *Acta Asiatica*, no. 45:1–26.

Mao Wen 毛汶
1936   "Chin-tai hsüeh-chih chih yen-chiu" 金代學制之研究. *Kuo-hsüeh lun-ts'ung* 國學論叢 7:26–36.

McMullen, David
1988   *State and Scholars in T'ang China*. Cambridge: Cambridge University Press.

Meng Hsien-ch'eng 孟憲承 et al.
1980   *Chung-kuo ku-tai chiao-yü shih tzu-liao* 中國古代教育史資料. Peking: Jen-min chiao-yü ch'u-pan-she.

Meng Ku-t'o-li 孟古托力
1991   "Liao-tai Han-tsu Ju-shih liang ta ch'uan-t'ung ch'ien hsi" 遼代漢族儒士兩大傳統淺析. *Pei-fang min-tsu wen-hua* 北方民族文化 2:57–69.

Miao P'o 苗潑
1991   "Lun Liao-tai tui Ju Shih Tao te chien-shou ping-hsü" 論遼代對儒釋道的兼收並蓄. Paper presented at the International Symposium on Liao-Chin and Khitan-Jurchen Histories, Tatung.

Mikami Tsugio 三上次男
1970   *Kindai seiji seido no kenkyû* 金代政治制度の研究. Tokyo: Chûô kôran bijutsu shuppan.
1972   *Kindai Joshin shakai no kenkyû* 金代女真社會の研究. Tokyo: Chûô kôran bijutsu shuppan.
1973   *Kindai seiji shakai no kenkyû* 金代政治社會の研究. Tokyo: Chûô kôran bijutsu shuppan.
1984   *Chin-tai Nü-chen yen-chiu* 金代女真研究. Trans. Jin Qicong 金啓琮. Harbin: Hei-lung-chiang jen-min ch'u-pan-she.

Mino, Yutaka
1980   *Freedom of Clay and Brush through Seven Centuries in Northern China: Tz'u-chou Type Wares, 960–1600 A.D.* Bloomington: University of Indiana Press.

Mu Hung-li 穆鴻利
1991   "Lun Chin-tai tsun-K'ung ch'ung-Ju chi ch'i tui Nü-chen

wen-hua fa-chan te ying-hsiang"論金代尊孔崇儒及其對女真文化發展的影響. Paper presented at the International Symposium on Liao-Chin and Khitan-Jurchen Histories, Tatung.

Murray, Julia K.
1981   "Sung Kao-tsung, Ma Ho-chih, and Mao Shih Scrolls: Illustrations of the Classic of Poetry." Ph.D. diss., Princeton University.

Niida Noboru 仁井田陞
1944   "Kindai keihô kô" 金代刑法考. Parts 1 and 2. *Tôyôshi kenkyû* 東洋史研究 9, no. 1:1–36; no. 2:20–59.

Nioradze, Georgii
1925   *Der Schamanismus bei den sibirischen Völkern*. Stuttgart: Strecker und Schröder.

Nishikawa Yasushi 西川寧, comp.
1966   *Seian hirin* 西安碑林. Tokyo: Kodansha.

Nogami Shunjo 野上俊靜
1953   *Ryô Kin no Bukkyô* 遼金の佛教. Kyoto: Heirakuji shoten.

Oguri Eichi 小栗英一
1963   *Gen Kômon* 元好問. Chûgoku shijin senshû 中國詩人選集, ser. 2, no. 9. Tokyo: Iwanami shoten.

Oyanagi Shigeta 小柳司氣太, comp.
1928   *Hakuunkan-shi* 白雲觀志. Tokyo: Tôhô bunka gakuin, Tôkyô kenkyûjo.

P'an Chieh-tzu 潘絜玆
1979   "Ling-yen ts'ai-pi tung hsin-p'o—Yen-shang-ssu Chin-tai pi-hua hsiao-chi" 靈巖彩壁動心魄—巖上寺金代壁畫小記. *Wen-wu* 文物, 1979, no. 2:3–10.

P'an Kuei-ming 潘桂明
1983   "Ts'ung Chih-yüan te Hsien-chü p'ien k'an Pei-Sung Fo-chiao te san-chiao ho-i ssu-hsiang" 從智圓的閑居編看北宋佛教的三教合一思想. *Shih-chieh tsung-chiao yen-chiu* 世界宗教研究, 1983, no. 1:78–94.

Po Sung-nien 薄松年 and Ch'en Shao-feng 陳少豐
1982   "Kuo Hsi fu-tzu yü *Lin-ch'üan kao-chih*" 郭熙父子與《林泉高致》. *Mei-shu yen-chiu* 美術研究, 1982, no. 4:62–69.

Pokora, Timoteus, trans.
1975   *Hsin-lun (New Treatises) and Other Writings by Huan T'an (43*

B.C.–28 A.D.). Michigan Papers in Chinese Studies, no. 20. Ann Arbor: Center for Chinese Studies, University of Michigan.

Preminger, Alex, ed.
1972   *Princeton Encyclopedia of Poetry and Poetics*. Enl. ed. Princeton: Princeton University Press.

Průšek, Jaroslav
1955   "Krieger und Abenteurer, das Burleske in der Volksliteratur." In his *Die Literatur des befreiten China und ihre Volkstraditionen*, pp. 507–15. Prague: Artia.

Pu Chin-chih 步近智
1983   "Lun Lü Tsu-ch'ien te Wu-hsüeh t'e-cheng" 論呂祖謙的婺學特征. *Chung-kuo che-hsüeh-shih yen-chiu* 中國哲學史研究, 1983, no. 2:89–98.

Rogers, Michael C.
1968a   *The Chronicle of Fu Chien: A Case of Exemplar History*. Chinese Dynastic Histories Translations, no. 10. Berkeley and Los Angeles: University of California Press.
1968b   "The Myth of the Battle of the Fei River (A.D. 383)." *T'oung Pao* 54:50–72.

Rossabi, Morris
1982   *The Jurchens in the Yüan and Ming*. Cornell University East Asia Papers, no. 27. Ithaca: China-Japan Program, Cornell University.

Roy, David T.
1977   Review of *Master Tung's Western Chamber Romance (Tung Hsi-hsiang-chi chu-kung-tiao): A Chinese Chantefable*, trans. and ed. Li-li Ch'en. *Harvard Journal of Asiatic Studies* 37:207–22.
1981   "A Confucian Interpretation of the *Chin P'ing Mei*." *Proceedings of the International Conference on Sinology, Section on Literature*, pp. 39–61. Taipei: Academia Sinica.

Sargent, Stuart H.
1993   "Contexts of the Song Lyric in Sung Times: Communication Technology, Social Change, Morality." In *Voices of the Song Lyric in China*, ed. Pauline Yu, pp. 226–56. Berkeley and Los Angeles: University of California Press.

Saso, Michael R.
1972   *Taoism and the Rite of Cosmic Renewal*. Pullman: Washington State University Press.

Schirokauer, Conrad
1978   "Chu Hsi's Political Thought." *Journal of Chinese Philosophy* 5:127–49.

Schneider, Lawrence A.
1980   *A Madman of Ch'u: The Chinese Myth of Loyalty and Dissent.* Berkeley and Los Angeles: University of California Press.

Sekino Tadashi 關野貞 and Takeshima Takuichi 竹島卓一
1934–35   *Ryô Kin jidai no kenchiku to sono butsuzô* 遼金時代の建築と其佛像. 2 vols. Tokyo: Tôhô bunka gakuin, Tôkyô kenkyûjo.

Serruys, Henry
1955   *Sino-Jürched Relations during the Yung-lo Period, 1403–1424.* Wiesbaden: Otto Harrassowitz.

Shan-hsi-sheng k'ao-ku yen-chiu-so 山西省考古研究所
1983   "Shan-hsi Chi-shan Chin-mu fa-chüeh chien-pao" 山西稷山金墓發掘簡報. *Wen-wu* 文物, 1983, no. 1:45–63.

Shan-hsi-sheng k'ao-ku yen-chiu-so Chin tung-nan kung-tso chan 山西省考古研究所晉東南工作站
1985   "Shan-hsi Ch'ang-tzu-hsien Shih-che Chin-tai pi-hua mu" 山西長子縣石哲金代壁畫墓. *Wen-wu* 文物, 1985, no. 6:45–54.

Shan-hsi-sheng wen-wu kuan-li wei-yüan-hui k'ao-ku yen-chiu-so 山西省文物管理委員會考古研究所
1960   "Shan-hsi Jui-ch'eng Yung-lo-kung chiu-chih Sung Te-fang, P'an Te-ch'ung ho 'Lü Tsu' mu fa-chüeh chien-pao" 山西芮城永樂宮舊址宋德方、潘德沖和'呂祖'墓發掘簡報. *Wen-wu* 文物, 1960, no. 6:22–25.

Shih Tao-kang 師道剛
1991   "Ts'ung hsin fa-hsien te Liu Ch'i teng san-p'ien i-wen k'an Chin Yüan chih chi Ju-hsüeh yü Ch'üan-chen-chiao te kuan-hsi" 從新發現的劉祁等三篇佚文看金元之際儒學與全真教的關係. Paper presented at the International Symposium on Liao-Chin and Khitan-Jurchen Histories, Tatung.

Shimada Hidemasa 島田英誠
1981   "Kisô chô no gagaku ni tsuite" 徽宗朝の畫學について. In *Chûgoku kaigashi ronshû: Suzuki Kei sensei kanreki kinen* 中國繪畫史論集：鈴木敬先生還曆記念, ed. Suzuki Kei sensei kanreki kinenkai 鈴木敬先生還曆記念會, pp. 109–50. Tokyo: Yoshikawa kobunkan.

Sickman, Lawrence, and Alexander Soper
1956   *The Art and Architecture of China*. Baltimore: Penguin Books.

Sinor, Denis, ed.
1990   *The Cambridge History of Early Inner Asia*. Cambridge: Cambridge University Press.

Sirén, Osvald
1956   *Chinese Painting: Leading Masters and Principles*. 7 vols. London: Lund, Humphries and Company.

Sontag, Richard Marton
1978   "Chang Te-hui and His Journey to Qaraqorum at the Summons of Qubilai Qan." Master's thesis, University of Arizona.

Soper, Alexander C.
1959   *Literary Evidence for Early Buddhist Art in China*. Artibus Asiae Supplementum, no. 19. Ascona: Artibus Asiae.

Steinhardt, Nancy Shatzman
1983   "The Plan of Khubilai Khan's Imperial City." *Artibus Asiae* 44:137–58.

Su Hsing-chün 蘇興鈞
1964   "Chi Chin-jen 'Wen-chi kuei Han t'u-chüan'" 記金人《文姬歸漢圖卷》. *Wen-wu* 文物, 1964, no 3:34–35.

Su Pai 宿白
1964   "Chao-ch'eng Chin-tsang ho Hung-fa tsang" 趙城金藏和弘法藏. *Hsien-tai Fo-hsüeh* 現代佛學, 1964, no. 2:13–22.

Sun Chin-chi 孫進己
1989   "Chin-tai Nü-chen te she-hui hsing-chih" 金代女真的社會性質. In *Liao Chin shih lun-chi*, ed. Ch'en Shu and Sung Te-chin, vol. 4, pp. 270–81.

Sun Chin-chi 孫進己 et al.
1987   *Nü-chen shih* 女真史. Ch'ang-ch'un: Chi-lin wen-shih ch'u-pan-she.

Sun K'o-k'uan 孫克寬
1968   *Yüan-tai Han wen-hua chih huo-tung* 元代漢文化之活動. Taipei: Chung-hua shu-chü.

Sung Te-chin 宋德金
1982   "Chin-tai Nü-chen tsu-su shu-lun" 金代女真族俗述論. *Li-shih yen-chiu* 歷史研究, 1982, no. 3:145–59.
1987   "Chin-tai te i-shih chu-hsing" 金代的衣食住行. In *Liao Chin*

shih lun-chi, ed. Ch'en Shu and Sung Te-chin, vol. 3, pp. 310–36.

1988   *Chin-tai te she-hui sheng-huo* 金代的社會生活. Sian: Shan-hsi jen-min ch'u-pan she.

1990   "Cheng-t'ung kuan yü Chin-tai wen-hua" 正統觀與金代文化. *Li-shih yen-chiu* 歷史研究, 1990, no. 1:70–85.

Suzuki Kei 鈴木敬

1981   "*Rinsen kochi shû* no 'Gaki' to Kaku Ki ni tsuite" 林泉高致集の畫記と郭熙について. *Bijutsushi* 美術史 30:1–11.

Suzuki Shûji 鈴木修次

1965   *Gen Kômon* 元好問. Kanshi taikei 漢詩大系, no. 20. Tokyo: Shueisha.

Ta-t'ung-shih po-wu-kuan 大同市博物館

1978   "Ta-t'ung Chin-tai Yen Te-yüan mu fa-chüeh chien-pao" 大同金代閻德源墓發掘簡報. *Wen-wu* 文物, 1978, no. 4:1–13.

Ta-t'ung-shih wen-wu ch'en-lieh-kuan 大同市文物陳列館 and Shan-hsi Yün-kang wen-wu kuan-li-so 山西雲岡文物管理所

1962   "Shan-hsi Ta-t'ung-shih Yüan-tai Feng Tao-chen, Wang Ch'ing mu ch'ing-li chien-pao" 山西大同市元代馮道真、王青墓清理簡報. *Wen-wu* 文物, 1962, no. 10:34–46.

T'ai Ching-nung 台靜農

1980   "Nü-chen-tsu t'ung-chih hsia te Han-yü wen-hsüeh—Chu-kung-tiao" 女真族統治下的漢語文學授—宮調. In *Chung-kuo ku-tien wen-hsüeh lun-wen ching-hsüan ts'ung-k'an (hsi-ch'ü lei)* 中國古典文學論文精選叢刊 (戲劇類), ed. Tseng Yung-i 曾永義, vol. 1, pp. 91–108. Taipei: Yu-shih wen-hua shih-yeh kung-ssu.

Takeo Giken 高雄義堅

1929   "Kindai ni okeru Dô Butsu nikyô no tokuchô" 金代に於ける道佛二教の特徵. *Shinagaku* 支那學 5:137–51.

Tamura Jitsuzô 田村實造

1971   *Chûgoku seifuku ôchô no kenkyû* 中國征服王朝の研究. 4 vols. Kyoto: Kyôto daigaku.

Tanaka Kenji 田中謙二

1954   "Bungaku to shite no *Tô Seishô*" 文學としての董西廂. Part 1. *Chûgoku bungaku hô* 中國文學報 1:93–112.

1955   "Bungaku to shite no *Tô Seishô*" 文學としての董西廂. Part 2. *Chûgoku bungaku hô* 中國文學報 2:75–100.

1968   "Imbun kô" 院本考. *Nippon Chûgoku gakkai hô* 日本中國學會

報 20:169–91.
1969　　　"Gendai sankyoku no kenkyû" 元代散曲の研究. *Tôhô gakuhô* 東方學報 40:1–114.

T'ang-shih san-pai-shou tu-pen 唐詩三百首讀本
1969　　　Annot. Ch'u Jao 劉苑. Taipei: Wen-yüan shu-chü.

Tao Jing-shen 陶晉生 (T'ao Chin-sheng)
1969　　　"Chin-tai te cheng-chih chieh-kou" 金代的政治結構. *Chung-yang yen-chiu-yüan li-shih yü-yen yen-chiu-so chi-k'an* 中央研究院歷史語言研究所集刊 41:567–93.
1970　　　"The Influence of Jurchen Rule on Chinese Political Institutions." *Journal of Asian Studies* 30:121–30.
1971　　　"Chin-tai te cheng-chih ch'ung-t'u" 金代的政治衝突. *Chung-yang yen-chiu-yüan li-shih yü-yen yen-chiu-so chi-k'an* 中央研究院歷史語言研究所集刊 43:135–61.
1976　　　*The Jurchen in Twelfth Century China: A Study of Sinicization.* Seattle: University of Washington Press.
1981a　　"Chin-tai te Chung-kuo chih-shih fen-tzu" 金代的中國知識分子. *Proceedings of the International Conference on Sinology, Section on History*, pp. 981–94. Taipei: Academia Sinica.
1981b　　*Nü-chen shih-lun* 女真史論. Taipei: Shih-huo yüeh-k'an ch'u-pan-she.

Teng Kuang-ming 鄧廣銘
1984　　　"*Ta Chin kuo chih* yü Chin-jen nan-ch'ien lu te chiu-ko" 大金國志與金人南遷錄的糾葛. Paper presented at the International Conference on Sung China, Hong Kong.

T'ien Hao 田浩 (Hoyt Tillman)
1988　　　"Chin-tai Ju-chiao: Tao-hsüeh tsai pei-pu Chung-kuo te yin-chi" 金代儒教：道學在北部中國的印跡. *Chung-kuo che-hsüeh* 中國哲學 14:107–41.

T'ien Hao 田浩 and Yü Tsung-hsien 俞宗憲
1989　　　"Chin-ch'ao ssu-hsiang yü cheng-chih kai-shuo" 金朝思想與政治概說. In *Ryû Shiken hakushi shôju kinen Sôshi kenkyû ronshû* 劉子健博士頌壽紀念宋史研究論集, ed. Kinugawa Tsuyoshi 衣川強, pp. 29–42. Kyoto: Dôbôsha.

Tillman, Hoyt Cleveland
1982　　　*Utilitarian Confucianism: Ch'en Liang's Challenge to Chu Hsi.* Harvard East Asian Monographs, no. 101. Cambridge: Council on East Asian Studies, Harvard University.
1992a　　*Confucian Discourse and Chu Hsi's Ascendancy.* Honolulu:

University of Hawaii Press.
1992b "A New Direction in Confucian Scholarship: Approaches to Examining the Differences between Neo-Confucianism and Tao-hsüeh." *Philosophy East and West* 42:455–74.

Ting Fu-pao 丁福保, comp.
1959 *Ch'üan Han San-kuo Nan-pei-ch'ao shih* 全漢三國南北朝詩. Peking: Chung-hua shu-chü.

Toyama Gunji 外山軍治
1955 "Ka Shidô ni tsuite" 賈似道について. *Shodô zenshû* 書道全集, vol. 16, pp. 25–27. Kyoto: Heibonsha.
1957 "Kin Shoso shuzo no shoga ni tsuite" 金章宗收藏の書畫について. In *Kanda hakushi kanreki kinen shoshigaku ronshû* 神田博士還曆記念書誌學論集, pp. 531–39. Kyoto: Heibonsha.
1975 *Kin shi* 金史. Tokyo: Meitoku shuppansha.
1978 *Kinchô shi kenkyû* 金朝史研究. 2d ed. Tokyo: Dôbôsha.

Trauzettel, Rolf
1964 *Ts'ai Ching (1046–1126), als Typus des illegitimen Ministers.* Bamberg: K. Urlaub.

Ts'ai Mei-piao 蔡美彪
1988 "Chin ch'ao" 金朝. In *Liao Sung Hsi-Hsia Chin shih* 遼宋西夏金史, ed. Teng Kuang-ming 鄧廣銘, pp. 125–43. Peking: Chung-kuo pai-k'o ch'üan-shu ch'u-pan-she.

Tsou Pao-k'u 鄒寶庫
1984 "Liao-yang-shih fa-hsien Chin-tai T'ung-hui Yüan-ming ta-shih t'a-ming" 遼陽市發現金代通慧圓明大師塔銘. *K'ao-ku* 考古, 1984, no. 2:175–77.

Tsui, Bartholomew P. M.
1980 "Li Ch'un-fu's Theory of Harmonization of the Three Teachings." Paper presented at the Congress of the International Association of the History of Religions.
1982 "Li Ch'un-fu and His Discussions of the Collected Plaints of Tao." Ph.D. diss., McMaster University, Hamilton.

Ts'ui Wen-yin 崔文印
1987 "Lüeh-t'an Chin Hai-ling-wang Wan-yen Liang te p'ing-chia wen-t'i" 略談金海陵王完顏亮的評價問題. In *Liao Chin shih lun-chi*, ed. Ch'en Shu and Sung Te-chin, vol. 1, pp. 357–70.
1990 "Chin shih" 金史. In *Chung-kuo shih-hsüeh ming-chu p'ing-chieh* 中國史學名著評介, ed. Ts'ang Hsiu-liang 倉修良 et al., vol. 2, pp. 165–82. Tsinan: Shan-tung chiao-yü ch'u-pan-she.

Tu Wei-ming
1982   "Towards an Understanding of Liu Yin's Confucian Eremitism." In *Yüan Thought*, ed. Chan Hok-lam and Wm. Theodore de Bary, pp. 233–77.

Tung K'o-ch'ang 董克昌
1991   "Ta Chin t'ung-chih ssu-hsiang chu-t'i te Ju-chia-hua lun" 大金統治思想主體的儒家化論. Paper presented at the International Symposium on Liao-Chin and Khitan-Jurchen Histories, Tatung.

Uchida Michio 內田道夫
1974   "Kôchu Ryû Chi-en shokyûcho" 校注劉智遠諸宮調. *Tôhoku daigaku bungakubu kenkyû nempô* 東北大學文學部研究年報 14:240–319.

Umehara Kaoru 梅原郁, ed.
1983   *Ken'en irai keinen yôroku jimmei sakuin* 建炎以來繫年要錄人名索引. Kyoto: Dôbôsha.

Van Gulik, R. H.
1961   *Sexual Life in Ancient China: A Preliminary Survey of Chinese Sex and Society from ca. 1500 B.C. till 1644 A.D.* Leiden: E. J. Brill.

Van Over, Raymond, trans.
1971   *I Ching*. New York: New American Library.

Velingerová, Milena
1960   "The Editions of the Liu Chih-yüan chu-kung-tiao." *Archiv Orientální* 28:282–89.

Waley, Arthur
1960   *Ballads and Stories from Tunhuang: An Anthology*. London: George Allen and Unwin.

Wang Chi-lin 王吉林
1971   "Liao-tai ch'ien-jen i yen-chiu" 遼代千人邑研究. In *Sung shih yen-chiu chi* 宋史研究集, ed. Sung-shih yen-chiu hui 宋史研究會, vol. 6, pp. 305–11. Taipei: Chung-hua ts'ung-shu pien-shen wei-yüan-hui.

Wang Chin-hsien 王進先 and Chu Hsiao-fang 朱曉芳
1990   "Shan-hsi Ch'ang-chih An-ch'ang Chin-mu" 山西長治安昌金墓. *Wen-wu* 文物, 1990, no. 5:76–85.

Wang Chung-min 王重民 et al., eds.
1957   *Tun-huang pien-wen chi* 敦煌變文集. Peking: Jen-min wen-

hsüeh ch'u-pan-she.

Wang, Elizabeth Te-chen, trans.
1961   *Ladies of the T'ang*. Taipei: Mei Ya Publications.

Wang Gung-wu
1962   "Feng Tao: An Essay on Confucian Loyalty." In *Confucian Personalities*, ed. Arthur F. Wright and Denis Twitchett, pp. 123–45. Stanford: Stanford University Press.

Wang Hung-chih 王宏志
1987a   "Chin Shih-tsung yü 'Lung-hsing ho-i'" 金世宗與"隆興和議." In *Liao Chin shih lun-chi*, ed. Ch'en Shu and Sung Te-chin, vol. 2, pp. 262–77.
1987b   "Lüeh-lun Chin chin-ju Chung-yüan hou cheng-ts'e te chuan-pien" 略論金進入中原後政策的轉變. In *Liao Chin shih lun-chi*, ed. Ch'en Shu and Sung Te-chin, vol. 3, pp. 243–60.

Wang Jen-fu 王仁富
1987   "'Ta Chin te-sheng t'o-sung' pei te chien-li chi ch'i yen-chiu" "大金得勝陀頌"碑的建立其研究. In *Liao Chin shih lun-chi*, ed. Ch'en Shu and Sung Te-chin, vol. 2, pp. 245–55.

Wang K'o-pin 王可賓
1987   "Nü-chen-jen ts'ung hsüeh-yüan tsu-chih tao ti-yüan tsu-chih te yen-pien" 女真人從血緣組織到地緣組織的演變. In *Liao Chin shih lun-chi*, ed. Ch'en Shu and Sung Te-chin, vol. 2, pp. 211–25.
1989   *Nü-chen kuo-su* 女真國俗. Ch'ang-ch'un: Chi-lin wen-shih ch'u-pan-she.

Wang Kuo-wei 王國維
1957   "Sung Yüan hsi-ch'ü k'ao" 宋元戲曲考. In *Wang Kuo-wei hsi-ch'ü lun-wen chi* 王國維戲曲論文集, pp. 1–148. Peking: Chung-kuo hsi-chü ch'u-pan-she.

Wang Li 王力, comp.
1982   *T'ung-yüan tzu-tien* 同源字典. Peking: Shang-wu yin-shu-kuan.

Wang Meng-ou 王夢鷗, comp.
1974   *T'ang-jen hsiao-shuo yen-chiu* 唐人小說研究. Vol. 1. Taipei: I-wen yin-shu-kuan.

Wang Ming-sun 王明蓀
1981   *Sung Liao Chin shih lun-wen kao* 宋遼金史論文稿. Taipei:

Ming-wen shu-chü.

1992 "Liao Chin chih shih-kuan yü shih-kuan" 遼金之史館與史官. In *Sung shih yen-chiu-chi* 宋史研究集, vol. 22, pp. 305–27. Taipei: P'an-an yin-shua-so.

Wang Pi-chiang 王辟疆, comp.
1955 *T'ang-jen hsiao-shuo* 唐人小說. Shanghai: Ku-tien wen-hsüeh ch'u-pan-she.

Wang Shih-lien 王世蓮
1989 "Chin-tai te k'ao-k'o yü lien-ch'a chih-tu" 金代的考課與廉察制度. In *Liao Chin shih lun-chi*, ed. Ch'en Shu and Sung Te-chin, vol. 4, pp. 236–47.

Wang Teh-yi (Te-i) 王德毅, Li Jung-ts'un 李榮村, and P'an Po-ch'eng 潘柏澄, comps.
1979–82 *Yüan-jen chuan-chi tzu-liao so-yin* 元人傳記資料索引. 4 vols. Taipei: I-wen shu-chü.

Wang Tseng-yü 王曾瑜
1983 *Sung-ch'ao ping-chih ch'u-t'an* 宋朝兵制初探. Peking: Chung-hua shu-chü.

Watson, Burton, trans.
1961 *Records of the Grand Historian of China*, by Ssu-ma Ch'ien 司馬遷. 2 vols. New York: Columbia University Press.

Weidner, Marsha Smith
1982 "Painting and Patronage at the Mongol Court of China, 1260–1368." Ph.D. diss., University of California, Berkeley.

Wen Yü-ch'eng 溫玉成
1981 "Shao-lin-ssu yü K'ung-men Ch'an" 少林寺與孔門禪. *Shih-chieh tsung-chiao yen-chiu* 世界宗教研究, 1981, no. 2:136–47.

Wen Yü-ch'eng 溫玉成 and Kung Ta-chung 宮大中
1975 "Ju Fo Tao san-chiao i-t'i te fan-tung pen-chih" 儒佛道三教一体的反動本質. *Wen-wu* 文物, 1975, no. 3:43–46.

West, Stephen H.
1974 "Shih Kuo-ch'i's Commentary on the Poetry of Yüan Hao-wen." *Ts'ing-hua Journal of Chinese Studies*, n.s. 10:142–69.
1977a "Jurchen Elements in the Northern Drama *Hu-t'ou-p'ai* 虎頭牌." *T'oung Pao* 63:273–95.
1977b *Vaudeville and Narrative: Aspects of Chin Theater*. Münchener ostasiatische Studien, no. 20. Wiesbaden: Franz Steiner Verlag.
1986 "Chilly Seas and East Flowing Rivers: Yüan Hao-wen's Po-

ems of Death and Disorder, 1233–1235." *Journal of the American Oriental Society* 106:197–21

West, Stephen H. and Wilt Idema
1992   *The Moon and the Zither: Wang Shifu's Story of the Western Wing.* Berkeley and Los Angeles: University of California Press.

Wixted, John Timothy
1981   "A Finding List for Chinese, Japanese, and Western-Language Annotation and Translation of Yüan Hao-wen's Poetry." *Bulletin of Sung-Yüan Studies*, no. 17:140–85.
1982   *Poems on Poetry: Literary Criticism by Yüan Hao-wen (1190–1257).* Calligraphy by Eugenia Y. Tu. Münchener ostasiatishe Studien, no. 33. Wiesbaden: Franz Steiner Verlag.
1990   "Some Chin Dynasty (金代) Issues in Literary Criticism." *Tamkang Review* 21:63–73.

Wolfe, Barnard
1980   *The Daily Life of a Chinese Courtesan, Climbing up a Tricky Ladder, With a Chinese Courtesan's Diary.* Hong Kong: Learner's Bookstore.

Wu, K. T.
1950   "Chinese Printing under Four Alien Dynasties." *Harvard Journal of Asiatic Studies* 13:447–523.

Wu Meng-lin 吳夢麟
1981   "Fang-shan shih-ching shu-lüeh" 房山石經述略. *Shih-chieh tsung-chiao yen-chiu* 世界宗教研究, 1981, no. 2:148–60.

Wu T'ien-jen 吳天任
1987   "Yüan I-shan chuan Ts'ui Li pei i-an" 元遺山撰崔立碑疑案. In *Yüan Hao-wen yen-chiu wen-chi* 元好問研究文集, ed. Shan-hsi-sheng ku-tien wen-hsüeh hsüeh-hui 山西省古典文學學會 and Yüan Hao-wen yen-chiu hui 元好問研究會, pp. 289–300. Taiyuan: Shan-hsi jen-min ch'u-pan-she.

Yang Mao-sheng 楊茂盛
1989   "Wan-yen chia-tsu tsai sheng Nü-chen she-hui fa-chan chung te tso-yung" 完顏家族在生女真社會發展中的作用. In *Liao Chin shih lun-chi*, ed. Ch'en Shu and Sung Te-chin, vol. 4, pp. 282–96.

Yang Shu-fan 楊樹藩
1974   "Liao-Chin wen-kuan jen-yung chih-tu" 遼金文官任用制度.

	Chung-kuo li-shih hsüeh-hui shih-hsüeh chi-k'an 中國歷史學會史學季刊 6:155–97.
1976	"Liao Chin ti-fang cheng-chih chih-tu yen-chiu" 遼金地方政治制度研究. *Chung-kuo li-shih hsüeh-hui shih-hsüeh chi-k'an* 中國歷史學會史學季刊 8:157–232.
1978	*Liao Chin chung-yang cheng-chih chih-tu* 遼金中央政治制度. Taipei: Commercial Press.
1983	*Liao Chin chung-yang cheng-chih chih-tu* 遼金中央政治制度. 2d ed. Taipei: Commercial Press.

Yao Ta-li 姚大力
1983	"Chin-mo Yüan-ch'u li-hsüeh tsai pei-fang te ch'uan-po" 金末元初理學在北方的傳播. In *Yüan-shih lun-ts'ung* 元史論叢, ed. Yüan-shih yen-chiu hui 元史研究會, vol. 2, pp. 217–24. Peking: Chung-hua shu-chü.

Yao Tao-chung
1980	"Ch'üan-chen: A New Taoist Sect in North China during the Twelfth and Thirteenth Centuries." Ph.D. diss., University of Arizona.
1986	"Ch'iu Ch'u-chi and Chinggis Khan." *Harvard Journal of Asiatic Studies* 46:201–19.

Yao Ts'ung-wu 姚從吾
1959	*Tung-pei shih lun-ts'ung* 東北史論叢. 2 vols. Taipei: Cheng-chung shu-chü.
1962	"Chang Te-hui *Ling-pei chi-hsing* tsu-pen chiao-chu" 張德輝《嶺北紀行》足本校註. *Wen-shih-che hsüeh-pao* 文史哲學報 11:1–38.
1963	"Chin Yüan chih chi Yüan Hao-wen tui-yü pao-ch'üan Chung-yüan ch'uan-t'ung wen-hua te kung-hsien" 金元之際元好問對於保全中原傳統文化的貢獻. *Ta-lu tsa-chih* 大陸雜誌 26, no. 3:1–12.
1970	"Yüan Hao-wen kuei-ssu shang Yeh-lü Ch'u-ts'ai shu te li-shih i-i yü shu-chung wu-shih-ssu jen hsing-shih k'ao" 元好問癸巳上耶律楚材書的歷史意義與書中五十四人行事考. *Wen-shih-che hsüeh-pao* 文史哲學報 19:225–75.
1971	*Liao Chin Yüan shih chiang-i: Chin-ch'ao shih* 遼金元史講議：金朝史. Vol. 3 of *Yao Ts'ung-wu hsien-sheng ch'üan-chi* 姚從吾先生全集. Taipei: Cheng-chung shu-chü.

Yeh Ch'ien-chao 葉潛昭
1972	*Chin-lü chih yen-chiu* 金律之研究. Taipei: Commercial Press.

Yin-hai 印海, trans.
1972   *Chung-Yin Ch'an-tsung shih* 中印禪宗史, by Kohô Chisan 孤峰智璨. Taipei: Hai-ch'ao-yin she. (A partial translation of Kohô's *Zenshû shi* 禪宗史.)

Yoshikawa Kôjirô 吉川幸次郎
1974   "Shushi gaku hokuden zenshi—Kinchô to Shushigaku" 朱子學北傳前史—金朝と朱子學. In *Uno Tetsuto sensei hakuju shûkuga kinen Tôyôgaku ronsô* 宇野哲人先生白壽祝賀記念東洋學論叢, pp. 1237–58. Tokyo: Uno Tetsuto sensei hakuju shûkuga kinenkai.

Yu Shao-ling, trans.
1977   "Tung Chieh-yüan: *The Romance of the Western Chamber*." *Renditions* 7:115–31.

Yü Chieh 于杰 and Yü Kuang-tu 于光度
1989   *Chin Chung-tu* 金中都. Peking: Pei-ching ch'u-pan-she.

Yu Yü-yen 于又彥 et al.
1989   *Nü-chen ch'uan-chi* 女真傳奇. Kirin: Shih-tai wen-i ch'u-pan-she.

INDEX

A-ku-nai, 146
A-ku-ta (Chin Ta'i-tsu, r. 1115–23), 27
A-shu, 26
Admonitions to the Court Ladies, 195
All-keys-and-modes. *See* Chu-kung-tiao
Ancient learning. *See* Ku-hsüeh movement
Assembled Worthies Collating the Classics, 184
Autumn Moon on the Music Terrace [at Kaifeng], 184
Avataṁsaka-sûtra (Hua-yen ching), 35

Book of Filial Piety, 34, 180 n. 25, 273
Buddhism: Confucians' hostility toward, 63; criticism of, 83; imperial patronage of, 147, 148, 159, 160; introduction to the Jurchen, 146; lay societies, 169; under the Liao, 146; in painting, 198, 206, 207; rivalry with Taoism, 158. *See also* names of individual sects
Bureau of Calligraphy and Painting, 208, 209, 210, 215 n. 12

Chaffee, John, 66 n. 4
Chan Hang-lun, 11
Chan Hok-lam, 11, 12
Chan, Wing-tsit, 72, 73
Ch'an Buddhism: Lin-chi branch, 150; popularity in the North, 146–47, 151; Ts'ao-tung branch, 147–48, 173–74; Yang-ch'i subbranch, 150
Chang Chien (late 12th cent.), 215 n. 12
Chang Chiu-ch'eng (1092–1159), 74, 75, 77

Chang Hsin-chen (1164–1218), 153
Chang Jou, 282
Chang Ku-ying, 80
Chang Kuei, 183, 184, 185, 209, 210
Chang Kung, characterization of, 246–47
Chang Po-ch'üan, 10, 72, 126
Chang Shih (1133–80), 44
Chang Yü, 183, 194, 195
Chao-ch'eng Chin-tsang, 174
Chao Chih-hui, 11, 216
Chao Fu (ca. 1206–ca. 1299), 71, 112
Chao I (1727–1814), 4
Chao Lin, 183, 188, 189, 194, 209
Chao Ling-chih (1061–1134), 241
Chao Meng-fu (1254–1322), 207, 211
Chao Ping-wen (1159–1232), 7, 10, 107, 115–144; on Buddhism and Taoism, 71, 87, 167; colophons by, 188, 209; on historians, 91–92; on legitimacy of Chin dynasty, 88–89; on Li Ch'un-fu, 83; on literature and calligraphy, 131–34; on Liu Pei and Ts'ao Ts'ao, 89–91; on political authority, 126–27; political career of, 120–21; on Southern Sung, 88; on Su Shih, 105–6, 137; on Tao-hsüeh and philosophy, 76–77, 87, 92, 105, 130–32, 134–39
Chen-i, Empress (1094–1161), 159, 177 n. 10
Chen-kuan cheng-yao, 107
Chen Ta-tao Taoism. *See* Ta-tao Taoism
Chen-ting, 3
Ch'en Kao-hua, 211
Ch'en, Li-li, 258, 260
Ch'en Liang (1143–94), 44

377

378 Index

Ch'en Lin [d.217] Drafting a Dispatch, 184
Ch'en Shan, 118–19
Ch'en Shih-cheng (d. 1194), 153
Ch'en Shu, 11
Ch'en Yüan, xxi, 157
Cheng Chen-to, 258
Cheng Heng, characterization of, 244
Cheng-t'ung Tao-tsang, 174
Ch'eng Hao (1032–85), 72, 76, 81
Ch'eng-hsiang, 30
Ch'eng I (1033–1107), 15, 72, 76, 80, 81, 125, 141–42, 144 n. 7
Chi-jang t'u, 274
Chi-lu chieh system, 32
"Chia-wu ch'u-yeh," 283, 301
Ch'iao K'uei-ch'eng (fl. 1270–1313?), 202
Chieh-fen ko, 217, 221
Chieh-tu shih, 26
Chien-hu, 31
Chien-tang kuan, 32
Ch'ien Chung-shu, 4
Ch'ien-hu, 26
Chih-chiu (d. ca. 1172), 35, 164
Chih-ying ssu, 194, 210–11
Chin Ai-tsung (r. 1224–34), 281, 291, 301
Chin Chang-tsung (r. 1190–1208), 37, 38, 148, 158, 159, 160, 161, 164, 165; poetry of, 232–33
Chin-chi, 299
Chin court and cultural policy: control of Buddhism and Taoism, 162–66, 173, 178 nn. 15, 16; court struggles, 29; historical sources, 2–3, 10; imperial painting academy, 208, 210–12; imperial sacrifices, 219; legitimacy of, 12–13, 37, 107, 287; military affairs, 36; as mix of northern and southern cultures, 1; painting, 183–215; patronage of Buddhism, 147–48, 159–60; patronage of Taoism, 157–60; political structure of, 126; relations with Southern Sung, 3–4, 40, 81, 226, 291; support of Chinese culture, 61–62; uprisings against, 35, 164; use of Chinese turncoats, 41, 46, 48; war with Mongols, 4, 81, 281
Chin Hai-ling (r. 1150–61), 29, 185, 224; attitudes toward religion, 165–66, 178 n. 15; poetry of, 224–26; promotion of schools, 50, 60–61
Chin Hsi-tsung (r. 1135–50), 29, 33, 147, 158–59, 223
Chin Hsüan-tsung (r. 1213–24), 6–7, 33
Chin-shih chü, 30
Chin Shih-tsung (r. 1161–89), 29, 34–35, 52, 147, 158–59, 161–62, 166–67, 227, 229–30
Chin-yüan chün-ch'en yen-hsing lu, 299
Ch'in Kou (late 11th cent.), 197
Ch'in Kuan (1049–1100), 197, 241
Ch'in Kuei (1090–1155), 42, 48–49 n. 1
Ching-ju (d. 1141), 150
"Ching-ti yin yin-p'ing," 273
Chinggis Khan, 154, 156
Ch'iu Ch'u-chi (1148–1227), 154, 158
Ch'iu Han-sheng, 113 n. 1
Ch'iu Hsing-kung (early 7th cent.), 188–89
Ch'iu Hsing-kung and Whirlwind Victory, 189, 190
Cho Wen-chün, 242
Chou Ang (d. 1211), 3, 80, 93
Chou Hui-ch'üan, 11
Chou Ssu-ming (d. 1211), 80, 93
Chou Tun-i, 74, 125
Chu Hsi (1130–1200), 72, 73, 89, 117
Chu Ju ming-tao chi, 18, 75, 77, 82, 113 n. 2
Chu-ko Liang (181–234), 90–91, 100
Chu-kung-tiao, formal characteristics of, 238–40
Chu Tun-ju (1081–1159), 213
Ch'uan-ch'i, 242–43
Ch'üan-chen Taoism, 82, 110, 153–56, 164, 174–76, 178 n. 14
Ch'üan Tsu-wang (1705–55), 71
Chuang-chia pu-shih kou-lan, 272
Chung-chou chi, 5, 120, 299, 300, 301–2

Chung-hua Ta-tsang-ching, 174
Ch'ung-yang li-chiao shih-wu lun, 154–55
Commission of Palace Services. See Chih-ying-ssu
Confucius, 50, 94, 107
Consort Ming Crossing the Frontier, 214 n. 6

De Bary, Wm. Theodore, 144 n. 1
De Harlez, Charles Joseph, xix–xx
De Rachewiltz, Igor, 149
Department of Painting. See T'u-hua shu
Description of Snow in the Liang Park [of Han], 184
Disciplinary school of Buddhism, 146, 150
Double-taxed households. See Erh-shui hu
Dream of Ssu-ma Yu, 183, 193, 196–98, 200, 202
Drum lyric. See Ku-tzu-tz'u

Erh-shui hu, 171–72
Examination system: and clergy, 35, 163–64 ; corruption of, 5–6; dual system, 33; numbers of degrees granted in, 33–34; poetic composition requirements, 72, 102, 108, 230; quotas in, 60; reform of, 7–8, 51, 103, 120–21

Fa-lü (1099–1166), 150
Fa-pao, 165
Fa-ts'ung, characterization of, 244–45
Fa-t'ung, 164
Fan Chung-yen (989–1052), 51, 65–66 n. 1
Fan Ning, 284–85
Five Elements or Powers. See Wu-hsing
Fo-chien Hui-ch'in (1059–1117), 150
Fo-kuo K'o-ch'in (1063–1135), 150
Fo-tsu li-tai t'ung-tsai, 147
Fo-yen Ch'ing-yüan (d. 1120), 150

Fourteen Images of Ancient Worthies, 184
Franke, Herbert, 11–12
Franke, Otto, xx
Fu Ch'i (late 12th cent.), 77, 108
Fu Chien (339–85), 39, 48, 221–22
Fu-yü (1203–75), 148

Hai-hui (d. 1145), 147, 159
Han Ch'i-hsien (1082–1146), 27
Han-lin Bureau of Painting. See T'u-hua yüan
Han-p'u (early 10th cent.), 25
Han Shao-yeh (late 13th cent.), 211
Han-shih p'ing-hua, 259, 263–64
Han Yü (768–824), 76
Hao Ching, 299
Ho Ch'eng (ca. 1218–ca. 1309), 211
Ho-li-po (1039–92), 25, 221–22
Ho, Wai-kam, 208–9, 214–15 n. 11
Honan, schools in, 56, 59, 67, nn. 7, 9
Hopei, schools in, 56–57, 59, 67 n. 9
Hou Yüan-hsien (1162–1230), 158
Hsi-hsiang-chi chu-kung-tiao, 239; compared with legend of the White Snake, 247–48; compared with Liu Chih-yüan chu-kung-tiao, 258–60, 274, 278; compared with "Ying-ying chuan," 242–43, 247; eroticism in, 249–56; as romantic comedy, 245–47
Hsi-wen. See Chu-kung-tiao
Hsiao Chih-ch'ung (1151–1216), 152
Hsiao Fu-tao (d. 1252), 152
Hsiao Pao-chen (d. 1166), 151–52, 158
Hsing-hsiu (1166–1246), 148–49, 151, 159, 174
Hsing-t'ai, 28
Hsü Heng (1209–81), 112
"Hsü hsiao-niang-ko shih-shou," 283, 290–91, 296–97
Hsü P'ing-fang, 179 n. 25
Hsü Tao-chen, 7
Hsü Yu-jen (1287–1364), 82
Hsüan-hsiao (1146–85), 230–31
Hsüan-hui yüan, 30
Hsüan-tu pao-tsang, 174

Hsüeh-t'ien, 60–61
Hu Li, 52
Hu Tzu (1082–1143), 4
Hu Ying-lin, 239
Hua-hsüeh, 208
Hua-yen Buddhism, 150
Huan-she, 221
Huan T'an, 124
Hui-chi (1148–1226), 150
Hung-fa tsang, 174
Hung Hao (1088–1155), 146
Hung Mai, (1123–1202), 4, 10
Hung-niang, characterization of, 244
Hunting in the Snow, 211
Huo-lang t'u, 274

I (Ch'an master), 159, 177 n. 11
Imperial Clothing Bureau. *See Yü-i chü*
Institute of Painting. *See Hua-hsüeh*

"January 1233: On Events after the Emperor's Departure on Eastern Campaign," 293
Jen-chen tsa-pien, 301
Jen Hsün (ca. 1110–ca. 1188), 215 n. 11
Jin Guangping, 10
Jin Qicong, 10
Johnson, Linda Cooke, 196
Jung-chai sui-pi, 4
Jurchen culture, decline of, 227, 229, 231–32
Jurchen literature: influence of Chinese liteature on, 217, 228–31; oral forms, 218–22, 227–28; origins of, 216–17; poetry, 224–26, 230–35; prose, 229
Jurchens: relations with Liao, 25–27; relations with northern Chinese, 28, 37; sincization of, 223–24, 226, 234–35

Kane, Daniel, 11, 216
Kao Shih-t'an (d. 1146), 37
Khubilai Khan (Yüan Shih-tsu, r. 1260–98), 148
Kiyose, Gisaburo Norikura, 11, 216

Ku-hsüeh movement, 103–4
Ku K'ai-chih (ca. 344–ca. 406), 195
Ku-liang chuan, 284–85, 297
Ku-tzu-tz'u, 241
Kuan-hu, 31
Kuang-en (1195–1243), 150
"Kuei-ssu ssu-yüeh erh-shih-chiu-erh ch'u ching," 282, 287, 291
"Kuei-ssu wu-yüeh san-jih pei-tu san-shou," 282, 295–96
Kung-chi chien, 31
Kung-wei chü, 30
Kuo Hsi (ca. 1010–ca. 1090), 185, 188, 212
Kuo-hsiang, 25
Kuo Mo-jo, 194
Kuo Shao-yü, 103
Kuo-shih, 35, 162
Kuo Ssu (d. after 1123), 188
Kuo-tzu chien, 34, 52
Kuo-tzu hsüeh, 34, 52
Kuo-tzu t'ai-hsüeh, 52

Laing, Ellen Johnston, 179 n. 20, 180 n. 25
Law codes, 31–32
Li (ritual), 128–29
Li Ch'ang-yüan, 9
Li Ch'in-shu, 7–8
Li Ching, 131, 134
Li Ch'iung, 42
Li Chün-min (1176–after 1256), 56, 62, 81
Li Ch'un-fu (1175–1231), 73, 83, 108; and Buddhism, 72, 149–51, 167; on Chin educational policy, 62; on Liu Chi, 80; on Liu Pei and Ts'ao Ts'ao, 89–91; on Tao-hsüeh, 74–76, 81, 84–87, 90, 114 n. 5; and the Three Teachings, 85–86
Li Hsi-an (d. 1266), 153
Li Hsi-ch'eng (1182–1259), 153
Li Hung-i, characterization of, 267–69
Li Jih-hua (1565–1635), 215 n. 12
Li Kuan-tao (late 13th–early 14th cent.), 215 n. 13

Li Kung-lin (1049–ca. 1106), 202, 206–7, 211, 274
Li San-niang, characterization of, 265–67
Li Shan (late 12th cent.), 210
Li Shen (d. 846), 241–42
Li Shu-t'ien, 11
Li Sung (ca. 1190–ca. 1230), 274
Li Tao-ch'un, 179 n. 21
Liao, relations with Jurchen, 25–27
Lieh-hsien chuan, 297
Lin Chao-en, 179 n. 21
Lin-ch'üan kao-chih, 185
Ling (director), 30
Liu Chih-yüan chu-kung-tiao, 238–39, 257–58; characterization of protagonist, 260–64; characterization of rural life, 269–72; comparison with *Hsi-hsiang-chi chu-kung-tiao*, 258–60, 274, 278; language of, 274–75, 277; as low burlesque, 276–79; references to other works, 273–74; relation to painting, 274; sources, 259–60
Liu Chih-yüan pai-t'u chi, 259, 264–65
Liu Ch'i (1203–50), 33; on Buddhism and Taoism, 167–68; on Chin literati, 7–9; on Chin military, 234–35; on dominance of northern Chin culture, 2; on examination system, 5–9, 114 n. 9; on the Green City, 291–92; on Hsüan-hsiao, 231
Liu, James T. C., 13, 19
Liu Pei (162–223), 89–91, 99–100
Liu Su-yung, 11
Liu Te-jen (1122–80), 152–53
Liu Ts'ung-i (1181–1224), 71, 83
Liu Yü (1073–1143), 40–42
Liu Yü-hsi (772–842), 49 n. 4
Liu Yüan, 183, 196–99, 212
Loyang, 289–90
Lü Wen-huan (d.1292?), 47
Lü Wen-te (d.1271), 47

Ma Chih-chi, 7
Ma Chiu-ch'ou (1174–1232), 80, 168
Ma Ho-chih (d. ca. 1190), 213
Ma T'ien-lai (1172–1232), 203, 210, 212–13
Ma Yün-ch'ing, 183, 202–3, 206–7, 209–10, 212
Ma Yün-han, 203
Making Music in Harmony, 184
Mao Hsi-ts'ung (1186–1223), 153
Mao P'ang, 241
Mao Wen, 66 n. 5
Men-shih hsin-hua, 118–19
Mencius, 288
Meng-an, 26, 166
Meng-an mou-k'o system, 26, 28, 31, 36
Meng Ch'i, 243
"Meng-kuei" 283, 295
Meng Yüan-lao, 272
Mi Chih-kuo, 11
Mi Fu (1052–1107), 208, 211
Mi-kuo, Prince, 233
Mi Yu-jen (ca. 1072–ca. 1151), 213
Miao-hsüeh, 50–52. See also Schools
Mikami Tsugio, 11
Ming-tao chi-shuo, 73–74, 77, 83, 85, 86, 113 n. 2, 150
Monasteries: Buddhist, 163, 169, 170, 177 nn. 10, 11; Taoist, 157, 163, 170
Mongols: conquest of China 47–48; use of Chinese turncoats, 4, 7–8; war with Chin, 4, 281
Monk certificates, sale of, 161–62
Mou-k'ou, 26, 28, 166

"Nan-hsing Ch'ien-chi hsü," 130
Nan-kuan lu, 300
Nan-mien, 28
Nei-shih chü, 30
Niida Noboru, 11
Northern Sung: Confucian reaction to fall of, 44–45; imperial painting academies, 198, 207–8; literati models, 125–26; painting, stylistic traditions, 197–98
Nu-pei hu, 31
Nü-chen kuo-tzu hsüeh, 34, 52

Office of Painting. See *T'u-hua chü*

Officials Going into Retirement, 184
Ou-yang Hsiu (1007–72), 37, 76

Pa-hei, 222
Pai-hu, 26
Pai-t'u chi. See *Liu Chih-yüan pai-t'u chi*
P'ai-t'i, 283
"P'ai-t'i: Hsüeh-hsiang-t'ing tsa-yung shih-wu-shou," 282–89, 292–93, 295
Painting, 183–215; Buddhist subjects, 198, 206–7; imperial academies, 207–8, 210–11, 213; symbolism in landscape, 185, 187; T'ang subjects and influences, 188–89, 194, 196
P'ang Yün, 61
Pao Chao, 286
Paper-clothed Recluse, 203
Pen-ch'ü, 217, 227–28
Pen-shih-shih, 243
Pien ku-kung chi, 283
Pien-liang, surrender of to Mongols, 281–82, 283, 286, 291–92, 299
P'ing-chang cheng-shih, 30
Po-chi-lieh, 27–28
Po-chin, 27
Po Chü-i (772–846), 271, 293
P'o-la-shu (1042–94), 25–26, 221–22
Political institutions, 26, 28; local government, 35–36; official titles, 32; protection (*yin*) system, 34; rule over Chinese, 28; structure of, 30; supervision of religious organizations, 35
Prestige titles. See *San-kuan*
Pu-yi (1906–67), 49 n. 5
Pure Land Buddhism, 151

Reading the Classics, 203
Rossabi, Morris, 11
Rural life, 271–72

Sacred Tortise, 183–84, 186, 188, 209–10, 214 n. 2
San-chiao ho-i, 145, 149, 151, 173, 178–79 n. 20
San-kuan, 32
San-kuo chih yen-i, 260

San-she system, 53
San-ta, 221
San-t'ang Wang, 198–99, 212
Sandalwood Buddha, 160–61, 178 n. 16
Schools, 34–35, 50–67; enrollment in, 53, 56; geographic distribution of, 54–56, 66–67 n. 6; impact of official recruitment, 63–64; land as a source of revenue, 60–61; local construction and repair of, 57–59, 62–65, 67 nn. 6, 7; in Northern Sung, 51, 66; in T'ang, 51; temple schools, 50–52; "three grades," 53; worship of Confucius in, 50
Sea, Chinese attitudes toward, 45–46
Seng-cheng, 162
Seng-lu, 35, 162
Shamanism, 219–20
Shang-shu sheng, 28, 30
Shang T'ing (1209–88), 202–3
Shansi, schools in, 56–57, 59, 64, 67 n. 7
Shantung, schools in, 56, 59–60, 63, 67 nn. 8, 9
Sheng Nü-chen pu-tsu chieh-tu shih, 26
Shensi, schools in, 56, 63
Shih (commissioner), 30
Shih-ch'i tai, 273
Shih-ching (sutras on stone tablets), 175
Shih Cho, 52
Shih-hsiang, 26
Shih I-sheng (d. 1159), 46
Shih Hsüeh-yu, 8
"Shih Hung-chao lung-hu chün-ch'en hui," 264
Shih-lu, 25
Shih-wen tzu-ching, 299
Shu-hu Kao-ch'i, 6
Shu-hu Sui, 234–35
Shu-hua chü. See Bureau of Calligraphy and Painting
Shu-mi yüan, 28, 30
Shuang Chien, 238
Shui-yün chi, 82
Sinor, Denis, 23

Six Horses, 183, 187, 188–89, 194, 209
Slaves and slavery, 31, 171–72
South Manchuria Railway Company, xx, 48
Southern Sung: imperial painting academy, 207, 213; relations with Chin, 43–44, 226, 291; relations with Liu Yü, 42–43, 48
Ssu (courts), 30
Ssu-ma Hsiang-ju, 242
Ssu-ma Kuang (1019–86), 125–26, 199
Ssu-ma Yu (late 11th cent.), 197
Su Hsiao-ch'ing, 238
Su Hsiao-hsiao (late 5th cent.), 197
Su Shih (1036–1101), 199, 285; influence of, 72, 103, 105, 110, 114 n. 9, 125, 129–30, 142
Sun Chin-chi, 10
Sung Chiu-chia (d. 1234), 71, 83
Sung Hui-tsung (r. 1100–1125), 38, 185
Sung Kao-tsung (r. 1127–62), 40, 213
Sung-mo chi-wen, 146
Sung Te-chin, 10
Sung Tzu-fang (late 11th–early 12th cent.), 208
Sung-Yüan hsüeh-an, 71–72, 80, 86, 92, 106, 117

Ta Chin hsüan-tu pao-tsang, 174
Ta Chin-kuo chih, 162
Ta-li ssu, 30
Ta-Tao Taoism, 152–53, 155–56
Tai-chao, 188, 209
T'ai-ch'ang ssu, 30
T'ai-fu chien, 31
T'ai hsüeh, 34, 51
T'ai-i Taoism, 151–52, 155–56
T'ai, Mt., 94–95
T'an Ch'u-tuan (1123–85), 82
Tanaka Kenji, 243, 273
Tang Huai-ying, 129–30
T'ang Kao-tsung (r. 650–83), 51
T'ang-kua, Madame, (1021–74), 220–21
T'ang T'ai-tsung (r. 627–49), 51
Tantric Buddhism, 151

Tao and *wen*, 104, 110, 116–18, 129, 140–42
Tao-cheng, 162
Tao-hsüeh fa-yüan, 77–78, 80
Tao-hsüeh, reception of in the North, 72–73, 80–81, 83, 108–12
Tao-hsün (1087–1142), 150
Tao Jing-shen, 11–12
Tao-lu, 162
Taoism, 145–51; Celestial Master sect, 156–57; Confucians' hostility toward, 63; imperial patronage of, 157–60; Mao-shan sect, 156–57; methods of self-cultivation, 156. See also Ch'üan-chen Taoism, Ta-Tao Taoism, T'ai-i Taoism
Teng Kuang-ming, 113 n. 1
Three Doctrines. See San-chiao ho-i
T'i-chü hsüeh-shih kuan, 35
T'i-tien, 30
T'iao-hsi yü-yin ts'ung-hua, 4
Tien-ch'ien tu tien-chien ssu, 30
T'ien-ch'ang Monastery, 157–58, 160, 162, 176 n. 8
T'ien Ch'üeh (d. 1147), 29
T'ien-pao i-shih chu-kung-tiao, 238–39, 249
Toyama Gunji, 11
Transmitting the Classics, 184
Ts'ai Kuei (d. 1174), 3
Ts'ai Sung-nien (1107–59), 29
Ts'an-chih cheng-shih, 30
Ts'ao Ts'ao (155–220), 89–90
Tso Ch'iu-ming, 292
Tso Yung, 51–52
Tsu-chou tz'u, 217
Tsu-lang (1149–1222), 151
Tsui, Bartholomew, 85, 113
Ts'ui, Lady, characterization of, 244
Ts'ui Li, 281–82
Ts'ui Wen-yin, 11
Tsung-kuan, 35
Tsung-kuan fu, 35
Tu-ch'eng chi-sheng, 272
Tu Jen-chieh, 272
Tu po-chi-lieh, 27

Tu-pu chang, 26
Tu-shih hsüeh, 299
Tu yüan-shuai fu, 30
T'u-hua chü, 208
T'u-hua shu, 194, 208
T'u-hua yüan, 207, 209
Tuan Ch'eng-chi, 198–99, 212
Tung Chieh-yüan, 241–43, 245–47, 251
Tung-p'o shih-ya, 299
Twenty-four Paragons of Filial Piety, 175, 179–80 n. 25
Tzu-chih t'ung-chien kang-mu, 89
Tzu-tu ko, 217

Vimalakirti Expounds Buddhist Sutras, 183, 201, 202, 204, 205
Vorob'ev, M. V., xx

Wan-yen Shou (1172–1232), 202–3, 207
Wan-yen Tsung-pi (d. 1148), 42
Wang An-shih (1021–86), 33, 125–26
Wang Che (1113–70), 153–54, 173, 180 n. 25
Wang Chen-p'eng, 202, 211
Wang Ch'u-i (1142–1217), 158, 160, 167
Wang Jo-hsü (1174–1243), 3, 4, 10, 78–79, 92–96, 100, 107; on Chu Hsi, 72, 80, 97–99; on Li Ch'un-fu, 83; on Liu Pei and Ts'ao Ts'ao, 99–100; on Ssu-ma Kuang, 99; on Su Shih, 105; on Sung Confucians, 97–98, 100; on Tao-hsüeh, 79–81, 101
Wang K'o-pin, 10
Wang K'uei, 198
Wang Ming-sun, 11
Wang Ni, 285
Wang O (1190–1273), 203
Wang Po-ch'eng, 238
Wang P'an (1202–93), 60
Wang Shih-chen (1634–1711), 202
Wang T'ing-yün (1175–1202), 209, 210, 211
Wang Tseng (978–1038), 60
Wang Wan-ch'ing (late 12th–early 13th cent.), 210
Wang Yü (fl. 1196–1201), 169

Wang Yü (1204–36), 105
Wang Yün, 203
Weidner, Marsha, 214 n. 7
Wen and *li*, 128
Wen and *tao*, 104, 110, 116–18, 129, 140–42
Wen-chi's Return to China, 183, 191, 192, 194–96
Wen T'ung (1018/9–79), 211
Whirling Snow in the North Wind, 185
Wixted, J. T., 12
Wu-ch'i-mai (Chin T'ai-tsung, r. 1123–35), 28
Wu-chu (d. 1154), 150
Wu Hsi, 46–47
Wu-hsing, 38
Wu-ku-nai (1021–74), 25, 221
Wu-lin-ta (d. 1154), 29
Wu-lin Ta-shuang, 235
Wu-tai shih, 273
Wu-tai-shih p'ing-hua, 259
Wu-ya-shu (r. 1103–13), 27
Wu Yüan-chih (late 12th–early 13th cent.), 209, 215 n. 12

Yang Huan, 283
Yang Li-chai, 238
Yang Pang-chi (d. 1181), 209
Yang P'u (Yang P'o, early 11th cent.), 27
Yang Shu-fan, 11
Yang Yün-i, 121, 128–29
Yao Ta-li, 72, 150
Yao Ts'ung-wu, 11, 24
Yeh Ch'ien-chao, 11
Yeh-lü Ch'u-ts'ai (1189–1243), 74, 83, 148–49, 151, 282, 298
Yen Te-yüan (1094–1189), 157
Ying-ko (r. 1094–1103), 26
Ying-ying, characterization of, 253
"Ying-ying chuan," 241–42
Yoshikawa, Kôjirô, 11, 72, 95, 106, 114 n. 9
Yu Shih-hsiung (1038–97), 189
Yü Chieh, 11
Yü Hsin, 285–86
Yü-i chü, 211, 215 n. 13

Yü Kuang-tu, 11
Yü-shih t'ai, 30
Yü-wen Hsü-chung (1080–1146), 37, 222
Yü Yu-yen, 10
Yüan Chen (779–831), 241
Yüan Hao-wen (1190–1257): on Buddhism and Taoism, 154, 164, 168; on Chao Ping-wen, 87, 120–24, 143; on Chin literati, 122, 298; epitaph of, 299–300; on Li Ch'un-fu, 73–74; poetry of, 3–5, 184, 203, 282–304; on poetry, 84, 114 n. 12; praise for Chin educational policy, 62; on Su Shih, 106; on Tao-hsüeh and *wen*, 74, 121–24, 125; on Wang Jo-hsü, 94–95
Yüan Hua (b. 1316), 184
Yüan-kai (1132–95), 150
Yüan-pen ming-mu, 272

www.ingramcontent.com/pod-product-compliance
Lightning Source LLC
Chambersburg PA
CBHW030125240426
43672CB00005B/25